The United Nations Global Compact

W9-BHB-074

The **United Nations Global Compact** is a strategic policy initiative that encourages businesses to support ten universal principles in the areas of human rights, labour standards, the environment and anti-corruption. It is the world's largest voluntary corporate responsibility initiative with more than 7,300 business and non-business participants in over 130 countries. This book reviews the first ten years of the Compact's existence (2000–2010) by presenting exclusively commissioned chapters from well-known scholars, practitioners from the business world and civil society, and Global Compact staff. They reflect on what the Global Compact has achieved, what trends it may have to respond to and what challenges are ahead. The book not only contains up-to-date reflections but also debates recent changes to the structure of the Compact, including the Communication on Progress policy, the role of Global Compact Local Networks and the role of emerging specialized initiatives.

ANDREAS RASCHE is Assistant Professor of Business in Society at Warwick Business School and, since 2007, has worked as a consultant to the United Nations Global Compact Office in New York. He received his PhD in Strategic Management and Corporate Responsibility from the European Business School, Germany. His research focuses on global governance and transnational organizational regulation in the context of contested global issues. He has published widely in leading international journals on corporate responsibility and has guest-edited special issues of various journals.

GEORG KELL is the Executive Director of the United Nations Global Compact. His career with the United Nations began in 1987 at the UN Conference on Trade and Development (UNCTAD) in Geneva. In 1997, Mr Kell joined the Office of the UN Secretary-General in New York, where he spearheaded the development of new strategies to enhance private sector engagement with the work of the United Nations. As one of the Global Compact's key architects, he has led the initiative since its launch in 2000. A native of Germany, he holds advanced degrees in economics and engineering from the Technical University of Berlin.

The United Nations Global Compact

Achievements, Trends and Challenges

Edited by

ANDREAS RASCHE

and

GEORG KELL

CAMBRIDGE UNIVERSITY PRESS
Cambridge, New York, Melbourne, Madrid, Cape Town, Singapore,
São Paulo, Delhi, Dubai, Tokyo

Cambridge University Press
The Edinburgh Building, Cambridge CB2 8RU, UK

Published in the United States of America by Cambridge University Press, New York

www.cambridge.org
Information on this title: www.cambridge.org/9780521145534

First published 2010

Printed in the United States of America

A catalogue record for this publication is available from the British Library

ISBN 978-0-521-19841-7 Hardback
ISBN 978-0-521-14553-4 Paperback

Contents

Figures

Tables

Boxes

Abbreviations

AACSB	Association to Advance Collegiate Schools of Business
ABERJE	Brazilian Association of Business Communication
ALNF	Annual Local Networks Forum
APIMEC	Association of Investment Analysts and Professionals of the Capital Market (Brazil)
ASrIA	Association for Sustainable & Responsible Investment in Asia
BMZ	German Ministry for Economic Development and Cooperation
BSR	Business for Social Responsibility
CEL	teChnology Enhanced Learning
CEO	chief executive officer
CFC	chlorofluorocarbons
CIO	chief investment officer
CIS	Commonwealth of Independent States
CITES	Convention on International Trade in Endangered Species
CLIP	Corporate Learning Improvement Process
CO_2	carbon dioxide
COP	Communication on Progress
COP	Conference of the Parties
CPI	Corruption Perception Index
CSR	Corporate Social Responsibility
CUT	Unified Workers Confederation
CVM	Security and Exchange Commission (Brazil)
DJSI	Dow Jones Sustainability Index
EABIS	European Academy of Business in Society
ECA	Statute of Children and Adolescents (Brazil)
ECLAC	Economic Commission for Latin America and the Caribbean
ECOSOC	United Nations Economic and Social Council

EFMD	European Foundation for Management Development
EH&S	environmental health and safety
EIASM	European Institute of Advanced Studies in Management
EITI	Extractive Industry Transparency Initiative
EMAS	Eco-Management and Audit Scheme
EMS	environmental management systems
EQUIS	European Quality Improvement System
EPA	Environmental Protection Agency (US)
EPAS	EFMD Program Accreditation System
EPG	Eminent Persons Group
ESCAP	United Nations Economic and Social Commission for Asia and the Pacific
ESG	environmental, social and governance
EuroSIF	European Sustainable Investment Forum
FDI	foreign direct investment
FIDES	Social and Business Development Institute Foundation (Brazil)
G8	Group of 8
GCAC	Global Compact Advisory Council
GCLN	Global Compact Local Network
GDP	gross domestic product
GFME	Global Foundation for Management Education
GHF	Global Humanitarian Forum
GHG	greenhouse gas
GRI	Global Reporting Initiative
GRLI	Globally Responsible Leadership Initiative
GTZ	German Technical Cooperation
HRCA	Human Rights Compliance Assessment
HRM	human resource management
IAT	Inter-Agency Team
IBAMA	Brazilian Institute of Environment and Renewable Natural Resources
IBASE	Brazilian Institute of Social and Economic Analyses
ICC	Citizen Charcoal Institute
ICC	International Chamber of Commerce
ICFTU	International Confederation of Free Trade Unions
ICT	information and communications technology
IEA	International Energy Agency
IETA	International Emission Trading Association

IIGCC	Institutional Investors Group on Climate Change
IISD	International Institute for Sustainable Development
ILO	International Labour Organization
IMF	International Monetary Fund
INCR	Investor Network on Climate Risk
IOU	Institute of Organization and Administrative Science
IPCC	Intergovernmental Panel on Climate Change
ISBM	International Schools of Business Management
ISE	São Paulo Stock Exchange Corporate Sustainability Index
ISO	International Organization for Standardization
ISS	Institutional Shareholder Services (now Risk Metrics)
IT	information technology
ITUC	International Trade Union Confederation
IUCN	International Union for Conservation of Nature
KPI	key performance indicator
LEED	Leadership in Energy and Environmental Design (Symantec)
MDGs	Millennium Development Goals
MNC	multinational corporation
MNE	multinational enterprise
MoU	memorandum of understanding
NCP	national contact point
NGO	non-governmental organization
NYSE	New York Stock Exchange
OECD	Organization for Economic Cooperation and Development
OHCHR	Office of the UN High Commissioner for Human Rights
OHSAS	Occupational Health and Safety Standard
PACI	Partnering Against Corruption Initiative
ppm	parts per million
PPP	public–private partnership
PR	public relations
PRI	Principles for Responsible Investment
PRME	Principles for Responsible Management Education
PSG	Pharmaceutical Shareowners Group
R&D	research and development
RESIST	Resisting Extortion and Solicitation in International Sales and Transactions

RFP	Requests for Proposals
RSE	Roundtables on Sustainable Enterprise
SA 8000	Social Accountability 8000
SAI	Social Accountability International
SCS	Scientific Certification Systems
SEC	Securities and Exchange Commission (US)
SEC	Security and Exchange Commission (Brazil)
SEE	sustainable enterprise economy
SER	Social and Environmental Reports (Petrobras)
SGSR	Secretary-General's Special Representative
SIF	Social Investment Forums
SME	small and medium-sized enterprise
SOE	state-owned enterprise
SRF	socially responsible fund
SRI	socially responsible investment
TI	Transparency International
TNC	transnational corporation
TRAC	Transparency in Recording on Anti-Corruption
TUAC	Trade Union Advisory Committee
UDHR	Universal Declaration of Human Rights
UKSIF	Sustainable Investment and Finance Association (UK)
UN	United Nations
UNCAC	United Nations Convention Against Corruption
UNCED	United Nations Conference on Environment and Development
UNCTAD	United Nations Conference on Trade and Development
UNDP	United Nations Development Programme
UNEP	United Nations Environment Programme
UNEP FI	United Nations Environment Programme Finance Initiative
UNESCO	United Nations Educational, Scientific and Cultural Organization
UNFCCC	United Nations Framework Convention on Climate Change
UNICEF	United Nations Children's Fund
UNIDO	United Nations Industrial Development Organization
UNODC	United Nations Office on Drugs and Crime
UN WSSD	United Nations World Summit on Sustainable Development

USP	unique selling proposition
WBCSD	World Business Council for Sustainable Development
WEF	World Economic Forum
WMO	World Meteorological Organization
WRI	World Resources Institute
WSSD	World Summit on Sustainable Development
WTO	World Trade Organization
WWF	World Wide Fund for Nature

Contributors

Ernst A. Brugger is President and managing partner of BHP – Brugger and Partners Ltd in Zurich, a consulting firm specialized in sustainability strategies. He is also chairman and member of the board of directors of numerous organizations as well as part-time professor for economic geography at the University of Zurich, Switzerland. As co-founder and CEO of The Sustainability Forum Zurich (TSF), and in his project work, he advocates the implementation of long-term strategy, corporate responsibility, sustainability and good governance in business and politics.

Eric Cornuel has been the Director-General and CEO of the European Foundation for Management Development (EFMD) in Brussels since 2000. Eric Cornuel is, among others, a Board Member of the EIASM (European Institute of Advanced Studies in Management), EBP (*European Business Journal*), IJBS (*International Journal of Business in Society*), EABIS (European Academy of Business in Society), ISBM (International Schools of Business Management) and GFME (Global Foundation for Management Education). He also sits on the board of several companies. From 1996 to the present, Eric Cornuel has been affiliate Professor at HEC Graduate School of Management, Paris. He has taught for fifteen years at various management schools in Europe and Asia.

Aron Cramer is President and CEO of BSR (www.bsr.org), a global non-profit business network and consultancy focused on sustainability. He advises companies on their sustainability strategies, and speaks frequently on the topic. He joined BSR in 1995 as founding Director of its Business and Human Rights programme, and has worked closely on several groundbreaking human rights initiatives related to business, as well as with the Global Compact Network.

Flavio Fuertes has been Programme Analyst at UNDP since 2002 and responsible for the Argentinean Global Compact Focal Point. He has represented the Argentinean Global Compact Local Network in many conferences (London, 2004; Barcelona, 2005, 2006; Geneva and Monterrey, 2007; Bonn, 2008; Istanbul, 2009). He has been a regular teacher at Universidad de Buenos Aires, on Comparative Politics from 2002 to the present and Electoral Regimes and Political Parties from 1999 to 2003 and visiting professor at University Torcuato Di Tella and Catholic University of Córdoba. He holds a Licentiate in Political Science (Universidad de Buenos Aires, 2000).

Claude Fussler is an expert in business innovation and issue management with a focus on sustainable development, climate change and corporate social responsibility. He is Senior Advisor to the United Nations Global Compact and organized the Caring for Climate initiative through 2008 and early 2009. He chairs the Sustainability Council of the EDF Group in Paris. As a vice president of Dow Chemical in Europe, where he worked for more than thirty years until 2001, he managed a number of international business units before moving to the World Business Council for Sustainable Development (WBCSD) where he was programme director until 2004. He and his family are living carbon positive on a farm in Provence thanks to energy efficiency, large-scale photovoltaic, green electricity feed and systematic reforestation (electric car wanted next!).

James Gifford is Executive Director of the United Nations-backed Principles for Responsible Investment (PRI) and has been guiding the initiative since its inception in 2003. He has a PhD from the Faculty of Economics and Business at the University of Sydney on the effectiveness of shareholder engagement in improving corporate environmental, social and corporate governance performance. He has a background in IT and forest protection, and degrees in Commerce and Law from the University of Queensland and a Masters in Environment Management from the University of New South Wales. He is a board member of the Melbourne-based Centre for Sustainability Leadership and is on the Advisory Council of the Responsible Investment Academy, an Australian industry training initiative.

Dirk Ulrich Gilbert is Professor of Management at the University of Erlangen–Nuremberg in Germany. After obtaining his PhD at the Johann Wolfgang Goethe-University in Frankfurt, he taught at the European Business School in Oestrich-Winkel, Germany, where he completed his postdoctoral thesis. He then became a Lecturer in International Business at The University of New South Wales in Sydney, Australia. He has published several books and articles in the areas of international strategy, international business ethics and organization theory.

Oded Grajew, entrepreneur, is the originator of Movimento Nossa São Paulo, and the founder, former president and current member of the Board of Instituto Ethos de Empresas e Responsabilidade Social. He is the originator of the World Social Forum, former president of Fundação Abrinq pelos Direitos da Criança e do Adolescente and former advisor to the President of Brazil (2003). In all his activities, Grajew works to mobilize society to promote socially responsible and sustainable economic development.

Ana Paula Grether Carvalho is the Coordinator of the Petrobras Social and Environmental Reports (SER), and has had responsibility for its development since 2005. She also represents Petrobras at the main international forums and initiatives on Corporate Social Responsibility (CSR). She is the Brazilian industry expert at the international working group of ISO 26000. In 2007, Ms Grether was nominated to be at the business sector representation of the Stakeholder Council of the Global Reporting Initiative (GRI), an international reference network to develop a sustainability reporting framework. She has participated in working groups and meetings of the United Nations Global Compact, the World Business Council for Sustainable Development (WBCSD), the Extractive Industry Transparency Initiative (EITI) and the Partnering Against Corruption Initiative (PACI).

Uzma Hamid is Corporate Social Responsibility Manager at KPMG Europe LLP, working across a number of sustainability issues ranging from human rights, environment, social inclusion to Corporate Social Responsibility (CSR) reporting, in both local and international contexts. In 2008 she undertook a secondment to the United Nations Global Compact Office in New York to help review the Communication on Progress (COP) requirement. Previous to this she specialized in employer branding and also diversity, working for the HSBC Group in London. Hamid holds a Masters from Glasgow University in History and Politics and a postgraduate diploma in Marketing from the Chartered Institute of Marketing in the UK.

Constanze J. Helmchen is a political scientist who has worked for ten years on corporate responsibility and sustainable development. Moving from management consultancy at the Boston Consulting Group she returned to her university focus on ethnic conflict, editing the *Berghof Handbook for Conflict Transformation*. At IFOK she then concentrated on cross-sector facilitation, negotiating public, private and civil society interests. After five years with the German Technical Cooperation (GTZ), she returned from Bolivia in January 2007 to coordinate the German Global Compact Network.

Paul Hohnen, a former Australian diplomat, is an independent expert on global sustainable development and corporate social responsibility issues. Hohnen is an Associate Fellow of Chatham House (London) and has worked on many of the leading international responsibility initiatives, including the United Nations Global Compact, the Global Reporting Initiative (GRI), the draft ISO Social Responsibility 26000 standard, and the OECD Guidelines for Multinational Enterprises. Hohnen has been a consulting Special Adviser to GRI and former Senior Adviser to the Global Compact.

Oliver Johner is a senior consultant with BHP – Brugger and Partners Ltd in Zurich, 2002–7 and again from August 2009. He focuses on topics such as corporate responsibility, sustainability and resource management. As a member of the Guilé Engagement Team he engages with companies that are included in investment funds based on their commitment to the Global Compact. From February 2007 to July 2009, Johner was a Communication on Progress Analyst at the United Nations Global Compact Office in New York. He holds a MSc in Geography from the University of Bern.

Georg Kell is the Executive Director of the United Nations Global Compact. Spanning more than two decades, his career with the United Nations began in 1987 at the United Nations Conference on Trade and Development (UNCTAD) in Geneva. In 1997, Kell joined the Office of the UN Secretary-General in New York, where he spearheaded the development of new strategies to enhance private sector engagement with the work of the United Nations. As one of the Global Compact's key architects, he has led the initiative since its launch in 2000, building the most widely recognized global business platform on human rights, labour, environment and anti-corruption. Prior to joining the

UN System, Kell worked as a researcher at the Fraunhofer Institute in Germany and as a financial analyst evaluating multinational companies' investment portfolios in Asia and Africa. He holds advanced degrees in economics and engineering from the Technical University of Berlin.

Birgit Kleymann is Associate Professor of Organisation Theory at IESEG School of Management, Catholic University of Lille, France, where she heads the Centre for Responsible Leadership. She holds a PhD from the Helsinki School of Economics. Her research interests include social systems theory, emerging organizational forms and pre-modern and non-traditional management approaches.

Huguette Labelle holds a PhD in Education. She is a Companion of the Order of Canada and has been awarded honorary degrees from twelve Canadian universities. She has served for nineteen years as Deputy Minister of different Canadian Government departments and on more than twenty Boards. She is Chancellor of the University of Ottawa, Chair of CRC Sogema, Board Member of the United Nations Global Compact, member of the Group of External Advisors for the World Bank Governance and Anti-Corruption Strategy Implementation and member of the ADB Advisory Group on Climate Change and Sustainable Development.

Klaus Leisinger heads the Novartis Foundation for Sustainable Development as CEO and President of its Board of Trustees. The Foundation (www.novartisfoundation.com) has consultative status with the Social and Economic Council of the United Nations. In addition he serves as Professor of Sociology at the University of Basel where he conducts research and teaches Business Ethics and Corporate Social Responsibility. Between September 2005 and December 2006, he served as Special Advisor of the UN Secretary-General for the Global Compact.

Malcolm McIntosh FRSA is Professor and Director of the Asia Pacific Centre for Sustainable Enterprise at Griffith Business School, Brisbane, Queensland. He is also a Visiting Professor of Human Security and Sustainable Enterprise in the Centre for Peace and Reconciliation, Coventry University, UK; Visiting Professor, Department of Civil Engineering, University of Bristol, UK; and Professor Extraordinaire, Sustainability Institute, Stellenbosch

University, South Africa. His most recent books are *SEE Change*, on the emerging low-carbon sustainable enterprise economy, written with Sandra Waddock (2010), and *Perspectives on Human Security*, co-edited with Alan Hunter (2010).

Peter Maurer is the Permanent Representative of Switzerland to the United Nations in New York. He studied History and International Law in Switzerland and has a PhD from the University of Bern. He joined the Swiss Ministry of Foreign Affairs in 1987 and was subsequently posted in Pretoria/Cape Town, Bern and New York. He has been involved in developing Swiss cooperation programmes in support of changes in South Africa in the late 1980s and Eastern Europe after 1989, relations between Switzerland and the European Union as well as Swiss–UN relations. In 2000 he became Head of the newly created Human Security Division in the Ministry of Foreign Affairs, which included oversight of Human Rights, Humanitarian Policy and Peace Support Programmes. He became Ambassador of Switzerland to the United Nations in 2004 and has since then focused on different areas of UN reform, mediation, and peace building and human rights issues.

Faris Natour is Director of BSR's research team, which produces independent, business-critical research to help companies anticipate emerging trends and implement sustainability strategies. Natour, who focuses on the intersection of human rights and business, has led research initiatives and training seminars on business and human rights and has advised a wide range of companies on managing their human rights impacts. Prior to working at BSR, he was a social research analyst with the Calvert Group focused on human rights. Natour has a master's degree in international law from George Washington University Law School and a law degree from University of Regensburg, Germany.

Guido Palazzo is Professor of Business Ethics at the University of Lausanne (Switzerland) and Visiting Fellow at the Universities of Oxford and Nottingham. His degree in Management is from the University of Bamberg, Germany, and his PhD in philosophy from the University of Marburg, Germany. His research is on the consequences of globalization for the role and responsibility of corporations.

Andreas Rasche is Assistant Professor of Business in Society at Warwick Business School and since 2007 a consultant to the United Nations Global Compact Office in New York. His PhD in Strategic Management and Corporate Responsibility is from the European Business School, Oestrich-Winkel, Germany. His research focuses on global governance and transnational organizational regulation in the context of contested global issues. He has published widely in leading international journals on corporate responsibility and guest-edited special issues of various journals. More information is available at www.arasche.com.

Guy Ryder is the General Secretary of the International Trade Union Confederation (ITUC), the world's largest trade union body with a membership of 170 million workers in 157 countries. The ITUC is in the forefront in defending trade union rights and promoting the economic and social conditions of workers around the world. Ryder has worked in the trade union movement at national and international level and was elected the General Secretary of the ITUC at its founding Congress in 2006. He is a member of the Global Compact Board.

Andreas Georg Scherer is Professor of Theories of the Firm and Director of the Institute of Organization and Administrative Science (IOU) at the University of Zurich (Switzerland). He has degrees from the University of Erlangen–Nuremberg, Germany, and has published on Business Ethics, Corporate Social Responsibility and Organization Theory. In particular he is interested in the political role of private business firms in global governance processes.

Matthias Stausberg joined the United Nations Global Compact Office in September 2002. As the Global Compact's lead spokesperson, he oversees the initiative's public affairs and media relations work and is a frequent speaker on issues of corporate responsibility and sustainability. Stausberg spent several years working in Germany's Internet industry, leading content development for one of Europe's largest interactive service providers. A German National Merit Scholar and a Fulbright Scholar, he holds a master's degree in Mass Communication from the University of North Carolina's School of Journalism.

Pierre Tapie is Dean and President of ESSEC Business School, Paris–Singapore. He holds an Engineer diploma from the École Polytechnique of Paris, France, a Master of Science in Biochemistry and a PhD in Biophysics from Paris XI Orsay University and an MBA from INSEAD. He studied Theology at the Catholic Institute of Paris. Among his other current responsibilities, Tapie is Chairman of the French Federation of Private Business and Engineering Schools, Vice-Chairman of the National Conference of Engineering and Management Colleges, Member of the National Evaluation Commission of French Business Schools and Member of the National Committee for Private Higher Education. He is member of the Board of Directors of the Association to Advance Collegiate Schools of Business (AACSB) and Vice-Chairman of the Globally Responsible Leadership Foundation.

Gregory C. Unruh is the Director of the Lincoln Center for Ethics at Thunderbird School of Global Management. Previously he was the Alumni Professor of Corporate Social Responsibility at the IE Business School in Madrid, Spain. He co-founded the Center for Eco-Intelligent Management with green architect William McDonough and has held positions at Columbia University in New York City, The Fletcher School in Boston, The Rotterdam School of Management and INCAE in Costa Rica. His research has appeared in academic and business journals including the *Harvard Business Review* and *Energy Policy*, as well as outlets such as the *Financial Times*, *Business Week* and the *Boston Globe*.

Nicolás Liarte Vejrup is an external consultant in Corporate Social Responsibility (CSR) and a consultant with the United Nations Development Programme (UNDP). He also teaches CSR at the Catholic University of Córdoba and is Director of PROETICA and In Company Training at the Institute of Administration Sciences, Catholic University of Córdoba. He holds a Master in Business Administration from the Institute of Administration Science, Catholic University of Córdoba and graduated in Political Science from the Catholic University of Córdoba.

Sandra Waddock is the Galligan Chair of Strategy and Professor of Management at Boston College's Carroll School of Management, and Senior Research Fellow at Boston College's Center for Corporate Citizenship. Widely published on corporate responsibility and citizenship, she holds MBA and DBA degrees from Boston University.

Patricia H. Werhane is the Wicklander Chair of Business Ethics and the Executive Director at the Institute for Business and Professional

Ethics at DePaul University, Chicago. She was formerly the Ruffin Professor of Business Ethics and Senior Fellow at the Olsson Center for Applied Ethics in the Darden School at the University of Virginia. She has published numerous articles and is the author or editor of over twenty books. She is the founder and former Editor-in-Chief of *Business Ethics Quarterly*, the journal of the Society for Business Ethics, and she is an Academic Advisor to the Business Roundtable Institute for Corporate Ethics.

Nessa Whelan has been a Network Coordinator with the United Nations Global Compact Office (2002–9). In this role she focused primarily on the development and facilitation of Global Compact Local Networks with particular emphasis on Europe and Asia. Nessa holds a MA in Comparative Ethnic Conflict from Queen's University Belfast.

Regina Wentzel Wolfe is Senior Wicklander Fellow at the Institute for Business and Professional Ethics, DePaul University, Chicago. She was Christopher Chair in Business Ethics at Brennan School of Business, Dominican University, Illinois, from 2004 to 2008 and Associate Professor of Theology at Saint John's University, Minneapolis, from 1994 to 2004. Wolfe has a BSBA from the McDonough School of Business, Georgetown University, an MTM from Loyola University Chicago and a PhD from King's College, University of London, UK.

Carolyn Y. Woo has been the Dean of Mendoza College of Business at the University of Notre Dame since 1997. Before then, she served as Associate Executive Vice President for Academic Affairs at Purdue University, Indiana. Woo's research focuses on strategy, entrepreneurship and organizational systems. She lectures regularly on individual integrity, ethical systems and corporate citizenship. She currently serves on a number of corporate and non-profit boards including AON Corporation, NiSource Incorporated, Catholic Relief Services and University of Portland. She was chair of the Association and Advance Collegiate Schools of Business (AACSB) International and co-convenes the United Nations Global Compact initiative Principles for Responsible Management Education (PRME).

Ursula Wynhoven is the Head, Policy and Legal and Special Assistant to the Executive Director of the Global Compact Office. A member of the Office's management team, she also handles its legal affairs and policy matters, and leads its work on human rights and labour. A lawyer by background, Ursula worked in private practice and government human rights agencies in Australia and the USA and for the OECD Secretariat on the Guidelines for Multinational Enterprises before joining the Office. Ursula has two Masters of Law degrees (Columbia Law School and Monash University) and is an Adjunct Professor in Business and Human Rights at Fordham Law School.

Acknowledgements

This book would not have been possible without the support and hard work of a number of people. Of course, it goes without saying that we very much appreciate the time and energy that all contributors invested in finishing their chapters on time. From the outset, it was clear that we wanted to produce a tightly integrated set of chapters on predefined topics and not a loose collection of essays around the United Nations Global Compact. We very much appreciate that all our contributors agreed to write their chapters while, at the same time, keeping the overall structure of the book in mind. We would also like to express gratitude for our contributors' patience and understanding while responding to our questions, recommendations and queries.

We very much appreciate UN Secretary-General Ban Ki-moon writing the Foreword for this book. We are also indebted to Eric Cornuel's (Director General and CEO, EFMD) very thoughtful reflections on 'Why This Book Matters!'. We would like to acknowledge the much-appreciated support by the European Foundation for Management Development (EFMD) and the Globally Responsible Leadership Initiative (GRLI). This book profited in many ways from the strong backing of both institutions.

Along the way, Rebecca Lewis (United Nations Global Compact Office) and Olubukola Okunnuga (Warwick Business School) provided support while preparing the final manuscript. We also wish to thank Barbara Docherty, who did an excellent job copy-editing the book. At Cambridge University Press, we benefited from the courageous support, energy and professionalism of Paula Parish and Phil Good.

We sincerely thank all involved parties. We trust that our combined effort has translated into an exciting and useful resource reflecting on the first ten years of the Global Compact, and also on the challenges lying ahead.

Andreas Rasche and Georg Kell
Coventry and New York, October 2009

Foreword

What began as a commitment by a few dozen inspired business leaders ten years ago has grown into the world's largest and most recognized platform for promoting responsible business practices. The Global Compact has evolved in substance, too, not just in size, as the debate it sought to spark and advance – on the environmental and social responsibilities of business – has emerged as an issue of strategic importance in boardrooms around the world.

As a unique partnership between business, civil society and the United Nations, the Compact has given inspiration and direction to the many efforts by business to improve their own performance and do their part in addressing the multiple global challenges we face, from abject poverty to climate change. This book offers a comprehensive analysis of the initiative's governance, its engagement mechanisms and, most importantly, its impact. I commend it to a wide global audience, and to all who want to learn more about the Compact's journey and its proven capacity to generate positive change for people and the planet.

Ban Ki-moon
UN Secretary-General

Why This Book Matters!

With over 7,300 business and non-business participants, the United Nations Global Compact is the largest corporate citizenship initiative in the world, and a unique one. This book provides a comprehensive overview of the Global Compact, discusses new aspects and offers a review of the first ten years of its existence. Why is it important?

First, it introduces three important issues that have hardly been dealt with in the literature before: (1) the Communication on Progress (COP) policy, (2) the role of Global Compact Local Networks (GCLNs) and (3) the role of emerging specialized initiatives. Second, because so many practitioners are involved, it contains many new and valuable case studies and examples. Third, it links responsible business practices and responsible management education, and paves the way towards a genuine partnership aligning mutual objectives. The management profession has indeed a fundamental responsibility to assume, to the benefit of society as a whole.

The book will be particularly valuable to three distinct, though linked, sets of readers.

Global Compact business and non-business participants: These readers will find much of interest in the book because it covers many issues that are of direct relevance to them. These include, for example, GCLNs and COP policy implementation. In addition, the book shows how the different parts of the initiative work together and offers a more detailed view and appraisal of the Compact that goes beyond any 'quick view' that has so far been available.

Academics researching the Global Compact: Academic interest in the Global Compact has grown strongly in recent years. This is especially true of some of the newer features of the initiative, for example specialized programmes such as Caring for Climate. And while this volume is not a 'theoretical resource', it is likely to become a much-used reference work by academics pursuing research on the impact of the Global Compact.

Students of corporate citizenship/corporate responsibility: Graduate and postgraduate students who work in the field of corporate responsibility/corporate citizenship will also find much of value in these pages. Many courses on corporate responsibility use or refer to the Global Compact and the book, which eschews the academic jargon often favoured by journal articles, will provide an accessible and appropriate student resource.

But whatever their background, I sincerely hope that all readers will find much to both enlighten and inspire them!

Professor Eric Cornuel
Director-General and CEO of the
European Foundation for Management Development (EFMD)

The Ten Principles of the United Nations Global Compact

The Global Compact asks companies to embrace, support and enact, within their sphere of influence, a set of core values in the areas of human rights, labour standards, the environment and anti-corruption:

Human rights
Principle 1: Businesses should support and respect the protection of internationally proclaimed human rights; and

Principle 2: make sure that they are not complicit in human rights abuses.

Labour standards
Principle 3: Businesses should uphold the freedom of association and the effective recognition of the right to collective bargaining;

Principle 4: the elimination of all forms of forced and compulsory labour;

Principle 5: the effective abolition of child labour; and

Principle 6: the elimination of discrimination in respect of employment and occupation.

Environment
Principle 7: Businesses should support a precautionary approach to environmental challenges;

Principle 8: undertake initiatives to promote greater environmental responsibility; and

Principle 9: encourage the development and diffusion of environmentally friendly technologies.

Anti-corruption
Principle 10: Businesses should work against corruption in all its forms, including extortion and bribery.

1 | Introduction: the United Nations Global Compact – retrospect and prospect

ANDREAS RASCHE AND GEORG KELL

About This Book

Much like the Global Compact, this book is based on the idea of collaboration between different stakeholders. We invited practitioners from a variety of areas and academics to share their views about the first ten years of the Global Compact, and to also reflect on what remains to come. From the outset it was understood that the different contributors would explain and reflect on the Global Compact in their own way. Instead of seeing this as a problem, we believe that a variety of perspectives can help to expose areas of agreement and disagreement. Over the years, the Global Compact has significantly profited from the ideas introduced by different parties and the tensions these ideas created. The unique blend of people involved in this book project serves to further develop the Global Compact by sustaining the existing discourse among practitioners and academics. Combining practical insights and lived experiences with recent academic reflections was one of the key motivations for this edited volume.

Bearing in mind that the Global Compact celebrates its tenth anniversary in 2010, we asked all contributors to take the theme of 'Achievements, Trends and Challenges' as a 'walking stick' to create their chapter contribution. While in some chapters a reflection on past achievements, current trends and future challenges is implicitly embedded in the discussion, other chapters address these three issue areas in a more explicit way. Looking back at the first ten years of the Global Compact, a reflection on what has been achieved and what issues are likely to influence the initiative during the next decade not only is necessary but most of all *timely*. Without doubt, the different chapters echo the complexity of the Global Compact as a Network-based, multi-stakeholder initiative working globally and locally. We believe that the rich reflections, which are presented in the chapters, give the reader a good grasp of what the initiative is about, where it came from, and where it is potentially heading.

The book should neither be understood as a comprehensive summary of the first ten years of the Global Compact nor as an offi-cially endorsed document. Our aim was to bring together academics and practitioners (and people who 'live' in both worlds) to reflect on their experiences researching, implementing as well as working for or with the Global Compact. While research on the Global Compact has expanded noticeably in recent years (see, for instance, Cetindamar and Husoy 2007, Rasche 2009a, Rieth *et al.* 2007, Runhaar and Lafferty 2009),[1] there is still much to learn from practitioners' on-the-ground experiences. For future research to be relevant, it needs to give con-sideration to the institutional embeddedness of the Global Compact and the constraints as well as opportunities this creates. Of course, the contributions in this book also show that practice can be inspired by the ideas developed through academic discourse. For instance, Dirk Ulrich Gilbert (chapter 19) emphasizes a variety of mechanisms to increase trust among participants in Local Networks. Whatever the relation between academic discourse and practice might be, this book aims to speak to 'both worlds'.

Achievements: the United Nations Global Compact in historical context

The underlying conviction of the Global Compact is very well characterized by UN Secretary-General Ban Ki-moon, who describes the relation between markets and societies as follows: 'Markets can flourish only in societies that are healthy. And societies need healthy markets to flourish' (United Nations 2008: 1). The Global Compact acknowledges that business, as a key agent driving globali-zation, can help to ensure that markets advance in ways that benefit society.

What is today the largest corporate responsibility initiative in the world, with currently more than 7,300 business and non-business

---

[1] We make no attempt to survey the rich academic and non-academic literature on the Global Compact. For a recent detailed overview and discussion, see Rasche (2009a).

participants in over 130 countries (as of January 2010), started out as a speech. When then-UN Secretary-General Kofi Annan went to the World Economic Forum in Davos in January 1999, he challenged the business leaders of the world to help fill the governance voids that the rise of the global economy had brought about, and thus become part of the solution. Based on the conviction that the goals of the United Nations and those of business can be mutually supportive, Annan declared: 'I propose that you, the business leaders gathered here in Davos, and we, the United Nations, initiate a Global Compact of shared values and principles, which will give a human face to the global market' (United Nations 1999: 1).[2]

The reaction to this speech was overwhelming. Annan received letters from CEOs and different ambassadors to translate these fine words into action. After non-governmental organizations (NGOs), labour and a variety of UN agencies had committed to the idea of setting up a Global Compact, where business makes a principled commitment to universal values, the initiative was operationally launched on 26 July 2000, at UN Headquarters in New York. The Global Compact went operational with only a handful of companies and non-business stakeholders but quickly attracted more participants and thus unfolded its own dynamic. The New York meeting brought together executives from around forty businesses and representatives from NGOs, labour, and partnering UN agencies.

Everyone who knows the history of the UN–business relationship is aware of the ideologies that had to be overcome to make the Compact a success story (for this, see also Sagafi-Nejad 2008). The Global Compact is the living example for a new era of cooperation between the business community and the United Nations; an era characterized by overcoming a recent past of mutual suspicion (Kell 2005). This rapprochement was reinforced by the rapid transformation of economic and social structures throughout the world, mostly driven by globalization and its discontents. The Global Compact was the creative answer to the many unaddressed governance gaps which deteriorated as a result of the worldwide expansion of value and supply chains.

---

[2] The full version of the speech, as well as a variety of other historical documents, can be accessed via the Global Compact website (www.unglobalcompact.org/NewsAndEvents/Speeches.html).

By launching the Global Compact, the United Nations successfully entered the corporate responsibility territory. Of course, providing a dictionary-like definition of what the Global Compact reflects is dangerous insofar as definitions are always static, while the initiative and its environment are dynamic. In its most general sense, the Global Compact is a call to companies to voluntarily align their operations with ten universal principles in the areas of human rights, labour standards, the environment and anti-corruption (the ten Principles are fully listed at the beginning of this volume, p. xxxi). By participating in the Global Compact businesses are expected to contribute to the fulfilment of the initiative's two major objectives: (1) to mainstream the ten Principles in business activities around the world and (2) to catalyse actions in support of broader UN goals (including the Millennium Development Goals or MDGs). It is obvious, but still needs to be emphasized again and again, that the Global Compact is neither a standard to measure corporations' compliance against predefined indicators nor a seal of approval for participating businesses. Without doubt, compliance-based instruments (e.g. certification standards for social audits) have their rightful place on the corporate responsibility agenda. Certification standards and principle-based initiatives, like the Global Compact, should be perceived as being complementary and not mutually exclusive. After all, the Compact is also no substitute for what governments seek to achieve through regulation.

Throughout its first ten years the Global Compact has proven to be a flexible and dynamic initiative, mastering growth with limited resources in a non-bureaucratic way – the addition of the 10th Principle on anti-corruption (2004), the launch of the Communication on Progress policy (COP, 2005), the first (2004) and second (2007) Leaders Summit, and the set up of issue platforms like Caring for Climate (2007) – are all landmark events in the history of the initiative and echo its vibrant and thought-leading character (see also the relevant chapters on these topics in this book). These and other events helped to achieve a lot: through its substantial outreach the Global Compact has helped to shape and widen the corporate responsibility movement – away from its limited emphasis on isolated philanthropic activities towards an understanding that responsible corporate action requires a redesign of value chain activities and corporate policies as well as strong leadership. Underlining the strategic significance of responsible business practices, the Global Compact has also helped to establish the business case for corporate responsibility, for instance by supporting the Principles for Responsible Investment (PRI). Nowadays, it is well understood that environmental, social and governance (ESG) issues are all drivers of corporate performance (see also chapter 11 by James Gifford).

Considering the plethora of corporate responsibility initiatives and their rapid proliferation over the last years (for overviews, see Leipziger 2003 and also Rasche 2009b), it is worth to take a closer look at some of the *distinguishing features* of the Global Compact:

1. The Global Compact, unlike other multi-stakeholder schemes aiming at certification (SA 8000) or reporting (GRI), is a principle-based initiative asking participants to align their operations and value chain activities with ten universally accepted principles. Commitment to the Global Compact has to be endorsed by the chief executive officer (CEO). This CEO-led character makes the initiative a leadership platform, which is based on a robust policy framework for the development and integration of corporate responsibility practices into a firm's value and supply chain.
2. The Global Compact, unlike other initiatives, is truly global. Half of all participants are based in developing or emerging economies (Global Compact 2008: 8). The worldwide reach of the Compact helps to fill governance voids through coordinated action across countries, regions, and continents. The Compact has a particularly strong foothold in essential economies like China and India, both of which play a significant role when looking at the challenges inherent in the ten Principles. By now, China and India are among the largest Local Networks and provide a significant share of the overall signatory base.
3. The Global Compact involves small and medium-sized enterprises (SMEs) *and* larger companies. Business participation is almost equally split between these two types of corporations. Considering that SMEs, which are often part of global supply chains, play a pivotal role when thinking about how to implement corporate responsibility practices in the local context, their participation in the Global Compact is inevitable.
4. The Global Compact enjoys wide government support. The General Assembly as well as the G8 have recognized the initiative. In addition, the mandate of the Global Compact Office has been renewed

and expanded through the General Assembly Resolution 'Towards Global Partnerships' (A/RES/64/223) of December 2009.

The combination of these characteristics makes the Global Compact unique when compared to other corporate responsibility initiatives.

Trends: shaping the corporate responsibility agenda

Corporate responsibility is a dynamic field. Many trends have shaped the agenda over recent years. Throughout its rather short history, the Global Compact (together with other initiatives) has witnessed a fundamental change in how, where and which businesses handle corporate responsibility issues. Considering these trends, it is necessary to look at what currently shapes the agenda:

First, *corporate responsibility has turned global.* As mentioned above, especially emerging economies like China and India have entered the corporate responsibility universe and started to build up localized knowledge and best practices. This development highlights the possibility for increased collaboration, not only among multiple stakeholders but most of all across continents and regions. The interconnected and interdependent nature of economies around the world (for example, as shown by the recent economic downturn) reflects a governance challenge. The Global Compact started from the premise that the existence of global governance gaps drives the need for corporate responsibility. This is nowhere more evident than in the early writings on the initiative (Kell and Levin 2003, Kell and Ruggie 1999, Ruggie 2001) and has also been acknowledged in the wider discourse on corporate responsibility (Scherer and Palazzo 2008, Scherer, Palazzo and Baumann 2006). Nowadays, this positioning of the Compact seems very timely and has surely contributed to its success.

Second, *corporate responsibility has turned into a strategic and operational concern.* Corporations join the Global Compact for reasons of risk mitigation and opportunity seizing. The 2008 Global Compact Implementation Survey finds that corporations are aiming at integrating ESG issues into their corporate strategies and value chain activities (Global Compact 2008: 10). Increasingly, corporate responsibility is proactively embedded in organizational processes and relates to concrete business practices; it is a strategic concern affected by and affecting the long-term positioning of an organization. The strategic concern for corporate responsibility is also reflected by the CEO-led nature of policies. While this shows that corporate responsibility has 'matured' insofar as it is perceived as being an 'internal' part of business activities (and not an 'external' add-on), top-level management commitment itself is not enough. Strategies and practices have to be communicated and 'lived' throughout the organization. This attitude is well reflected in the remarks by Bo Miller (Global Director, Corporate Citizenship, The Dow Chemical Company) who was interviewed for Carolyn Woo's chapter 7 on 'Implementing the United Nations Global Compact'. Miller states: 'Our view of the Compact is significantly more than a declaration or document – it is a living, active process for continuous, practical improvement.'

Third, the *link between financial markets and corporate responsibility* is growing stronger. The Global Compact, through its partnership with the PRI, has significantly supported this process. A swiftly growing community of asset owners and asset managers commits to considering ESG issues in their investment decisions. As discussed in chapter 11 by James Gifford, the link between financial markets and corporate responsibility is central as initiatives like the PRI encourage businesses to either join the Global Compact or improve their performance and level of implementation with regard to corporate responsibility issues. The recent global financial crisis has reinforced the need for long-term, sustainable investment strategies over short-term considerations. While improved governance of financial markets cannot solely rest on voluntary initiatives like the PRI, but needs to be backed up by legislation, there is no doubt that a further recognition of ESG issues by the investment community acts a strong driver of the corporate responsibility agenda.

Last but not least, the *environmental and corporate responsibility agendas are conflating*, largely due to business' pivotal role in shaping a future low-carbon economy. The Global Compact realized this development early on by creating the Caring for Climate and CEO Water Mandate specialized engagement platforms (see also the chapter by Claude Fussler). While a few years ago social issues largely dominated the corporate responsibility field, environmental issues are increasingly recognized as being an integral part of corporate responsibility. Companies that choose not to accept the challenge of integrating sustainability-related issues into their strategies and operations do so at their peril.

Staying ahead of the curve implies the need to recognize that environmental challenges – like lowering carbon dioxide (CO_2) emissions, fresh-water availability and water pollution – cannot any longer be managed in a disconnected manner. There is an urgent need not only to put these issues on the corporate responsibility agenda but to also understand existing and emerging linkages: (a) among these environmental problems, (b) between these problems and the wider corporate responsibility agenda (e.g. social issues and anti-corruption) and (c) between these problems and a company's business policy and value chain activities. For instance, it is widely accepted that there are strong connections between the climate, energy and water agendas (e.g. climate change affects water scarcity and sustainable supply because of the decreased natural water storage capacity from glacier/snowcap melting; see Pacific Institute and United Nations Global Compact 2009).

Challenges: the need for further action

The Global Compact is a dynamic initiative, promoting learning, but also able and willing to learn itself. While almost all chapters reflect on the future of the Global Compact in one way or another, we would like to highlight four challenges in particular.

Improving implementation of the ten Principles

The 2008 Global Compact Implementation Survey revealed different implementation gaps (Global Compact 2008). In a world of globally interconnected value and supply chains, the Compact's Principles have to move beyond corporate headquarters. The contribution of subsidiaries and supply partners has to be deepened when thinking about how to put the ten Principles into practice. This, however, will require advancing businesses corporate responsibility policies and further developing existing management practices. The Global Compact – as an initiative representing a range of companies from a variety of sectors, sizes and regions – attracts companies with different expertise regarding corporate responsibility issues. The 2008 Implementation Survey identified only 8 per cent of all participants as 'advanced' performers (Global Compact 2008: 12), with the majority of participating businesses ranking as 'intermediate' performers.

The key challenge will be helping 'beginners' to scale up their corporate responsibility performance, while maintaining the strong position of the 'advanced' companies. This challenge needs to be addressed from two sides: the Global Compact itself can recommend and develop tools and guidance, help to share good practices and promote multi-stakeholder dialogues and learning. Companies, through top-level management commitment and allocation of ample resources, have to integrate the ten Principles into their core operations and supply chain management (for a comprehensive discussion of implementation, see chapter 7 by Carolyn Woo and also Fussler, Cramer and van der Vegt 2004).

Advancing Communication on Progress (COP)

As discussed throughout this book, disclosure on implementation progress is one important way for corporations to demonstrate commitment to the Global Compact. The Global Compact requires annual reporting on progress and delists all participants which fail to communicate their ongoing implementation efforts. While more than 7,000 COP Reports are already available on the Global Compact website for public review (as of January 2010), it is also clear that the overall quality of reporting has to improve. Only a minority of companies is using established disclosure frameworks, like the GRI G3 Reporting guidelines. The challenge is to not only report on corporate policies and unconnected projects, but to show clear evidence of impacts 'on the ground' based on measurable and transparent indicators. So far, the Global Compact has been forced to delist over 1,000 companies (as of January 2010) for failure to submit a COP Report.

Of course, we need to bear in mind that, while most multinational and large national companies have experience in non-financial reporting, disclosing information on the implementation of the ten Principles is 'new territory' for many SMEs. The Global Compact is working hard to provide practical guidance to those seeking further information and help (see, for instance, the 2008 edition of the 'Practical Guide to UN Global Compact Communication on Progress'). The bottom line is that without a more rigorous approach towards annual disclosure, it will be hard for stakeholders (especially investors) to judge whether and how a company performs with regard to the ten Principles. Establishing the link between ESG performance and long-term value requires more comprehensive disclosure.

Further developing specialized engagement platforms

The Global Compact, together with other organizations, has developed engagement platforms to give participants a chance to demonstrate leadership regarding climate change (Caring for Climate platform) and water sustainability (CEO Water Mandate). Both platforms already enjoy a number of supporters from developed, emerging and developing economies – 370 firms have signed on to Caring for Climate, while 57 companies have signed the CEO Water Mandate (as of January 2010). Participating companies are engaged in individual and collective action and annually report on progress. While both initiatives have gained momentum, it is also clear that supporters of these platforms represent only a small fraction of the overall signatory base of the Global Compact. Considering the urgent need for large-scale action to address climate change and water sustainability, it is necessary to broaden these specialized engagement platforms. Change comes from well-coordinated individual and collective action; expanding the signatory base of such engagement platforms is inevitable if this change is to occur.

Coping with changing global economic realities

While it is still unclear what precise long-term effects the multiple global crises will have had on corporate responsibility practices, there is no doubt that – as businesses around the world adjust to changing economic realities – new challenges are being created. Many of the issues covered by the ten Principles and also the MDGs are likely to be negatively impacted by the crises. For instance, the conditions which perpetuate poverty (e.g. missing out on basic education) are further compounded by the global economic slowdown. The challenge is to not let short-term thinking drive out long-term practices. Addressing this challenge is even harder in an environment where many people have lost trust in corporate activities. According to the 2009 *Edelman Trust Barometer*, 62 per cent of people around the world say they trust corporations less than they did a year ago (Edelman 2009).

The Global Compact is well positioned to cope with the changing global economic realities. More than 1,400 businesses joined the initiative in 2008, reinforcing the notion that in times of crises there is, despite all the problems, also an increased search for sustainable business practices. Restoring confidence in the marketplace cannot happen overnight – it requires long-term solutions, transparent actions, ample financial and non-financial resources, measurable impacts and top-level management commitment. As mentioned above, not all Global Compact participants currently perform at this level. The Compact and its Local Networks have to ensure that the progress which has been achieved over recent years is sustained and extended, by: (1) recognizing and sharing best practices to let 'beginners' catch up, (2) offering contextualized guidance, especially for SMEs in developing and emerging economies and (3) delisting participants which fail to fulfil the annual disclosure requirement.

With every challenge comes an opportunity to learn and instal changes. As with the last ten years, the Compact's ability to make use of the arising opportunities will depend on its ability to promote learning, dialogue and collective action through its Network-based style of organization. While the initiative has achieved a lot in rather a short period of time, there is no doubt that addressing the identified challenges will require strengthening both the quantity and the quality of participation.

Organization of the book

The first ten years of the Global Compact can be explored from different angles. We decided to structure this book in four parts. In part I, chapters 2–6 present reflections on the four key issue areas (i.e. human rights, labour, the environment and anti-corruption). In part II, chapters 7–13 discuss different participant groups and engagement mechanisms. The key objective is to understand how different actors (i.e. businesses, investors, academic institutions and NGOs) relate to and engage with the Compact. In part III, chapters 14–17 discuss Global Compact governance and the COP policy. Our aim was not only to 'simply' introduce the COP policy, but also to show how firms produce COP Reports and how the COP policy fits into the broader framework of the Compact's integrity measures. In part IV, chapters 18–21 discuss the role of Global Compact Local Networks (GCLNs) in connecting the broad policy goals and initiatives at the global level with concrete action on the local and regional level. Finally, chapter 22 summarizes some of the findings presented in this book and outlines currently existing challenges which the Global Compact has to address.

Part I: Achievements, trends and challenges: reflections on the Principles

The ten Principles constitute the 'heart' of the Global Compact. The acknowledged universal legitimacy of the Principles offers an institutional advantage to the initiative, particularly when considering the need to clarify which issues and problems corporate responsibility should address. Through its four issue areas – human rights, labour standards, the environment and anti-corruption – the Compact offers a robust and internationally accepted framework of values. The contributions in part I discuss these four issue areas.

Klaus Leisinger, Aron Cramer and Faris Natour in chapter 2 draw our attention to human rights principles. Based on a solid discussion of the roots of human rights and their applicability to non-state actors, the authors put a special emphasis on the 'protect, respect and remedy' framework which was introduced by the Secretary-General's Special Representative (SGSR) on the Issue of Human Rights and Transnational Corporations, John Ruggie. They discuss how the different parts of the framework relate to the Compact's human rights principles and, in particular, discuss corporations' responsibility to respect human rights. Acknowledging the need to put the Global Compact human rights principles into practice, they also discuss a variety of measures which can support implementation and reporting on progress.

Taking a more critical perspective while, at the same time, acknowledging the potential value of the Compact, Guy Ryder in chapter 3 discusses the role of the global trade union movement and its relation to the Global Compact labour principles. Ryder draws our attention to the limits of corporate responsibility and argues that, to further unleash the potential of the Compact, there needs to be further integration among its many stakeholders. Referring to the necessity to protect labour standards around the world, he critically discusses the stakeholder concept and its relation to the Global Compact. Rather than accepting the status quo, Ryder challenges the initiative to live up to its full potential.

Discussing the environmental issue area, Gregory C. Unruh in chapter 4 gives a detailed analysis of the origins of the Global Compact environmental principles and their embeddedness in international environmental policy. Looking at the functioning of global environmental governance, Unruh explores the meaning behind the

Compact's environmental principles (e.g. the precautionary approach) and thus illustrates the range of phenomena they address. His analysis is based on a variety of real-life examples which show how corporations give meaning to the Compact's environmental principles in their day-to-day business practices and strategic planning. Considering the variety of environmental challenges which Global Compact participants have to address, this chapter offers inevitable background knowledge on what it means to work towards creating a sustainable business in the twenty-first century.

Complementing Unruh's remarks on the environmental principles, and linking them to the Compact's emphasis on working towards a low-carbon economy, Claude Fussler in chapter 5 discusses the significance of the Caring for Climate issue platform. He not only reveals the urgent need for leadership and collective as well as individual action but also discusses how Caring for Climate can act as a platform to identify and share best practices. Caring for Climate signatories make a commitment to performance (e.g. by lowering the carbon burden and increasing energy efficiency) and annually report on progress to the public. Fussler's inspiring discussion demonstrates the usefulness of issue platforms under the umbrella of the Global Compact.

Huguette Labelle in chapter 6 discusses the history and current context of the 10th Principle on anti-corruption. Looking at the status of implementation, she discusses some of the most important tools available to Global Compact signatories to fight against corruption. Labelle recognizes the need to strengthen the work of Local Networks while implementing the 10th Principle. Local Networks can help to better understand the idiosyncratic context in which corruption happens and can be avoided; Networks are well suited to identify those companies and stakeholders which can make a difference on the ground. Regarding future challenges, Labelle stresses the need for deepening the engagement of the Global Compact and its signatories in fighting corruption. The communication and application of available tools is just one important step in this direction.

Part II: Participants and engagement mechanisms

Part II turns our attention towards the different participants in the Global Compact and available engagement mechanisms. While chapters 7–11 give a detailed discussion of selected actors (i.e. businesses,

NGOs, the investment community and academic institutions), chapters 12 and 13 take a closer look at learning, dialogue and the exchange of best practices.

Carolyn Woo focuses in chapter 7 on how businesses implement the Global Compact and also reviews the general status of implementation. She starts by discussing the business case for the Global Compact and finds much evidence that customers and financial markets increasingly value companies' participation in the initiative. Woo also draws our attention to the variety of practices which can support implementation of the ten Principles. Based on an empirical assessment of three Global Compact signatories (i.e. PricewaterhouseCoopers, Symantec and Dow Chemical), the chapter illustrates how corporations embed the ten Principles into their strategy and operations. The three case studies tell interesting stories from different sectors and show that reflection and commitment are essential drivers of implementation.

Moving from businesses to academic institutions, Regina Wentzel Wolfe and Patricia H. Werhane discuss in chapter 8 the role of business schools in supporting the Global Compact agenda. Focusing on the Principles for Responsible Management Education (PRME), which are co-convened by the Global Compact, this chapter illustrates that business schools have an important role to play when thinking about corporate responsibility in the long term. Educating leaders who truly understand the need for corporate responsibility and who are familiar with the institutional environment shaping sustainable business practices is both necessary and timely. This chapter, by empirically assessing PRME signatories' practices, makes an important contribution to better understanding how business schools can best approach this task. Wolfe and Werhane's analysis shows that while many business schools have courses on corporate responsibility issues, there is not much integration of these topics into the broader business school curriculum.

Based on the PRME agenda and the apparent need to educate responsible leaders, Birgit Kleymann and Pierre Tapie in chapter 9 discuss reasons for business schools' failure to teach responsibility and ethics in an effective way. Their argument is based on the assumption that business schools are still following a narrow educational approach based on 'quick' (and apparently practically relevant) programmes and stand-alone ethics modules. Educating responsible leaders, however, requires a set of skills (e.g. managing complexity) which is hardly supported by such programmes. Kleymann and Tapie outline a different approach to education, an approach which can act as an important stimulus to the PRME community. Their arguments are put into perspective by Eric Cornuel's comment. Cornuel emphasizes the need to strengthen the relation between the business and academic world. To this end, he discusses the role of accreditation agencies (like the European Foundation for Management Development, EFMD) as well as partnerships between business and academic institutions (like the Globally Responsible Leadership Initiative, GRLI).

Next, Oded Grajew in chapter 10 looks at the relation between NGOs and the Global Compact. The chapter reveals the rich variety of possible contributions that NGOs can make to the initiative and its participants. According to Grajew, NGOs can help to point out routes where future collective and individual action is needed. In addition, NGOs can also help to create a favourable environment for the implementation of the ten Principles by corporations and, at the same time, carry out a 'watchdog function' to restrict practices which can harm such Principles. Interestingly, Grajew also points out that NGOs themselves have to act as examples of how to put the Global Compact Principles into practice.

Moving from NGOs to financial markets, James Gifford in chapter 11 discusses the Principles for Responsible Investment (PRI) and what financial markets – and, in particular, investors – can do to support the Global Compact agenda. The chapter not only tells the story of the UN-backed PRI initiative but also, and maybe most of all, demonstrates that there are important linkages between the investment community and corporate responsibility. Strengthening and deepening these linkages is vital for the future success of the Global Compact and the corporate responsibility discourse in general. Gifford's reflections are invaluable to help us better understand how investors' consideration of ESG issues can influence corporate practices.

Looking closely at how learning among different stakeholders happens in practice, Malcolm McIntosh and Sandra Waddock in chapter 12 report the results of a series of Roundtable discussions held in different parts of the world between 2007 and 2009. Asking what the world would look like if the Global Compact Principles were fully implemented, this chapter takes a close look at available and desired practices to put the Global Compact into practice and also discusses how the initiative is viewed differently in a variety of countries.

Based on the results of the Roundtables, McIntosh and Waddock develop the notion of a 'sustainable enterprise economy' (SEE), which is founded on the Principles underpinning the Global Compact. Their discussion underscores the need to better understand the change, which the Global Compact desires, as a transformation affecting the interaction among different systems.

Last but not least, Guido Palazzo and Andreas Georg Scherer in chapter 13 conceptualize the implementation of the Global Compact as an organizational learning process. Pointing to the deficits of management theory, this chapter demonstrates that we need to understand corporations' involvement in corporate responsibility in general, and the Global Compact in particular, as an ongoing learning process. Businesses have much to learn when it comes to developing and implementing responsible practices in their sphere of influence (e.g. about changing societal expectations and their own impact on supply chain activities). Palazzo and Scherer conclude that the Global Compact is the right forum to initiate and further develop such learning processes, especially when considering the multi-stakeholder nature of the initiative and its nested Network structure.

Part III: Governance and Communication on Progress

Part III takes a close look at the Compact's disclosure requirement (i.e. the so-called COP policy). While chapter 14 discusses the COP policy as part of the more general integrity measures which the Global Compact has installed, chapters 15–17 offer reflections about the origins and challenges of the COP policy, its implementation by corporations and, finally, its relation to the Global Reporting Initiative (GRI).

Ursula Wynhoven and Matthias Stausberg in chapter 14 discuss and introduce the governance structure of the Global Compact. Most importantly, they explain the evolution of governance from the early Global Compact Advisory Council (GCAC) to the 2004–5 governance review, and the resulting multi-centric governance model of the initiative. Based on this, Wynhoven and Stausberg discuss the Global Compact's integrity measures by putting a special emphasis on the necessity and possibility of social vetting mechanisms. Social vetting – i.e. the critical examination of the information provided by companies on their engagement in the Global Compact – is an important procedure to safeguard the quality of COPs and to foster public debate on corporate responsibility issues.

Uzma Hamid and Oliver Johner in Chapter 15 introduce the origins and current context of the COP policy. Besides discussing the need for and achievements of this policy (e.g. that the COP requirement introduced many firms to non-financial reporting), Hamid and Johner also address several future challenges. In particular, they discuss the need to improve the quality of COP Reports – for instance, by establishing clearer and simpler guidance on how to report on the implementation of the Global Compact's Principles. In this context, they highlight the need to work out specialized disclosure requirements for SMEs. Their chapter is enlightening for everyone interested in the rationale, context and future directions of the COP policy. Considering that governments like Denmark have started to introduce legislation requiring companies to include ESG issues into their financial reporting, a further discussion of COP reporting seems indispensable and well timed.

Next, Ana Paula Grether Carvalho in chapter 16 gives practical insights into how one company, Petrobras, creates its COP Reports. She describes what operational procedures and policies had to be set up to gather the data for the final report and how Petrobras defines reporting indicators. Grether also explains how COP Reports can be used as management tools (e.g. to develop a company's risk management practices). Her remarks are invaluable as they demonstrate the need to conceive COP Reports as change management tools and not solely as data gathering. This case study of one company can serve as an inspirational guide for other reporters seeking to improve their reporting practices.

Closing the section on COP reporting, Paul Hohnen in chapter 17 looks at the interplay between the Global Compact and the GRI. Based on an in-depth explanation of the current policy context around both initiatives, Hohnen outlines a range of challenges both initiatives have to address (e.g. further strengthening compatibility and improving their level of uptake). His discussion also emphasizes the need for enhanced policy support at the national and international level. Considering the remarks by Hamid and Johner in chapter 15 regarding the need to further improve the quality of COP reporting, Hohnen's chapter increases our understanding of how the GRI framework can contribute to produce better COP Reports, and what issues/ problems might impede such cross-fertilization.

Part IV: Local Networks: the emerging global–local link

Local Networks – clusters of participants advancing the Compact's Principles in a specific country or region – are key when thinking about how to embed global policies and universal values into idiosyncratic local contexts. Part IV brings together different perspectives on Local Networks. While chapter 18 gives a comprehensive review of the history of Local Networks and their current status, chapter 19 conceptualizes the Global Compact itself as a 'Network of Networks' and discusses trust as an important steering mechanism within and between Local Networks. Chapter 20 and 21 lead us to the local level, discussing the German and Argentinean network, respectively.

Nessa Whelan, in chapter 18, gives an up-to-date introduction to the role and functioning of Local Networks. She discusses which activities are undertaken by Local Networks, why these activities are carried out and how the activities shape the Global Compact agenda. Interestingly, Whelan finds that many Networks have matured in the sense that they are moving away from an 'outreach and awareness-raising phase' to a more established phase allowing them to focus on more substantive issues related to continuous quality improvement. Whelan also discusses how Local Networks have developed over time. This history is of particular importance as it shows why Local Networks were formed and that problems had to be overcome to involve them in the Compact's overall governance structure. Understanding the role of Local Networks as 'translators' of global values is critical when trying to make sense of how the Global Compact attempts to achieve measurable impact on the ground.

Based on Whelan's general introduction, Dirk Ulrich Gilbert in chapter 19 offers a fine-grained analysis of what social Network Theory can teach us about the functioning of Global Compact Local Networks (GCLNs). Based on a review of Network Theory, Gilbert argues that trust is the glue that holds networks in general, and GCLNs in particular, together. His analysis reinforces the need to build robust formal and informal governance structures around Local Networks. Trust on the interpersonal and interorganizational level acts as an informal governance structure leading to stable collaborative agreements between multiple actors. Gilbert's analysis is necessary and timely as it systematically identifies a variety of options for a successful management of Local Networks.

Constanze J. Helmchen in chapter 20 discusses the unique history and current operating practices of the German Local Network. Based on her own practical experience, she describes how the Network developed from a small cluster of committed companies to a well-managed multi-stakeholder Network undertaking a variety of activities in support of the Global Compact. The chapter identifies a variety of best practices which can serve as vivid examples for other Networks (e.g. focusing on selected topics and developing contextualized tools). Whereas the story of the German Global Compact Network is a rich and inspiring one, Helmchen also emphasizes the need for Local Networks to differentiate themselves in order to survive in the crowded marketplace of partly competing corporate responsibility initiatives.

Next, Flavio Fuertes and Nicolás Liarte-Vejrup in chapter 21 take a fine-grained look at the COP Reports of members of the Argentinean Local Network. They analyse COP Reports with regard to a variety of dimensions: report content, communication of reports and also characteristics of reporting organizations. Their analysis reveals that while Argentinean Global Compact participants have improved their reporting practices over time (e.g. with regard to reporting scope), firms still need to intensify their reporting practices to provide more detailed information to interested stakeholders.

Closing the book, Ernst A. Brugger and Peter Maurer in chapter 22 present a summary of the Global Compact's future challenges. Considering the institutional environment of the initiative, they point out that the role of governments will be critical to the further evolution of the Compact. Furthermore, they also highlight the necessity to recognize, respect and protect the brand value that the initiative has created over the last ten years. Brugger and Maurer rightly conclude that, whereas much has been achieved within the last decade the future of the Compact will depend on its ability to respond to swiftly evolving trends and to address both forthcoming challenges and expectations.

PART I

Achievements, trends and challenges: reflections on the Principles

2 Making sense of the United Nations Global Compact human rights principles

KLAUS LEISINGER, ARON CRAMER AND
FARIS NATOUR

Introduction

The ten years in which the United Nations Global Compact has been in existence have been watershed years with respect to business and human rights. Never before has as much attention been paid to the many ways that businesses impact human rights conditions, and it is safe to say that the Global Compact is one of the main reasons why this is so. Specifically, more companies have pledged their support for human rights than ever before, and the Compact is perhaps the single greatest catalyst for these commitments. In addition, the Compact has reminded businesses and stakeholders that human rights principles are indeed universal, and not merely the product of Western or wealthy nations. Finally, the Compact has provided a unique and essential platform for dialogue, enabling business, government, civil society and trade unions to discuss, debate and create progress.

At the same time, the link between business and human rights remains unclear for many. At the policy level, there are questions about the relationship between public and private responsibilities, as well as whether and how well national accountability systems fit with globalized business activities. And at a practical level, many business people continue to grapple with the precise meaning of human rights as they relate to daily commercial activities. This chapter traces the development of human rights as a business matter; the impact of the Global Compact, the Special Representative's mandate; practical applications of human rights by business; and, finally, a look ahead at what the future may hold.

The establishment of the universality of human rights

The start of a long journey

In late 1945, world leaders met in San Francisco to establish the United Nations. Vividly aware of the atrocities committed in the Second World War they included in the preamble to the Charter of the United Nations a reference to human rights: 'We the peoples of the United Nations [are] determined . . . to reaffirm faith in fundamental human rights, in the dignity and worth of the human person, in the equal rights of men and women and of nations large and small' (United Nations 2009a).

In April 1946, a group of experts started to work on a first draft of an international bill of human rights and on 10 December 1948 the UN General Assembly solemnly proclaimed the Universal Declaration of Human Rights (UDHR) 'as a common standard of achievement for all peoples and all nations' (United Nations 2009b): all human beings are born free and equal in dignity and rights and are entitled to all the rights and freedoms set forth in the UDHR 'without distinction of any kind, such as race, colour, sex, language, religion, political or other opinion, national or social origin, property, birth or status' (United Nations 2009b).

The UDHR identifies a comprehensive range of rights: *civil and political* are primarily designed to protect the individual against illegitimate state interference (e.g. right to life, freedom from discrimination, provision on fair trials, right to freedom of thought, conscience and religion and political rights, including the right to vote and be elected). *Economic, social and cultural rights* prohibit authorities to deny access to available food, work, education, health services, etc. and entitle individuals to get protection from the state from third parties who interfere with access to these rights (Kaelin, Mueller and Wyttenbach 2004: 23). These rights also oblige states to take concrete measures to progressively improve socio-economic conditions in order to reach a level which allows everyone to fully enjoy these rights. Specifically, they are understood as *economic* (e.g. right to work, right to form and join trade unions, equal pay for equal work), *social* (e.g. right to an adequate standard of living, including the right to adequate food, clothing and housing and right to medical care) and *cultural* (e.g. right to education, right to participate in the cultural life of the community).

The UDHR is today the most widely accepted and influential statement of norms for civilized societies: many countries have ratified the two covenants that establish binding duties for states on the rights listed in the UDHR, and have adopted national human rights laws. And yet, studying the annual reports of Amnesty International or Human Rights Watch, human rights continue to be gravely violated around the world – the fight against human rights abuses remains an urgent and ongoing task for the world community.

The application of the UDHR to non-state actors: 'every individual and every organ of society. . .'

The drafters of the Universal Declaration sought to apply its provisions in the first instance to nation-states. Indeed, only the state is entitled to enforce the law, through the police and the courts, and it is widely understood that the Universal Declaration above all calls upon national governments to fulfil their duty to safeguard the fundamental human rights and liberties and fulfil the obligations set out in human rights conventions. The two implementing covenants are international treaties to be signed and ratified by governments.

It is equally clear, however, that the provisions of the Universal Declaration are intended to apply more widely. This notion is most clearly and explicitly stated in the preamble of the UDHR: The 'common standard of achievement for all peoples and all nations' requests '*that every individual and every organ of society,* keeping this Declaration constantly in mind, *shall strive* by teaching and education to promote respect for these rights and freedoms and by progressive measures, national and international, *to secure their universal and effective recognition and observance*, both among the peoples of Member States themselves and among the peoples of territories under their jurisdiction' (United Nations 2009b, emphasis added). This language, established at the dawn of the human rights era, makes clear that private enterprises and private citizens have responsibilities with respect to human rights. It is only fairly recently, however, that the application of these principles to business has been widely and seriously debated.

The business and human rights debate takes hold

As such, the specific application of human rights to business is a relatively new development. It was only in the 1990s, during the rise of the global economy era, that human rights became a significant part of the mainstream discussion of corporate responsibility. Several factors led to this development, including the flowering of civil society; the rise of information and communication technologies, especially the Internet; consumer outrage about high-profile allegations of corporate wrongdoing; advocacy by national governments and international leaders, and the rise to positions of influence of business leaders who came of age during the 1960s. Within the UN system, leaders, notably including Secretary-General Kofi Annan and High Commissioner for Human Rights Mary Robinson, made business and human rights a priority. Yet, while businesses, civil society organizations and governments began acknowledging the relevance of human rights as a matter for business, the precise nature of this link remained unclear.

It was in this context that the United Nations Global Compact arrived. The Compact's inclusion of two human rights principles legitimized and accelerated the adoption of human rights policies and practices by companies across the globe. The two human rights principles of the Global Compact call on signatory companies to:

- *Principle 1*: Business should support and respect the protection of international human rights within their sphere of influence; and
- *Principle 2*: make sure that they are not complicit in human rights abuses.

The establishment of these principles had both a direct and indirect impact on the acceptance of human rights as a business issue. The direct impact has been the fact that Global Compact signatories, which grew from an original 50 to 6,500 today, are now obligated to apply these two principles and report on their progress towards implementation. It is highly unlikely that as many companies would have adopted corporate human rights policies without this step. The large number of businesses, including several global leaders, committing themselves to the Global Compact and its two human rights principles has also had the indirect impact of legitimizing human rights as a business issue. Through the international platform of the United Nations, adoption of human rights principles has globalized, which makes it less likely that businesses outside the OECD would assert that human rights are solely a 'Western' or developed world concept.

Human rights and business: a conceptual challenge

As referenced above, the practical definition and application of human rights principles to business has proven elusive even with the significant increase in attention to the subject in the past fifteen years. This is for a variety of reasons:

- First, as noted earlier, human rights principles were established with a view to the role of nation-states, rather than private actors. This has resulted in a lack of clarity about which principles apply to business, how they apply to business and how to understand situations in which private and public responsibilities intersect – as they often do.
- Second, human rights principles are often violated even where national laws, regulations and customs are followed. Even where striving to go beyond compliance is part of corporate culture, misalignment of human rights and local laws can present companies with seemingly unsolvable dilemmas.
- Third, jurisdictional questions cloud the application of human rights principles relevant to business. Lack of clarity about whether and how cross-border liability is justified has further complicated the situation.
- Fourth, responsibilities as they relate to business are sometimes clouded by the presence of complex value chains in which numerous actors are seen to have an impact on human rights.
- Fifth, today's spectrum of the discussion on human rights and business is extremely broad, covering questions of free trade and investment (UN–ECOSOC 2003) as well as bioethical issues concerning the human genome (UNESCO 2009a, 2009b), research priorities of the pharmaceutical industry (Swithern 2003) and emerging issues including what constitutes the fair use of natural resources such as water.[1] Some authors even discuss the question whether access to credit should be a human right (Hudon 2009).

---

[1] See, for example, the story at www.pbs.org/newshour/bb/asia/july-dec08/waterwars_11-17.html.

• Finally, and significantly, many business managers running their 'normal daily business affairs' with integrity consider an association with the whole human rights and business debate not to be of direct relevance for them and their institutions. Human rights remain, in the minds of many, an abstract, political concept. This cognitive dissonance bears high risks for companies: on the one hand, companies must stay far away from anything that could be associated with such violations, on the other hand, there is lack of sensitivity.

Filling the conceptual gap

Within the UN system, efforts have been made to define further what companies' human rights responsibilities are, and how they can best fulfil them.

The first such effort ended in deadlock. The UN Commission on Human Rights, through its sub-commission on the promotion and protection of human rights, developed a draft set of *Norms on the Responsibility of Transnational Corporations and other Businesses on Human Rights*,[2] which were intended by its authors and supporters to establish ground rules for companies, as well as initial mechanisms for enforcement. The Norms were not endorsed by the full UN Commission. While all the major industrial countries rejected the 'Draft Norms' in 2005, most developing countries and human rights organizations, as well as many UN bodies, supported them. Amongst other reasons, the rejection was based on the perception that the Norms would impose obligations on companies akin to the state duty to protect. Further, the idea behind the Norms that only a sub-set of human rights would be relevant to business proved misguided. For example, the human rights issues around privacy and free expression faced today by Internet companies were not among the rights included in the Norms as business-relevant.

---

[2] See in this context Merieau (2008) and also Laufer Green Issac (2004). The research finds that the problem is twofold. First, many non-profit leaders and business executives harbour serious negative stereotypes about one another that undermine the trust necessary for successful partnership. Second, the cultural dynamics and linguistics of for-profit and non-profit organizations are so distinctive that executives and non-profit representatives unknowingly reinforce many of the negative perceptions held by their counterparts. These dynamics create a dysfunctional backdrop against which even organizations with common goals have difficulty forming successful partnerships.

To overcome the political deadlock, a position of 'Special Representative on the Issue of Human Rights and Transnational Corporations' was created, and John Ruggie of Harvard University was appointed to this post in July 2005. His mandate included the direction to:

- Identify and clarify standards of corporate responsibility and accountability for transnational corporations (TNCs) and other business enterprises with regard to human rights.
- Elaborate on the role of states in effectively regulating and adjudicating the role of TNCs and other business enterprises with regard to human rights.
- Research and clarify the implications for TNCs and other business enterprises of concepts such as 'complicity' and 'sphere of influence'.
- Develop materials and methodologies for undertaking human rights impact assessments of the activities of TNCs and other business enterprises.

Ruggie submitted the result of his and his teams' first three years of work, a conceptual framework for business and human rights, to the UN Human Rights Council on 3 June 2008 (Ruggie 2008). The Council endorsed his report and, on 18 June, extended Ruggie's mandate for a period of three more years, *inter alia* 'to elaborate further on the scope and content of the corporate responsibility to respect all human rights and provide concrete guidance to businesses and other stakeholders . . . in coordination with the efforts of the human rights working group of the UN Global Compact' (United Nations Human Rights Council 2008a: 3).

The Ruggie framework: an emerging benchmark

Over the course of his mandate, John Ruggie has successfully navigated through a topic that has proven extremely complex in political, legal and operational terms. At this stage in his work, many believe that he has succeeded in providing a conceptual framework that has been widely – if not universally – accepted, and is considered the *de facto* benchmark against which companies and other institutions can define and assess the business commitment to human rights. Importantly, Ruggie has undertaken efforts to clarify and distinguish between the respective responsibilities of state actors and private actors. In addition, the process through which he has operated, utilizing numerous stakeholder dialogues, broad-based workshops and advice from legal experts and practitioners, has enriched both the quality and credibility of the work undertaken through his mandate.

The core elements of the framework are:

- *The State has a 'duty to protect human rights'*: The state's obligation to protect people against human rights abuses by non-state actors, including business, within their territory or jurisdiction has been a well-recognized core element of international human rights law. The Special Representative has reasserted the pre-eminence of this state obligation: states are expected to take all necessary steps to protect against such abuse, including to prevent, investigate and punish abuse and to provide access to redress. This clear delineation helps to prevent a State from using companies as scapegoats for their own failings in the duty to protect against human rights breaches – it also helps to put into perspective requests by human rights stakeholders which could be interpreted as shifting duties away from (unable or unwilling) States.

- *The corporate sector has the 'responsibility to respect human rights'*: This responsibility 'essentially means not to infringe on the rights of others – put simply, to do no harm' (Ruggie 2008: 9). Very importantly, the 'responsibility to respect' exists independently from the quality of a state's willingness or ability to deliver on its duty to protect human rights. It is true that the most egregious violations of human rights occur in countries with poor governance, weak governance, or endemic conflict – but none of these circumstances relieves a company from its duty to respect human rights. The responsibility to respect covers all human rights. Meeting this responsibility requires proactive management of human rights impacts.

- *Access to remedy* in cases of violations of human rights *must be facilitated*: Both judicial and non-judicial remedies are necessary and need to be made more accessible and effective in cases where human rights are impacted. Depending on the severity and other circumstances, company mechanisms, such as anonymous hotlines, mediation, ombudsmen and alternative dispute resolution can contribute to effective remediation.

The Special Representative has also aimed to provide clarity about the meaning of long-ambiguous terms in the business and human rights debate, such as *'sphere of influence'* and *'complicity'*. Ruggie rightly views these three pillars of his framework not as a new standard but as the manifestation of existing practice, widely accepted standards and expectations for corporate human rights practices. The definition of a corporate responsibility to respect all human rights, for example, is in part based on the fact that most corporate human rights policies include such a commitment, and that the 6,500 signatories of the Global Compact have made a similar commitment via Principles 1 and 2.

The corporate responsibility to respect

On first glance, it appears unnecessary to have to state the responsibility to respect the human rights of a company's employees, customers, or community neighbour: it appears to state the obvious. It is worth remembering, however, that recognition of the relevance of human rights to business remains a recent phenomenon. The Ruggie (2008) framework did not create new international legal obligations, for governments or business, and defined the corporate responsibility to respect human rights to be basically a 'duty to do no harm'. This is entirely consistent with the general ethical approach most companies consider themselves to take.

In contrast to the attempt by the Draft Norms to select a sub-set of rights relevant to business, Ruggie makes clear that the responsibility to respect, to do no harm, applies to all human rights. While in practice, business will and should prioritize key areas of impact, the universe of rights considered applicable to business under the framework covers all rights listed in the UDHR, the International Covenant on Civil and Political Rights, the International Covenant on Economic, Social and Cultural Rights and the ILO Core Conventions.

While Ruggie and his team continue to develop clear operational guidance based on the framework, Ruggie's basic recommendations in this context are clear: 'To discharge the responsibility to respect requires due diligence' (Ruggie 2008: 17). This means that companies are expected to take conscious, proactive steps to become aware of, prevent and address adverse human rights impacts.

'Sphere of influence'

The *sphere of influence* concept most often used in the past worked with a set of concentric circles mapping stakeholders in a company's value chain. Mary Robinson's remark 'Clearly, the closer the company's connection to the victims of rights violations, the greater is its duty to protect. Employees, consumers, and the communities in which the company operates would be within a first line of responsibility' (Robinson 2002) is still valid. However, according to Ruggie, the concept of proximity used in isolation is inappropriate to assign or define responsibility, as it conflates two very different meanings of influence: one is *impact*, where the company's activities or relationships are causing human rights harm; the other is the *leverage* a company may have over actors that are causing harm. According to the Special Representative the first (*impact*) falls within the corporate responsibility to respect human rights; the second (*leverage*) may do so only in particular circumstances.

Companies, Ruggie argues, cannot be held responsible for the human rights impacts of every entity over which they may have some influence, because this would include cases in which they were not a causal agent, direct or indirect, of the harm in question. And yet, the 'court of justice' applies here different standards than the 'court of public opinion'. Therefore, the sphere of influence concept remains useful for companies to assess risks and opportunities and develop management systems for the human rights impacts along the value chain.

'Complicity'

The term 'complicity' in the present context usually refers to an indirect involvement by companies in human rights abuses, i.e., the actual harm is committed by another party, including governments and non-state actors. It is not possible to specify definitive tests for what constitutes complicity in any given context, but the Ruggie Report offers the following considerations:

- Mere presence in a country, paying taxes, or silence in the face of abuses is unlikely to amount to the practical assistance required for legal liability – but acts or omission in narrow contexts may carry negative implications for companies in the public's perception.

- Deriving a benefit from a human rights abuse is not likely on its own to bring legal liability, but may also carry negative implications for companies in the public's perception.
- Legal interpretations of 'having knowledge', when applied to companies, might require that there be actual knowledge, or that the company 'should have known' that its actions or omissions would contribute to a human rights abuse. Complicity does not require knowledge of the specific abuse or a desire for it to have occurred, as long as there was knowledge of the contribution. Therefore, it may not matter that the company was merely carrying out normal business activities, if those activities contributed to the abuse and the company was aware or should have been aware of its contribution.
- The fact that a company was following orders, fulfilling contractual obligations, or even complying with national law will not necessarily protect it in the 'court of public opinion'.
- Companies can avoid complicity by using the due diligence processes which apply not only to their own activities but also to the relationships connected with them.

Corporate leadership for human rights

One of the most valuable contributions of the Global Compact has been as a forum for companies to exchange and share best practices. In the area of human rights, the Global Compact published several volumes with best practice examples of corporate leadership for human rights and interesting case studies (Global Compact 2004a) as well as a number of very valuable Business Reference Guides[3] helping companies to learn about and to contextualize human rights and their management in daily business practices. These efforts not only helped countless managers to find their way in hitherto unknown territory but also prevented a 'reinvention of the wheel' in an area that needed fast and coherent development.

Analysing the relevant literature and websites and studying the Communication on Progress (COP) which companies are asked to

---

[3] See, for instance, the following three publications: Business Leaders Initiative on Human Rights *et al.* (2006), International Finance Corporation *et al.* (2007) and Monash University *et al.* (2007).

submit annually to the Global Compact Office, one finds a large variety with regard to what companies are willing to do throughout their 'hierarchy of corporate responsibilities' (Leisinger 2007). From sector to sector, corporate leadership for human rights is expressed by various proactive measures to avoid negative human rights impacts, or going beyond the baseline of 'do no harm' to help strengthen human rights protections. For instance, companies from the extractive industry engaged in training human rights lawyers, pharmaceutical companies applied differential pricing for essential medicines, while banks and companies producing infrastructural equipment committed themselves to transparency measures. As always with corporate responsibility, there are only restrictions with regard to not 'going through the floor' of the acceptable norms corridor – but no limits to stretch the ceiling.

Managing corporate human rights responsibilities

While the Global Compact and the Special Representative have helped bring considerably greater clarity to the debate about business and human rights, neither provides precise definitions that offer a clearly defined roadmap that companies can implement on human rights. As such, companies continue to look for ways to translate Global Compact Principles and other relevant human rights principles into operational terms that enable them to implement within their own operations, convey to business partners, and measure their performance.

As Peter Drucker (1993: 57f., 80, 97–101) observed many years ago, successful companies focus on responsibility rather than power, on long-term success and societal reputation rather than piling short-term results on top of short-term results (see also Avery 2000). This philosophy underlines the importance of getting the human rights dimension of business right, not only as a moral question but also one of good management practice. Good managers realize that it is impossible to be a world-class company with a second-class human rights record, and they act accordingly.

We believe that a human rights management system should include the following four elements:

- Human rights policy,
- Human rights impact assessment,

- Human rights strategy and implementation and
- Measuring and reporting on performance.

In addition, at each step, companies should consider two concepts: integration and stakeholder engagement. Every function of the company and every local operation could potentially impact human rights, positively or negatively. Ensuring decentralized ownership and integration of human rights into existing business processes is critical. Stakeholder engagement is an essential ingredient for all corporate responsibility efforts, and is a bedrock principle of the Global Compact. It is arguably most important when it comes to assessing and addressing human rights impacts. The engagement can itself be an exercise in human rights, and hearing from those whose rights could be impacted will lead to better decisions and will help the company better understand what still are very complex issues.

Ruggie outlines similar steps when describing what human rights due diligence could look like under the corporate responsibility to respect. We expect Ruggie's final report to comment further on each of these steps.

Adopting a human rights policy

Adopting a human rights policy allows companies to publicly affirm their commitment to respect human rights and enables proactive management of human rights impacts internally. The policy statement should commit to respect for all human rights as referenced by the UDHR, the two International Covenants and the ILO Core Conventions. Referencing these external human rights standards has two benefits for the company: (1) it demonstrates that the company's commitment is serious and that the company understands the international human rights framework; and (2) it clearly defines the boundaries of what the company means – and does not mean – by 'human rights'. Signatories of the Global Compact should also reference the commitments made by signing on to the Compact and its first two Principles.

The policy should detail governance of human rights and highlight priority areas – the right to health for pharmaceutical companies, for example. The chief executive officer of the company should sign the policy. By including the CEO signature, the policy becomes a vehicle to express executive support for human rights, which in turn facilitates local ownership and buy-in from key operational and functional leaders throughout the company.

To develop the policy, the company should form a cross-functional and cross-regional task force. This not only ensures a more holistic, and ultimately effective, corporate policy, but also begins to distribute ownership for human rights to key functions and regional staff throughout the company.

Assessing human rights impacts

In retrospect, it seems clear that many of the companies that initially pledged support to the Global Compact – in good faith – had no clear idea what it meant for them 'to support and respect the protection of internationally proclaimed human rights within their sphere of influence' as well as 'to make sure they are not complicit in human rights abuses' (see Global Compact Principles 1 and 2). Most companies make an intuitive assumption that they are operating lawfully and ethically, and therefore there are no human rights violations through their own activities.

Nonetheless, experience shows that it is inadvisable to assume that there are no issues. The wisest course of action is to conduct a thorough human rights impact assessment. Through a process of (1) defining 'material' human rights issues, (2) assessing risks and opportunities associated with those issues and (3) obtaining the views of important stakeholders on a company's risks and opportunities *vis-à-vis* human rights. These steps can enable a company to develop a strategy and operational practices that translate international human rights principles, certainly including the Universal Declaration, into practical guidance.

When conducting the assessment, there are three broad factors to consider:

- *The country context* in which their business activities take place, in order to highlight any specific human rights challenges they may face.
- *Their own human rights impacts*, e.g. in their capacity as producers, service providers, employers, or neighbours.
- *Potential human rights impacts of others* with which they may be associated, such as with business partners, suppliers, state agencies and other non-state actors.

We have begun to see the development of assessment tools that companies can implement for this purpose. Some companies have adapted pre-existing environmental and political assessment tools to include human rights considerations.[4]

One of the authors of this chapter participated in several human rights assessments of the pharmaceutical corporation Novartis using the Human Rights Compliance Assessment tool developed by the Danish Institute for Human Rights. In a nutshell, this was the experience undergone: while no unpleasant surprises requiring immediate corrective action were found, a number of issues that had their roots in local cultures or religious practice (e.g. no equal benefits for 'non-traditional families'; 'imported' grievance mechanisms that were inappropriate in the local cultural context; limitations on cultural dress and religious practices in sensitive areas) were found. Part of the issues found were minor, others were clearly of a temporary and technically explainable nature and could be solved by minor changes. The most important result, however, was that after the HRCA there was a much higher degree of understanding of the 'human rights and business' challenges and a much higher sensitivity with regard to differences in judgement due to differing cultural backgrounds.

The very process of conducting human rights assessments plays a significant role in sensitizing managers to non-traditional questions like human rights. It may be that this impact, while intangible, is the single most important change resulting from a human rights impact assessment. It is also valuable for companies to undertake their own assessment, proactively, rather than responding defensively to challenges from outside.

Equally, however, it is essential to integrate external perspectives into company assessments. Human rights is a new topic for business, and few – if any – companies have all the perspectives, skills, or networks needed to assess human rights conditions effectively on their own. This is especially true in light of the fact that human rights dilemmas often arise in highly complicated – and sometimes conflict-ridden – political environments. Interestingly, many companies have also come to appreciate that their judgements are significantly enhanced through dialogues with human rights and other relevant civil society organizations that have in the past been adversaries.

---

[4] See, for example, www.humanrightsbusiness.org.

This is in part because of the fact that such organizations can help companies get a grasp of the 'opinion and judgement market' on which opinions and judgements about company actions are based. Finally, this kind of partnership can also lead to collaborations that can expand a company's latitude for effective action, as multistakeholder efforts can sometimes unlock solutions that business alone is unable to achieve.

Collaborative dialogue is central not only between companies and civil society actors, but also *within* companies. Within companies, opinions and judgements about human rights often differ. Managers whose workplace is located in countries with poor human rights conditions will have different perspectives than those in other, calmer locations. Purchasing managers will have a view of things that differs from that of communications officers, and so forth. Significantly, the view of the legal department may be quite different, especially in light of the risk of cross-border liability in some jurisdictions, notably the US, by virtue of the way in which US courts currently interpret the Alien Tort Statute of 1789. A serious analysis of potential vulnerabilities and corresponding guidelines for corporate activities in sensitive areas are a credible first 'good faith effort'. For all these reasons, companies also benefit from adopting a cross-functional approach to mapping human rights issues and identifying systematic company efforts that cut across all relevant functions.

Internal consultation processes are not only valuable to gather the heterogeneity of views available in the company but also necessary to eventually broaden ownership for what has been decided as guidelines and management processes. Experience shows that when something is perceived as being imposed 'from above' it will have a smaller effect in daily practice than if something is perceived to be 'our' decision. If a policy change is perceived as a threat (to investment plans, marketing policy, customer relations and so on), it may – despite the decision being taken at the level of corporate policy – lead to passive resistance, cover-up practices and refurbishment of some Potemkin façades.

Developing and implementing a human rights strategy

After a thorough human rights impact assessment has identified the company's human rights risks and opportunities, and assigned a degree of materiality to each one, the company is ready to develop a strategy and implementation plan. The company should clarify the scope and limits of corporate human rights responsibilities, and identify key priorities – not to disregard lower priority impacts entirely, but to allocate resources strategically.

Effective human rights strategies will differ not just from sector to sector, but from company to company. An oil company may prioritize human rights impacts related to security, while an Internet company is likely to prioritize privacy and free expression. Even within a specific sector different problems will lead to different decisions regarding corporate human rights policy. A look at the different COP submissions to the Global Compact Office can help potential Global Compact participants to learn from other companies' experiences.

To implement the company's human rights strategy, which has identified the most material human rights risks and opportunities, a 'normal' management process has to be implemented – that is, managing the human rights impacts in compliance with the company's human rights policy becomes part and parcel of normal business activities. These processes will vary from company to company. Some key elements of this process are (see also Amnesty International and The Prince of Wales Business Leaders Forum 2000: 30):

- Appoint a senior manager/member of the Executive Committee to have executive oversight for human rights, and serve as an executive sponsor and spokesperson for human rights internally and externally.
- Designate an operational manager with day-to-day responsibility for human rights.
- Raise awareness for human rights throughout the company by launching an interactive communication and learning campaign targeting all employees in all major corporate languages.
- Deliver internal training of key personnel, including corporate functions and operational or 'field' managers, using best practice case studies.
- Conduct ongoing engagement with key human rights stakeholders to provide an 'out-of-the-box view'. Alternatively, integrate human rights into existing stakeholder engagement processes.

Measuring and Reporting on Performance

A comprehensive system to measure and report on performance will ensure that human rights impacts are effectively managed and that stakeholders – both internal and external – remain informed. In addition, reporting regularly on human rights performance can serve as an early warning system for the company. Human rights impacts evolve constantly and quickly – transparency and stakeholder engagement can help the company spot these changes as they happen, allowing for proactive management of emerging challenges.

The company should take the following steps:

- Develop *measurable indicators* – qualitative and quantitative benchmarks that are relevant to the human rights impacts the company has identified and that allow the company to measure progress on implementation. The Global Reporting Initiative's (GRI) G3 Reporting guidelines include a set of human rights indicators that can be used as a guide. The GRI, along with the Global Compact, has developed more specific guidance on human rights reporting (Global Reporting Initiative 2010).
- Set *key performance indicators* (KPIs) to measure progress on implementation and address the most material human rights impacts. Human rights performance is often very difficult to measure – especially on a quantitative basis. Training units delivered, or complaints received, investigated and resolved are examples of possible KPIs for human rights.
- Create *incentive systems* related to human rights performance for staff with operational or executive responsibility.
- *Measure performance* against the established indicators and KPIs. The data collection process for the annual or Corporate Social Responsibility (CSR) report could serve as a good mechanism to collect this data.
- Develop and implement an *auditing system* with external verification.
- *Report on the performance annually*, using the CSR report or a separate reporting mechanism. Human rights reporting should include performance against KPIs and other relevant indicators, and provide context where necessary.

Implementing a comprehensive strategy and management system for human rights will take some time. The company should set milestones to ensure completion. If this is done, the promise 'to support and respect the protection of internationally proclaimed human rights' as well as 'to make sure they are not complicit in human rights abuses' (see Global Compact Principles 1 and 2) will become part of normal business activity.

It is important to note that human rights management is not a project that has a clear beginning and end, but is an ongoing process of continuous improvement: As the circumstances change, as the debate on human rights and business progresses, and as new insights and innovative ways of dealing with human rights-related business challenges appear, corporate management must regularly reassess its approach and take corrective action if and when necessary.

Conclusions, outlook and recommendations

A great deal has changed since fifty companies gathered in New York in 2000 and adopted, amongst other things, the human rights principles of the Global Compact. The 'business and human rights' discussion will continue along with and beyond the work of the Special Representative. Companies are well advised not to leave the further elaboration 'on the scope and content of the corporate responsibility to respect all human rights and provide concrete guidance to businesses and other stakeholders' (United Nations Human Rights Council 2008a: 3) exclusively to John Ruggie and his team but to actively participate in the academic, political and public debate on the issue. Ruggie's initial framework has been so successful in large part because of the widespread active participation from business, civil society, academia and government. Again, the Global Compact can contribute immensely by organizing more regional and sector-specific learning forums and inviting a mix of leading and 'beginner' companies in order to enhance cross-corporate learning.

Companies are likely to face increasing public expectations, more political pressures and more intensive requests to proactively manage human rights impacts. At the same time, those impacts will continue to evolve quickly. One of the key drivers, information and communications technology (ICT), continues to progress, reshaping the associated human rights impacts for business. The 2009 Business for Social

Responsibility (BSR) series 'Human Rights in a Wired World' sheds light on the impact of technology on human rights, and the resulting challenges for business.[5] Highlighting many human rights impacts for companies in all sectors that were not part of the business and human rights debate even a few years ago, the series illustrates the need for ongoing reassessment and, most importantly, continued dialogue between business and the stakeholder community.

Enlightened companies will not define their mission too narrowly. Being aware of their responsibilities as corporate citizens, they will measure their success more comprehensively than just in terms of quarterly profits. The Global Compact's Principles of support and respect for human rights, for fair social and environmental standards, as well as for a commitment against corruption is not only the 'right thing to do' – there is a plausible 'business case' as well. It is about more than safeguarding the company's reputation: decent and safe workplaces, treating employees with dignity and respect, fighting discrimination and promoting diversity in all layers of employment and creating constructive and supporting relationships with the neighbouring communities – all these elements of human rights-related corporate responsibility are good for sustainable business success. All four elements of the Global Compact will remain pillars of any relevant corporate responsibility concept – but human rights will continue to play a special role as their respect is non-negotiable, not relative and thus expected to be absolute. This is especially true for times of economic crisis.

For sustainable progress in human development, there is an immense need for collective action by all who can make a contribution. Investing capital, improving productivity, creating employment and thus income, developing human resources, transferring technology and skills, as well as empowering people by providing a broad range of products and services: there can be no doubt that the private sector can play an important role in achieving the MDGs.[6]

The 'human factor' within management may well be the single most important aspect: the UN Global Compact does not offer a concrete standard to be met but challenges companies to reflect on its principles and innovate ways to implement them effectively (and

---

[5] The complete series can be downloaded at www.bsr.org/research/human-rights-wired-world.cfm.

[6] See, for example: Commission on the Private Sector and Development (2004) and Witte and Reinicke (2005).

be accountable for them). This reflection process can be narrow or enlightened, it can involve considerations beyond the limited definition of business and its responsibilities and it can stop at the factory gate. It ultimately depends on the existing corporate culture and value system. Enlightened and imaginative managers are needed to fill the two Global Compact human rights principles with life. Creativity and innovation is a normal part of management success – why not test it for human rights and business purposes? Maybe leaders come up with 'Islands of Respect for Political and Civil Rights' or 'Social Contracts for Economic, Social and Cultural Rights'?

The complexity of human rights and business endeavours can be shown, for example, by its employment dimension. Beyond the obvious essentials such as eliminating forced and child labour, an enlightened approach will include attention to the issues of a living wage, promotion of the right to equality of opportunity, the right to work in healthy and safe working conditions, and improving the employability of working poor – to mention just a few.

Business is a major engine for economic growth and – in combination with good governance – an essential element for social development and the fulfillment of economic and social human rights. Corporate management is therefore most often a force for good in many respects (Birkinshaw and Piramal 2005). The most crucial precondition for this is that corporate successes are not achieved with collateral human rights damages. There are signs that those who 'care' are starting to win on the financial markets.[7] Our hope is that civil society and the media will increasingly and publicly differentiate their judgements on multinational corporations (MNCs) and will provide reputation capital to those that have a measurably superior corporate responsibility record.

Last but not least, with human rights as much as with global social and ecological issues, one imperative has to be stressed – namely, the imperative of collective action. Sustained improvements in the global human rights situation can be achieved only if all relevant actors, government, civil society and the private sector are addressing the human rights challenge collaboratively. None of the actors can do the job alone – but together, we may get it done.

---

[7] See, for example, Global Compact (2004b). Some pension funds, e.g. the Dutch APG group, have explicitly asked companies to publish a human rights policy (see also Umlas 2009).

3 The promise of the United Nations Global Compact: a trade union perspective on the labour principles

GUY RYDER

Introduction

The special value of the Global Compact at its inception was its engagement with major actors, its Principles, its association with the United Nations and its commitment to operate through dialogue. It engaged business with the United Nations. Its principles were rooted in universal and legitimate international standards. And it was to be 'driven' by dialogue. It was, in particular, that aspect of the Global Compact that resulted in the decision of the international trade union movement to participate.

This chapter will explore the rationale for the original trade union involvement in the initiative. It will also examine the risk, present from the beginning, that the Compact could be derailed and lose its direction and become a 'super-Corporate Social Responsibility (CSR)' initiative, a sort of 'feel-good' drug for large companies. Most importantly, it looks at the potential which the Global Compact still has to add balance to globalization. The 2008 economic crisis is the culmination of decades of mistaken policies and actions. The Global Compact, like financial and economic decision-making, needs to be examined critically if we are not to exit the crisis with 'business as usual'. The involvement of private parties in dialogue remains an essential component for a sound and prosperous economy, for respect for rights, for social justice and for a healthy environment. The Global Compact must renew its original promise if it is to contribute to the fundamental changes that must be made if we are to shift direction and move more towards sustainable development.

In the beginning . . .

Although not implicated in the Global Compact at the beginning, the international trade union movement had the opportunity to discuss with the United Nations and consider participation not long after the Compact was launched. At the time, the independent, democratic trade union movement at the global level comprised the International Confederation of Free Trade Unions (ICFTU, replaced in 2006 by a new organization, the International Trade Union Confederation, ITUC), the Global Union Federations representing unions by sector and occupation and the Trade Union Advisory Committee to the OECD. There were vigorous debates among those organizations as to whether trade unions should participate in the initiative. Following a meeting with then-Secretary-General Kofi Annan about trade union concerns and need for clarification and the assurances given, it was agreed, in spite of substantial differences of opinion, to support the Global Compact. The major concerns were:

- The Global Compact should not be seen as a voluntary offset or alternative to intergovernmental action. The WTO Ministers meeting in Seattle was about to take place and there were indications that the Compact was seen by some as an excuse for government refusal to discuss the relationships between trade and international labour standards.
- The Global Compact should not be seen as a cut-rate or sub-standard 'code of conduct' for companies. At the time, the OECD Guidelines for Multinational Enterprises (MNEs) were being reviewed and, ultimately, were improved. That instrument, as well as the ILO Tripartite Declaration of Principles concerning Multinational Enterprises and Social Policy (see the explanation of both instruments in box 3.1) provided more detailed guidance for business. And, unlike the Global Compact, although they were also not legally binding, they were not 'voluntary' in their coverage or application.
- Trade unions are, at the same time, part of industry and part of civil society. They were not willing to simply be lumped together with other civil society actors. Among other reasons, they did not want companies to fulfil their dialogue functions, particularly with regard to the labour principles, while avoiding talking with trade unions that represented workers.

Box 3.1: International instruments on corporate responsibility

---

ILO Tripartite Declaration of Principles Concerning Multinational Enterprises and Social Policy (MNE Declaration)

The OECD Guidelines for Multinational Enterprises are 'recommendations addressed by governments to multinational enterprises' (OECD 2008a: 9); they are complementary to, and consistent with, the ILO MNE Declaration. The MNE Declaration contains more guidance on employment issues, whereas the OECD Guidelines cover a wider range of subjects. The ILO MNE Declaration is the most universally applicable and authoritative statement concerning the relationship of business to social development. The stated purpose of the Declaration is 'to encourage the positive contribution of multinational enterprises to economic and social progress' and 'to minimize and resolve difficulties to which their operations may give rise' (ILO 2006: 2). The declaration consists of fifty-nine paragraphs organized into four sections: General policies, Employment, Conditions of work and life and Industrial relations.

The Declaration was adopted by the Governing Body of the International Labour Conference in 1977; it was revised in 2000. Both processes involved extensive consultation and negotiations between representatives of governments and employers' and workers' organizations. The instrument reflects an agreed understanding by governments, employers and workers that, although ILO Conventions and Recommendations address the responsibilities of governments and are intended to be applied by governments, many of the underlying principles of these instruments can be applied by business as well.

The Declaration does not expect corporate management to define or implement their social responsibilities unilaterally. Instead, it envisions consultations between governments and national employers' and workers' organizations. Moreover, it calls for MNEs to take 'established policy objectives into account', as well as to be 'in harmony with the development policies' of the country concerned (ILO 2006: 3).

The ILO MNE Declaration recognizes the important social role of corporations to create employment. Too often, many people forget that the creation of decent jobs is also a social responsibility of business. It was envisioned that the ILO MNE Declaration would have two adequate and credible follow-up mechanisms. The first was to be an interpretation procedure, which would provide an opportunity to 'clarify' the meaning of the Declaration in specific instances. The second mechanism was to be a periodic 'survey of the effect given to the Declaration'. Although neither has proved to be very effective, the Declaration remains a unique and compelling standard for business conduct.

The OECD Guidelines for Multinational Enterprises

The OECD Guidelines were adopted in 1976 and revised in 2000. They are part of the 'OECD Declaration on International Investment and Multinational Enterprises' and are organized into the following chapters: Concepts and principles; General policies; Disclosure of information; Employment and industrial relations; The environment; Combating bribery; Consumer interests; Science and technology; and Competition and taxation. Although the Guidelines are recommendations, and not legally binding, they are applicable to all enterprises that fall within their scope. Nonbinding, therefore, is not the same as optional. Similar to the ILO MNE Declaration, it is not necessary for a company to 'sign up' to the Guidelines first. The Guidelines are the authoritative expectations of governments. Furthermore, they need to be taken as a complete set. Companies cannot 'pick and choose' provisions.

The scope of the Guidelines is large. All MNEs that are based in the territories of the adhering governments (the OECD countries, as well as other adhering countries) are expected to observe the Guidelines wherever they operate. In addition, they also apply to companies from non-adhering countries for their operations inside countries that do adhere to the Guidelines. Taken together, the OECD member countries are already home to most of the world's MNEs. Under the Guidelines, the enterprises that fall within its scope are also expected to encourage their business partners, including suppliers and sub-contractors, to apply compatible principles.

The OECD Guidelines have a more useful follow-up procedure than the ILO MNE Declaration. Every country adhering to the

Guidelines is obliged to establish a national contact point (NCP), responsible for promoting the Guidelines. The NCP is also obliged to contribute to the solution of problems that are brought to its attention. The procedure allows trade unions, or other concerned parties, to raise a case concerning the behaviour of an enterprise with respect to the Guidelines with an NCP. This procedure also obliges the NCP to follow-up according to well-defined steps, the objective being to resolve the problem. Unfortunately, some governments adhering to the Guidelines have failed to establish credible or effective NCPs.

The Trade Union Advisory Committee (TUAC) to the OECD has prepared a Users' Guide to the OECD Guidelines. It has, so far, been translated into twenty languages: French, Spanish, Portuguese, Italian, Hungarian, Czech, Russian, Estonian, Latvian, Lithuanian, Croatian, Romanian, Georgian, Korean, Japanese, Bahasa–Indonesian, Thai, Bulgarian, Turkish and Chinese. In addition to trade unions, a number of businesses and employer organizations have used it.

A subsequent joint statement with the United Nations reaffirmed what had already been contained in their joint position with the International Chamber of Commerce (ICC), that 'global markets need global rules'.

The Global Compact was to be built around four 'engagement mechanisms'; dialogue, learning, Local Networks and project development. Of course, dialogue is the key to all four, but particularly learning and Local Networks. Unfortunately, the orientation rapidly narrowed to becoming an 'insider' CSR game, hermetically sealed off from the real world. The inherent weaknesses in corporate responsibility have, therefore, become weaknesses of the Global Compact. And the opportunities have never been seized to deepen and make this work more serious through real links with the OECD Guidelines and the ILO Tripartite Declaration.

The unique role of trade unions has been clearly understood by many major corporations and business organizations. In recent years, there has been an explosion of global social dialogue, but neither the basis of such dialogue nor the shared concerns of trade unions and employers have ever been fully understood by the Global Compact or by their allies in the corporate responsibility industry. The Global Compact is foreign to that world. It is, of course, a vicious circle. The less relevant the Global Compact is to trade unions, the less incentive there is to participate. That, in turn, means that the Compact becomes even more distant from the concerns of trade unions and their members.

The ILO has put together a publication entitled, 'The Labour Principles of the United Nations Global Compact: A Guide for Business' (ILO 2008). It is hoped that this will generate not only greater understanding of those principles, but also of the importance of trade union recognition and the need for productive social dialogue.

Corporate responsibility

Corporate responsibility is a limited concept with many built-in weaknesses. It looks at companies as if they function in isolation rather than being part of a larger society. One way to broaden the concept is to speak of the 'social responsibilities of business'. The ICFTU, one of the predecessor organizations of the ITUC, in its 'Trade Union Guide to Globalisation' (ICFTU 2004: 56) defined it in the following terms:

The social responsibilities of business are the set of widely accepted expectations on how business should behave. These are the expectations of society as a whole. They can come in the form of laws or they can take non-legally binding forms. They can be legitimately defined in both formal and informal ways. For instance, they are set out formally where a democratic government, acting as the instrument of the entire society, adopts laws or regulations. They can also exist informally as widely shared cultural values expressed in various ways.

Among other things, this definition differs from one common view – that social responsibility is only voluntary and goes beyond legal obligations. However, in many countries, obeying the law is too often disregarded, sometimes by companies that claim to be socially responsible. One of the countries where corporate responsibility was born is the USA. But, in spite of the fact that labour laws in that country are very lenient and weak, corporate lawlessness is rampant. Every year, in the USA, there are tens of thousands of workers illegally fired for trade union activity. A major American-based multinational retailer prefers to close its stores rather than obey the law and recognize their trade union if its workers decide to form one. And, yet, at the same time, it polishes and relishes a 'socially responsible' image.

Corporate responsibility is often, if not always, paternalistic. Rather than respecting the rights of workers to protect their interests as they define them, it prefers to 'take care' of workers as if they were just like the world of nature – which is, after all, without a voice and not capable of defending itself. And, yet, it is unusual in sustainability reporting, the preferred method of the Global Compact, to dwell on the effective rights of workers to organize or bargain, much less to speak of the promotion of sound industrial relations.

To the extent that there is room for dialogue in the reporting processes, it is through 'stakeholder consultation'. That does not mean that it is empty of value, just not very ambitious. It may help companies get their different departments and divisions to talk, if for no other reason than to prepare the report, but its degree of real engagement with the larger society is limited. The trade union movement does not dismiss social and environmental reporting. It has, in fact, developed a guide for trade union involvement in the Global Reporting Initiative (GRI) at company level. However, it considers the contribution of such reports to be modest and it does not expect that large numbers of trade unions will drop their real work to engage in a process that requires so much effort for questionable results.

Another disservice that corporate responsibility has rendered is its contribution to the degradation of language. It might be laughable, but, as George Orwell said, 'if thought corrupts language, language can also corrupt thought'. There are such inane phrases as 'doing well by doing good', and the linked 'business case' for social responsibility, as if following the road to the highest profits automatically leads to ethical behaviour, not to mention the endless series of 'win–win' situations. There may still be a few business people who believe in the natural virtue of business, but to those taxpayers and workers who will have to pay, and for generations, the cost of a crisis that sprang from the greed of the most privileged among us, it rings hollow.

There is no more striking example of language abuse than the misuse of the word 'stakeholder'. The word has come to mean everything; therefore, it means nothing. It may mean groups or people with a stake in a company, as well as those without one. It may make companies stakeholders in governments, or even make governments stakeholders in companies. But, the most offensive use of the term is to refer to citizens as stakeholders in their governments. In democratic governments, citizens would be, as a minimum, shareholders rather than stakeholders. After all, government is supposed to belong to them. It would only be in dictatorships that citizens might be considered stakeholders, if not shareholders with non-voting stock (an explanation of what stakeholder means and what it does not mean is given in box 3.2).

Corporate responsibility was spawned by public relations. Although it has grown more sophisticated and some companies are sincere and serious in their efforts, it suffers from its origins – a public effort to prove virtue and/or correct (or distort) images. One does not talk about despoiling the land in open caste mining or cutting down all of the trees in a forest, but only about restoration, if only partial, of the land or replanting some of the trees. Similarly, one sought to prove that labour practices, even in dictatorships, were good and workers were happy to obscure the fact that all that really mattered in global supply chains, particularly at the beginning before consumers mobilized, was the cheapest possible production of garments based on sweated labour and the lowest possible labour costs.

In the social area, this PR approach contrasts markedly with the practice of industrial relations. The assumption in collective bargaining is that no company will be perfect. It takes into account normal, human failures and, practically and realistically, tries to resolve problems and repair damage. And, if possible, it does it quietly so as not to injure the firm. Elements of global industrial relations are emerging with an important expansion of global trade union recognition, including in the form of international or global framework agreements that have been signed by Global Union Federations with scores of MNCs. They have in common the desire to solve problems and cooperate based on shared values and agreed procedures (see box 3.3 on global framework agreements).

Rule of law, governance and the ten Global Compact Principles

Although what a firm does inside its own enterprise and supply/production/service chains is important, companies do not, individually or collectively, have the legitimacy to 'govern' society, nor can their 'good conduct' compensate for flaws and weaknesses in governance by

Box 3.2: Who are the real stakeholders?

CSR has popularized the term 'stakeholders', which is now used extensively when the relationship of business to the rest of society is considered. The term, therefore, exerts a strong influence on our thinking. Unfortunately, its meaning has changed and, as the word is most often used, it obscures more than it clarifies relationships. The term 'stakeholder', which has an important use in the debate over corporate governance, was intended to contrast with the term 'shareholder'. In this view, stakeholders, like shareholders, are those who have an identifiable interest in the success of a corporation. As with shareholders, the interests of stakeholders need to be taken into account. In this sense, workers and communities can often be considered as important stakeholders in specific companies.

In the new CSR language, however, the meaning of the term 'stakeholder' changed to include anyone that is affected, in any way, by the activities of business. The term no longer referred to a specific party in a specific relationship. In its new use, it is not expected that stakeholders name the specific company in which they hold a 'stake'. In practice, the term usually is used as a synonym for 'organization', or for 'NGO'. Sometimes the term replaces words such as 'workers', 'consumers', or 'environmentalists'. In these cases, the term has less meaning than the words that it is replacing.

There is a moral dimension to stakeholders' claims in the term's earlier and more precise use. The reason why the claims of stakeholders should be taken into account is that it is in the interest of society. The interest of society as a whole includes, among other things, secure employment, the fairness of contracts and financial transparency. Some claims are going to be more important than others in this regard. One implication of this is that not every stakeholder is equal and therefore not entitled to the same treatment. These important distinctions are rarely appreciated by those using the term in its newer, broader and less meaningful sense.

Trade unions, which are among the most important representative organizations in society, are usually treated as 'just one of many' stakeholders. Worse, they are often overlooked. The result is that the term 'stakeholder', ill defined as it is, may help business avoid responsibilities.

Box 3.3: Global framework agreements

A growing number of companies have found a better way to act responsibly than making declarations and reports. They deal with workers' rights at the international company level through global trade union recognition, dialogue and, in some cases, international agreements. These agreements are concluded between international companies and Global Union Federations.

The content of some framework agreements, particularly many of the earliest ones, is often similar to the language found in some of the codes of conduct that companies have adopted for their suppliers and which cover some, or all, of the fundamental rights at work. However, that does not mean that a framework agreement is the same thing as a code of conduct. It is not. There is a fundamental difference between a code of labour practice, which is a unilateral management pledge, mainly made to address public concerns, and a framework agreement, which is a recognition that the company will recognize and engage the global trade union organizations and discuss issues of fundamental concerns to both parties.

Whereas most CSR exercises are voluntary efforts (promises or claims), the adoption of framework agreements can be seen as the start of international industrial relations with provisions that are negotiated and agreed. Global agreements are also a way to resolve conflicts or problems before they become serious or damaging. Most problems that have been resolved so far, through global social dialogue or with the help of agreements, have been worked out informally and quietly. Unlike campaigns and other public action, the intention is to implement common, agreed principles in a way that leads to a speedy resolution of conflicts or even anticipation of conflicts, partly with the aim of preventing damage to the reputation of a company. Nevertheless, dialogue and agreements have also been used to resolve conflicts that have become public.

government in any society. Corporate responsibility is often inspired by the need to do business in nations where governance is poor. Some of the connections between corporations and governance were outlined in an online article by Jim Baker, Coordinator of the Council of

Global Unions, entitled 'The Future of the Global Compact', which appeared in the Global Compact newsletter for Local Networks (Baker 2007). Four excerpts from that article now follow:

> What do all of the principles have in common? In addition to being based on universal principles, they are all about governance. Rule of law and legitimate, functioning institutions are necessary to resolve conflicts. Something so fundamental, does not lend itself to purely technical solutions. It requires making right choices based on an understanding of the nature of the principles and of our common challenges.
>
> How can human rights be respected without rule of law, due process, and an independent judiciary? Can the Global Compact seriously expect to ensure that human rights are respected or deal with human rights violations if rulers subject the ruled to arbitrary arrest, detention, torture or assassination? Isn't that about governance?
>
> The rights of workers, especially the enabling rights to organize and bargain collectively must be, first and foremost, respected, protected, and promoted by governments. Even if those principles were 100 per cent honoured by multinational enterprises, which is not the case, most of the world's workers do not work for such enterprises or even in their supply, production or service chains. There is no substitute for good laws, well enforced. Isn't that about governance? And, will the planet survive through targets and technologies alone? Or, only through the good intentions of private parties? Don't citizens need to be free to force governments to clean up their act? And, isn't that governance?
>
> As for the 10th principle on corruption, is it enough for companies to refrain from bribing government officials to end corruption in the world? The principle is, as it must be, much broader and calls for engagement in the fight against corruption. Action on the supply side alone, as important as that is, will not solve the problem. So, this one, like the nine original principles, is also about governance.

There is no society in history that has fully respected human rights, including allowing workers to form unions free from fear and intimidation, or cleaned up its environment without an important role for law and government. There are severe limits on what companies can do in isolation to contribute to positive changes in society. However, if they work with others to achieve improvements in rule of law and governance, they can make a difference. Collective action, often through employer associations, enables them to better address governance problems and the need for basic public services such as education and health care and other services.

It makes no sense to think that adequate health care can be provided in society if only some of those employed by MNEs are covered, or that those private health services can be expanded without limit to the entire community. Similarly, training for specific tasks to be performed at work will never replace the knowledge and skills that can only come from a good, universal system of free public education. The specific needs of companies can only be efficiently provided by the whole community.

Civil society and democracy

Businesses, as such, are not part of civil society. But they are when they join together as members of employer organizations. Then, they have a collective role in policy development and implementation. They are no longer only producing and selling goods and services, but are defending broader interests by participating in representative organizations in the same way that workers join civil society when they form unions. When they come together, first among themselves and then with others, companies can play a serious role in promoting the creation of decent societies that work for everybody. And, representative organizations (often working with other representative organizations like trade unions), by their very nature and role, contribute to democracy.

The Global Compact, as do many others groups and individuals, confounds 'civil society organizations' with 'non-governmental organizations' (NGOs). Many NGOs are, in fact, part of civil society because they represent people, have governance structures and are accountable. But others, although they may make valuable contributions like delivering services or providing expertise, do not play that vital and fundamental representative role so crucial to making democracy work. Real, living democracy must mean a lot more than periodic free elections. It must provide a permanent way for people to participate in their societies and in their own futures.

Although it may not be fashionable to say it in the corporate world and, too often, in the United Nations, democracy provides some controls at the national level that are prerequisites for global progress. The global warming that threatens us all cannot be effectively dealt with through government negotiations to fix quotas or targets alone. At the end of the Cold War, many were shocked to see the environmental degradation and bad health and safety conditions in the former Soviet bloc. That was not because they lacked capitalism and 'free markets', but rather because the ruled had little or no control over their rulers. When democracy came, in part though the work of free trade unions like Solidarność, civil society was born, people were able to organize and act and the horrendous pollution to which they had been exposed became a problem for governments and began to disappear.

Part of the dialogue that needs to take place should be about the value of democracy for employers, for workers and for all citizens. Stimulating the awakening of democracy and strengthening it where it exists should be among our common goals. It is implied in all of the Global Compact Principles. It is foolish and misguided to think that human, including trade union, rights will be respected, and environmental progress happen, in some of the cruellest most oppressive dictatorships in the world. It is like pretending to enjoy a gourmet meal in a sewer.

Sustainable development and 'short-termism'

The three pillars of sustainable development (i.e. a balance between economic, social and environmental goals) require medium- and long-term thinking. They require a flexible and innovative form of 'planning', a word that was recently considered to be obscene. Global warming and other related problems cannot be remedied in the short term and 'on the cheap'. Problems that took generations to develop will take generations to resolve. Sustainability in the form of social justice also requires long-range vision and commitment to rights that goes beyond the adoption of a mission statement or the issuance of a press release. Injustice in the form of growing gaps between the tiny elite of super-rich and the teaming ranks of the poor will, unfortunately, take time to undo.

In corporate responsibility circles, there is much talk about risk and about 'managing risk'. In fact, many of the firms that pledge their undying devotion to the Global Compact have been managing risk by shifting it onto the shoulders of workers. They have in many cases organized their work using sub-contracting, contracting out, short-term contracts, phony self-employment and precarious work so as to avoid employment relationships and ensure that they never have to bargain with workers whose rights they claim to honour. In at least one major firm supporting the Global Compact, management training combines constant reminders of the importance of workers' rights and of Global Compact Principles with instructions as to how things can be organized so as to avoid the exercise of those very rights. The fear that is being fostered among 'disposable' workers is not only creating precarious work, but also precarious societies with exclusion and marginalization.

The need for a long-term approach to the environmental and social pillars of sustainable development may be obvious, but the crisis since 2008 has revealed that it is equally important in the economic sphere. Leveraged buy-outs profited the few, but did not leverage prosperity for the many. Astronomical financial returns that make no sense in the real economy are not a foundation for solid and sustainable economic growth. They are an economic house of cards subject to destruction by the slightest breeze.

The future of the Global Compact: making its promise a reality

There is one aspect of the Global Compact that remains the same as it was when it was launched a decade ago. It has tremendous potential. If it takes its principles seriously and works in a steady, serious and long-term manner, it can prove to be a vital and crucial initiative. Sustainable development will only happen if its three pillars can be integrated. That will require real discussions, real interaction and real understanding of the interdependence of economic progress, social justice and a healthy and safe environment. It will not be achieved with 'smoke and mirrors', but through a real dialogue beyond slick sustainability reports and simulated dialogue with 'stakeholders'.

If the Global Compact is to make a real and sustainable difference for the world in which we live, it should become a compact of social forces that can serve as a catalyst for change. The Compact's legitimacy comes from its principles and its power comes from the actors it brings together. It must bring together parties who do not always find it easy to discuss. It must bridge different interests and habits and help to break down barriers between real actors rather than building a corporate responsibility Potemkin village. It means involving, improving and respecting government, including government regulation, rather than thinking that private is always better.

The Global Compact is too good an idea to abandon in tough times. But it will not be this Global Compact that can carry out this mission, but rather one designed to deepen understanding and support for its principles and enable a quantum leap in the quantity and quality of the indispensable dialogue that must take place. Working together, we can deepen the roots and practice of democracy. We might even be able to bring it out of the closet. We can set into motion the momentum necessary to build the kind of decent, fair and sustainable societies that we all seek.[1]

---

[1]   All boxes in this chapter are based on material that was previously published in ICFTU (2004).

4 | The United Nations Global Compact Environmental Principles: achievements, trends and challenges

GREGORY C. UNRUH

Introduction

The environmental principles of the United Nations Global Compact represent recognition by the community of nations of the role corporations must play if we are to successfully address pending global environmental concerns. This chapter will explore the environmental principles of the Global Compact by first examining their roots in international environmental diplomacy and sustainable development discourse. It will then review the rising importance of multinational corporations (MNCs) in the global economy and the contributions that private enterprise can offer in achieving established global environmental goals. The Global Compact environmental principles will then be surveyed with a special emphasis on their prospective role in addressing one of the most complex and challenging environmental issues: global climate change. Finally current trends in environmental management will be traced with specific examples of companies implementing the Global Compact environmental principles in their strategy and operations.

Many business people see the UN Global Compact as another, albeit authoritative, set of sustainability guidelines produced by government and civil society to influence corporate behaviour *vis-à-vis* the natural world. This view, however, misunderstands the significance of the Global Compact in the evolution of global governance. Since the Treaty of Westphalia (1659), which most scholars pinpoint as the beginning of the modern system of international law and relations, the only recognized entity in international policy-making – as the name implies – has been the nation-state (Gross 1948). Only legitimized national governments have been recognized as having standing and competence to engage in diplomacy and in the process of establishing

59

and advancing the international regulatory regimes. The Global Compact, however, signifies an important new development in this tradition. As will be discussed, the Global Compact Principles are in fact derived directly from foundational international law. In this sense, then, the Compact can be interpreted as an implicit recognition, by nation-states and international organizations, of the need to translate the norms of international law into a guiding philosophy for the private sector of the global economy. It is the recognition that the international community's greatest challenges and highest common principles cannot be fulfilled to their potential without the active participation and contribution of global businesses that makes the Global Compact an historic institution. In effect, the Global Compact has asked private sector firms to sign up to international law and become a positively contributing member to the process of global governance. For students of international relations and diplomacy this is an important development and perhaps the most revolutionary aspect of the Global Compact. And while this subject is not the focus of this chapter, it should not go unremarked.

It should also be noted that this chapter is not intended to be an exhaustive survey of the impact of the environmental principles on business, nor their success in fostering improvements in environmental management. It is too early in the process to draw scientifically defensible conclusions along these lines. Instead the focus of the chapter is upon understanding the diplomatic origins of the environmental principles, their recent translation to MNCs, and where the principles might speculatively guide corporate environmental management in the future.

The origins of the Global Compact environmental principles

The environmental principles of the Global Compact are an example of the ongoing process of codification of global norms pertaining to environmental protection and preservation, a process that has its roots in the rise of the so-called 'environmental movement', which emerged in the post-war era. Environmental concerns entered the popular public conscience largely through organized events like the first Earth Day (22 April 1970) and subsequently became a persistent feature of policy-making in the 1960–1970s (Dunlap and Mertig 1992, Shabecoff 1993). In reality, however, concerns about the environmental impact of commercial activity predate the environmental movement and are closely associated with the rise of the industrial economic development model.

Industrialization paralleled the tapping of fossil fuel for energy generation in the nineteenth century, a process that greatly accelerated our extraction and exploitation of natural resources and with it a concomitant increase in environmental degradation (Tarr 1996). With rising populations and new more efficient manufacturing methods like factory production, traditional renewable energy supplies – which include fluvial sources, agricultural crops, natural forest biomass and animal products like whale oil – came under scarcity pressures as economies grew and new technologies accelerated the harvesting rates of natural inputs for manufacturing. The rising shortage of natural inputs (especially for energy production) and rising prices led to an accelerated search for new supplies and substitutes for traditional sources. One of the first countries to experience this was the UK in the early nineteenth century (TeBrake 1975). Coal had long been recognized as a potential energy substitute for traditional biomass in England, but was seen as a less desirable 'dirty' fuel when compared with firewood. However, as deforestation of the country's woodlands progressed, more and more citizens and businesses turned to coal for their energy needs (Mosley 2001).

The economic exploitation of coal was followed in short order by the exploitation of petroleum reserves, which began in earnest in the USA in 1959 when the first oil well was successfully completed in Pennsylvania by 'Colonel' Edwin Drake. Refined 'rock oil', as petroleum was first called, was initially used as a substitute for increasingly scarce and expensive whale oil used in lamps for illumination (Black 2000). However, the successful development of the internal combustion engine in the 1860s and the rise of the automobile as a primary mode for personal transportation dramatically increased the uses and demand for petroleum (Flink 1975). This combined with the development of synthetic petroleum-based chemistry, which included the invention of plastics, transformed the industrial economy and made fossil fuel exploitation a primary driver of economic growth.

The development and use of fossil fuel energy sources was fundamental in creating the modern economic landscape and fostering the entrepreneurial opportunity and wealth accumulation that powered the globalization of the corporate model. It has allowed businesses to become truly global enterprises that can coordinate on a transnational basis. However, fossil fuel-driven economic development and resource exploitation has also had unintended environmental implications. The increased rate of energy use and greatly accelerated harvesting and processing rates of minerals, biomass and animal products has brought about a concomitant degradation of ecosystems and their ability to provide necessary ecosystem services such as water purification, pollination, etc. (Daily 1997). In addition to the consumption of natural resources, the expansion of industrial chemistry has fostered a proliferation of synthetic compounds which natural ecosystems have only a limited ability to absorb, disperse, or degrade (Clark 1999). The unsurprising consequence has been increasing environmental degradation that eventually fostered a social and political response that would have important implications for business as new policies became codified into environmental laws and regulations.

The earliest examples of environmental policies are often found at the national or local government level, arising in response to urban and industrial pollution that accompanied local industrial development. The famous London 'killing fogs' of 1952, for example, were the result of coal smoke and soot mixing with London's infamous fog bank, a condition in one case that lasted for four days and killed an estimated 12,000 Londoners (Brimblecombe 1987). The 1952 tragedy led to UK Clean Air Act of 1956 which restricted industry's use of polluting coal fuels (Bowler and Brimblecombe 2000). This sequence of increasingly evident environmental degradation leading belatedly to mitigating regulation would be repeated numerous times in many countries and, in fact, continues today.

It was environmental degradation like that seen in London that instigated what is commonly called the *environmental movement* in the second half of the twentieth century (Szasz 1994). Motivated by press coverage of environmental disasters, like the oil spills from the Torrey Canyon, UK, and in Santa Barbara, California, as well as popular books like Rachel Carson's *Silent Spring* (1962) and Paul Erlich's *The Population Bomb* (1968), the environmental movement gained momentum as a political force. By the mid-1970s extensive environmental regulations were in place in many industrialized nations. In the USA, for example, the regulatory regime included the creation of the US Environmental Protection Agency (EPA) and a series of specific laws such as the 1970 Clean Air Act, the 1972 Clean Water Act and the 1976 Resource Recovery Act.

For firms, the new regulations had implications for business activity, often raising the costs of operations and adding the burden of demonstrating legal compliance to regulators. In many cases the economic impact has been significant. In the USA, for example, the costs for complying with the Superfund regulations, legislated to clean up polluted industrial sites, are estimated to be five–ten times the annual revenues of the chemical industry itself (Hird 1993). Business responded to these new requirements and costs in several ways. First, many impacted industries developed lobbying and strategic political competencies so that they could engage in and influence political debates over environmental regulations. In this way businesses became a more active and important stakeholder in the national environmental policy process, gaining influence and the ability to defend economic interests (Coen 1999). Secondly, many companies developed extensive regulatory compliance functions within the organization. These environmental health and safety (EH&S) functions were new additions to the organizational structure and were often perceived as obligatory cost centres (Reinhardt 2000). By the 1980s, in part because of the political actions of business, the pace of new environmental regulation in industrialized countries slowed. The deregulation trend of the Reagan and Thatcher eras gave environmental regulatory relief in many industries. But at the dawn of the new millennium, environmental regulation has been reinvigorated, largely due to the process of regulatory harmonization and modernization in the European Union (Hix 2005).

The rise of international environmental policy

While early efforts to minimize environmental pollution began at the national level, by the 1970s it was recognized that many environmental problems ignored national borders and that an effective policy response required multinational cooperation (Haas 1990). This understanding led to the development of a new field of international law – international environmental diplomacy – and the establishment of the first multilateral environmental regimes. Following the 1972 International Conference on Human Development held in Stockholm, the meeting that established the United Nations Environmental Program (UNEP), international environmental policy efforts accelerated. Within a decade several international regimes had been established including the 1973 Convention on International Trade in Endangered Species (CITES), the 1977 International Convention to Combat Desertification and the 1979 Convention on Long-range Transboundary Air Pollution. The development of these regimes was done mostly under the auspices or the support of the UN system of organizations (Susskind, Moomaw and Gallagher 2002).

As international environmental governance advanced, the complexities of global environmental policy became apparent and in some cases proved more challenging than historic international diplomatic concerns. Part of the reason for this complexity was due to the constantly evolving scientific understanding of global environmental problems. Another challenge lay in the changing and complex landscape of actors that had a stake in global environmental regimes. As discussed, the nation-state has historically been the undisputed structuring force in global governance. The diplomatic representatives of countries, motivated by national interests, would agree to global norms codified into international law through a formal treaty or convention. The treaty's intentions would then be translated through national parliaments into laws, regulations and standards for society. But the end of the Cold War signalled a shift in the relative structuring power of nation-states, and new actors like activist non-profit organizations and private businesses increasingly sought and gained influence in the international regime formation process (Newell 2000).

In dealing with global environmental challenges it became clear that nation-states had some limitations. Many smaller countries, for example, often did not have the capacity to effectively engage in the diplomatic process, meaning that the interests of larger industrialized countries could dominate or impede international policy that threatened vested economic interests (Victor, Raustiala and Skolnikoff 1998). In other instances, specialist non-governmental environmental organizations were better informed about environmental issues than the diplomatic representatives from many countries. With the tools of globalization, including the Internet, many environmental NGOs thus became influential actors in regime formation, including organizations like the European-based World Wide Fund for Nature (WWF) and environmental think tanks like the US-based World Resources Institute (WRI) and the Canadian-based International Institute for Sustainable Development (IISD). By the late 1980s these organizations were influential in defining the issues, proposing new international agreements and pressuring national governments into action. A symbolic recognition of the new importance of NGOs came in 1996 when the World Trade Organization (WTO), historically a guarded institution that preferred decision-making outside of public scrutiny, officially recognized the role of NGOs and 'civil society' through a process of systematic consultation (WTO 2009).

As discussed, the rise of global environmental policy also had economic impacts which drew the private sector into the process of regime formation. Historically, business tended to derivatively engage in international diplomacy by lobbying their home governments in an effort to influence the national negotiating position. Some of the early international environmental regimes like CITES or the International Convention to Combat Desertification had a limited impact on most industries and did not draw substantial business concern or input into the regime development process. However, other regimes had important economic consequences and thus drew corporations more actively into the international policy process. The Montreal Protocol on Substances that Deplete the Ozone Layer, for example, required changes to existing economic and technological structures, something that fostered the active participation by chemical manufacturers and their representative industry associations in regime formation (Benedick 1991). These and parallel social processes ultimately altered the role global corporations play in international environmental issues, as discussed in the following section.

Business and global environmental governance

Today many experts and practitioners recognize corporations as important and influential actors in global economic structuring and international governance. This influence has grown over the last decades as a result of economic policy developments – motivated by liberal market philosophy – that have empowered the corporations globally. Financial and trade liberalization, for example, removed the constraints on a company's ability to build and assemble a multinational production, distribution and marketing organization (Cerny 1994). This, combined with the rise of the Internet and the collapse in the costs of transnational communications, has lowered the expense of managing and coordinating a global organization. Companies now assemble global supply chains and reach global markets wherever the superior economic conditions are found with limited interference, and often incentives, from most host governments.

Global corporations are therefore arguably freer and more capable global institutions than many nation-states, a fact that has not escaped those interested in addressing many global social and environmental concerns. Non-governmental activists, for example, have historically preferred to lobby governments for environmental protection policies, but the global reach of many corporations has become an attractive attribute for activists (Crane 1998). Many activists recognize that convincing a global multinational to adopt environmental protection policies can facilitate their implementation in every country where the company operates. And unlike the representative parliamentary democracies of many nation-states, activists have learned that corporations have centralized decision-making hierarchies. Where parliamentary processes often slow decision-making and ensure that minority views have a hearing, corporations are based on largely unilateral executive decision-making. This unitary decision structure can foster rapid global change in company policy, something that is attractive to activists.

It is also widely recognized, both inside and outside the business world, that corporations are important players in both creating and solving environmental problems. As discussed, industrial processes and resource use are usually at the centre of environmental concerns. Solving many environmental challenges requires innovative new ways of operating and corporations, being one of the primary sources of innovation and technology, are thus well positioned to help create the solutions to environmental problems. While it is not universally accepted that corporations have responsibilities beyond legal and fiduciary duties, the above factors have combined to create a relatively new focus on business as an international actor with the potential to play a constructive role in addressing global environmental issues. It is from within this context that the Global Compact environmental principles have emerged.

The Global Compact environmental principles

The Global Compact environmental principles help establish a foundation for considering the impact of corporate operations on the environment in decision-making and strategic planning. As discussed, the principles are adapted to a corporate context from their original source in international environmental law. The following subsections will introduce each principle, discuss its purpose and validity and explore how companies have interpreted and implemented the principle in the business environment.

Global Compact Principle 7

'Business should support a precautionary approach to environmental challenges.'

This Principle, known in business circles as the 'precautionary approach', forms the foundational logic for the Compact's subsequent environmental principles and finds its regulatory roots in European environmental policy-making (McCormick 1995). When serious environmental damage is suspected, the precautionary principle calls for rational preventive actions even before conclusive proof is found. The need for the principle arises from the nature of Earth's ecosystems and the complexity of understanding the impact of human interventions on ecosystem health. As discussed, the scale and impact of human economic activity has become large relative to ecosystems and their function. In fact humans, by many measures, have become a dominating planetary force comparable in scale to some geological processes. The dynamism of industrial science and technology and our globally integrated economies means that the rate at which new innovations can be produced and deployed has constantly accelerated since the industrial revolution. In contrast, our understanding of the earth's biogeochemical systems, while progressing, is still quite limited, and the scientific process of discovery – hypothesis generation, data collection, analysis and verification/falsification – is complex and time-consuming. Thus our ability to understand the environmental implications of new technologies and commercial innovations generally lags our ability to produce and diffuse them across the globe.

History is rich with examples of new commercial conveniences that were rapidly adopted in the marketplace only to belatedly discover the environmental damages they produced (Wargo 1996). It wasn't until seven decades after the Model T entered the marketplace that scientists understood the car's role in creating photochemical smog and the health risks of ground-level ozone production (Sperling 1995).

Similarly, large-scale centralized coal-fired electricity generation had existed for decades before it was recognized that it could cause acid rain and undermine the health of terrestrial and aquatic ecosystems. Chlorofluorocarbons (CFC) were welcomed as wonder chemicals, but their impact on stratospheric ozone was accepted only after the so-called 'ozone hole' was demonstrated over the Antarctic (Benedick 1991). It is this inability to predict the environmental implications of human interventions and alterations of ecological systems that forms the justification for the precautionary approach. And while the precautionary principle is most often associated with political discourse it actually has a long colloquial history. Traditional sayings like 'an ounce of prevention is worth a pound of cure' and 'better safe than sorry' both capture the understanding that humans should use foresight and rational prevention in their endeavours.

It was the 1969 Swedish Environmental Policy Act that was responsible for introducing the idea that constraints on potentially ecologically damaging activities could be imposed on the basis of risk alone, stating that some environmentally hazardous activities 'for which the mere risk (if not remote) is deemed enough to warrant protective measures or a ban on that activity' (Anderson 1997: 163). Similarly, as German regulatory officials developed clean air policies in the 1970s the 'Vorsorgeprinzip' or 'forecaring' principle was invoked, arguing that foresight and planning were required (Anderson 1997). The precautionary principle entered into the realm of international law during the 1992 UN Conference on Environment and Development (UNCED), also known as the 'Earth Summit', where several of the agreements signed at the conference invoked the 'precautionary principle' including the United Nations Framework Convention on Climate Change (UNFCCC) and the UN Convention on Biological Diversity. But it was perhaps Principle 15 of UNCED's Rio Declaration that best captured the concept:

In order to protect the environment, the precautionary approach shall be widely applied by States according to their ability. Where there are threats of serious or irreversible damage, lack of full scientific certainty shall not be used as a reason for postponing cost-effective measures to prevent environmental degradation. (UNEP 2009)

During the Earth Summit and afterwards, the precautionary principle was greeted with some trepidation by many in the business community. In some industries, like tobacco, scientific uncertainty about the health effects of products had been exploited by firms to delay restrictive regulation and protect lucrative product markets. The precautionary principle, if strictly interpreted, would undermine such political strategies. For other companies there were two additional concerns. The first was that the principle could be invoked in an absolutist manner, with little or no flexibility in the way companies could respond to new environmental concerns about their products or technologies. Companies worried that the principle would have legal implications and could force them to abandon costly investments and assets prematurely.

Secondly, there was an implied shift in responsibility for determining whether or not a given product or technology was environmentally benign. Historically, the most profitable products and technologies were treated like criminal suspects in modern legal systems: innocent until proven guilty. An extreme interpretation of the precautionary principle could imply that the responsibility had shifted and the burden of proof now lay with the company to demonstrate that a product was environmentally benign before it was commercialized. Most companies felt that the responsibility for understanding the environmental risk of products and technologies needed to be more broadly shared across society, with scientists, regulators and environmental groups playing a role alongside business. Given these concerns, business argued for the term 'precautionary approach' instead of precautionary principle, to indicate that it was not a legal requirement but an acceptable industry practice (O'Riordan and Cameron 1994). The term was ultimately adopted in the language of the Global Compact and is commonly used by business executives today.

Global Compact Principle 8

'[Businesses should] undertake initiatives to promote greater environmental responsibility.'

Principle 8 is a logical next step once companies have accepted the precautionary principle and the responsibility that attends it. The Principle calls for action on the part of business to integrate environmental concerns into managerial processes, strategic planning and investment. Like the precautionary principle, Principle 8 has its roots primarily in the 1992 Earth Summit agreements. *Agenda 21* (chapter

30) states that business can demonstrate environmental responsibility through the:

> responsible and ethical management of products and processes from the point of view of health, safety and environmental aspects . . . Towards this end, business and industry should increase self-regulation guided by appropriate codes, charters and initiatives integrated into all elements of business planning and decision-making and fostering openness and dialogue with employees and the public. (United Nations 2009c)

Most companies have responded to this principle by adopting and implementing voluntary environmental assessment and management systems. Called generically an environmental management system (EMS), these organizational innovations extended traditional environmental health and safety functions into strategic planning, operational decisions and new product development (Unruh and Konolla 2007). Environmental management systems were influenced by the 'quality movement' of the 1980s, which codified quality management principles into imitable standards (Hackman and Wageman 1995). The ISO 9001, for example, became a widely accepted quality standard. A similar process has ensued with environmental management systems, leading to the establishment of standards like the ISO 14001 and the European Eco-Management and Audit Scheme (EMAS).

The adoption of voluntary environmental management tools and greater corporate accountability to the public found in Global Compact Principle 8 also coincided with the rise in a wider acceptance of the stakeholder view of the firm by many business organizations. The stakeholder perspective holds that corporations are accountable not only to their shareholders, but also to broader constituencies that can include employees, the community, customers and the natural environment (Freeman 1984). Principle 8 likewise calls for openness and engagement with the public stakeholder groups. In addition to the establishment of consultative relations with identified stakeholders, many companies have developed non-financial reporting functions that detail their social and environmental performance in public documents. There is a good deal of dynamism and innovation going on with companies producing a broad array of 'Corporate Social Responsibility' (CSR) or 'sustainability' reports. Some analysts see a standardization process that will lead to comparable measures of non-financial performance in the future. Efforts along these lines include the Global Reporting Initiative (GRI), which has emerged as the leading source of reporting guidelines (Hedberg and von Malmborg 2003) and has been adopted by a significant number of Global Compact signatories (see also chapter 17 by Paul Hohnen).

Global Compact Principle 9

'[Businesses] should encourage the development and diffusion of environmentally friendly technologies.'

In many ways Principle 9 is the expected outcome as businesses implement Principles 7 and 8. As discussed throughout this chapter, many of our important environmental challenges have their roots in the types of industrial technologies and processes that businesses have developed and commercialized since the industrial revolution. Many of these technologies manifested their unintended environmental externalities only after they were broadly adopted and diffused throughout the economy. Addressing the environmental consequences of this situation requires commercial change and industrial innovation in which business can play a leading role.

Management processes to foster environmentally friendly technologies have tended to focus most successfully on the new product design and development phase in the commercialization process. A variety of design and management tools have emerged for integrating corporate environment concerns into new product decision-making (Allenby 1999). Many of these tools can be collectively categorized as 'Design for X', where 'X' can stand for recycling, efficiency, disassembly, etc. In many cases these practices have made products easier to recover and recycle and reduced their material and energy demand in operation and production.

While environmentally responsible product development is still at an early stage in most industries, it seems to be an area that promises the greatest environmental gains for the business sector. The potential can be illustrated in the changes that have occurred in a common durable good like the refrigerator. Today's refrigerator is bigger and 75 per cent more energy efficient than its counterpart produced a decade ago, but costs 50 per cent less (Unruh 2008). Design improvements like this are obviously a plus for both consumers and the environment as well as manufacturers. Because this is a growing trend in business environmental management, it will be discussed in greater detail in the trends section of this chapter (p. 74).

Global climate change and the impact of business

For a more comprehensive illustration of how business can implement the Global Compact environmental principles, and in doing so have a positive impact on the environment, we can take the example of global climate change (see also chapter 5 by Claude Fussler). Global climate change, which is the unwanted alteration of the Earth's heat balance by the accumulation of industrial greenhouse gases, is one of the most pressing global environmental problems today. In the business response to climate change, all three of the Global Compact environmental principles come into play. The goal of this section is not to assess whether companies are comprehensively employing the principles in addressing global climate change, but rather to look at the potential impact on global climate change were companies to fully execute the principles.

The basic science of global climate change, and the role of greenhouse gases in climatic regulation, has been understood since the nineteenth century. But it wasn't until the 1980s that the issue emerged as an international environmental policy concern. The World Meteorological Organization (WMO) and UNEP established the Intergovernmental Panel on Climate Change (IPCC) in 1988 as an authoritative international scientific body responsible for consolidating the existing research and scientific understanding into guidance for policy-makers. As the science was slowly understood it became increasingly obvious that regulatory action to address the issue would have important economic and business implications. The businesses most impacted by potential regulatory control of greenhouse gas (GHG) emissions were the fossil fuel energy sector (coal, oil and gas) and other energy-intensive businesses like automobiles, petrochemicals, cement and heavy industry. As diplomats began moving towards an international convention to prevent unwanted climate disruption, businesses organized to influence the process and in many cases to protect commercial interests (Kolk and Pinske 2005).

An influential association of energy interests called the Global Climate Coalition actively worked to frame the global climate change policy debate in ways beneficial to their members as well as to water down any regulations that would impose costs on their industries (Rowlands 2000). Following the failure of countries to meet their voluntary commitments to reduce greenhouse gas emissions agreed to as part of the 1992 Earth Summit agreements, negotiations were begun on a new treaty that would become the Kyoto protocol. This protocol would require mandatory cuts in industrial country emissions. As with previous diplomatic efforts, the business groups like the Global Climate Coalition began a public media and lobbying campaign to weaken any Kyoto commitments that would impose costs on industry. However, responding to a shift in public awareness of the issue and growing scientific understanding, one of the founding members of the coalition – BP, a signatory of the Global Compact – made a break with its industry peers and withdrew from the organization (Rowlands 2000). In a 1997 speech at Stanford University, BP CEO John Browne, justified the company's actions on the basis of what is embodied in the Compact's Principle 7, the precautionary approach:

The concentration of carbon dioxide in the atmosphere is rising. And the temperature of the earth's surface is increasing . . . there is now an effective consensus among the world's leading scientists . . . that there is a discernible human influence on the climate. The time to consider the policy dimensions of climate change is not when the link between greenhouse gases and climate is conclusively proven but when the possibility cannot be discounted. We in BP have reached that point. (BP 2009)

Acting on the precautionary principle, BP took action to mitigate the company's climate impact and in doing so demonstrated environmental responsibility as required by Principle 8. To fulfil its environmental responsibilities, the company also had to act on the Compact's Principle 9 by encouraging the development and diffusion of environmentally superior technologies within the company. In 1998 BP committed to a 10 per cent reduction in their greenhouse gas emissions by 2010, something that would require substantial technological and process innovations throughout the company. To foster these innovations, BP established a global emissions trading system within the company that mirrored and demonstrated the feasibility of the mechanisms negotiated in the Kyoto protocol (Akhurst, Morgheim and Lewis 2003). BP's demonstration that the policy mechanism of cap and trade could work and that reductions in emission could be captured at minimal economic cost, or perhaps even net benefit, had some effect. To the surprise of many both inside and outside of the company, BP achieved its 10 per cent reduction nine years ahead of schedule and in doing so fostered $650 million in business value creation (Akhurst, Morgheim and Lewis 2003).

BP's actions during the period are a good illustration of all three of the Compact's environmental principles in action. However, it needs to be recognized that BP has run into trouble in other areas of environmental management, most notably an important oil spill in the Alaskan wilderness and an explosion in a Texas refinery that killed fifteen employees. It is also been reported that, given the current economic downturn, BP has recently begun backing away from its renewable energy investments, something that illustrates the challenge of maintaining commitments over the long term in the face of unpredictable market and economic shifts (*New York Times*, 'Oil Giants Loath to Follow Obama's Green Lead', 8 April 2009). In recognition and acknowledgement of these challenges, the following sections explore some trends in how companies are implementing environmental principles and the spirit which they embody.

Trends toward the future: case examples

As the issue of climate change indicates, business can play a positive role in moving forward on environmental challenges and fulfilling the principles embedded in the Global Compact, but it requires a proactive attitude on behalf of business and the corps of professional managers. The real business challenge is fulfilling the aspirations of the Compact's Principles, but doing so in ways that create business value. Across the spectrum of businesses there are encouraging examples of companies working to these ends. It is recognized, however, that these are anecdotal cases and provide no conclusions to the extent to which the Compact's environmental principles are comprehensively impacting business behaviour. These successful cases instead can provide encouragement and serve as an example to firms and their management that sign onto and accept the Global Compact.

As discussed, the precautionary approach embedded in Principle 7 is in many ways the foundational norm of the other environmental principles. By accepting this Principle, firms commit to using ecological foresight in all decision-making and incorporating the recognition of humanity's fundamental ignorance of the totality of the environmental implications of technological and material innovations in their dealings. One of the administrative decision areas where this principle is currently at the forefront in business management is in the area of toxic materials management. As discussed earlier there are numerous examples of 'wonder materials' that were later discovered to have unintended negative environmental consequences. Thus toxic materials management is an excellent place for companies to manifest their commitment to Principle 7.

An example of a company acting in the spirit of Principle 7 in terms of materials management is the Swedish textile retailer and Global Compact signatory Hennes & Mauritz, Inc. (H&M). Founded in 1947, H&M is a $9.2 billion clothing company with over 1,200 retail outlets worldwide. In addition to a variety of chemical dyes, the company is a major user of cotton and synthetic fibre such as polyester and nylon. Beginning with Azo dyes, a common chemical in the textile industry, H&M established a chemical restriction policy to govern the use of chemical inputs in their production operations. The restriction policy was overtly motivated by the precautionary approach. According to Ingrid Schullstrom, H&M's Environment & CSR Manager, 'we decided to adopt the strictest of any country policy for any sales country and later adopted the precautionary principle' (Greiner *et al.* 2006: 30). The company currently has over 170 chemicals or chemical categories in its restricted chemical list and continues to follow changes in the scientific understanding of chemical and materials risk. The company updates its list every two or three years, adding new substances to the list or lowering the allowable limits of already listed chemicals, thus providing an ongoing process of incremental improvement (Greiner *et al.* 2006).

The H&M chemical policy is a relatively simple approach to implementing the precautionary approach, requiring just a list of chemicals and a set of restrictions pertaining to their use in H&M products. The implementation of the policy, however, has important implications that extend beyond H&M itself outward into the company's supply chain. In order to implement the policy H&M has to engage its suppliers who are responsible for production and materials sourcing tasks. To do so, H&M presents its suppliers with its restricted chemicals list at the beginning of each contract period and asks them to sign the H&M Chemical Restriction Commitment as a way to guarantee their compliance. The suppliers are further provided with acceptable testing procedures and a list of approved laboratories where they are required to screen samples of their input materials (H&M 2003). The compliance cost of the H&M processes can be substantial, requiring approximately 70,000 sample analyses annually with an associated cost of nearly $1.75 million (H&M 2003). Surprisingly to some observers, many suppliers are unaware of the detailed chemical compositions of their own products. This means that the H&M policy has the effect of extending the precautionary approach to the supply chain. In order to fulfil H&M's expectations, the company's suppliers must pass on the restrictions to their own suppliers, which include dye mills, tanneries and basic chemical producers. This extends the impacts of the policy through the supply chain well beyond H&M.

Another example of proactive precautionary action can be found in the US-based consumer goods company S.C. Johnson, Inc. The 117-year-old family-managed firm has a history of precautionary environmental management, including being the first company to remove ozone-depleting chlorofluorocarbons from its aerosol products. In 2001, S.C. Johnson launched a materials management system it called Greenlist to guide the raw material choices of its product formulators and designers (Martin 2009). The Greenlist evaluation process begins by categorizing the function of materials used in product formulations and then setting acceptable environmental and human health criteria for each of the categories (Martin 2009). For example, cleaning compounds that are likely to be disposed of down a drain and thus enter into riverine or marine ecosystems needed to be biodegradable and not demonstrate aquatic toxicity. Data pertaining to hazards for each of the identified criteria are collected from publicly available sources including commercial databases, published scientific studies, or material suppliers themselves and used to rank input materials on a 0–3 scale, with 0 meaning that the use of the material must be carefully restricted. Greenlist is then applied at the product design and formulation stage, embedding a precautionary approach at the very beginning of the new product innovation process and helping to ensure that each generation of new offerings will incorporate the latest scientific understanding.

Similar business applications of the Global Compact can be seen in Principle 8. By adopting Principle 8, companies commit to demonstrating environmental responsibility in decision-making and when planning the strategic and operational future of the company. The essence of the principle might be understood as self-regulation – that is, proactively recognizing the environmental insults created by a company's operations and acting to mitigate them even in the absence of government regulation. An example of an industry acting in the spirit of Principle 8 in both the USA and Europe can be found among the carpet manufacturing companies.

At the beginning of the new millennium, the carpet industry was growing substantially and by 2003 was producing more than 4.5 billion pounds of carpet worldwide. However, the overwhelming majority of discarded carpet was ending up in municipal landfills. Less than 5 per cent of all waste carpet was recycled and much of it was being used for waste-to-energy conversion (see also the standard for sustainable carpets issues by Scientific Certification Systems (SCS)). Concern about carpet waste began being voiced by local municipalities in the USA and Germany who were concerned about the volume that carpets were contributing to city landfill. Carpet manufacturers and industry groups recognized that if the industry did not take responsible voluntary action to address the carpet waste issue they risked potential future regulation. This led to a variety of environmental responsibility initiatives by carpet companies on both sides of the Atlantic, including the creation of industrial-scale recycling facilities and carpet recycling networks.

The response in the USA provides an interesting example because of the fact that companies addressed the waste carpet problem from both competitive and collaborative perspectives. Competitively, companies like Interface, Mohawk and Shaw Industries launched heavily advertised 'sustainable carpet' initiatives that included product redesigns and innovations in the manufacturing process to foster recycling (Realff *et al.* 1999). The companies were clearly competing on the relative sustainability merits of their market offerings, a competition that continues broadly across the carpet industry today. At the same time most executives recognized that the waste carpet problem was not just an individual firm problem, but a challenge to the industry as a whole. Responsibly solving the problem meant that all companies in the industry would need to commit to addressing the carpet waste issue, a situation demanding collective action (Kibert 2003). The forum for fostering the collective action in the USA was the Carpet and Rug Institute, which engaged in a search for an industrywide solution with a broad set of stakeholders that included state governments, NGOs, and the US EPA. The result was the National Carpet Recycling Agreement which was signed in January 2002 by carpet and fibre manufacturers. This agreement established a ten-year schedule to reduce the amount of waste carpet going to landfill and increased the amount of recycling and the reusing of post-consumer carpet. By signing the agreement the stakeholders hope to reach their common goal of diverting 40 per cent of end-of-life carpet from landfill disposal by 2012. This example of voluntary action by individual companies and collective self-regulation by the entire industry provides a suitable example of how companies can adopt Principle 8.

By accepting Principle 9, companies are asked to rethink their current product portfolio and production processes in light of environmental concerns. A good example of a company doing so, however not under the umbrella of the Global Compact, is the sports equipment and apparel retailer Patagonia. Founded in 1972 by Yves Chouinard, the company has had a commitment to high-quality, long-lasting products but also recognized a need to take responsibility for its end-of-life products. The company first began addressing this in 1981 through a partnership with New England textile manufacturer Wellman, Inc. Wellman had developed a technology that could create a recycled polyester fleece fabric from waste soda bottles. Branded as Polartec, the mill collected the bottles, then shredded, melted and re-extruded them as a soft fleece which would then go into Patagonia's jackets, jerseys and pants allowing Patagonia to reduce its use of virgin natural resources and also reduce the amount of waste plastic entering landfill.

Building on the success in the late 1990s Patagonia partnered with Teijin, a Japan-based textile manufacturer (Unruh 2010). Teijin had developed a depolymerization process that allowed it to convert wastes like bottles and shower curtains into a quality filament fibre perfectly suited to Patagonia's high-performance applications. Making the partnership work meant that Patagonia had to make design changes to their clothing in order to produce a stream of waste fabric that would work well with the Teijin processes. After substantial innovation, Patagonia was able to launch the Common Threads Recycling Program in 2005 as a new closed-loop, clothing-to-clothing manufacturing process. The inaugural product was their 'Capilene baselayers', Patagonia's brand of long underwear. Despite the long-distance transport, Patagonia has published a detailed study showing that the process creates a net beneficial environmental benefit by consuming 76 per cent less energy than virgin processes. The company is now leveraging the Common Threads Recycling Program more broadly across their product line, expanding into new garments and products in 2007.

Challenge and opportunities

The above examples are heartening illustrations of what companies can achieve when they adopt the Global Compact environmental principles and embed them into their decision-making processes. But while the examples indicate that companies can achieve a good deal, it must be recognized that business cannot be expected to solve environmental problems alone. Importantly, managers have an undeniable fiduciary responsibility to the providers of capital and cannot be expected to abandon that responsibility. There are, furthermore, numerous external drivers that are out of managerial control and that need to be aligned to facilitate proactive business behaviour. The examples above indicate that companies can do much within their existing constraints, but unless policy corrects for environmental externalities and market failures, companies will be challenged in situations where profitability and environmental quality conflict. In this sense, companies are one of many contributors to the broader social challenge of achieving environmental sustainability. By signing on to the Global Compact environmental principles companies accept these responsibilities and take their respective place amongst nation-states, intergovernmental organizations and civil society at large in the collective task of preserving the global environment.

5 | 'Caring for Climate' – The Business Leadership Platform

CLAUDE FUSSLER

Introduction: a moral issue

The way we consume and produce changes the composition of the planet's atmosphere and, thus, creates a global warming trend that destabilizes our climate. This warming is faster than in any previous era. Climate events like storms, floods, or droughts get fiercer and more frequent. Many species cannot adapt at this speed and biodiversity declines while links in our food chains weaken. Many human infrastructures and activities are also vulnerable to sudden extreme weather events.

The balance between emissions of gases forcing climate change and the planet's ability to absorb and neutralize them has been disturbed by our massive combustion of fossil fuels. Take carbon dioxide: 15–30 per cent of any release persists for centuries and, therefore, adds a factor of certainty to the global risks.[1] Now make the connection: anyone in charge of a source of CO_2 or causing someone to release CO_2 (or any other greenhouse gas) shares a moral responsibility in the current and future consequences of climate change, even in the most remote places of the world. Because every person has a right to a safe environment, to energy, work and comfort that neither weaken our living planet nor endanger the prospects of future generations, the Global Compact signatories should feel compelled to act. Their duty not only arises from the obvious precautionary approach, the support for environmental responsibility and the promotion of climate-friendly technologies, but more fundamentally from their core commitment to the respect of human rights, their engagement to fight poverty and contribute to a better society.

At the Global Compact Leaders Summit in July 2007, UN Secretary-General Ban Ki-moon formulated this connection into a special

---

[1] See, for instance, www.globalwarmingart.com/wiki/Image:Carbon_Dioxide_Residence_Time_png.

initiative – Caring for Climate – launched jointly with the United Nations Environment Programme (UNEP) and the World Business Council for Sustainable Development (WBCSD) (Global Compact 2007a). The timing was good. Seven years after its launch, the Global Compact was growing as a wide Network of, then, more than 4,000 committed organizations in 116 countries. It had given the fuzzy territory of Corporate Social Responsibility (CSR) a clear basis of ten universal Principles. It had also overcome initial scepticism by delivering on its promise to press business signatories for more discipline in communicating on implementation and progress. At the same moment the international climate agenda was dominated by the conjunction of several high points. The publication of the Stern Review argued for the overwhelming economic advantage of early climate action (Stern 2006). Al Gore's intensive public campaigning, spearheaded by the Academy Award winning documentary *An Inconvenient Truth*, led to a Nobel Peace Prize.[2] He shared it with the Intergovernmental Panel on Climate Change (IPCC) which had also just released its 4th Assessment Report (IPCC 2007a). The IPCC expressed in this report the consensus of thousands of scientific studies that unequivocally affirm the warming of our climate system and link it directly to human activity. The Synthesis Report of the 4th Assessment was particularly relevant for the policymakers due to meet in December in Bali at the thirteenth Conference of Parties to the United Nations Framework Convention on Climate Change (UNFCCC); there they would prepare and agree on a Road Map to prepare the successor to the Kyoto protocol (UNFCCC 2008).

Leadership and early action

Mid-2007 was therefore the moment to call Global Compact signatories for a special focus on the climate issue, and Ban Ki-moon spelled out the expectations: 'The Caring for Climate platform sets the stage for individual and collective actions on climate change, and sends a powerful message to businesses, governments and consumers everywhere about the need for *leadership and early action*' (United Nations 2007).

'Leadership and early action' are the operative words. Caring for Climate invites chief executive officers (CEOs) who have already

---

[2] For more information on Gore's movie, please visit www.climatecrisis.net.

committed their company to the ten Principles of the UN Global
Compact to take an additional formal step and sign a comprehensive
document of engagement (Global Compact 2007b). They thus make
a triple commitment: first commitment to performance by changing
towards higher energy efficiency and a lower-carbon burden in the
company's production and services, in its supply chains and in shaping
its consumers' and the public's attitudes; a second commitment to
measuring and annual reporting of progress to the public; a third commitment to supporting policy-makers towards a successful outcome
of the current climate negotiations through the examples of successful practices and by speaking out for the need of a binding ambitious
climate policy. With these three conditions Caring for Climate is
demanding and different. It is not something to sign lightly. Three
years later, in January 2010, the Global Compact had convinced 370
companies to join. Every third signatory is headquartered in an emerging economy, proof that climate leadership is shifting well beyond
Europe and other richer countries.

Let's think over the case for leadership and early action. In recent
years, books, conferences and reports, articles and news, documenta-
ries and websites have challenged the capability of anyone to embrace
the breadth and complexity of the climate change question and keep
up with its technical and political solutions. Yet, leadership is about
deciding on what is so important that it comes first in the line of
action. But it is tricky to understand and deal with a situation that
cannot be explained concisely. Can we reduce the climate brief to a
few points, the length of a ten minutes' coffee or tea break, to stir up
a business colleague for action now?[3]

The 10 minute case for action

We are changing the composition and properties of our planet's
atmosphere by emitting gases that trap a fraction of the sun's radiation reflected by the earth. This greenhouse effect has enabled life as
known on the earth. But the more greenhouse gases, the higher the
effect. CO_2 accounts for about 80 per cent of this greenhouse effect. It

[3] Of the numerous reliable sources available on the subject the author, when not
otherwise stated, drew data from Greenfacts – clear summaries of scientific
publications produced by an independent non-profit organization (see www.
greenfacts.org/en/climate-change-ar4).

comes first in all climate debates and actions. Of every 100 molecules of carbon dioxide, 19 are released by the destruction of irreplaceable forests and burning/decay of other biomass; 76 by the combustion of fossil fuels to produce the heat and energy at the core of human activity; the other 5 from reactions in cement kilns and the gas flaring by oil companies (International Energy Agency 2009: 398–9).

For million of years, vegetation, oceans and rocks removed carbon dioxide from the atmosphere. This positive carbon cycle cooled the climate to a range ideal for the expansion of civilizations. Then, the industrial revolution started the ever-increasing growth of fossil carbon through the exponential proliferation of domestic and industrial combustion devices. The natural carbon cycle is overwhelmed. Of 100 molecules released now about 50 remain in the atmosphere long enough to force climate change and leave 20 practically forever.[4]

In 1958, scientist Charles David Keeling initiated the continuous recording of the build-up of CO_2 in the atmosphere. There is no doubt about its steady rise (see figure 5.1). This has a profound implication: long seen as practically inert and simply valuable for the growth of vegetation, CO_2, beyond a limit, is also hazardous. Therefore no one causing its emission, at any level, to the atmosphere can assume that they are being harmless. Action or inaction is then a moral dilemma. At least, it should be.

CO_2 hazardous? What is the solid evidence? For one, its radiation absorption and heat-trapping properties are a long-established scientific fact. It is estimated that all the CO_2 (plus the cohort of other greenhouse gases) emitted since 1750 has caused the earth to retain, for every m², 1.6 watts more sun radiation than what it should radiate back to the cosmos. So, it is as if the molecules of CO_2 (and other greenhouse gases) aggregated into a powerful 1,600 kilowatt radiator over every km² of the planet. As if there were now 510 million of them for the whole planet, always 'on' and still growing in power. No surprise that we have global warming. As a fact the earth's mean surface temperature, monitored by thousands of weather stations, has already increased by 0.74°C in the past 100 years (Henson 2008).

But the greenhouse energy is not distributed evenly across every m² of the earth. It depends highly on the sun's angle and whether it

[4] See: www.globalwarmingart.com/wiki/Image:Carbon_Dioxide_Residence_ Time_ png.

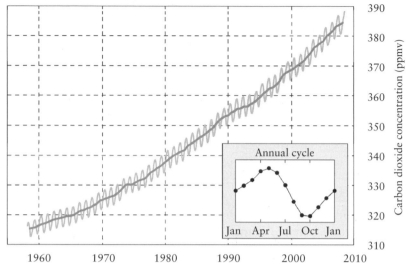

Note: Measured in Mauna Loa, Hawaii.
Source: Reproduced under the terms of the GNU Free Documentation License.

Figure 5.1 Keeling curve: atmospheric CO_2, 1960–2010

hits snow, water, forest, desert, concrete or clouds and the multitude of materials of our natural and man-made areas. As a result there is not only a warming trend but we get stronger and longer climate turbulences like storms, floods and droughts. 2008 was again a record year for losses of life from cyclones and hurricanes. The cost of weather-related catastrophes was at an estimated $200 billion, 50 per cent higher than the year before. The Arctic ice level dropped to its second-lowest level (UNEP 2008).

The correlation between CO_2, temperature and climate instability is strong. Scores of scientific studies converge to the same conclusion: as long as we continue to emit CO_2 at or over the current rate we increase the probability of large-scale dangerous impacts on the natural systems that sustain our economies and societies (IPCC 2007b).[5] The climate models also show how impacts worsen with temperature. In particular, beyond 2°C (over preindustrial temperature, or about

[5] The IPCC assessed the scientific studies and presented at the end of 2007 a summary for policy-makers on the correlation between greenhouse gases concentrations, temperature predictions and impacts. It remains a basis for the discussion on mitigation and adaptation strategies.

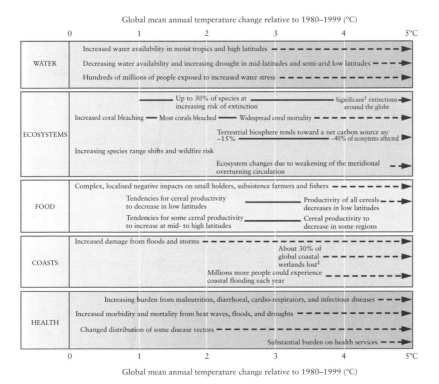

Global mean annual temperature change relative to 1980–1999 (°C)

Figure 5.2 IPCC assessment of temperature impacts, 1980–99

Notes: †Significant is defined here as more than 40%.
‡Based on average rate of sea level rise of 4.2 mm/year from 2000 to 2080.
ICE = Internal combustion engine.
Gt = Giga-ton.
Source: International Panel on Climate Change.

1.2°C over current average) several irreversible effects could accelerate climate change (see also figure 5.2).

With the melting of ice sheets the earth loses the cooling power to reflect the sun's radiation; heat waves are bound to devastate larger areas of forests that protect ground water and biodiversity; the water from melting continental ice runs to oceans that also swell up as they warm; rising sea levels flood coastal areas and cities as storms push them over inadequate shore protections. Electricity and gas networks, airports, harbours and bridges, riverside and coastal cities and factories are amongst the most exposed infrastructures. A few major climatic catastrophes could ruin entire regions and wipe out their biodiversity and food supplies. The Global Humanitarian Forum (GHF), a Geneva-based foundation, tried to connect the IPCC assessment to present and future impacts on human life. It concludes that several hundred million people, of the poorest and most vulnerable, are already severely affected by weather-related disasters including droughts and floods. This number could double in the next twenty years (Global Humanitarian Forum 2009).

The scientific warning about the 2°C threshold is stern. It correlates with about 450 parts per million (ppm) of CO_2 on the Keeling curve. At 380 ppm now and a growth rate of 2 ppm yearly we have only thirty-five years before we saturate the last 70 ppm headspace under this probable point of no return. A number of scientists, alarmed about the momentum of the climate system, even recommend an urgent return to 350 ppm as a safe limit.

At the other side of the debate, there are a few voices that doubt the severity of the climate risk and the importance of human responsibility. Gambling on their denial of basic physics and mainstream science would betray the commitments to precaution and care at the roots of the Global Compact. We have come to a time when CO_2 emissions cannot grow further but must come down. Leadership and early action are about getting it done.

Government leaders also seem more determined than ever to protect their citizens from climate risk. They have been on the case for decades with an awful track record. In 1992, based on the first scientific assessments, 166 heads of states in Rio de Janeiro signed the UNFCCC. It declared a precautionary approach to prevent dangerous human interference with climate stability. It recognized the shared but differentiated responsibility of nations at various stages of their economic development. It instituted a Secretariat and a Conference of the Parties (COP) to put the convention's principles into targets and action plans. This difficult debate culminated in 1995 with the Kyoto protocol. While the Parties agreed to keep global greenhouse gases emissions at the 1990 level, the treaty required Annex I countries (developed and economies in transition) to achieve collectively a 5.2 per cent cut over 1990 by 2008–12 while developing countries, to satisfy their development plans, avoided compulsory limits. The Kyoto protocol became legally binding with the ratification by fifty-five Annex I governments. This only happened ten years later; by then, global emissions were already 20 per cent over 1990.

Yet government leaders express more resolution than ever to deal with the complexity of a global binding agreement before the Kyoto protocol runs out in 2012. In 2008 the EU leaders sealed a twenty-seven-party deal that requires them to reduce by 20 per cent in 2020 with a vision to achieve 80 per cent by 2050. Other governments and several US governors have also endorsed the need for this 80 per cent cut. The USA has initiated a process with the world's seventeen major emitters to provide helpful impetus to the UNFCCC mainstream negotiations between its 196 parties. Are such declarations and meetings any more decisive than the host of past intents, particularly when we have not yet recovered from a deep and brutal financial crisis?

Next to the alarming scientific climate forecasts, this financial crisis is a sobering lesson about the sudden large-scale collapse of a seemingly resilient system. There is also a view that the huge financial rescue packages should benefit the taxpayers who fund them. While environmental and climate risks continue to be high on the list of public concerns, promoting a green recovery is an intelligent solution. It fosters clean technologies, enterprises and jobs that create environmental quality. These programmes also increase our energy security and avoid future fuel purchases and costs from air and water pollution as well as their related maintenance and health bills.

Such sensible assumptions are now supported by a body of serious economic studies. In particular the International Energy Agency (IEA) (2008) as well as the McKinsey Global Institute developed detailed large-scale mitigation scenarios that establish the possibility of a low-cost, immediate reduction of CO_2 emissions (see figure 5.3).

Building and transport efficiency, reduced deforestation, efficient power generation from gas as well as wind, photovoltaic and nuclear can bring emissions back to the recommended 450 ppm limit by 2020. The highest cost for the last ton of CO_2 avoided would reach 60€/ ton. But the combination of all options would be cost neutral because of the short payback time of energy efficiency measures. Each year of delayed action and additional emissions makes it harder to close the gap between reality and target.

If action is possible and affordable, where are the last difficulties? The scenarios also show that the largest opportunities for reductions are in developing countries. Even if all richer countries took all

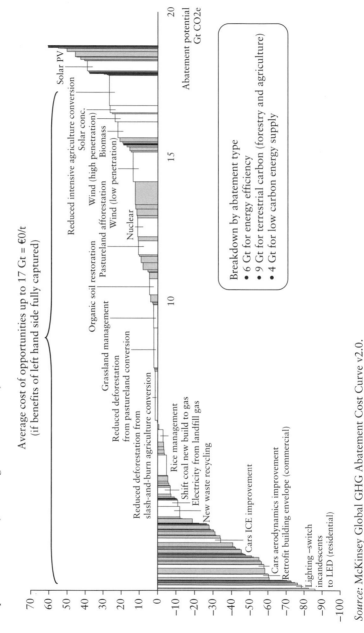

Up to costs of €60/t, excluding transaction costs, 4% discount rate

Average cost of opportunities up to 17 Gt = €0/t
(if benefits of left hand side fully captured)

Abatement potential
Gt CO2e

Breakdown by abatement type
- 6 Gt for energy efficiency
- 9 Gt for terrestrial carbon (forestry and agriculture)
- 4 Gt for low carbon energy supply

Solar PV
Reduced intensive agriculture conversion
Solar conc.
Wind (high penetration)
Biomass
Pastureland afforestation
Wind (low penetration)
Nuclear
Organic soil restoration
Grassland management
Reduced deforestation from pastureland conversion
Rice management
Shift coal new build to gas
Electricity from landfill gas
New waste recycling
Cars ICE improvement
Cars aerodynamics improvement
Retrofit building envelope (commercial)
Lighting –switch incandescents to LED (residential)
Reduced deforestation from slash-and-burn agriculture conversion

Source: McKinsey Global GHG Abatement Cost Curve v2.0.

Figure 5.3 McKinsey abatement potential and cost curve, 2020

possible measures they would only achieve the third of the worldwide potential reductions. Even if they managed to reduce emissions to zero, rapid-emerging emitters would still take the world over the limit in the near term. The political challenge is then to create a deal with incentives for all to take a binding commitment. This also requires firm and tangible support for finance and technology cooperation from developed, traditional large emitters towards developing and poorer parties to the agreement.

As the climate negotiation deadlines get closer it seems difficult to sort out the public posturing of some large emitters from the less visible forces that concentrate on a positive outcome. We have come to a point, however, where business should expect a tighter, more inclusive policy framework to succeed the Kyoto protocol. It should also expect a steady increase of the cost to emit carbon; it will gradually catch up with all emitters.

In summary, the business context is changing fast. The risk that extreme climate events batter operations and markets increases with carbon emissions. Governments are bound to limit them and carbon emissions will show up as real costs and liabilities in business results. On the other hand, emission reductions through efficiency measures, forest and land management and renewable energy sources present large opportunities for short paybacks and no-regret strategies. The more internationally inclusive the climate treaties with higher financial and technical cooperation, the lower the trade and competitive distortions. Early action will therefore avoid risks, secure competitive advantage and create brand strength with customers who deeply desire to deal with companies that they respect not only for price and quality but for their integrity and dedication to a better future.

A business call for an ambitious climate treaty

As a matter of fact a growing cluster of influential business leaders stands out from the crowd of those adverse to change. They encourage governments to conclude an ambitious climate treaty that provides long-term clarity on technology opportunities and investment choices while reducing the risks to society. One of the most articulate business declarations is the 'Copenhagen call' that concluded a summit of more than 500 business leaders with government and civil society leaders in May 2009 (see box 5.1).

Box 5.1: The Copenhagen call

The Copenhagen call, presented at the World Business Summit on Climate Change Copenhagen, 24–26 May 2009

As global business leaders assembled at the World Business Summit on Climate Change, we call upon our political leaders to agree an ambitious and effective global climate treaty at COP15 in Copenhagen. Sustainable economic progress requires stabilizing and then reducing greenhouse gas emissions. Success at COP15 will remove uncertainty, unleash additional investment, and bolster current efforts to revive growth in a sustainable way.

By addressing the magnitude of the climate threat with urgency, a powerful global climate change treaty would help establish a firm foundation for a sustainable economic future. This would set a more predictable framework for companies to plan and invest, provide a stimulus for renewed prosperity and a more secure climate system. Economic recovery and urgent action to tackle climate change are complementary – boosting the economy and jobs through investment in the new infrastructure needed to reduce emissions.

Business is at its best when innovating to achieve a goal and the goal of reducing greenhouse gas emissions is vital to our common social, economic and environmental future. At the Summit we* agreed that this will require:

*1. Agreement on a science-based greenhouse gas stabilization
   path with 2020 and 2050 emissions reduction targets*
We support the scientific evidence of the IPCC's 4th. We are concerned that some recent scientific evidence suggests the problem may be worse than many of the IPCC estimates.

---

* The views expressed here have been informed by discussions at the World Business Summit on Climate Change. They do not necessarily reflect the views of all participants.

Presented by the Copenhagen Climate Council, informed by discussions with the World Business Council on Sustainable Development; 3C; the World Economic Forum Climate Change Initiative; the United Nations Global Compact and The Climate Group, and deliberations among participants at the World Business Summit on Climate Change, 26 May 2009.

An effective global climate treaty must establish an ambitious goal and set emission targets that protect us and future generations from the risks of climate destabilization. Limiting the global average temperature increase to a maximum of 2 degrees Celsius compared to pre-industrial levels would entail abatement of around 17Gt versus business-as-usual by 2020. This will require an immediate and substantial change in the current global greenhouse gases emission trend: it must peak and begin to reduce within the next decade. Longer-term targets must be informed by the evolving science, but the IPCC's 4th Assessment Report indicates that global emissions must fall by at least half of 1990 levels by 2050. We believe that working to reduce emissions now is less costly than delaying our efforts. There is nothing to be gained through delay. The deepest reductions should initially be made by developed economies though global emissions reduction will require all nations to play a part.

Emissions reduction at this scale will profoundly affect business, and business is already taking action to drive down greenhouse gas emissions. We are ready to make those changes and support ambitious political decisions to address the climate challenge wherever we operate. If policies are well designed and implemented, the benefits of early action will outweigh the short-term adjustment costs. This early action can only be achieved by setting an ambitious 2020 target.

2. Effective measurement, reporting and verification of emissions

Achieving and tracking greenhouse gas emissions reduction is vital to measuring convergence towards the objectives of an effective climate treaty. As businesses we can set an example by contributing to a unified, coherent and reliable measurement, reporting and verification discipline leading to mandatory reporting. Accounting for the emissions we are responsible for will provide the basis for emissions reduction beyond what may be required by regulation and allow our performance to be properly judged and rewarded by investors and the public.

3. Incentives for a dramatic increase in financing low-emissions technologies

To promote effective, efficient, equitable and ambitious action to address climate change the world will need to mobilize the scale of investment necessary to achieve the emissions reduction required. Properly established, an international carbon market framed around ambitious reduction targets can enable both cost-effective abatement and create the carbon price stability to drive the deployment of technologies that will deliver large-scale emissions reductions. The first steps to establishing a global market will be to enable linkage between national and regional carbon markets. An international agreement will help secure investor confidence in the carbon market, and national actions will help generate new financial flows for climate investment.

The new climate treaty must 'push' the development of new technologies through the use of public funds to leverage private finance in early stage demonstration and deployment. This will require policy measures that create clear, predictable, long-term incentives to stimulate private investment and enable the global diffusion of capital and technology.

4. Deployment of existing low-emissions technologies and the development of new ones

The private sector is already the source of over two-thirds of the world's investments in clean technology innovation, and is the most effective source of know-how and technology dissemination and transfer. Many low carbon technologies already exist and can significantly reduce global emissions. Significant emissions reduction can be achieved through energy efficiency, much of it with positive financial returns. Standards and regulations are the best way to achieve this. A new treaty must support deployment of low carbon solutions by encouraging incentives for public and private purchasers to choose the lowest emissions infrastructure and technologies and for investors to account for climate risk in their decisions.

Government and business must work together to ensure that all nations have equitable access to new clean energy technologies and other innovations by, among others, working with developing countries to improve the infrastructure required for effective deployment.

An effective global climate treaty must provide the means to fund research, development and the deployment of new clean energy technologies. Pricing can help 'pull' these technologies through the innovation chain, generate revenue and enhance the flow of investment to developing countries. Governments should strive to end the current perverse subsidies that favour high emissions transport and energy infrastructure and promote deforestation.

A shift to a low-carbon economy, supported by private sector participation and government, has the potential to drive the next generation of technological innovation, address the environmental and economic challenges that climate change presents, and contribute to global development.

5. Funds to make communities more resilient and able to adapt to the effects of climate change

We recognize that adaptation is as important as mitigation in an effective global climate treaty. Adaptation planning will require a holistic and long-term planning perspective, which will require different levels of activity at the international, national and local levels. Businesses will be responsible for building much of the infrastructure needed to protect us from climate impacts. An effective global climate treaty will mobilize funding that supports public–private partnerships to enhance development, adaptive capacity, climate resilience and management of risk.

6. Innovative means to protect forests and balance the carbon cycle

Because a significant proportion of the CO_2 reduction required by 2020 comes from the sequestration of carbon in forests and agriculture lands, an effective climate treaty must facilitate such sequestration. If emissions reductions targets are to be met, there is an immediate need to protect forests and enhance carbon sequestration. The private sector can play an important role in reducing deforestation, particularly in developing countries, through mechanisms structured to value conservation.

We believe these elements should form the core of the international climate change treaty agreed at Copenhagen. As business leaders we stand ready to innovate and operate within the framework established through that treaty and national policies.

Reducing the emissions that until now have been so linked to our economic growth and betterment will be an enormous, unprecedented global challenge but will also provide significant opportunities for sustainable growth, development and innovation. Acting together, we owe it to future generations to meet this challenge. Now is the time to create the foundations for long term, low carbon prosperity. We are willing to work with government to do so.

And now 10 minutes for implementation guidance

So much for the case for leadership and early action. What is the best way to go about it? It starts with fully understanding one's emissions and impact on climate; it goes on right away with reducing them to insignificance for the next thirty years and, thus, being an example to employees and business partners, customers and markets as well as policy-makers.

It seems that many companies do not even know their carbon dioxide emissions and do not understand how they play their part in driving up the climate risks. The largest initiative on carbon disclosure – the Carbon Disclosure Project – invited, in 2009, 3,700 of the largest publicly quoted corporations around the world to fill its yearly information request on carbon emissions and climate strategy. It only received 1,800 full responses (less than 50 per cent).

A detailed analysis of the 500 largest companies (the Global 500 ranked yearly by *Fortune* magazine) shows that 82 per cent agreed to respond and only 68 per cent disclose emissions (see figure 5.4). But the disclosure level is up from previous years. In 2009 Professor Robert Bailis of the Yale School of Forestry and Environmental Studies presented the analysis, on behalf of the Global Compact, of disclosure performance by the signatories of Caring for Climate. From a sample of 145 signatories, 89 (61 per cent) reported at least one year of emissions, 70 (48 per cent) enough years to look at an emission

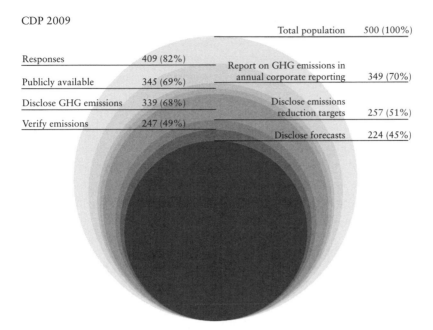

CDP 2009		Total population	500 (100%)
Responses	409 (82%)	Report on GHG emissions in annual corporate reporting	349 (70%)
Publicly available	345 (69%)		
Disclose GHG emissions	339 (68%)	Disclose emissions reduction targets	257 (51%)
Verify emissions	247 (49%)	Disclose forecasts	224 (45%)

Source: Carbon Disclosure Project.

Figure 5.4 Carbon Disclosure Project, Global 500 carbon disclosure analysis, 2009

trend and 57 (39 per cent) had set a form of reduction target. But only 20 reported that they had actually reduced emissions (Bailis 2009).

These are just two spot checks on company disclosures in a universe of some 50,000 large public, private and state companies. There may be a few reasons for not publishing emissions and yet measuring them. But the simple obvious reasons for non-disclosure are ignorance or the inability to aggregate emissions from a complex system of sources.

Nonetheless, clear guidance is available in the form of a voluntary reporting and accounting standard established by a decade-long partnership between the World Resources Institute (WRI) and the WBCSD: the Greenhouse Gas (GHG) Protocol.[6] This has become a foundation for every reporting initiative on climate change. It is also a perfect guidance for the essential first step in judging a company's responsibility for CO_2 impacts. Measurements are not even necessary at this stage. It needs at least some time for joint thinking by the

[6] For further information, see www.ghgprotocol.org.

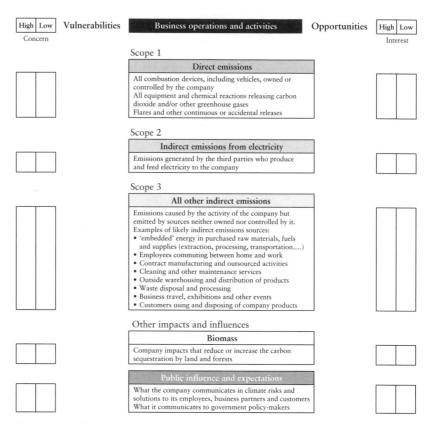

Figure 5.5 Climate opportunities and vulnerabilities scan

leaders most knowledgeable about the company's operations and supply chain. They mentally scan every aspect of their business. With experience, intuition and common sense they can, in no time, identify what makes their business most vulnerable to the risks of climate change, what solutions they would be particularly able to turn into business opportunities and, also, where they worry about important knowledge gaps. They could also agree on their level of interest to seize opportunities.

This first leadership step to face climate responsibility could be based on the Climate Opportunities and Vulnerabilities Scan (or any version tailored for the activities of the company). It starts the company on the journey of action with meaningful priorities and shared awareness among the leadership (see figure 5.5).

If this is the first act of a journey of change the second should be about setting a goal without waiting for policies and laws. The world economy needs to achieve carbon neutrality before 2050 in order to match the natural systems' capacity to remove and fix CO_2. All carbon emitters should therefore organize to contribute their fair share and anticipate a drastic reduction of their direct emissions (Scope 1, figure 5.5) rather than waiting for a crisis that collective inaction would only precipitate. By virtue of an 'impossible' target many companies have set free a boost of creativity. The mindset needs to stretch to a range between the 80 per cent reduction goal that a number of industrialized countries' leaders have already declared for 2050 and the ultimate *zero-carbon* target. An Internet search for *zero-carbon* brings forth increasing numbers of serious commitments for housing projects, factories, whole companies and cities as well as for regional industrial policies. Traditional incremental and single-digit goals are out of touch with the scale and speed required by the situation.

Is a zero-carbon pathway possible between now and 2050? Not for all, but we need many to get close in order to bring the transfer of fossil fuels to the atmosphere below the level compatible with the 2°C–450 ppm CO_2 limit.

Energy efficiency is the best weapon in the zero-carbon quest. One cannot lose pushing efficiency to new peaks by relentless innovation. It also improves energy security and eliminates collateral health and maintenance costs from exhaust and smoke stack pollution. Yet it also runs into trivial barriers like the economic gap between those who should make the investment into new efficient features and those who use them and would benefit from the efficiency. Technology creativity may well be the easier part. What is required is also commercial, financial and policy creativity to share the benefits of energy efficiency across multiple agents.

As operations, products and value chains are redesigned and reinvented for significant efficiency gains it becomes ever easier to take carbon out of the electricity system (Scope 2, figure 5.5). Many utilities already offer certified renewable electricity contracts. Supply generally exceeds demand for lack of takers. More takers would encourage faster investments in zero-carbon electricity. At their early stage wind, solar and other weather and daylight-dependent sources are handicapped because of the need for 'firming' their variable output with stand-by

gas- or coal-fired generators. A massive proliferation and intercon-
nection of renewable sources through long-distance low-losses trans-
mission lines and computer-operated grids can significantly reduce
this handicap and the need for firming capacity. This is where public
policies and subsidies are needed. Photovoltaic looks more and more
promising thanks to recent efficiency breakthroughs. With its infinite
sizing and easy installation features it can be integrated into the energy
users' facilities. While capital per kilowatt is high, but falling with
technology progress, it is a low barrier for distributed user installa-
tions. Combined with minimal operating costs and risks photovoltaic
can reach parity with grid tariffs from other sources in sunny regions in
less than ten years. It can also bring synergy with the switch to battery-
powered vehicles. Therefore a zero-carbon approach not only pushes
electricity suppliers to accelerate their transition to higher efficiency
and lower carbon but also considers the integration and ownership of
renewable sources as a substitute for electricity purchases.

Companies aiming at zero-carbon Scope 1 and 2 also consider carbon
offsets as part of the solution. They ensure that the CO_2 emissions that
they cannot eliminate in their own operations are eliminated elsewhere
by a certified operator. This entails a purchase of carbon 'credits' with
a certification that they are unique and additional – that the carbon
elimination would not happen under other normal circumstances. The
Kyoto protocol has instituted such a Clean Development Mechanism.[7]
It generates funding of technology transfers and implementation of
carbon/greenhouse gas reductions in developing countries. It creates
a controlled market mechanism that can ensure the most effective
use of finance for carbon reduction. There are also a number of voluntary carbon offset markets with operators who can provide access
to certified offset projects.[8] It is essential to get quality assurance for
such projects to protect credibility. When it comes to large emitters
they anyhow are likely to face, as in the European Union, a cap and
trade scheme instituted by governments with a serious commitment to
extensive climate mitigation. The interesting side of a carbon market
is that it does not trade carbon. It exchanges commitments to avoid
carbon. Therefore it stimulates the movement and dissemination of

---

[7] For further information see http://cdm.unfccc.int.
[8] A good place to start for information on carbon offsets is the International
Emission Trading Association (IETA) in Geneva (http://ieta.org).

low-carbon practices and technologies. Combined with commitments to carbon caps it creates access to capital and technology. Introduced where the carbon avoidance potential is largest and based on reliable, verifiable carbon emission registries, carbon markets have the capability to reach environmental objectives with cost efficiency while bringing capital and technology where it is needed most.

One of the safest and cheapest proven CO_2 offsets is realized by photosynthesis. We need to turn forests into net carbon sinks instead of setting them on fire for short-lived and shortsighted land productivity. We also need them for biodiversity, ground water and soil protection, landscapes and a host of sustainable socio-economic activities. The quality assurance for slow-growth and climate-vulnerable resources like trees is, however, problematic and still being discussed. Nevertheless reforestation and sustainable forest stewardship have their place in an organization's climate strategy in the form of offset programmes and forestry products purchasing policies.

For Scope 3 business activities we cannot reduce the climate risk without a strong commitment to zero-carbon mobility. Large managed fleets and logistics systems are the right place to start. Any corporate climate strategy should ask the question of how long it wants and can afford to have the company logos on the road, on the seas and in the air trailing exhaust pipes. The conjunction of high gas prices in 2008 and the intensity of the climate discussion have woken the transportation industry as well as drivers to the possibility of retiring the combustion engine. Fleet owners like postal services have started to seriously experiment with fully electrical vehicles. Several carmakers have announced new models as of 2010 with consumer appeal and normal daily-use autonomy. While mileage and maintenance costs are most attractive, the purchase price would be a strong deterrent unless public policies step in to lift the electric car on a level playing field with combustion models.

These are but a few ideas to show that a zero-carbon approach is not complete utopia. Specific pathways depend on each company in proportion to its current carbon intensity and in relation to its sector and markets, to its location and its economic and public policy context. One common factor, though, is the commitment to communicating on progress, a fundamental feature of the Global Compact integrity measures. This entails the adoption of a carbon emission measurement scheme (again according to the GHG standard). What is most desirable is communicating on progress towards a target. Strategy is about the future. It is more interesting to understand how an organization converges with its long-term goals instead of only learning around July where it was last December in relation to December in previous years.

A revolution without chaos and crisis?

Moving to a carbon neutral economy that provides quality of life for all within our shrinking climate safety headroom is technically feasible. It is even hailed as a new industrial revolution. 'Revolution' sounds great, it sounds like progress, a better life, a new era. But history of industrial change is showing that revolutions take time, meet resistance and proceed by improvisation and chaos. Ultimately technologies prevail because they satisfy the needs of their users more efficiently at a lower cost; then, more investors join to support them in anticipation of better future cash flows. The revolution wins.

But how on earth can we imagine that low-carbon technologies will ever prevail spontaneously and only through voluntary action? The previous industrial revolution was won by fossil-fuelled horsepower over human and animal energy. It established a free licence, and even many subsidies, to connect indefinitely all chimneys and exhaust pipes to our common atmospheric headroom; a towering barrier of entry to alternative sources. A century later we now know that nature is only robust and resilient to a point because we have gotten so close or even beyond that point. Maintaining, for anyone, free usage of a limited resource – our shrinking atmospheric headroom – is a titanic man-made market failure.

Leaders supporting the Global Compact and Caring for Climate – many of the largest enterprises and most visible brands of our global economy – are expected to take side early and round up their performance and communication on progress with an action towards policy support. Governments need to hear that an influential fraction of business is ready with solutions for rapid change and welcomes a new ambitious inclusive climate framework to replace the weak Kyoto protocol. Otherwise we all remain exposed to a crisis we never experienced and that will mainly affect our children. We may believe that we have still time on our hands but climate change is happening and requires immediate, innovative, large-scale action.

6 | *Anti-corruption: challenges and trends*

HUGUETTE LABELLE

Businesses should work against corruption in all its forms, including extortion and bribery.

United Nations Global Compact 10th Principle

The history of the 10th Principle

Corruption is a global problem that requires global action. This makes the United Nations the organization best positioned to be at the vanguard of the ongoing battle against corruption and explains why the inclusion in 2004 of the 10th Principle against corruption in the United Nations Global Compact is so important. Since its inception in 2000, the United Nations Global Compact had always envisaged a need to address the issue of corruption. It was not included in the first nine Principles for the simple reason that the United Nations had no legal instrument in place to enforce its provisions. The ratification of the United Nations Convention Against Corruption (UNCAC) in 2003, and its introduction in 2005, provided this framework.

On 24 June 2004, during the United Nations Global Compact Leaders Summit, participants unanimously agreed to add a 10th Principle to the Global Compact: 'Businesses should work against corruption in all its forms, including extortion and bribery.' Speaking on the day the announcement was made, Peter Eigen, founder and then chairman of Transparency International (TI), who was on the UN advisory board to the Global Compact, put it succinctly: 'By tackling corruption, you also strike at a root cause of environmental, human rights and labour abuses.' He also noted 'the recent corporate scandals, from Enron and Tyco to Parmalat, have clearly shown that corruption is bad for business'. Five years on, with the global economy shattered by corporate mismanagement, poor regulation and corruption on a grand scale, those words ring truer than ever.

Call it enlightened self-interest or an acceptance of Corporate Social Responsibility (CSR) – the business embrace of the anti-corruption agenda is a major step on what has been, and will be a long road to eradicate corruption from business. Now, the global legal framework established through the UNCAC, to be implemented by the UN Office on Drugs and Crime (UNODC), can provide a wider mechanism to punish bribery, kickbacks and corruption across the world. The goal is to level the playing field so that all businesses benefit.

TI was an instrumental part of the multi-stakeholder Global Compact working committee that worked towards the adoption of a 10th Principle. TI argued that the other nine Principles required a commitment to anti-corruption and transparency to make their implementation achievable. The facts are irrefutable: corruption impacts significantly on all areas of development and human rights. It wastes money and resources that could be used to alleviate poverty, fund development and education and make lives more bearable for the billions of people who still eke out an existence on just $1 a day. The World Bank estimated that 'bribery has become a $1 trillion industry' (Kaufmann 2004). Corruption adds up to 10 per cent to the total cost of doing business globally, and up to 25 per cent to the cost of procurement contracts in developing countries. Citing a study on foreign direct investment (FDI), Alan Boeckmann, the Chairman & CEO of the US-based Fluor Corporation, noted that moving business from a country with a low level of corruption to a country with medium or high levels of corruption is found to be equivalent to a 20 per cent tax on foreign business.

In 2004 when the 10th Principle was added, the Global Compact had 1,457 signatories. Today (January 2010) there are nearly 7,300 signatories across the globe, of which more than 5,000 are corporations, a 30 per cent increase over the previous year. More than half of these signatories employ between 10 and 250 people. This anti-corruption initiative can boast a wide range of supporters and a broad geographical reach, which makes the Global Compact a singularly important instrument for tackling corruption in the private sector across the globe.

This surge to become part of the global fight against corruption is evidence of the change that is happening with the emergence of CSR as a key component of business policy and management strategy. CSR has now become a major part of maintaining business reputations and a key element in a company's risk management strategies. Civil society has played a significant role in advancing these issues but the damage a corruption scandal can do to a corporation's brand and bottom line has sounded the wake-up call to others. This has been evidenced by the débâcles at Enron, Parmalat, British Aerospace, or Siemens, to name just a few high-profile cases. The private sector is well aware that falling back on 'it's just the way business is done' will not win acquittal in the courts or support from investors.

For the private sector to acknowledge the damage done by corruption is a good first step; developing the mechanisms to wipe it out is significantly harder. The collective approach that unites the various efforts worldwide to fight corruption is at the heart of implementing the 10th Principle globally. The Global Compact works through and with the various civil society and governmental efforts to eradicate corruption both globally and by sector. The Global Compact, as a voluntary initiative, relies heavily on the strength of its participants and the support structures that are developed to further its mission. These two pillars will provide the impetus to continue the truly remarkable surge in acceptance.

In January 2008 at the second Conference of States Parties to the UNCAC, the Global Compact Office helped convene a special private sector meeting to reflect on the potential of UNCAC as a new market force. Co-conveners of the Business Coalition meeting included TI, the ICC and the Partnering Against Corruption Initiative (PACI) of the World Economic Forum (WEF). A wide range of representatives from civil society, business and government participated in the session. The special session culminated in a declaration acknowledging, among other things, that fighting corruption was a shared responsibility between government, civil society and business and reaffirming support for the 10th Principle and the measures needed to implement it globally. The participants also urged the Conference of States Parties to establish an effective mechanism to review its implementation 'as a matter of great importance and urgency', and to include participation of business in such a mechanism. More groundwork was laid for further discussions that, despite opposition from some UNCAC signatories, will hopefully lead to the adoption of a robust review mechanism. This global convention will be most important to support the work of the Global Compact.

Initiated by the Global Compact, the ICC, PACI and TI in May 2009, CEOs from some of the world's leading companies called on governments to more effectively and robustly implement the UNCAC. In a letter to UN Secretary-General Ban Ki-moon, they voiced their support for the UNCAC, underlining at the same time the need for the establishment of an implementation review mechanism at the next Conference of States Parties (Transparency International 2009b). In particular, this letter was meant to have an impact on governments' negotiation processes in the run-up to the Conference of States Parties which took place in Doha in November 2009.

The Global Compact from the outset identified the Business Principles for Countering Bribery (Transparency International 2003), a dedicated anti-bribery code for business, as a well-designed instrument to provide a framework for companies undertaking to implement the 10th Principle. The Business Principles were developed by TI in partnership with leading global companies, experts, unions and civil society to consider whether a consensus framework could be produced for use by the private sector in the fight against bribery. This multi-stakeholder approach is consistent with the spirit of the Global Compact and reflects the belief that it is only through cross-sector negotiations and discussions that a workable solution can be achieved. TI has since worked closely with the Global Compact to further the concrete implementation of the 10th Principle. In 2005, TI worked with the Global Compact and the International Business Leaders Forum to produce a practical guide for business, *Business Against Corruption: A Framework for Action* (Global Compact, International Business Leaders Forum and Transparency International 2005), to assist business in the challenging task of implementing the 10th Principle. The following year, TI contributed to a follow-up Global Compact publication focused on company efforts and dilemmas in tackling corruption (Global Compact 2006a).

The Global Compact, as an overarching global umbrella, brings together organizations to disseminate information about how to fight corruption. In the last few years, the issue of corruption and bribery and what role the private sector plays in combating it, has risen to the top of the private sector agenda. The current global crisis only heightens the need for a global approach to eliminate corruption and a global commitment to transparency in reporting corporate strategies to achieve it. There is no lack of information already in the public domain to guide businesses committed to fighting corruption. The tools exist to make best practice universal; the goal is to continue to ensure commitment and compliance. The Global Compact has made great strides towards making this happen.

Current status of implementation of the 10th Principle

Practising what you preach is a significant challenge. According to the 2008 *Global Compact Annual Review*, the 10th Principle was considered the hardest to implement by those responding to the annual survey (Global Compact 2008). All Global Compact signatories commit to reporting on how they are applying its principles. These Communication on Progress (COP) documents are expected to be written annually. As of spring 2009, more than two-thirds of the participating companies were up to date with their COPs. Only five of the 165 *Financial Times* 500 companies that have pledged to comply with the Global Compact have not submitted reports.

The Global Compact is continually working to help companies reach the highest standards of compliance. In 2004 it introduced Notable COPs, highlighting best practice, and by mid-2009 there were more than 270 examples of Notable COPs identified on the Global Compact website. In May 2009, as mentioned above, as a result of the coordination and cooperation within the network of civil society organizations committed to fight against corruption, the Global Compact launched its pilot reporting guidelines (Global Compact 2008) that will both bolster the reputation of the Global Compact and provide a framework for disclosure on the 10th Principle for companies large and small. The reporting guidelines propose key reporting elements that reflect comprehensive anti-bribery measures. They emphasize the need for zero-tolerance policies towards corruption and illustrate how best to implement them. They also advocate swift action against those found guilty of corruption. These pilot guidelines for reporting on anti-corruption are being field-tested by a selection of Global Compact signatories.

Companies now have a selection of resources aimed at helping them negotiate the pitfalls of doing business in a world where corruption is still rife. In addition to the new Global Compact reporting guidelines, these include:

1. Resisting Extortion and Solicitation in International Sales and Transactions (RESIST) (International Chamber of Commerce *et al.* 2009), a practical guide based on real-life scenarios designed to help companies and individual employees respond to inappropriate extortions and solicitations. RESIST, which is a collaborative effort among civil society organizations, helps answer simple questions such as how to react if a bribery demand is made within different contract bidding scenarios.
2. TI's Business Principles for Countering Bribery, which come in two versions, with one designed specifically for small and medium-sized enterprises (SMEs) (Transparency International 2008a) taking into account their more limited resources.
3. TI's Integrity Pact (Transparency International 2002), a tool developed for the public sector procurement process, which commits governments or government departments and all bidders for a public contract to work without bribes and provides for sanctions should either side violate the pact.

Motivated by the belief that meaningful disclosure of anti-bribery measures is a key to improved corporate transparency and good governance, TI published its first Transparency in Reporting on Anti-Corruption (TRAC) survey in 2009 (Transparency International 2009a). This survey analysed the reporting practices of the 500 leading corporations regarding bribery and corruption. TRAC analysed the extent to which a company reports on the strategy, policies and management systems it has in place for combating bribery. It did not, however, assess how effective these tools are.

The results, though generally disappointing, provide a benchmark going forward. Of the 500 companies surveyed, only seven achieved the top score in a 1 to 5-star rating system developed by TI. Slightly more than one-quarter of the sample companies (127), are Global Compact signatories. It is encouraging to note that overall the Global Compact signatories scored higher than the non-signatories, giving them an average 3-star rating compared to a 2-star rating for the remaining companies.

This kind of information is necessary both to monitor progress and to encourage others to commit to the fight against corruption. It sets global standards. TI uses its network of local TI chapters to disseminate this research and advocate for change. The Global Compact can count on its Global Compact Local Networks (GCLNs), which have as wide a reach and a dedicated business focus, to do the same.

GCLNs bring together Global Compact signatories in a particular country who then identify specific strategies tailored to their environment. It is this kind of targeted grassroots approach that has been a leading factor in the rapid growth of Global Compact signatories, because those on the ground are best placed to identify companies and leaders who can make a difference. Today there are more than eighty Local Networks globally, available to provide resources to new and current signatories.

This community-orientated approach has fostered the rapid expansion of the organization. It has built a constituency that identifies itself as opposed to corruption. It is now for the stakeholder community to hold companies accountable. GCLNs, with support from the Global Compact Office and the partner organizations within the UN family and civil society in general, must and can deliver the message that compliance and transparency are the bedrock on which the future reputation of the Global Compact will be based.

Challenges for voluntary initiatives and private sector corruption

The challenge is to keep the momentum going in four key areas. First, more companies must commit to zero-tolerance of bribery and corruption. Second, once they have done that, they have to demonstrate compliance with their commitment. Third, they must be aware of different types of corruption practices that are constantly emerging and finally, they must publish fully their efforts to live up to their commitment.

Communications is key. Not surprisingly more than half the resources GCLNs have are spent on outreach events to introduce the Global Compact to their communities. These activities have great benefits. In just five years since it started, the Local Network in Argentina now has over 300 participants, 82 per cent of which are businesses (see also chapter 21 by Flavio Fuertes and Nicolás Liarte-Vejrup). In 2006 more than 120 different organizations and companies attended workshops and seminars organized under the Global Compact umbrella across Canada. This resulted in a burst of signatories to the Global Compact and the development of a Canadian GCLN. Today there are 70 Global Compact signatories in Canada, of which 48 are corporations. In April 2009 China formally launched its GCLN, which has a core constituency of 200 organizations of which 129 are businesses. The vast majority of these have signed up since 2007. Events and outreach programmes are happening all over the world, every week, explaining the benefits of fighting corruption and enlisting a cadre of new converts to the cause of zero-tolerance for corruption.

Commitment and compliance – which require dedicated management systems and personnel – come at a cost. But the downside of corruption can be far more devastating. It is a message that needs to be publicized. Take the example of Siemens, the multinational German electronics and telecommunications giant. In 1999 Siemens claimed tax deductions in its accounts for bribes, and listed some of these as 'useful expenditures'. According to Dr Mark Pieth, chairman of the OECD Working Group on Bribery: 'People felt confident that they were doing nothing wrong' (*The Economist*, 18 December 2008). Less than a decade later Siemens admitted that it operated a slush fund and was forced to pay fines totalling €1.2 billion in the USA and Germany. As Alan Boeckmann, chairman of Fluor and a key person behind PACI, said: 'It's hard to measure the benefit you get from a good reputation, and sometimes it's hard to imagine the danger of the disaster that can befall you if you run afoul of that' (PricewaterhouseCoopers 2008a: 5).

In 2007 Siemens, an early Global Compact signatory, submitted a comprehensive COP Report. This admits past errors, the damage the corruption scandal has done to its reputation, and recommits the company to uphold the Global Compact Principles, including the 10th Principle. Its section on anti-corruption measures now includes a detailed strategy to inform and educate its workforce on what constitutes bribery and how to avoid it. A compliance help desk introduced in September 2007 received 1,783 requests in the first nine months of operations. The Siemens example is now highlighted in the 2008 *Global Compact Annual Review* (Global Compact 2008).

The steady stream of press reports about business scandals worldwide is forcing pockets of the private sector to rethink their risk management strategies to recognize the benefits of transparent, anti-corruption policies. The OECD noted that in 2003 MNCs were twice as likely to publish their anti-corruption policies as they had been in 1999 (Global Compact 2004d). A survey conducted by the accounting firm PricewaterhouseCoopers, of 390 senior executives, found that

80 per cent said that their companies had some form of programme in place to prevent and detect corruption (PricewaterhouseCoopers 2008a). The increase in the number of companies that have signed the Global Compact is further evidence of this.

Nevertheless, the broader battles against corrupt practices are far from won. Since 1995 TI has published its Corruption Perception Index (CPI) (Transparency International 2008b), which ranks 180 countries by their perceived level of corruption. In 2008 the results were disappointing. Several wealthy exporting countries turned in poorer performances than the previous year, most notably the UK, which dropped from 12th to 16th place and France from 19th to 23rd. In 2007 TI published an assessment of the OECD Convention on Combating Bribery of Foreign Public Officials, a crucial international legal instrument that focuses on the supply side of international bribery, and found that of the 37 signatories only fourteen enforce the rules with any vigour. This probably accounts for another disturbing fact: TI's 2008 Bribe Payers Index surveyed more than 2,700 senior business executives worldwide. A staggering 75 per cent were not familiar with the OECD's Convention at all.

This is a message not lost on civil society, and clearly shows that despite the successes, there is much work yet to be done. Awareness and vigilance are half the battle in confronting corruption, particularly at a time when the murky waters of corruption are becoming harder to define, despite the best efforts of high-profile international treaties and initiatives. No longer is it good enough to identify the obvious bribe – cash for services rendered – as corruption's sharpest weapon. Situations, which allow individuals, businesses or sectors to coopt or 'capture' the regulators, who are supposed to oversee their business, have contributed to the current crisis.

Take some of the issues raised by the recent financial crises. Daniel Kaufman, formerly senior manager for Governance, Finance and Regulatory Reform at the World Bank and now a senior fellow at the Brookings Institute, noted on the World Bank's Governance Matters blog (World Bank 2009) several incidents of 'capture' that led directly to the financial crises. For example, citing sources from the *Wall Street Journal*, he points to how Freddie Mac and Fannie Mae, the large now-state-controlled mortgage companies at the heart of the sub-prime mortgage débâcle, spent millions of dollars lobbying members of Congress to reduce the capital reserve requirements, thereby exposing them to huge future losses when the sub-prime loans turned bad.

Is it possible to define this as corrupt, or just working within the system? Clearly the global economy, the US taxpayers and by extension the world's poorest people are paying a high price. In the past decade much has progressed towards a world that both identifies and understands the need to publicize and enforce anti-corruption polices. As regulators grapple with the state-level strategies to eradicate corrupt practices, the Global Compact 10th Principle, and other initiatives, go to the heart of the private sector's responsibility in this battle. They encourage companies to stand up and be counted. For the Global Compact signatories this means publishing a regular COP Report, a comprehensive account of action plans and practices that encompasses all ten Principles.

As of 1 July 2009, companies have one year from the time they join the Global Compact to produce a COP. This is then posted on the Global Compact website. The Global Compact is working hard to strengthen the content of the COPs. Those who are looking for free publicity and standing in the community by virtue of having signed the Compact are not tolerated. The Global Compact delists companies that do not submit satisfactory COPs within the two-year framework. In 2008 more than 400 companies were delisted, bringing the total to 800 over the past decade. If a company is delisted it cannot use the Global Compact logo. The Global Compact is in the process of implementing tougher measures to sanction non-compliance or superficial COP reporting. Also, a company becoming a participant as of 1 July will be required to report on at least two of the four issue areas and all the issue areas after five years.

Going forward

The Global Compact is fully cognizant of the challenges it faces and it is aware that success can be achieved with a consistent, focused approach. Recent history proves that mobilizing support is vital. Given that it has only been five years since its adoption, the Global Compact 10th Principle is still a new mechanism, a recent and welcome reinforcement to the anti-corruption forces. Going forward, because of its wide scope and outreach, it is likely to be key in the battle to maintain pressure on the private sector to ensure that anti-corruption policies are adhered to worldwide. With huge amounts of money earmarked for government bailouts across a wide range of industries – not only for banks and financial institutions – ordinary taxpayers are demanding accountability and transparency.

The Global Compact, with its global reach and high profile, can fulfil an important role in bringing about collective business action to make the 10th Principle second nature. Implementation of the UNCAC and the adoption of a strong review mechanism would further enhance the 10th Principle – it would not only be desirable to abide by it, but the UNCAC with a review mechanism would also offer the right legal incentive. The Global Compact has become popular and widespread fast; it needs to remain credible while continuing to increase its reach.

There is enormous will to make this happen. TI is part of the sub-working group that produced the pilot guidance document on reporting on anti-corruption for the COP. The group has recommended a structured and comprehensive tool that allows for thorough and consistent reporting of anti-corruption matters across companies (Global Compact 2009a). The Global Compact and TI released in December 2009 a Global Compact–TI Reporting Guidance which allows for thorough and consistent reporting of anti-corruption matters across companies. This document was produced by a Global Compact working group chaired by TI after an extensive public consultation.

Goodwill and results will enable the Global Compact to flourish. The last decade has shown how success can breed success. The emergence in such a short time of such a wide-reaching network is evidence enough. Across the world those committed to eradicating corruption in the private and public sectors are spreading their message and providing the tools for others to follow suit. One need only to look at the maps on the Global Compact website to see the tremendous geographic spread the movement has already achieved. Multi-stakeholder commitment has galvanized this process, and will surely move us further towards a world where business can be conducted on a level global playing field. It is clear that the momentum that brought the 10th Principle to life will sustain and strengthen it as the Global Compact enters its second decade.

PART II

Participants and engagement mechanisms

7 | *Implementing the United Nations Global Compact*

CAROLYN Y. WOO

Introduction

In 1999, then-UN Secretary-General Kofi Annan addressed the World Economic Forum in Davos, Switzerland, and from his words was born the concept of collaboration between the United Nations and the private sector in the United Nations Global Compact (Global Compact 2009b). This invitation urged corporations to abide by ten Principles pertaining to human rights, labour rights, environmental sustainability and anti-corruption. This would be a transnational, voluntary engagement whereby signatory companies would embrace and advance these principles in their strategies and operations. Accountability would be sought through self-reporting or through Communication on Progress (COP) reports made available to the public.

With full support, Secretary-General Ban Ki-moon has continued to advocate the importance of the United Nations Global Compact's role in promoting Corporate Social Responsibility (CSR). In his remarks to the Korean Global Compact Local Network (GCLN) in 2008, Ban asserted:

In the end, the United Nations Global Compact is not only about the moral imperative to treat workers well, to respect human rights and to embrace transparency and good governance as guiding principles. It is also about the business case: attracting skilled workers; saving costs; enhancing productivity; creating trust; and building brands. By implementing corporate practices which respect the Compact's 10 principles, you can create sustainable value and benefits for your companies, workers, communities and society at large . . . Taking steps to address climate change, uphold workforce standards, or achieve higher levels of corporate accountability is not just about the financial success of companies or rewards from the market. It is also about building a better future for our children, our country and our planet. It is a call to our humanity. (United Nations 2009d)

Ban's statement rose from the recognition that businesses possess unmatched influence in the achievement of the eight Millennium Development Goals (MDGs). According to Bruce Piasecki, of the world's 100 largest economies, 51 are corporations. In addition, 300 multinational companies (MNCs) account for 25 per cent of the world's total assets (Piasecki 2007: 37–8). The potency of business' impact lies in the reality that it plays a significant role in setting conditions for trade, savings rate, domestic and foreign investment and job creation. It engenders capacity development along multiple dimensions as in financial markets, regulatory frameworks, physical infrastructures, education and civil society.

Businesses can also set up trading parameters relating to revenue distribution policies, reporting requirements that promote transparency and multilateral collaboration between local governments, non-governmental organizations (NGOs) and transnational agencies such as the United Nations, International Monetary Fund (IMF) and the World Bank. There is no question that business can accelerate the pace of development and enlarge the scope of actions. Responsible conduct by corporations can bring genuine benefits of globalization to all populations, including those which are most disadvantaged. As the three primary causes of conflict are corruption, poverty and social inequality, it is not difficult to see the potential influence of business over peace and stability (Williams 2008).

The remaining sections of this chapter will address the business case for the Global Compact, implementation of the Compact and future challenges. The final section presents three illustrative case reports of companies from different industries and in various stages of adoption of the Global Compact Principles.

The business case for the United Nations Global Compact

The pressure for companies to demonstrate CSR in their actions has gained unprecedented intensity and scrutiny. Extensive surveys have revealed that a high percentage of customers would purchase the more 'green' option when presented with products where all other factors were comparable. Customers are increasingly educated about fair trade, green labelling and the impact of their consumption on upstream providers. There is an emerging connectedness that consumers embrace between their behaviour and the welfare of the people whose resources and labour they consume. Strong and forward-looking competitors seize opportunities for differentiation and for building brand equity through products which serve as solutions to these problems. Suppliers of capital, regulatory agencies, rating bodies and the new 'watchdog' agencies are recalibrating risks and seeking unprecedented levels of accountability. In a 2007 McKinsey survey of close to 400 CEOs from Global Compact-participating companies, 93 per cent of CEOs were now more likely than five years ago to incorporate environmental, social and governance issues into their core strategy (Oppenheim *et al.* 2007).

In a survey of *Fortune* 100 firms across consumer goods, pharmaceuticals, electronics and airlines ranging in revenues from $1 billion to $70 billion, AT Kearney and the Institute for Supply Management found that 58 per cent of the surveyed firms had a sustainability strategy. The primary reasons given for the creation of a sustainability strategy were to improve brand (54 per cent) and to differentiate products (50 per cent) as well as to achieve compliance (46 per cent) and to manage risk (33 per cent). Only 21 per cent of companies in this report implemented a sustainable strategy for efficiency and 17 per cent for cost improvements (Mahler, Erhard and Callieri 2007).

While data on the level and variability of returns to socially responsible funds (SRFs) do not yet yield consistent trends, analyses by Goldman Sachs shed light on the potential benefits to companies. The Goldman Sachs report concludes:

While there is no evidence that ESG or SRI investing on their own add value, incorporating our proprietary ESG framework into long-term industrial analysis and return-based analysis of the sectors covered to date (energy, mining, steel, food, beverages, and media) has enabled us to select top picks that have outperformed the MSCI [a worldwide stock market including 1,500 stocks] by 25 percent since August 2005. Of these, 72 percent have outperformed their peers over the same period. (Goldman Sachs 2007: 1)

This conclusion correlates with the large number of signatories of the Principles for Responsible Investment (PRI) from financial services. The PRI now counts 470 members representing $18 trillion under management (see also chapter 11 by James Gifford).

A force to note is the explosion of organizations which serve as 'watchdogs' of corporate actions. Piasecki noted that in the last twenty years, more than seventy rating groups have sprung up. These include agencies which perform credit rating and governance scoring, and provide advisory to voting and proxy agents. Institutional Shareholder Services (ISS), renamed Risk Metrics, has expanded the evaluation of financial risks to include corporate governance, compliance, legal, transactional, environmental, social and reputational exposure. Public scepticism about self-reporting by companies has fostered reporting protocols by third parties such as the Global Reporting Initiative (GRI) and the Dow Jones Sustainability Indices which provide a standard-ized format and a high bar for disclosure. The family of Dow Jones Sustainability Index (DJSI) employing the Zurich-based SAM's com-prehensive risk evaluation system, now provides ratings for companies across all three major industrial regions of the world: the Americas, Asia-Pacific and Europe. For corporate boards, practices gaining popu-larity are director training, recruitment of environmental experts for the board and creation of a separate committee for managing climate and social risks. Corporate responsibility has become a global phenomenon across firms of all sectors, sizes and regions (Piasecki 2007: 231).

The United Nations Global Compact in action

Scope of participation

Signatories of the Global Compact now number 6,500 in total and include 5,000 businesses and 1,500 civil society and other non-business organizations (as of May 2009). These span 135 countries. In 2008, 1,473 new businesses became signatories, amounting to a 30 per cent increase in corporate membership and a dramatic expansion from the 50 new signatories in 2000. The distribution between small and large companies is about equal. With 250 employees as the divid-ing point, small and large businesses account for 53 per cent and 47 per cent of Global Compact signatories, respectively. Participation information for selected countries is listed in table 7.1 and reported in the *Global Compact Annual Review* from 2007 and 2008 (Global Compact 2007c, 2008)

Reasons for participation

In the survey of Global Compact members from the *2007 Annual Review*, 400 firms responded. Not surprisingly, the survey revealed

Table 7.1 *Participation information, selected countries*

	Number of participants in 2007 Global Compact Annual Review (15 May 2007)	Rank of participation in 2007 Global Compact Annual Review (15 May 2007)	Number of participants in 2008 Global Compact Annual Review (31 Dec. 2008)	Rank of participation in 2008 Global Compact Annual Review (31 Dec. 2008)
France	370	1	512	1
USA	104	6	203	5
Mexico	151	4	278	3
Brazil	137	5	205	4
China	75	11	171	6

that a major motivation for corporate participation emanates from the desire to increase trust in the company (63 per cent) and to improve public relations (46 per cent). Additional important sets of drivers for signing the Global Compact were to address humanitarian concerns (52 per cent), become more familiar with CSR (40 per cent) and acquire practical know-how for implementation (34 per cent). Companies also welcomed the opportunities for networking (53 per cent) and for establishing links with the United Nations (34 per cent). Only 20 per cent of survey respondents cited improved market access as a relevant reason (Global Compact 2007c).

In the interviews conducted for the three company case reports discussed in the final section of this chapter, the companies often highlighted the draw of being part of a global network with local connections that enable the exchange of ideas with like-minded businesses. In addition, the companies utilized and appreciated the access to activities and interactions within the Local Networks, tools and guidance, problem-solving exercises and guidance documents. Members also use the Networks to promote multi-stakeholder dialogue and mutual understanding.

In addition, another theme that arose from the interviews pointed to the importance of rigour in Global Compact reporting practices.

Credibility of the Global Compact rose significantly when stricter measures were implemented in the annual reporting process associated with the COP. When 404 companies were delisted from their signatory status in 2008, bringing the total number of delisted companies to 800 by the end of 2008, and another 184 were placed on notice, member signatories we spoke with cited the importance of this practice in signifying rigour and commitment.

Implementation practices

Leadership and governance responsibility

For the 707 signatories that responded to the 2008 Global Compact survey, corporate responsibility policies and practices were largely developed or managed by the CEO (69 per cent). The Board of Directors played an active role in the creation and implementation of these policies in a little less than 60 per cent of the respondents' corporations. Actions to operationalize corporate responsibility include developing specific policies (69 per cent), conducting internal evaluations (63 per cent) and identifying non-financial strategic issues (57 per cent). Companies also sought external expertise, input and reference points by joining voluntary initiatives (55 per cent), participating in multi-stakeholder dialogues (39 per cent) and engaging the services of CSR experts (38 per cent) as well as benchmarking against others (36 per cent).

Communication of corporate responsibility policies, actions and progress usually takes place on the website (78 per cent). Slightly less than 50 per cent reference this information in annual reports while 47 per cent publish a separate corporate responsibility or sustainability report. In 2008, when a family of Global Compact logos was made available to signatories, 628 firms requested the use of the logo.

Living the UN Global Compact Principles

In regards to human rights, 68 per cent of the 707 respondents to the Global Compact 2008 survey indicate that they incorporate human rights in their corporate codes of conduct. Only one-third included a specific corporate statement of human right principles and 27 per cent reported a specific human rights code. Only one of four companies from the survey indicated that operational guidance notes were available although half of the companies provided some degree of employee training and awareness. In addition 30 per cent of respondents reported an increase in risk assessments of human rights issues, 28 per cent in multi-stakeholder dialogues and 36 per cent in the availability of complaint mechanisms. Ongoing assessment occurs at a rate of 31 per cent of survey participants in the area of employee performance assessment and 17 per cent in the overall impact. Human rights principles and practices generally encompass employees (85 per cent) and suppliers to a lesser extent (45 per cent).

The most frequent elements covered in corporate policies regarding human or labour rights are generally workplace health and safety (82 per cent) and non-discrimination (77 per cent). Freedom of association is included in 63 per cent of the policies of survey respondents. Restrictions on child labour and forced labour are in about half of the policies. Policies also include the guarantee of certain rights such as the right to health (70 per cent), privacy (51 per cent), life, liberty and security (68 per cent) and an adequate standard of living (46 per cent).

With respect to environmental principles, about 60 per cent of the respondents have established sustainable consumption or responsible use objectives. More specific targets relating to environmental performance as well as to sustainable production and consumption are reported by 59 per cent, 58 per cent and 60 per cent of the companies, respectively. About half of the companies indicated the presence of measurement and tracking systems. Application of these policies by groups are as follows: employees (88 per cent), production sites owned or under significant control (52 per cent), subsidiaries (49 per cent), downstream clients or consumers (30 per cent), significant contracted supplies (52 per cent) and surrounding communities (36 per cent).

The tools for implementing environmental initiatives include employee training (64 per cent), following good industry practices (58 per cent) and adopting programmes on the three 'R's of reduction, re-use and recycling (55 per cent); 59 per cent of the companies undertake impact assessments while another 52 per cent address risk assessments. Respondents that adopt an environmental lens in the design and manufacturing of products do so through technology assessment (36 per cent), eco-design (25 per cent) and life-cycle assessment (24 per cent). Approximately a quarter of the companies engage in emissions trading. A third of the companies engage in multi-stakeholder dialogue, while sustainability reporting has risen from 33 per cent of respondents in 2006 to 44 per cent in 2008.

For 67 per cent of companies participating in the survey, anti-corruption is incorporated in their corporate code of conduct. In addition, 42 per cent have established explicit anti-corruption policies and compliance mechanisms while 44 per cent have adopted a zero-tolerance policy. Only 2 per cent of companies allow facilitation payments without pre-approval while one out of four permits payments with pre-approval. Policies also exist within companies to limit gift values (39 per cent), set parameters on charitable donations (33 per cent) and publicize political contributions (12 per cent); 14 per cent of respondents require suppliers to have anti-corruption policies in place. Implementation of anti-corruption policies takes place through public dissemination and posting (42 per cent), training (48 per cent), anonymous hotlines for reporting (27 per cent) and sanctions for policy breaches (28 per cent). One of four companies records cases of corruption and facilitation payments while 38 per cent report that a supplier would be terminated if corruption occurred. 14 per cent of respondents require country managers to sign 'no-bribery' certifications.

Implications for the future

The implementation practices reported above indicate that seldom have more than half of the respondents put in place formal policies and programmes to forge advances in human and labour rights. Implementation across subsidiaries and suppliers remains inconsistent. Since respondents to the survey represent only 14 per cent of Global Compact business signatories and are likely to be more engaged, adoption of the Global Compact Principles remains an area that requires serious attention and offers significant opportunity for improvement.

While signatories may embrace the Global Compact with enthusiasm, enthusiasm itself is not sufficient. Intentions do not equal actions. The gap between intention and action, when dismissed, will erode commitment, trust and effectiveness. This deficit is prevalent and can lure participants to derive a sense of satisfaction before significant progress is achieved. A 2007 study of 391 CEOs by McKinsey confirmed significant gaps between what companies say they should do and what actually gets done. Table 7.2 shows the prevalence of these gaps (see Oppenheim *et al.* 2007 for the full study).

Table 7.2 *Gap between responses and actions of companies, per cent*

Percentage of CEOs responding/Actions	Should do	Actually does	Gap
Fully embed ESG into strategy and operations	72	50	22
Board engagement and oversight	69	45	24
Engage in industry collaborations and multi-stakeholder partnership/ dialogue	56	43	13
Fully embed into strategy and operations of subsidiaries	65	38	27
Incorporate into investor relations and engaging financial analysts	51	31	20
Embed into global supply chain	59	27	32

CEOs were also questioned about the obstacles for implementing environmental, social and governance (ESG) principles. The obstacles most frequently cited were competing strategic priorities (43 per cent) and the complexity of driving principles across business functions (39 per cent) and across regional cultures (22 per cent), which have vastly different characteristics and operating systems. In addition, 18 per cent of respondents cited failure to make the business case by linking ESG to value drivers as a major challenge and 25 per cent of respondents pointed to their struggle with gaining recognition from financial markets. The absence of an effective communication infrastructure was also listed as a difficulty by 13 per cent of the respondents.

In a subsequent survey by McKinsey, the results shed some light on the actions required for achieving meaningful change. The study probed for actions taken by CEOs who were highly successful (166 out of 2,500 respondents) in enacting significant organizational transformations. Of this high-performing group, 64 per cent cited the importance of ongoing communication that conveys and celebrates short-term wins and milestone achievements. These CEOs also presented emotionally compelling messages for the transformation (54 per cent) and reinforced change through performance targets and incentives (52 per cent). Commitment by leaders is demonstrated through executive sponsorship and systematic monitoring (62 per cent), and modelling the desired behaviour (57 per cent). Over half of the CEOs had developed clear structures for implementation, with 50 per cent reporting ownership by frontline staff (Meaney and Pung 2008).

Finally, it is necessary that reporting and accountability move to a deeper level of specificity and rigour. It is critical that the Global Compact continues to tighten its policy on COPs and on screening for breaches of the Global Compact Principles by signatories. However, heightened reporting by firms for the general public, independent of their connection to the Global Compact, will also need to occur. With the work of organizations such as the DJSI, Global Reporting Initiative (GRI), and a new guidance standard (ISO 26000) on corporate responsibility, reporting is raised to a different level of rigour and expectations. Such standardizations, which provide definitions and criteria for assessment, will level the playing field for firms that want to demonstrate their ESG leadership and provide reliable indicators of progress.

Businesses must be vigilant and continue to advance on the ESG issues such as the universal principles embedded in the Global Compact. We are reminded, 'Notwithstanding the current economic turmoil, sustainability remains firmly on investor agendas. As many commentators have pointed out during the last months, nature doesn't do bailouts. Issues such as climate change, water scarcity and risk management will continue to drive corporate success – and increasingly so' (Barkawi 2009).

Implementation of the Global Compact Principles: company cases

PricewaterhouseCoopers LLP
About PricewaterhouseCoopers
PricewaterhouseCoopers (PwC) provides industry-focused assurance, tax and advisory services to build public trust and enhance value for its clients and their stakeholders. More than 155,000 people in 153 countries across the company share their thinking, experience and solutions to develop new perspectives and practical advice.

- Net sales: $28.2 billion in revenue (2008)
- UN Global Compact global signatory since January 2008

Reasons for joining the Global Compact
In 2002, the US firm of PricewaterhouseCoopers LLP became a
Global Compact signatory as an individual territory. From 2002 to
2007, a total of eight PwC member firms from the USA, Europe and
Africa become Global Compact members. In 2007, recognizing that
PwC values, brand and reputation aligned very well with the Global
Compact, PwC's global leadership decided that instead of individual
member firms, PricewaterhouseCoopers International Limited would
became the Global Compact signatory. Interest also grew when the
Global Compact became more rigorous in enforcing its reporting
standards and took action against those signatories which did not
provide the proper COP Reports. By that time, clients also looked to
PwC to communicate its corporate responsibility credentials. Some
Requests for Proposals (RFPs) from clients began requiring information on carbon footprints and impact on community benefit. The PwC
organization saw in the Global Compact the opportunity to be part of
a learning network and to engage in surveys and findings pertaining
to emergent trends.

*Integration of Global Compact Principles in the company's goals and
mission statement*
The Principles of the Global Compact are reflected in the pillars of
PwC's globally embraced corporate responsibility framework. The
intent was to adopt the Global Compact as a complementary framework for the behaviours and responsible leadership demonstrated by
PwC. This was not a departure or 'add-on' to PwC's existing values
and priorities but a way to achieve integration of the initiatives, to
provide the same platform for engagement across all of PwC's member
firms, and to be a part of a dynamic network to continuously learn
and improve. In a recent statement, Samuel A. DiPiazza, Jr, CEO
of PricewaterhouseCoopers International, described the core role of
corporate responsibility for PwC: 'As trusted advisors in the business
community, we have a responsibility to consider all aspects of social
and environmental sustainability. Our advice cannot be based solely
on the drivers of change for today; we have a responsibility to help
shape the drivers of the future' (PricewaterhouseCoopers 2008b: 4).

Implementation of UN Global Compact Principles in strategy and operations

PwC demonstrates its commitment and support for the Global Compact by incorporating the spirit of its ten Principles into its corporate responsibility framework. Additionally, references to the Global Compact relationship are included in presentations and reports, and visibly endorsed through the use of the Global Compact logo on websites and in other deliverables. The partnership with the Global Compact is also demonstrated through timely and robust COPs, participation in topic-specific surveys and local involvement and sponsorship in territory-driven Global Compact networking events. Across PwC, implementation of corporate responsibility around the world is organized around four pillars: (1) *Marketplace*, which refers to the principles behind client service and demonstrating integrity in the organization's work practices, (2) *People*, which relates to diversity and the development of PwC staff, (3) *Community* and (4) *Environment*.

Marketplace focuses on ethics, integrity and governance. This encompasses actions to drive trust both internally and externally through a code of conduct for employees and vendors, training on ethics and compliance and development of thought leadership on major trends and situations (climate change, downturns). While vendor codes of conduct vary by individual country laws, PwC in the USA uses the UN Global Compact Principles as the foundation for their mandatory vendor assessment survey, which is given to suppliers of travel services, office supplies and facilities. PwC globally has also embedded client-facing services related to sustainability and corporate responsibility into their existing lines of service. The assurance practice has the capability to audit non-financial information; tax professionals evaluate the tax implications of carbon offsets and the carbon tax versus cap and trade scheme; and advisory professionals calculate carbon footprints and measure the risk of limited resources while also offering services to promote inclusion and employee development. This work is supported by a global network in more than forty territories with more than 800 practitioners.

Governance is achieved through internal structures to assure independence, ethical decision-making and assessment of client satisfaction and individual firm performance. Internal structures are also in place at PwC to enhance the development of its *people* and their leadership through processes for performance, evaluation, rewards and training, as well as valuing and enhancing diversity. PwC cultivates a high-performance culture which calls for excellence and balance. The firm supports its employees through policies that promote wellness, non-discrimination, unlimited sick time and safety labour standards. Employees also are educated about corporate responsibility and PwC's impact on communities during new-hire orientations and in various career milestones, such as new-manager training.

PwC's contribution and commitment to local *communities* is extensive and multi-faceted. The organization has a strong focus on youth education, with diverse implementation across different PwC territories – for example, it has conducted green literacy training in schools. For the past eight years, PwC has also supported Project Ulysses to develop responsible leaders. This programme assembles a global network of PwC leaders committed and trained to build trust-based relationships with diverse stakeholders and to gain expertise on integrating stakeholder collaboration with business operations. In June 2008, the 'Power of 10' was undertaken in the ten days leading up to PwC's tenth anniversary. In this programme, the PwC community in over 100 countries contributed $4 million to the UN refugee agency to build and operate schools for some 20,000 of Darfur's refugee children.

PwC maintains a practice of local purchasing and hiring to reflect the make-up of the local community. It also reaches out to its local communities by forming partnerships and conducting robust dialogue with various social service organizations. PwC created Global Communities within its offices to provide professional services, volunteers, funds and corporate community leadership in support of these organizations. Different offices have launched PwC Transparency Awards for high-quality reporting in the not-for-profit sector. In terms of work time permitted for volunteering, the policy differs by territories. The US firm permits unlimited hours of volunteer time when participating in firm-sponsored and organized community events. Employees are also given an additional 10 hours, which can be used during the work week, to focus on personal causes and charities. Last fiscal year, these efforts amounted to about 100,000 hours, a value of approximately $19 million. PwC has hosted different forums to speak about the benefits of corporate responsibility from The Conference Board and the Service Nation Summit to the World Economic Forum.

CEO Samuel A. DiPiazza, Jr serves as Chair of the World Business Council for Sustainable Development (WBCSD).

With respect to *environmental* initiatives, PwC member firms work within each territory to define the appropriate goals and methodology to measure and assess their environmental impact. Many territories have calculated their carbon footprint and publicly communicated reduction goals. To engage their people in this effort, PwC actively communicates their strategy and individual actions that can be taken to be more respectful of the environment as well as to contain costs. A formal training for partners, Forward Thinking, was created through Cambridge University to educate partners on the impact of climate change and the opportunities for providing sustainability services to clients to help them effectively address this emerging concern. In addition, several territories have Green Week, which provides communications, videos and interactive tools to promote environmental awareness. PwC has also implemented strategies to improve energy efficiencies and ways to assist clients in reducing their carbon footprint. Emphasis on the environment also permeates recruiting activities. With its most recent Extreme Tax Competition for students, the case challenged students to address how a tax credit would be structured for green construction. PwC made available a carbon calculator on Facebook for the public to use as a way to educate in an entertaining and interactive manner.

Leadership, governance and metrics

Accountability for corporate responsibility is placed with the Global Corporate Responsibility Board reporting to the Global Strategy Officer who works directly under the CEO. In addition, the Global Climate Change Response Group, comprising representatives from the eight largest PwC member firms, provides support to members in developing goals and plans, and driving the pace of change. Goals are different across territories with measurements taken at the local levels. In 2008, PwC US announced a goal to reduce its carbon footprint by 20 per cent by 2012 without the use of offsets. Offices in the UK, Netherlands and Australia, with the use of offsets, have been carbon neutral since July 2008. The UK firm has been very progressive in their carbon measurement and evaluates partners and staff at the individual level. The reporting protocol also differs by territories, with the GRI format serving as the consistent basis for measurement.

Some territories go beyond the GRI format to include additional elements like commuting. A few territories have created formal corporate responsibility reports and the US firm will join that list in March 2010. The goal is to formalize the reporting to include more tangible quantitative and qualitative indicators of progress, more of a report than a brochure. This will enable roll-up of data across different territories.

Challenges moving forward

Both Bill Harrington and Shannon Schuyler, who were interviewed for this case study (see appendix 1 for full list of sources for all three case studies), view the biggest challenge to be engaging and focusing the actions of 155,000 partners and staff across the globe. As Shannon said:

When we signed the UN Global Compact, we committed as a global network of firms to embed the ten core principles of the Compact into our corporate responsibility efforts and more broadly into the distinctive experience that we deliver to our client and our people. This commitment can be challenging to manage due to the size and scope of our organization, but we continually witness actions initiated across our global network where we are investing more dollars and resources in an effort not just to do business, but to do good business and do the right thing even in tough times. This commitment further enhances our brand and the reputation that we have as being responsible leaders in the global marketplace.

PwC notes that more companies are issuing corporate responsibility reports. The scope of these reports has broadened beyond mostly environmental reporting to comprehensive coverage along the triple-bottom-line dimensions (people, planet, profit). It sees increasing quality of reporting as global standards emerge. While some clients use reviews by external advisory boards, these will be increasingly supplemented by third-party verification through assurance services. Outside of the USA, there is movement for corporate responsibility reports to become a part of the annual report. These cases would require sign-off by the CEO and audit partner. This shift to include a corporate responsibility report alongside a company's annual report demonstrates how corporate responsibility has simply become part of doing business and sharing the level of accountability expected of a company.

Symantec
About Symantec
Symantec is a global leader in providing security, storage and systems management solutions to help consumers and organizations secure and manage their information-driven world. The software and services is supposed to protect against more risks at more points, enabling confidence wherever information is used or stored.

• Net sales: $5.9 billion in revenue (2008)
• UN Global Compact signatory since 3 March 2006

Reasons for joining the Global Compact
Around the 2004–5 timeframe, Symantec was encouraged by a European board member to start thinking about a more formal sustainability programme. In 2006 Symantec decided it needed an approach to frame its responsibilities more broadly and globally. In March 2006, John Thompson (then CEO) signed the United Nations Global Compact on behalf of Symantec at Symantec's offices in Silicon Valley. In our interview, John Thompson observed that:

Symantec's core values were already aligned with UN Global Compact Principles and how it would want to be known in our communities around the world. We had a very active community outreach program where we encouraged employees to get involved site by site, location by location. We had other activities such as an environmental management system in our Dublin, Ireland manufacturing center and a newly released employee code of conduct. What we needed was a comprehensive approach in which we could tie all these activities together. External stakeholders were also looking at these issues and wanted Symantec to be responsive in addressing corporate social responsibility issues across the spectrum. We saw more of this from customers: they were looking at the corporate responsibility practices as well, and not just products and services. Since our mission is about securing and protecting the world's information, we need strong credibility as a good steward and good corporate citizen. This extends beyond the quality of the products and services that we deliver. It's also about how responsible we are on all the important dimensions.

Integration of Global Compact Principles into Symantec's goals and mission statement
According to John Thompson, '[o]ur stated core values are Innovation, Customer-driven, Action and Trust. Hence UN Global Compact

Principles align not only with the importance of trust to the company, but with all of our values'. John Thompson further emphasized that 'corporate responsibility at Symantec is intertwined with the company's core purpose of securing and managing your information-driven world. We define corporate responsibility as the way in which we fulfill this purpose: with full attention and respect to ethical operation, the environment, and commitment to positive societal impact.' Progress on these fronts has enjoyed ongoing visibility and vigilance. For some initiatives, quantitative goals such as a 15 per cent carbon footprint reduction globally across all Symantec sites by 2012 would be stated. The company intends to do some real hard quantification on current status to establish a meaningful baseline for other initiatives.

Implementation of Global Compact Principles in strategy and operations

While specific actions and programmes are necessary, it is important to note the importance of 'consistency' to John Thompson:

Influence in the behaviour and culture in an organization is about consistency in what you declare to be important and the expectations you set and uphold. We urge our people to be involved in their communities, to help the company be more environmentally responsible, and to act in a manner consistent with the ethics and values put forth by the company; we want to see good financial performance but there is a way in which good financial performance is produced. Over the course of the ten years of my term, it's the consistency by which we have emphasized the importance of these actions that has influenced the way people behave and the results of the company.

As signatory of the Global Compact, Symantec has referenced the Global Compact in its standard service provider agreements and expects suppliers to adhere to the corresponding principles. In so doing, it incorporated baseline standards for social and environmental practices of suppliers. It also encourages enterprise customers to participate in the Global Compact. Cecily Joseph (Director of Corporate Responsibility) serves as the Business Representative/Focal Point for the US Network of companies to the Global Compact. The US Network provides the forum for knowledge sharing among US Global Compact signatories. Symantec has co-hosted several forums for US

Network members on topics ranging from human rights to responsible procurement and climate change.

With respect to people development, Symantec has identified the advancement of women and minorities as one of the highest priority. It took a leadership role in women initiatives as an adopter of the Calvert Women's Principles™, the first global standard for women in the workplace. The Symantec Supplier Diversity Team coordinates with the Global Procurement Group to ensure progress in supplier diversity and has asked the largest non-diverse suppliers to report on the minority representation among their second-tier suppliers. It has outsourced 100 per cent of manufacturing of consumer, availability and enterprise software products in the USA to certified Minority Business Enterprise/Small Business Enterprise.

Symantec's environmental programmes are comprehensive and include internal energy reduction as well as products and services that increase efficiency. It completed a global greenhouse gas inventory. Data centre closures saved over 300,000 kWh per month. The company adopted reduced material usage through software packaging which delivers products electronically. Reduced employee commuting and business travel through increased video conferencing shrank the carbon footprint. The company was able to improve server efficiency by leveraging server virtualization, consolidation and life-cycle management. Energy use reduction was also achieved through an end-point power management tool that turns off employees' idle PCs. A new policy called for the application of sustainable building practices and Leadership in Energy and Environmental Design (LEED) certification (when practicable) for existing owned buildings and new construction.

To assist customers on the energy front, Symantec prepared the Green Data Center Report which indicates opportunities for customers to cut electricity costs by 25 per cent. As of 2007, only 30 per cent of US-based companies had corporate green policies in place for computing. Symantec's Green IT solutions are supposed to enable customers to reduce energy use in data centres and computer systems, identify inactive data, de-duplicate data, improve storage utilization and control energy costs.

In terms of community outreach, Symantec donates software and refurbishes computers for underserved populations. It provides free access to Symantec software products for data and system protection to non-profit organizations. In particular, its assistance for youth education is broad and multi-faceted. This includes cash and software donations, partnerships with Teach for America and other community organizations and such things as being a founding sponsor of Computer Science Area of Science Buddies.

Leadership, governance and metrics
Symantec's Ethics and Compliance Committee and Global Risk Committee hold monthly meetings and report to the Audit Committee of the board every quarter. The Nomination and Compensation Committee revised its charter in 2007 to include corporate responsibility issues and performance. The Symantec Code of Conduct was updated in 2007 and included expectations on fair labour, diversity, health and safety, human rights, global citizenship, environment and guidelines to prevent corruption; 95 per cent of all employees completed the ethics training. Within the company, sixteen Diversity and Inclusion Councils worldwide are charged to review corresponding strategy and progress. The Environmental Stewardship Council, comprising executives across different functions, sets companywide goals and targets, identifies environmental impacts and develops policies. Symantec's score on corporate governance from Institutional Shareholder Services (ISS, now Risk Metrics) is at the 96.9 per cent level of S&P 500. It is also listed on the DJSI and FTSE4Good.

In terms of reporting, Symantec adopted the GRI standards for its first unaudited Corporate Responsibility Report in 2008. Different efforts exist for data collection. A Global Diversity and Inclusion Survey measures progress on diversity. US operations have set up targets to increase the number of women in various functions and leadership positions. Symantec also participates in industry benchmarking reports and surveys that compare Symantec's diversity progress. The company measures employee engagement on a quarterly basis.

Challenges moving forward
John Thompson stated in our interview the challenges facing the company as follows:

I think the single most significant challenge for us is sustaining the focus. In a time of tight economics, it is easy to become occupied with the problem du jour. We must make sure that we don't lose sight of our broader set of goals and aspirations. Consistent with that, we're going through a leadership change and the new CEO would need to put his own stamp on how we step up in terms of corporate responsibility.

While there will likely be more regulation as a result of the current economic turmoil, I think the role of CSR is to look beyond regulations. For example, we had Sarbanes–Oxley, but for the companies that messed up, they found a way to get around Sarbanes–Oxley. I think the biggest stride is made when companies realize we need to do even without regulation.

The Dow Chemical Company

About Dow Chemical

With sales of $58 billion in 2008 and 46,000 employees worldwide, Dow is a diversified chemical company that combines the power of science and technology with the 'Human Element' to constantly improve what is essential to human progress. The Company delivers a broad range of products and services to customers in around 160 countries, connecting chemistry and innovation with the principles of sustainability to help provide everything from fresh water, food and pharmaceuticals to paints, packaging and personal care products. On 1 April 2009, Dow acquired Rohm and Haas Company, a global specialty materials company with sales of $10 billion in 2008 and 15,000 employees worldwide. References to 'Dow' or the 'Company' mean The Dow Chemical Company and its consolidated subsidiaries unless otherwise expressly noted.

- Net sales: $58 billion in revenue (2008)
- Global Compact signatory since May 2007

Reasons for joining the Global Compact

Dow's corporate strategy focuses on growth through expansion into emerging geographies, through new joint ventures and in downstream businesses closer to end users. Each of these broadens exposure and increases the number of stakeholders across the world; as such, Dow anticipates strong social expectations of their operations along the dimensions of human rights, environmental protection and governance.

When Dow first examined the Global Compact in 2000, there were several hundred codes in circulation. One concern the company had regarding the Compact was that if the company signed one code, it would likely encounter pressure to endorse many others including those advocated by customers and suppliers, and risk dilution of its own values and internal code of business conduct. By mid-2004–5, while the company had held high standards and adopted rigorous sustainability goals for its operations, it recognized the need to look at corporate responsibility from a business perspective and to incorporate external expectations in light of its growth strategy. External expectations were highly dynamic and the scope would be extended to Dow's suppliers and vendors. Joining the Global Compact would validate the company's existing values while connecting it to like-minded organizations from which it could learn best practices and stay attuned to changing expectations. The Global Compact in that time had greatly improved in terms of procedures, measurements and reporting. The decision to sign the Compact in 2007 was vetted with the internal sustainability team, external advisory board and the appropriate committee of the board of directors and signed by the CEO. During our interview, Bo Miller stated: 'Our view of the Compact is significantly more than a declaration or document – it is a living, active process for continuous, practical improvement.'

Integration of Global Compact Principles in the company's goals and mission statement

Dow's mission is to 'constantly improve what is essential to human progress by mastering science and technology'. The mission relates directly to the Global Compact Principles as its purpose is to elevate the human condition and to ensure development for all peoples and respect for their rights. In 2005, Dow Chemical had accomplished the ten-year environmental health and safety (EH&S) goals launched in 1996. These goals were largely focused on operations defined in terms such as reduction of emissions and worker injuries, improvements in wastewater and energy efficiency. It was time to establish goals for the next ten years. The process took a year and a half and engaged both internal and external stakeholders. Senior management and outside councils challenged the team working on the goals to stretch and think outside of the box. These engagements elevated the focus from operational performance to broad-based sustainability goals.

The goals were organized in aligned support of the company's four strategic themes: (1) Drive financial discipline and low cost-to-serve, (2) Set the standard for sustainability, (3) Build a people-centric performance culture and (4) Invest in strategic growth. Of these, theme (2) speaks directly to the Global Compact Principles. Precise metrics for implementation and performance measurement with regard to the second theme are listed in appendix 2.

Implementation of Global Compact Principles in strategy and operations
Theme (2) of the 2015 Sustainability Goals sets the aspiration to be the standard-bearer for sustainability. Sustainability encompasses a broad scope beyond environmental initiatives to include Citizenship, Solutions and Footprint. *Citizenship* focuses on the protection of local human health and safety in all Dow locations and contributing to the wellbeing of the local communities. The purpose is to support the local community's vision of success in terms of its social and environmental standards.

Solutions are to be achieved through (a) product safety leadership, (b) advances in sustainable chemistry and (c) 'breakthroughs'. Dow aims for major pushes in energy-efficient housing, cost-effective approaches to purifying water and new technologies that advance production of food and agricultural goods. The company focuses on sustainable chemistry to produce new or re-engineer current products to be more sustainable from an environmental perspective. As 95 per cent of products manufactured embed chemicals, this would be a large area of potential impact. The breakthrough goal is to achieve, between 2006 and 2015, three game-changing inventions in the areas of water, affordable housing and food, as well as human health and safety. Breakthrough can be in the form of a product, technology or business model that represents a paradigm shift and greatly enhances people's wellbeing.

Two prongs, (a) energy efficiency/conservation and (b) climate change, define the activities under *Footprint*. Between 1996 and 2005, the company reduced energy consumption by 22 per cent. This would be the baseline from which a 25 per cent reduction would be sought in the next ten years. It will also turn to its products and processes to advance energy alternatives such as biofuels, photovoltaics and wind, as well as develop less carbon-intensive material sources. Dow intends to increase its R&D investments beyond historical levels and to advocate for an international framework and for fair markets for carbon trading.

Leadership, governance and metrics
The EH&S committee of the board, chaired by an outside director, operates by a broad charter which includes sustainability goals, corporate citizenship, a philanthropy strategy and a human rights policy. There is a well-defined chain of responsibility from the EH&S board committee to the corporate sustainability team, individual executive sponsors for each of the seven goals, implementation leader and project leader.

Progress against the 2015 Sustainability Goals is reported on a quarterly basis on dow.com, reporting by the G3 format of the GRI standard. Dow uses the Operating Discipline Management System to collect and aggregate data. Measurements are established to allow for tracking progress against goals. The 2007 GRI report was reviewed by an external firm – Environmental Resources Management. Specific metrics are established for evaluating progress under the following sections: environmental management, labour practices disclosure, human disclosure, social disclosure and product responsibility disclosure. As this reporting protocol adheres to the highest standards, the metrics are reported in appendix 2 as an illustration of leading practices.

Challenges moving forward
The biggest challenge is to achieve greater integration between the Global Compact Principles and the existing systems and procedures. How does one get a process-orientated culture to implement something that may be seen by certain employee segments as a 'softer' thing? As Bo Miller stated in our interview:

> How do we engage more colleagues to see these practices as not a 'nice to do' or 'add on' but as an integral part of the business case? We need to increase their understanding of how the Compact matches with our code and values. We need to engage at least two more levels in beyond corporate officers and senior executives to the levels of country managers, business and marketing directors. Dow will benefit through their increased participation in Local Networks. Right now it rests with a small number of people. We are building from that base. The UN Global Compact has

to be seen as compatible, synergistic, and supportive of existing values and priorities and not 'here's another thing that I have to do'.

Appendix

Appendix 1: Sources for case studies

PwC sources:

- Interview with Shannon Schuyler (US Managing Director of Corporate Responsibility); Bill Harrington (Assurance Partner)
- PricewaterhouseCoopers 2008 *Annual Global Review*
- *Corporate Responsibility at PricewaterhouseCoopers*: *Taking Responsibility in our Communities* (PricewaterhouseCoopers 2008b)
- *The Right Combination: Corporate Responsibility Reports: The Role of Assurance Providers and Stakeholder Reports* (PricewaterhouseCoopers 2007)

Symantec sources:

- Interview with Mr John Thompson (former CEO and current Chairman); Cecily Joseph (Director of Corporate Responsibility); Linda Smith (Symantec Public Relations)
- 2007–8 Global Compact Communication on Progress Report
- 2008 *Corporate Responsibility Report*

Dow Chemical Company sources:

- Interview with Mr Bo Miller (Global Director, Corporate Citizenship, The Dow Chemical Company and President, The Dow Chemical Company Foundation)
- *Global Reporting Initiative Report* 2008 (year-end 2007)
- 2007–8 Global Compact Communication on Progress Report
- Dow Chemical Company *Annual Report* 2007

Appendix 2: Metrics used by Dow Chemical

Environmental disclosure on management approach

- EN1 Materials used
- EN2 Percentage of materials used that are recycled input materials
- EN3 Direct energy consumption by primary source
- EN4 Indirect energy consumption by primary source
- EN5 Energy saved due to conservation and efficiency improvements
- EN6 Initiatives to provide energy-efficient or renewable energy based products and services
- EN7 Initiatives to reduce indirect energy consumption and reductions achieved
- EN8 Total water withdrawal by source
- EN9 Water resources significantly affected by withdrawal of water
- EN10 percentage and total volume of water recycled and reused
- EN11 Location and size of land owned, leased, managed in, or adjacent to, protected areas and areas of high biodiversity value
- EN12 Description of significant impacts on biodiversity in protected areas and areas of high biodiversity value
- EN13 Habitats protected or restored
- EN14 Strategies, current actions and future plans for managing impacts of biodiversity
- EN15 Number of IUCN Red List species and national conservation list species with habitats in areas affected by operations, by level of extinction risk
- EN16 Total direct and indirect greenhouse gas emissions by weight
- EN17 Other relevant indirect greenhouse gas emissions by weight
- EN18 Initiatives to reduce greenhouse gas emissions and reductions achieved
- EN19 Emissions of ozone-depleting substances by weight and by CFC-11 equivalence
- EN20 NO_X, SO_X, and other significant air emissions by type and weight

- EN21 Total water discharge by quality and destination (Dow tracks wastewater with an intensity metric)
- EN22 Total weight of waste by type and disposal method (Dow tracks waste with an intensity metric)
- EN23 Total number and volume of significant spills
- EN24 Weight of transported, imported, exported or treated waste deemed hazardous under the terms of the Basel Convention Annex I, II, III, and VIII, and the percentage of transported waste shipped internationally
- EN25 Identity, size, protected status and biodiversity value of water bodies and related habitats significantly affected by the discharges of water and runoff
- EN26 Initiatives to mitigate environmental impacts of products and services, and extent of impact mitigation
- EN27 Percentage of products sold and their packaging materials that are reclaimed by category
- EN28 Monetary value or significant fines and total number of non-monetary sanctions for non-compliance with environmental laws and regulations
- EN29 Significant environmental impacts of transporting products and other goods and materials used for the organization's operations and transporting members of the workforce
- EN30 Total environmental protection expenditures and investments by type

Labor practices disclosure on management approach

- LA1 Total workforce by employment type, employment contract and region
- LA2 Total number and rate of employee turnover by age group, gender, and region
- LA3 Benefits provided to full-time employees that are not provided to temporary or part-time employees
- LA4 Percentage of employees covered by collective bargaining agreements
- LA5 Minimum notice periods regarding operation changes, including whether it is specified in collective agreements
- LA6 Percentage of total workforce represented in formal joint management–worker health and safety committees that

help monitor and advise on occupational health and safety programmes

- LA7 Rates of injury, occupational diseases, lost days and absenteeism, and the number of work-related fatalities by region
- LA8 Education, training, counseling, prevention, and risk-control programmes in place to assist workforce members, their families or community members regarding serious diseases
- LA9 Health and safety topics covered in formal agreements with trade unions
- LA10 Average hours of training per year per employee by employee category
- LA11 Programmes for skills management and lifelong learning that support the continued employability of employees and assist them in managing career endings
- LA12 Percentage of employees receiving regular performance and career development reviews
- LA13 Composition of governance bodies and breakdown of employees per category according to gender, age group, minority group membership and other indicators of diversity
- LA14 Ratio of basic salary of men to women by employee category

Human rights disclosure on management approach

- HR1 Percentages and total number of significant investment agreements that include human rights clauses or that have undergone human rights screening
- HR2 Percentage of significant suppliers and contractors that have undergone screening on human rights and actions taken
- HR3 Total hours of employee training on policies and procedures concerning aspects of human rights that are relevant to operations, including the percentage of employees trained
- HR4 Total number of incidents of discrimination and actions taken
- HR5 Operations identified in which the right to exercise freedom of association and collective bargaining may be at significant risk, and actions taken to support these rights
- HR6 Operations identified as having significant risk for incidents of child labour, and measures taken to contribute to the elimination of child labor

- HR7 Operations identified as having significant risk for incidents of forced or compulsory labor, and measures to contribute to the elimination of forced or compulsory labor
- HR8 Percentage of security personnel trained in the organization's policies or procedure concerning aspects of human rights that are relevant to operations
- HR9 Total number of incidents of violations involving rights of indigenous people and actions taken

Social disclosure on management approach

- SO1 Nature, scope and effectiveness of managing impact on communities
- SO2 Percentage and total number of business units analysed for risks related to corruption
- SO3 Percentage of employees trained in organization's anti-corruption policies and procedures
- SO4 Actions taken in response to incidents of corruption
- SO5 Public policy positions and participation in public policy development and lobbying
- SO6 Total value of financial and in-kind contributions to political parties, politicians and related institutions by country
- SO7 Total number of legal actions for anti-competitive behavior, anti-trust, and monopoly practices and their outcomes
- SO8 Monetary value of significant fines and total number of non-monetary sanctions for non-compliance with laws and regulations

Product responsibility disclosure on management approach

- PR1 Life cycle stages in which health and safety impacts of products and services are assessed for improvement and percentage of significant products and services categories subject to such procedures
- PR2 Total number of incidents of non-compliance with regulations and voluntary codes concerning the health and safety impacts of products and services during their life cycle, by type of outcomes
- PR3 Type of product and service information required by procedures, and percentage of significant products and services subject to such information requirements

- PR4 Total number of incidents of non-compliance with regulations and voluntary codes concerning product and service information and labeling, by type of outcomes
- PR5 Practices related to customer satisfaction, including results of surveys measuring customer satisfaction
- PR6 Programs for adherence to laws, standards, and codes related to marketing communications, including advertising, promotion and sponsorship
- PR7 Total number of incidents of non-compliance with regulations and codes concerning marketing communications, including advertising, promotion and sponsorship, by type of outcomes
- PR8 Total number of substantiated complaints regarding breaches of customer privacy and losses of customer data
- PR9 Monetary value of significant fines for non-compliance with laws and regulations concerning the provision and use of products and services

8 | *Academic institutions and the United Nations Global Compact: the Principles for Responsible Management Education*

REGINA WENTZEL WOLFE AND
PATRICIA H. WERHANE

> As teachers, you can ensure that tomorrow's leaders understand
> that the long-term growth of business is tied to its environmental
> and social impact. As scholars, you can produce research that
> drives innovation and helps management to recognize the
> benefits of being a responsible business. And as thought leaders
> and advocates in your communities, you help advance awareness
> of broader challenges, opportunities and responsibilities.
>
> UN Secretary-General Ban Ki-moon (see United Nations
> 2008)

Introduction

The United Nations Global Compact was created both to close global
governance gaps in commerce and as a means to set universal standards for moral behaviour, globally. The goals of the United Nations
Global Compact are to encourage the adoption of the ten business
principles worldwide and to promote support of broader United
Nations initiatives, in particular the Millennium Development Goals
(MDGs) aimed at worldwide poverty reduction. Although focused on
commerce, the membership of the Global Compact is wide-ranging
and includes non-governmental organizations (NGOs), academic
institutions and governments, as well as corporations.

There has never been a time, historically, when commerce has not
faced serious ethical issues. As early as 1800 BC the Mesopotamian
ruler, Hammurabi, developed a code of ethics for the conduct of trade
and commerce, an obvious reaction to some questionable behaviours
that occurred at that time. Regrettably, questionable behaviours

144

in business practices continue to occur. The scandals of 2001 – exacerbated by the Enron scandal, the monumental corrupt activities of Parmalat and Siemens in Europe, and the global financial meltdown of 2008 – are among the most recent examples. In response, codes of conduct, such as the Caux Principles, principles developed by Transparency International (TI), the World Economic Forum (WEF) Partnering Against Corruption Initiative (PACI), the Organization for Economic Cooperation and Development (OECD), and others illustrate an ongoing effort to encourage, if not require, less corrupt practices. Given all these efforts, it is tempting to view the Principles of the Global Compact as just another in the series of codes and principles developed by various international and national bodies. But there is a difference.

The United Nations is a global organization. Its human rights principles, outlined in the *United Nations Universal Declaration of Human Rights* (UDHR, hereafter: the Declaration) written in 1948 reflect the global nature of this organization, as well as set up the moral foundations for its thinking and practice. Thus, the perceived legitimacy of the Compact's Principles is greater as they are based on widely accepted UN conventions and declarations. Moreover, the Global Compact Principles apply to the developing world in a way that the other principles do not, at least not explicitly. A careful study of these Principles, many of which evolve from the Declaration, would conclude they are normative standards that have universal appeal across religions, ethnic and cultural diversity, gender, race, political differences and economic systems. While the implementation of the Principles, particularly Principle 7, the precautionary environmental principle, presents challenges to many companies, they should serve as ideals towards which every organization should strive. Organizations that do so will be better placed to survive and do well in the long term in light of the new (or renewed) emphasis on corporate responsibility worldwide.

As recent corporate scandals have demonstrated, the long-term wellbeing of any organization is inexorably linked to its moral as well as economic performance. In a global economy this is particularly true, where pressures to act with integrity, treat labour with respect and dignity and work toward environmentally clean technologies are inescapable and come from a variety of sources including NGOs, civil society and governments. The Global Compact Principles are merely a philosophical reflection and standardization of these global aspirations. The goal, of course, is to stamp out corrupt practices worldwide, improve labour and environmental standards and initiate a universal recognition of human rights. It is perhaps too much to expect achievement of these lofty aims in the near future, but they set the bar high; if operationalized in even a few companies, they will become models for corporate behaviour in the future.

The Principles for Responsible Management Education (PRME)

Given past and recent scandals, and the efforts of multinational companies (MNCs) to become global, responsible and even environmentally more sustainable, business education today has a mandate to adopt and teach the Global Compact Principles. If we are to develop business leaders who can function and function well in what Tom Friedman (2006) calls the 'flat world' of a global economy, then we must educate leaders to be sensitive to and to strive for the creation of value-added for their employees and for the communities in which they operate, as well as to decrease their environmental footprint. Such education will help future leaders recognize that concern for profitability alone is not sustainable over the long term.

Fortunately, we are finding more and more global companies working to adopt the Global Compact Principles and to reform their own activities, such as corruption, in the communities in which they operate. Sadly, however, not all business education, either in North America or in other parts of the world, has adapted or is developing curricula that embrace these mandates. While in the past university education has prided itself in being in the forefront of creating knowledge, we find today that many business schools are merely reactive. The Principles for Responsible Management Education (PRME) aim to correct this educational lag by encouraging this new emphasis on corporate responsibility in business school education.

Inspired by the Global Compact, the PRME are voluntary standards that management schools interested in developing future leaders should adopt and integrate into management education, at both the undergraduate and MBA levels (see box 8.1 for the PRME). According to the PRME document, 'The mission of the Principles for Responsible Management Education (PRME) initiative is to inspire and champion

Box 8.1: The Principles for Responsible Management Education (PRME)

As institutions of higher learning involved in the education of current and future managers we are voluntarily committed to engaging in a continuous process of improvement of the following Principles, reporting on progress to all our stakeholders and exchanging effective practices with other academic institutions:

Principle 1 Purpose: We will develop the capabilities of students to be future generators of sustainable value for business and society at large and to work for an inclusive and sustainable global economy

Principle 2 Values: We will incorporate into our academic activities and curricula the values of global social responsibility as portrayed in international initiatives such as the United Nations Global Compact.

Principle 3 Method: We will create educational frameworks, materials, processes and environments that enable effective learning experiences for responsible leadership.

Principle 4 Research: We will engage in conceptual and empirical research that advances our understanding about the role, dynamics and impact of corporations in the creation of sustainable social, environmental and economic value.

Principle 5 Partnership: We will interact with managers of business corporations to extend our knowledge of their challenges in meeting social and environmental responsibilities and to explore jointly effective approaches to meeting these challenges.

Principle 6 Dialogue: We will facilitate and support dialogue and debate among educators, business, government, consumers, media, civil society organizations and other interested groups and stakeholders on critical issues related to global social responsibility and sustainability.

Source: Global Compact (2007d).

responsible management education, research and thought leadership globally' (PRME 2009). This is a global appeal that parallels the Global Compact Principles and applies to management education's contemporary global reach as these institutions educate managers for the growing global economy. The PRME address this global dimension directly, when stating: 'In the current academic environment, corporate responsibility and sustainability have entered but not yet become embedded in the mainstream of business-related education. The PRME are therefore a timely global call for business schools and universities worldwide to gradually adapt their curricula, research, teaching methodologies and institutional strategies to the new business challenges and opportunities' (PRME 2009).

As of May 2009, only 229 institutions have adopted the PRME principles, of which 219 are academic institutions (see appendix for PRME and Global Compact academic partner membership data). The remaining PRME participants are foundations, NGOs and other organizations that support academic endeavours. Although academic institutions can be both participants in the Global Compact and adopters of the PRME, not all who have signed on to the Global Compact have also opted to adopt the PRME. In both instances, the majority of participants are from Europe with similar levels of participation (see figures 8.1 and 8.2). North American participation in the PRME is significantly higher than participation in the Global Compact. Asian and South American participation levels are just the opposite, with greater participation in the Global Compact.

The 219 academic institutions that have adopted the PRME at the time of writing represent less than 20 per cent of the membership of the Association to Advance Collegiate Schools of Business (AACSB), the foremost agency for business education.[1] This relatively small number highlights the need for greater adoption of the six principles put forward by the PRME initiative. In our view, every business school and management programme *should* adopt these principles. Our reasoning for this conclusion is not original, but critical nevertheless.

The PRME are not merely a set of ideal standards. They challenge business schools to change a mindset that focuses primarily on profitability, a mindset that defines 'value-added' as shareholder returns rather than returns for or enrichment of the various stakeholders and communities with which an organization interacts. The PRME require that ethics and moral principles not merely be 'add-ons' in the educational process – that is, taught as 'soft' courses. Rather, ethics

---

[1] As of May 2009 there were 1,127 member schools listed on the AACSB website; 568 of these were accredited by AACSB (see www.aacsb.edu).

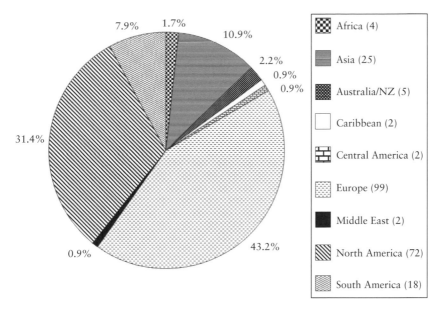

Figure 8.1 Geographical distribution of PRME academic partners

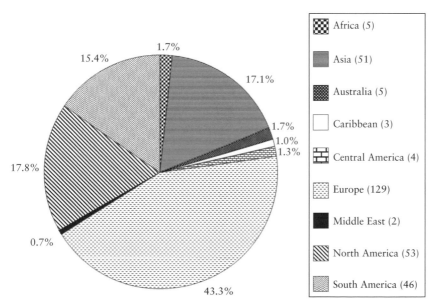

Figure 8.2 Geographical distribution of UN Global Compact academic partners

and moral principles are to be embedded in the curriculum, thus highlighting the integral relationship between ethics and economics. In addition, the PRME require that the reasoning skills taught in management classes include forms of moral reasoning as well. The logic for this emphasis should be transparent.

Companies create or respond to markets, develop strong labour pools and produce products and provide services that are needed or desired; in doing so, they affect other human beings. The core activities of successful companies are integral to the wellbeing of human communities. For example, the current focus on environmental sustainability demonstrates this proposition. As the planet becomes smaller, it is critical for its survival and the survival of its inhabitants that we all take the warnings of environmental scientists seriously. Businesses play a crucial role in these efforts. Similarly humane treatment of employees and respect for their equal rights, and working fairly with suppliers and communities in market exchanges are, or should be, part of 'business-as-usual'. This is because, if for no other reason, causing harm to these human communities violates the commercial agenda. However, we do not always teach these ideas in business schools. By avoiding these topics and continuing to frame commerce and business only in terms of owner or shareholder profitability, we do not prepare our students for the increasing global pressures to be socially responsible. Moreover, by not addressing these topics, we increase the possibility of more scandals and more financial meltdowns, activities which the world can no longer afford to tolerate.

There are a number of paths that a school of management can take in institutionalizing the PRME principles. In the following we will outline some of the programmes from institutions that are adopting the PRME and highlight a few ideas or activities that might serve as models for others to adopt or adapt. We can all learn from each other, and we are grateful for these models as starting places for what should be an ongoing effort to share best practices and to learn from each other's mistakes and challenges.

PRME participant profiles and reports: learning from each other

One of the requirements for institutions adopting the PRME is the submission of an annual progress report. As we mentioned earlier, there are 229 PRME participants, of which 219 are academic institutions.

The PRME website provides each participant with a webpage that contains basic information about the type and location of the institution. In addition, each participant webpage has a section in which the institution can list achievements in the integration of Corporate Social Responsibility (CSR) and sustainability into the curriculum as well as achievements in research in those areas. Of the 219 academic institutions, 111 have posted information on a separate participant webpage (i.e. PRME participant profile). These webpages vary greatly in the data provided when considering the categories for assessing PRME reports which are discussed below. Given the structure of the webpages, most organizations focus narrowly on curricula and research. However, some webpages provide extensive information that may be useful to other academic participants, as they consider how to enhance implementation of the PRME. It should be noted that similar activities may very well be taking place at other institutions but simply have not been reported.

It should also be noted that those leading the PRME initiative are in the process of developing a policy for sharing information on activities and accomplishments. In fact, a few member institutions have posted comprehensive stand-alone annual reports. As of May 15, 2009, seven academic institutions had filed such reports. Without doubt, this number will continue to grow. These more extensive reports will be valuable to academic institutions that are considering signing on to the PRME. An example of this is the approach of Martin-Luther University in Halle-Wittenberg, Germany, found in the comprehensive report posted to the PRME website; it reflects how PRME can be critical to the education of future business leaders in countries that do not have significant legislative mandates that incentivize responsible behaviour:

Education in these [PRME] competencies should be integrated into the bachelor and master programmes, not with a separate degree for 'ethicists,' but as a possible major within classical management education. Unlike the US (with its [Federal] Sentencing Guidelines or the Sarbanes–Oxley Act), German legislation cannot be expected to create massive incentives for a new profession of 'ethics officers'. Therefore, especially in Germany [and we would suggest, in many parts of the world outside the USA] Economic Ethics and Business Ethics must choose the path to strengthen general managers' education in the area of 'strategic management'. (Martin-Luther University Halle-Wittenberg 2008: 7)

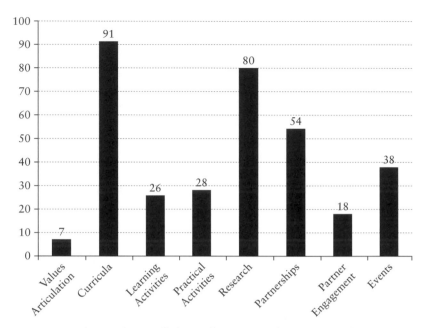

Note: Because the sample is small, the graph points to only tentative conclusions.

Figure 8.3 Assessment of 111 reports of PRME participants, according to activity categories

In other words, ethics must be integral to all facets of management education as part of strategic management, broadly conceived, and not as a separate, compartmentalized area of interest. We wholeheartedly concur, and suggest that this should be the aim of business education at all levels to create values-based leaders (see also Holland 2009: 15). As our evaluation of participant profiles indicates, some schools are moving toward this more integrated approach.

To ease the evaluation of the information posted by 111 institutions in their participant profiles on the PRME webpage, we have used eight categories as criteria with which to measure achievement. From the available participant profiles and based on the categories for assessment listed below, we have documented achievements by category alone (see figure 8.3) and by category and geographical distribution (see figure 8.4). The eight criteria for assessment are as follows (adopted from Waddock *et al.* 2009: 18–19):

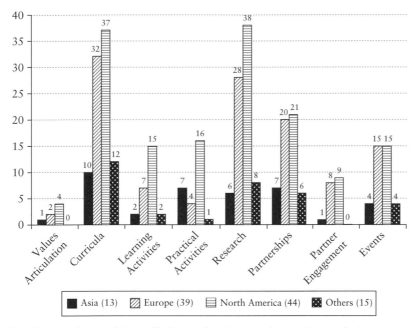

Note: Because the sample is small, the graph points to only tentative conclusions.

Figure 8.4 Assessment of 111 reports of PRME participants, according to activity categories and geographical distribution

1. Ability of students to articulate their values and the values of the Global Compact and the PRME, and assess how their own values reflect or do not match the principles of the Global Compact and the PRME.
2. Curricula development and extracurricular activities that focus on sustainable management as a key part of the learning processes.
3. Development of new learning activities aimed at stimulating interest and learning for responsible leadership.
4. Ability of students to engage in practical activities aimed at operationalizing some of the PRME values; these could be social outreach projects, environmentally green initiatives, internships in sustainable companies or NGOs, school leadership, etc.
5. Substantial faculty research outputs that advance knowledge about sustainable social, environmental and economic outcomes for MNCs.
6. Development of partnerships with local community leaders in both the corporate and non-profit sectors.
7. Engagement with partners in symposia and classroom settings so that students see the importance of the PRME in their work experiences.

8. Facilitation of seminars, speaker series, classroom exchanges and media events aimed at dialogue about the PRME and the Global Compact Principles.

In our examination we found that very few schools engage in values articulation, but many schools do at least one or more of the following: (1) Emphasize CSR and environmental sustainability in new student orientation activities, although there are differences in definitions of CSR and in the scope of what is to be considered as 'environmental sustainability'. Those differences are to be expected and encouraged. (2) Require business ethics and/or CSR courses; some US business schools have courses in corporate compliance that include studies of the Federal Sentencing Guidelines for Organizations, the Sarbanes–Oxley Act, the Securities and Exchange Commission (SEC), and/or other regulatory mandates or governmental bodies. (3) Integrate ethics across core subjects in the required business or management curriculum. This does apparently show that North American business schools are a bit ahead in integrating the PRME principles in their curricula and research agendas, but the latter might be due to the focus of English-speaking management journals on ethics and CSR issues.

Although we cannot comment on all of the participants here, we shall illustrate some of our findings with a few case examples:[2]

- Thunderbird School of Global Management (USA): Thunderbird was one of the earliest subscribers to the PRME and its president, Angel Cabrera, helped to formulate the PRME principles. At Thunderbird students drafted the 'Professional Oath of Honour' an oath that mirrors the PRME principles. Faculty, administrators and students are strongly encouraged to sign this oath (for a detailed discussion of this case see also Waddock *et al.* 2009).
- Ramon V. del Rosario, Sr, Graduate School of Business, De La Salle University (Philippines): Teaching evaluation forms were revised to include questions that assess 'how well faculty incorporate ethics and social responsibility considerations in their teaching practice.'

---

[2] The following case examples and quotations are derived from the participant profiles of PRME adopters available at www.unprme.org/participants/index.php (all data as of May 2009).

- Aston Business School (UK): MBA core module requires students 'to submit a reflective account of their own values and comment upon whether their future decision making and actions may be influenced by their studies.'
- Hull University Business School (UK): An audit was conducted to determine 'where CSR/Sustainability principles are being taught (or not) across the Business School's offering. This will be used to identify future areas for development.'
- Heller School of Management Brandeis University (USA): MBA core courses are 'taught from the perspective of mission-driven organizations and the special skills needed to lead these organizations. Students also take non-traditional courses like Social Justice and Management to develop their own perspective on social justice and to incorporate that perspective into their role as managers; and Social Policy Frameworks, to develop their ability to analyse, evaluate and advocate for the policies that are critical to the social mission of their organization.'
- The School of Business Administration, University of San Diego (USA): An annual international consulting project targets 'business development and wealth creation at the base of the pyramid. In 2008 the project was in Uganda to assist an NGO in developing sustainable business initiatives with the local community.'
- Hanken School of Economics (Finland): 'We encourage critical thinking including towards the mainstream notion of corporate responsibility . . . used as an opportunity to discuss environmental and social issues.'
- Audencia School of Management (France): Students define team projects 'either in cooperation with one of the partner companies of Audencia's Centre for Global Responsibility or with other stakeholders [in which students examine] the complexity of Global Responsibility issues, define the issues, do documentary research, and identify best practices in other organizations or companies, interview people inside and outside of the company. They write a final report with strategic proposals, recommendations and evaluation criteria for the follow up and implementation. They then take part in the implementation.'
- Mendoza College of Business University of Notre Dame (USA): A multi-faceted Ethics Assessment Project 'analyses the outcomes

associated with a required undergraduate course in ethics . . . studies results from the Business Education Survey . . . as well as case study responses from all students [and conducts a] survey, given during students' sophomore and senior years, [to determine] student attitudes toward and conceptions of business, business and society, and business education.'

• Grenoble École de Management (France): 'Students in Free Enterprise . . . submitted a Corporate Social Responsibility project . . . aimed to raise awareness of CSR and help SMEs in the Greater Grenoble area to implement CSR initiatives.'

Assessing the categories of achievement criteria

We very much appreciate the efforts by Waddock *et al.* (2009) for taking the lead to set out criteria for assessing achievement. We have some suggestions for expanding those criteria and for encouraging institutions to be clearer in their participant profiles so that we can all learn from and model these ideas. These include:

(1) Add a criterion that focuses on faculty development for teaching and research based on the PRME.

(2) Ask about evaluation/audit methods for assessing the curriculum in light of the PRME.

(3) The reporting process should be more systematized and directed (perhaps using the criteria for assessment listed above). This would enable the participant profiles (and also the required annual reports) to be more useful to partner institutions as a means for measuring their own progress as well as learning from the successes and challenges of others.

(4) Only a few of the participant profiles will provide helpful models or ideas for others to emulate. Participants should be encouraged to give practical examples of implementation of the principles. Such models are great learning tools for institutions, particularly those that either have recently adopted the PRME principles or are considering adopting them.

(5) Distinguish between efforts to stimulate research – e.g. summer research grants – and research accomplishments, which should include some sense of how research is disseminated and impacts student learning.

(6) In cases where modifications or upgrades have been made to courses perhaps 'before and after' course descriptions and/or syllabi can be appended.

(7) Syllabi and other teaching resource materials should have a distinct and easily accessible place on the PRME website.

(8) Clearer definitions of terms are needed. For example, a few PRME participants focus on identifying courses that deal narrowly with environmental issues; in some cases, the way this is done can lead readers to conclude that these institutions understand sustainability in narrow environmental terms – a conclusion which is not necessarily correct.

(9) Taking a brief from the Lilly Endowment, reporting should go beyond descriptions of successful activities and achievements to identify challenges that were experienced and how they were overcome as well as to describe activities or initiatives that were tried but were not successful and the reasons why they were not successful; this might help to avoid repeated failures and to optimize use of limited resources.

(10) Participant profiles and reports should clearly distinguish what is happening from what is being planned.

(11) Participant profiles and reports should distinguish between providing opportunities for continuing education for business practitioners and events and activities that provide students with the opportunity to observe and learn from practitioners who participate in symposia and other continuing education activities.

(12) Participant profiles should clearly indicate when they were last updated. With the development of more detailed PRME reporting standards, this weakness should be alleviated.

Despite what might be perceived as shortcomings of the PRME participant profiles, we found each profile to be indicative of academic institutions that are wrestling successfully with broadened educational reform aimed at creating business leaders who will exemplify the PRME in their practice. We applaud the efforts of these institutions that are models for educational change. We recognize that integrating the PRME into business education is challenging and hard work. However, it is also creative and rewarding. Participation in this project will make a difference to the future of commerce and free enterprise, and we encourage all schools of management to accept the challenge of adopting the PRME.

Conclusions: some tentative proposals for assessment

Let us conclude with some very tentative practical proposals for programme assessment. Programme assessment and assessment of student progress in internalizing and engaging practice with the PRME is very difficult to judge. Because the PRME is in its early stages of development, assessment tools have yet to be definitively developed. The criteria set out by Waddock *et al.* (2009) and used in our evaluation of participant profiles provide a workable framework for an initial assessment programme. As conceived by those authors, the various criteria reflect particular principles. Criteria (1)–(4), which focus on values articulation, curricular modifications, learning activities and practical engagement, respectively, assist in assessing principles (1)–(3). Criterion (5) addresses principle (4), which is concerned with research. Criteria (6) and (7) focus on principle (5)'s emphasis on partnerships with businesses and community leaders, while criterion (8) focuses on principle (6)'s emphasis on promoting dialogue on CSR and sustainability. 'While each school and each professor will approach these topics differently and measure outcomes differently, these objectives [or criteria] are general enough not to interfere with academic freedom, and whether a school is working toward implementing them should not be an onerous task to evaluate' (Waddock *et al.* 2009: 18–19).

The PRME are aimed at changing some of the traditional mindsets that have dominated business and management education for almost a century. In the last decade, however, these traditions have been criticized by a number of management educators including the late Sumantra Ghoshal from the London Business School (Ghoshal 2005), Jeffrey Pfeffer of Stanford University (Pfeffer 2007), and Rakesh Khurana from the Harvard Business School (Khurana 2007). According to these and other critics, what is usually taught in a traditional business school focuses primarily on profit maximization to the exclusion of other human and organizational stakeholders who influence or are affected by the organization; the focus is on training rather than education, and the training is management-focused rather than leadership-orientated. As Khurana states it baldly, the education of business leaders has shifted 'from higher aims to hired hands'.

The PRME challenge these traditions and offer positive principles and methods with which to engage students and change these worn-out mindsets. The principles encourage values-based leadership education that is grounded in the ten Global Compact Principles while being practitioner-orientated. Such forms of education suggest an approach that defines management as a principled profession that integrates values with sustainable management practice. The term 'sustainability' here refers not merely to sustaining the natural environment, but also to producing corporate thinking and practice that integrate principles, a social agenda and environmentally sound practices with creating economic value-added for its stakeholders – including, of course, its shareholders. Such a systems-based method does not view these elements as disparate or discrete, each with its own agenda; rather its approach is integrative and responsive to the interconnected nature of today's global economy. In this environment, business schools that choose not to accept the challenge of integrating the PRME into their programmes do so at their peril.

Appendix: PRME and Global Compact academic partner membership data

There are 475 educational institutions affiliated with one or both of these initiatives (as of May 2009).

PRME: 229 academic partners (52 are also Global Compact participants)

- 175 listed as Business School or Department of Management
- 44 listed as University or College
- 10 as NGO, foundation, network, or association

Geographical distribution

- 4 African partners
- 25 Asian partners (5 are also Global Compact participants)
- 5 Australian/New Zealand partners

- 2 Caribbean partners (1 is also a Global Compact participant)
- 2 Central American partners
- 99 European partners (30 are also Global Compact participants)
- 2 Middle East partners
- 72 North American partners (11 are also Global Compact participants)
- 18 South American partners (5 are also UN Global Compact participants)

111 have filed information at their participant profiles and 7 institutions have submitted annual progress reports

UN Global Compact: 298 academic partners

Geographic distribution

- 5 African partners
- 51 Asian partners
- 5 Australian partners
- 3 Caribbean partners
- 4 Central American partners
- 129 European partners
- 2 Middle East partners
- 53 North American partners
- 46 South American partners

24 have filed an activity report under the Compact's COP programme.

9 Corporate responsibility and the business school agenda

BIRGIT KLEYMANN AND PIERRE TAPIE
(WITH A COMMENT BY ERIC CORNUEL)

A situation of real failure

In times of an acute moral and material crisis such as the one we are witnessing today, it is a very sobering experience to come across work dating from years ago where the tendencies which eventually led to the present crisis had been clearly identified. One such sobering read is the autumn 2002 issue of *Administrative Science Quarterly*. A large section of that issue was dedicated to a discussion on the role of the organization in society, and the function of teaching and research in this. An article by Hinings and Greenwood (2002) first gives a historical overview of the times when there was no Organization Theory but a budding discipline called Sociology of Organizations. Soon, however, the sociological focus was lost, giving way to more pragmatic, managerial perspectives. The Sociology of Organizations, a discipline dedicated to the understanding of a system, moved towards what in a rather unfortunate choice of terminology is today frequently called 'Management Science', often dedicated to pragmatic questions of 'usefulness'. The viability of this trend was questioned by the authors contributing to the issue: 'In particular, the question of consequences, i.e., efficient and effective for whom?, is usually left unasked' (Hinings and Greenwood 2002: 413). A follow-up article by Bartunek (2002) in the same issue then builds on this to ask a number of questions about the role (and the character) of business school professors: '(1) Who are the appropriate stakeholders of research on business and organizations and their impacts on society? (2) What are the implied relationships between organizational scholars and those who manage organizations, as well as other stakeholders of scholarly work? and (3) How is research about organizations and their impacts likely to have, or not have, an impact on its stakeholders?' (Bartunek 2002: 424).

These questions seem to have gained in urgency in view of the current crisis. The increasing number of signatories to the United Nations Global Compact's initiative of six Principles for Responsible Management Education (PRME), which we will briefly introduce later, is one powerful example of a will to profoundly change the very fabric of business education.

It is becoming increasingly clear that the role of education must go beyond the mere teaching of knowledge: places of education should be first of all the places where students are educated to become adult citizens; in other words, men and women who are aware of their double role as both actors and stakeholders. Without simplifying too much, one can say that one problem with business schools' failure to turn out graduates who act in a contextually responsible manner is that the schools have been too often focused on *training*, but not enough on *education*. In a world which is increasingly interconnected, where systems – both technical and social – are becoming more and more complex and non-linear, there are two things in which students first and foremost need to be educated: the first is a *contextual understanding* of the main mechanisms that underlie the dynamics of social and industrial development, and the second is *concern for the common good*. This requires teaching students an awareness of the interdependence between any organization and its physical and social environment. We also need to provide them with the ability to handle managerial tools with the discernment necessary to provide for the good not only of the organization or part of it within a fixed timeframe, but for the good of any stakeholder in the organization itself.

An education that instils in future leaders a concern for the common good cannot be considered as optional today, for two reasons: First, the end of the Soviet Union twenty years ago, and the transformation of China, have established the free market economy as the dominant if not unique economical system in our world, and any striving for justice has to be generated from within the system itself – in other words, from the people who generate and manage it. Second, the powers of private corporations have never been so large, and these powers are ever-increasing. Today more than half of the 100 largest economic entities are corporations, not nation-states, and this proportion is increasing. The frontiers between public and private goods or matters handled by companies are increasingly blurred, as private firms deal with public utilities, health services, research and even armament and defence. Educating executives for the common good is an essential remedy, one that resides and acts from within the company, to protect the free market economy against its own excesses – from excessively greedy behaviour, which would jeopardize the political legitimacy of the liberal economy itself, causing it to be rejected by voting citizens or elected politicians.

Like other places of higher learning, business schools are, for better or worse places of socialization. It is no good to advocate smaller or larger adjustments to business school curricula – an ethics module here, an elective on Corporate Social Responsibility (CSR) there. This, however well intentioned it may be, just treats the symptoms, over and over again, as the recent proliferation of case studies on the subject shows. But these kinds of additions to curricula, well meant as they are, remain at a surface level and amount to highly insufficient, and ultimately ineffective, *bricolage*. What is needed is a profound change in the way business schools contribute to academia, and to society at large.

Business schools are missing the point

As an interesting paradox, it can be noted that within the academic community at large, business schools are lagging dramatically behind in terms of awareness of, and commitment to, action in response to current problems – be they acute, as the recent financial crisis, or slowly but surely advancing, such as global warming or the increasing scarcity of natural resources. One should expect that these issues are known to the educated population of any Western country, but clearly there is a wide gap between theoretical knowledge and actual certainty, and an even wider gap from there to taking action. Consciousness of the urgency with which remedial action must be instigated is in the greater academic community much higher among engineers and natural scientists (scholars and students), in terms of both values, information and commitment, than among scholars and students at business schools. There are rational reasons for this situation.

In the natural sciences, increasing efforts and monies are directed to research measuring global environmental changes, and in the engineering sciences we can observe a strong upsurge in R&D work on new green technologies. Compared to this, it is quite interesting to see how little business schools have reacted to the recent dramatic changes in our social and physical environment. At the risk of greatly simplifying a complex matter, one can say that the aim of the sciences is the development and extension of knowledge about the world, of technologies to create new options. They are on a quest for understanding – while business academia has been increasingly concentrating on *production and operation*: the production of 'functional elites' – in other words, technocrats, servants to a system. While business schools say that they take their clues from the demands of industry and pride themselves on their links with the corporate world, the information on what kind of student to educate, which they get from industry, is frequently very short-term orientated. Business schools are quick to come up with electives and whole new Masters' programmes whenever an industry, or a technology, appears to gain prominence – one only needs to look at the upsurge in programmes catering to the telecommunication-related sectors or modules in event management.

This certainly bears testimony to their fast reaction times, and more deeply to their commitment of educating graduates who have *relevant* competences, as expressed by their employers. This situation creates an 'egg and chicken issue' where, if the education system is just providing what the economy asks for, the system tends to be structurally conservative. We are reminded here of Streeck's analysis of vocational education training going 'from low-skill equilibrium to wrong-skill equilibrium' (Streeck 1989). This trend, rooted in a noble commitment (providing relevant education), counteracts – if it does not actually forbid – business schools' commitment to the education of mature and responsible men and women who have acquired solid thinking skills enabling them to act with wisdom in an increasingly complex world. We would like to make the provocative point here that wisdom in action might in fact not consist at all in jumping onto the ever-faster-moving bandwagon of organizational entanglements and the pursuit of growth for its own sake, but possibly in a slowing down of the whole process, or in inventing other forms of development. This requires *courage* and *discernment* – something no current highly specialized intensive and narrow-focused executive programmes can teach.

Business schools are missing the point, and the reasons for this can be found in the way that they are embedded within, and interact with, corporations and society at large, and also in the way they recruit and groom their academic staff. A large proportion of the business schools around the world have behaved as almost exclusive servants to the paradigm of shareholder value, much in line with Milton Friedman's famous postulate: 'there is only one social responsibility of business – to use its resources and engage in activities designed to increase its profits so long as it stays within the rules of the game, which is to say engage, in open and free competition without deception or fraud' (Friedman 1970). Students are mostly taught methods and mindsets geared to the maximization of this one core criterion and the optimization of ways to reach it, while the majority of their fellow citizens are challenging this principle.

A similar picture emerges when one browses through a typical business school's course catalogue. Courses are increasingly taught in highly compressed ('intensive') modules, leaving students no time for reflection, consideration, or further reading around the topic. There is a strong focus on the teaching of technical skills and hence the increasing offering of high-tech teaching methods, the flood of textbooks filled with ever-more attractive graphics, the surge of case studies and the proliferation of course titles all promising to impart, within a fixed timeframe and with minimal pain inflicted to the student, immediately 'useful' knowledge on topics ranging from 'Doing Business in India' to 'Motivation and Rewards Systems'. Of course modules like these do have their place in a business school curriculum. But practically relevant though these types of courses certainly are, the knowledge they impart is detailed and limited, and ultimately even useless beyond the very narrow confines of their topic, especially when the students exposed to such concrete knowledge have never been trained in understanding the larger context of the world in which they are supposed to deploy their tools. It is almost as if foremen on a construction site were trained in the handling of tools without ever giving them a feel for architecture, nor an idea of the climate in which the building will stand, nor any hint on the kind of function the building is meant to provide. In short, what has been crucially missing is attention to teaching students the appropriate *wisdom of using* these tools.

The question we dare to ask here is whether business academics are acting truly according to their initial vocation as scholars and educators, or whether in reality they are mainly marketing themselves and their institutions, incurring in the process the risk of pandering to the lowest common denominator. The harsh truth is that we as business schools are, on average, no better or worse than the business leaders we have educated. Our mission should be that of providers of a public good – we give actors in business and society an education, knowledge, ideas and – ideally – the capability to act with discernment and wisdom. Many business schools do, however, behave as producers of a private commodity in the form of more and more streamlined degrees – from MBAs to PhDs and the increasingly popular, because it is supposedly more 'functional', Doctor in Business Administration (DBA). Especially on the research side, doctoral students and professors alike pursue their work on the basis of pragmatic concerns such as the 'usefulness' of the research to industry or its publishability in a small set of journals. Very little work in business schools is done out of a thirst for knowledge or a desire for the understanding of a system: Many courses are offered, and many papers are written, on topics that discuss 'how-to' questions: how to manage a merger, how to pursue a policy of employee diversity, etc. But too little research work, and almost no teaching, is dedicated to understanding the system itself: questions like 'what is the *raison d'être* of the firm?' or 'how and why do organizations develop?' receive little interest. They are not taught because they are of no apparent immediate use to students. They are not easily publishable in key journals because these kinds of topics defy the general requirements for quantitative, testable and empiria-driven research wedded to frequently wholly inappropriate but popular paradigms that are typically a precondition for publication.

What we need in business schools is more critical and detached thinking. Business schools and the corporate world currently form a closed, self-referential system; and such systems are ultimately destined to stagnate or to be forced into drastic changes by new key actors. If we want to educate business leaders for the common good, scholars have to re-address the purpose of the company itself, the yardsticks of their successes, of our students' successes and of our own success. Educating wise, not greedy leaders is a matter of global public concern. Business schools must be educators of thought leaders – and not purveyors of 'operational' staff with little fantasy or courage to seize the status quo and strive to change it for the better. We would like to point out here that the founding fathers of economic thinking in the eighteenth century were philosophers as well as economists.

It would be too easy to blame the malaise of business schools on the corporate world alone. In fact, much of it is home-made: if we take a critical look at the way most business schools are organized and run, we face a significant contradiction. While desiring to educate responsible businessmen and women and cater to academic excellence in research, the business models of our academic institutions are such that they require a never-ending race to raise more funds, to pay academic staff, to ever improve on advertising and to generally compete with one another. We are creating a prisoner's dilemma situation for ourselves, imposing huge tuitions fees on students, eventually graduating them with heavy debts, and encouraging greed among our own faculty through highly competitive remuneration schemes which all too seldom take into account the quality of teaching and dedication to a role as educators and mentors.

This attitude is encouraged and proliferated through the press who, in an attempt to ever-improve their ranking systems of business schools, often use students' salaries upon graduation and their increase during their time at the business school as a yardstick for business school quality. The lack of a direct link between a manager's salary and his or her ability to do the job well, or his or her social usefulness and leadership potential, has become all too clear in the light of the recent corporate scandals, but the obsession with graduates' salaries continues to hurt our freedom as educators.

Often our institutions have become slaves of rankings – with the only beneficiary of this being the press, knowing that magazines with rankings in them sell well. European schools resisted these trends up to the late 1990s. They have since given in to them with a relish.

Towards a new approach to education

The purpose of business should become again the creation of economic and social progress in a sustainable way: the present crisis should encourage us to overcome the short-termist and reductory – myopic – focus on shareholder value and return to wisdom. There is, however, a very real impediment to this with many companies just struggling for life in the current climate. A major risk of the current crisis is that nothing will change, because companies are engaged in a daily fight for survival and the reconstitution of their financial position as quickly as possible. There is a real risk that over the next five years to come, firms will deny the need for a profound cultural change.

If firms do not have the time, the foresight, or the resources to re-think themselves, change must come from the men and women who will eventually join their workforces. Business schools must assume the role of a spawning ground, and a catalyst, for corporate change. How can this be done? We still sound provocative if today we say that, for example, eighteenth-century philosophers and the wisdom of the East must have their place in a business school curriculum, but the proposal is not as other-worldly as it might sound to many. We need a deep review of the instrumental approaches we have been locked in for so long. We need to re-instate contextual understanding, discern-ment, courage and a sense of stewardship in the way we train our stu-dents. A business school education should contribute to what can be subsumed under the twin headings of 'Knowledge' and 'Stewardship', which we consider to be the key characteristics of a responsible and effective business leader which a business school can and must help to develop.

Knowledge

In an age where terms such as 'knowledge management' and 'learn-ing organization' are highly popular labels used very liberally by management schools and consultants alike, it might be interesting to call to mind the German philosopher Max Scheler (1874–1928) who distinguished between three closely related and mutually contingent kinds of knowledge, namely '*Bildungswissen*' (knowledge acquired through formation and training), '*Leistungswissen*' (knowledge for achievement, such as science) and '*Heilswissen*' (knowledge for salva-tion, knowledge of the essentially Good, the basis of discernment). This distinction is remarkable in that it disconnects knowledge from immediate social or material contingencies. Knowledge is a value in itself; it is what makes a man or a woman a fully human being. Knowledge goes beyond the mere know-how of the praxis of surviv-ing in a certain environment. Knowledge, in the way Scheler and many other philosophers understand it, is a man's or a woman's participa-tion in the *Noosphere*, the sphere of thought; it is through knowledge that he or she participates in the co-creation of the world. Never has this been felt more intensely than in today's so-called Information Age. Information needs knowledge – the 'Bildungswissen' to acquire and handle the information, the 'Leistungswissen' to use the information and the 'Heilswissen' to do so with discernment and an awareness of an ultimate Good. Information without knowledge is just chatter, and blind reaction to this information takes away much of the dignity we assume when we call our species *homo sapiens*.

Stewardship: the steward as co-creator of an evolving social system

Related to this is the requirement for students to conceive of organizational systems as something dynamic. Snapshot approaches such as the much-loved matrices are nice initial stocktaking tools, but do little to foster an understanding of evolutionary dynamics and non-linear systems behaviour. Rather than reducing it to a few bullet points on a matrix, students should be encouraged to actually *embrace* complexity. One way of bringing this home to students is to physically expose them to this complexity: business schools cannot overemphasize the importance of life experience to their students. Students must be required to experience, and live with, different cultures. Exposure to different countries and a requirement for at least two foreign languages is very important, but we must go further: students must get to know the context of society. Exposing them to the 'other' by making them experience less favoured strata of society or, for example, by requiring them to engage in humanitarian projects or take the 'opposite' point of view by working for an NGO will help them to see their own ambitions in context, understand the interconnectedness and interdependence of *all* strata of society, and take stock of the full measure of responsibility they will hold once in a corporate position. We could also introduce them to other ways of conceiving of the world around them, by exposing them to the actual production and appreciation of arts, music, paintings, dance or poetry. The idea is to invite them to discover *beauty*. An appreciation of what is beautiful gives a sense of contextual harmony – a sense very much needed by anyone who aspires to lead a complex social system.

Embracing complexity and acquiring a feel for what co-creation actually means requires learning how to choose. It is through choice and living with that choice that a person gets to know himself or herself. There must be a dialogue with oneself prior to engaging in dialogue with the environment. Wisdom requires self-knowledge, and self-knowledge can arise only out of the progressive construction of freedom. In that perspective, students should be exposed to a flexible programme, allowing them to create their own learning experience within a challenging and high-standard framework. A leader can lead only if he or she knows freedom with its possibilities, its limits and its restrictions: Encouraging students to construct and pursue their own challenges can help in this.

Linked to the last point is the immense value of a mentor: sadly, as schools have become larger and teaching has all too often acquired the forms and procedures of a mass-processing practice, this feature of a classical humanist education has all but been lost in most institutions. It is high time to revive the tutor who accompanies, challenges and encourages the student, who does not judge but who holds a critical but well-meaning mirror up to the student and thereby induces him or her to take a detached – but not non-attached – look at his or her own place and path in the system. This requires certain changes in the way we rate our academics. Being a first-rate researcher and producer of concepts, or an inspiring teacher, or an excellent mentor are very different things, grounded in different attitudes and talents. Business schools must recognize this, and introduce a wider plurality of criteria for their staff excellence.

Lastly, a capable leader is a whole human being. A business school cannot stop at conveying knowledge without making sure that this knowledge will have the soil to take root. As humans are mental as well as physical beings, a certain harmony between the two aspects is required. Students should be actively encouraged to seek a certain fitness for life, in terms both of life-style to retain physical health and stamina (stamina does not come from vitamin supplements, as many students appear to think, rather it comes from an inner attitude – the Eastern traditions have much to teach us there) and in terms of mental resistance to outside aggression: this aggression comes in many shapes, in a constant bombardment with ideas, fads, institutional pressures and all sorts of physical and conceptual noise. A leader must learn to be himself or herself in spite of this sort of aggression. Physical and moral courage – and, importantly, an outlook of tender if slightly melancholic irony towards the follies of the world – are qualities that any actor in the modern world will dearly need. We are strongly reminded here of Plato's call for 'philosopher kings', and the study of this concept would certainly be a worthwhile addition to any business school curriculum.

Business schools as catalysts of a paradigm shift: the PRME ambition

Importantly, it is not just the brain's capacity for knowledge that made the human being truly human. The hands were just as important in the evolutionary process, and it is here that we see a chance for the role of business schools – with their rather praxis-orientated outlook – to become incubators and catalysts of a new approach to organizational citizenship. While, traditionally, universities have concentrated on theory development based on experimental or conceptual research and the subsequent bestowing of this knowledge on to students, business schools have followed a more hybrid model in that they were more closely interlinked with business – in other words, knowledge produced here frequently comes from interaction with students (especially those who are taking post-experience courses) and the outside world.

There is more of a push–pull relationship between business schools and their environment, and while there is the danger of the establishment of a closed system mentioned above, this set-up can also be a great opportunity: schools can assume the role of catalysts, and co-creators, of a paradigm shift. Co-creation rests on two conditions: interdependence and differentiation. In other words, business schools can and must benefit from their entwinement with the corporate world, but they must also retain their difference as places of reflection, experimentation – and, importantly, as places sheltered from the immediate pressures of time, shareholders and marketing fads. The place of a business school is neither in the ivory tower nor in the boardroom, and certainly not on the trading floor – be it the trading floor of money or that of fashions, rankings and quick fixes. Our plea is not so much one for a complete and revolutionary change in business schools, but rather one for the *return of the business school to itself*. We need hands *and* brains, method *and* wisdom, as Indian philosophy has it, and the *raison d'être* of a business school is that of a meeting place of these requirements for sustainable social evolution.

How can this concretely be done? First of all, we would like to go back to our argument for a focus on an improvement in students' contextual understanding. Tools are useless – and often outright dangerous – unless the practitioner understands what their use will do to the whole system. Without wanting to digress too much into pedagogical detail, we think that a prime immediate target for classroom change can be in the way case studies are used. The problem with the way most case studies are currently set up and used is that they tend to invite reductionist approaches: students are trained to identify problems, and find solutions, within the much-reduced micro-universe of twenty or so pages and more or less large attachments with graphics and concrete but narrow statistics. We would advocate a different case methodology which requires students to do their own research on an organization and, importantly, on its contextual environment. The focus should be on the context and embeddedness of the firm and stakeholders: using perspectives such as the Resource Dependence Theory or Neoinstitutionalism could be helpful. We have to train our students both to *read* the complex world, and to be at ease in *thinking* the world.

We would also like to advocate an increase in more contextually orientated modules in the curriculum. Much can be learned from history and philosophy; a course on the comparative history of capitalist systems, a module in inter-religious studies, a workshop on Plato for managers, or a reading seminar on the writings of Dag Hammarskjöld, one of the great models of a responsible leader, are just a few examples.

Taking up again the twin requirements for knowledge and stewardship, we can sum up the seven key tools which a business school can give to a student in order to prepare them for a truly useful, and personally satisfying, role in society:

1. Experience at international and intercultural level
2. Exposure to the 'other', dealing both with human suffering and the beauty of the Arts
3. Encouragement of creativity in thought and action
4. Alternating exposure to work and academia, 'thinking' and 'doing' (e.g. through internships, etc.)
5. Encouragement of choice: giving students the opportunity to personalize their course
6. Personal mentoring to train discernment
7. Training mental and physical stamina: this includes self-discipline and the courage to preserve independence of thought.

Conclusion

Business schools should go beyond teaching. They should raise aspirations in the sense that they must provide the mental grounding and self-confidence in students to go beyond the immediate and the short term, to seek more than a small set of criteria. So far, we have been too busy producing skilled operators for a system that has proven to be ultimately unstable and dysfunctional. We should now look to produce leaders in the sense of the word. A man or a woman can be a capable leader only if he or she has the will, the creativity, the skill and the courage to transcend the status quo.

This challenge is demanding and difficult. We have grown and developed ourselves in tight symbiosis with our business environment, and thus strong reactions on our part could be perceived as jeopardizing this proximity. As business schools, we have to reinvent how to manage our ambivalence: proximity to the real organizational world without losing our academic character, which resides neither in the ivory tower nor on the trading floor. Because the business world is changing quickly, and because the political legitimacy of the free market economy is at stake, the key question is whether business schools will be foresighted and brave enough to tackle these massive challenges, or whether they will stay in their present narrow-minded instrumental approach which is becoming more and more obsolete. If they manage to change quickly enough, they will enlarge their scope and credibility; if, however, they refuse, they will be eventually overtaken in credibility by other academic players such as colleges of arts and sciences or schools of political sciences, because economic leaders today have to understand deeply both technology and politics.

This invitation to change has been at the core of the writing, by a group of academics, of the PRME in 2007, under the umbrella of the Global Compact. The main aim of these six principles is to propose that business schools enlarge their mission and the goals they are implicitly educating their students towards. Principle 1 summarizes the spirit: 'Purpose: we will develop the capabilities of students to be future generators of sustainable value for business and society at large and to work for an inclusive and sustainable global economy' (see also chapter 8 by Regina Wentzel Wolfe and Patricia H. Werhane). The proposal of a mission statement for business schools as a community to educate future leaders creating sustainable value for business and society obviously broadens the traditional scope of business schools, and emphasizes their *de facto* political horizon.

An interesting and encouraging observation is that the very best students among the new generation do ask for such changes. They are more open to issues concerning the common good, and more demanding for *meaning* in what they undertake. The finest employers are paying attention to those trends to attract the best talents. It is likely that those business schools that will be perceived as the leading ones in the twenty-first century will be those able and committed to engage in mastering the challenge of social complexity and responsible leadership in a creative and proactive way.

Welcome to a world that moves towards sustainability.

Management education and corporate responsibility: the role of EFMD and the GRLI (a comment by Eric Cornuel)

Introduction

The European Foundation for Management Development (EFMD), though a quintessentially European organization based in the European 'capital', Brussels, is also truly international, with over 700 members in 80 countries. These members cover academia, business, public service and consultancy. Over the past forty years EFMD has provided them with a unique network offering information, research and debate on innovation and best practice in management development. Key to this endeavour is EFMD's determination (reflected in its wide-ranging membership) to encourage cooperation and dialogue between academia and business. And as part of its overall remit it has always been committed to creating a relevant and diverse network that shared a common objective of developing effective and socially responsible leaders and managers.

It was in this context that in 2003 it signed a partnership agreement with the Global Compact that subsequently led to the innovative international Globally Responsible Leadership Initiative (GRLI) and the development and formulation of the Principles for Responsible Management Education (PRME), which were presented to UN Secretary-General Ban Ki-moon in July 2007. During the same period EFMD has also been a strategic partner with the European Academy of Business in Society (EABIS) and together they have conducted two surveys on 'Business in Society and Corporate Responsibility Research, Education and other Initiatives in Business Schools and Universities'. The findings from the latest survey feature in the European Business in Society Gateway which was launched in 2009.

EFMD's long-standing interest in and support for issues around CSR, business ethics and the like also informs its role as a leading figure in the drive for quality standards in higher management education through accreditation processes such as EQUIS (European Quality Improvement System), EPAS (EFMD Program Accreditation System), CEL (teChnology Enhanced Learning) and CLIP (Corporate Learning Improvement Process). In all cases, quality assessment is defined not just as compliance with minimum standards, but as the attainment of a high threshold of quality or excellence as measured against best international practices.

Launched in 1997, EQUIS is central to EFMD's mission of improving the standard of management education worldwide. Covering all programmes offered by an institution from first degree to PhD, EQUIS accreditation has been awarded to 117 institutions from 34 countries, all of which have demonstrated an overall high quality in all their academic activities, a large degree of internationalization, a balance between high academic quality and the professional relevance provided by close interaction with the corporate world, and commitment to responsible leadership in the academic and business worlds (see box 9.1 for a discussion of CSR within EQUIS).

The definition of transnational quality standards and quality assurance processes provided by these accreditation schemes will allow European and other institutions to learn from one another and to advance more quickly up the quality curve. In Europe specifically, the aims of the Bologna-inspired reforms can be achieved only if quality improvement and institutional development are placed at the heart of the national legislation that is being introduced in each participating country.

Responsible management education: the impact of GRLI

EFMD's interest in the firm's role in society and the implications for management education and development goes back to the 1970s and 1980s. But it has gained a new impetus with the partnership agreement with the Global Compact and the creation of GRLI and the PRME. GRLI was launched in 2005 by a global group of schools and companies convened by EFMD and the Global Compact. Today the initiative has concluded its 6th General Assembly and produced outcomes and results that will drive the development of a future generation of

Box 9.1: CSR within EQUIS

EQUIS standards and criteria are based upon the EQUIS framework, which consists of eleven separate areas for assessment. One of the areas covers 'Contribution to the Community' and pays attention to the issue of CSR, as a matter of both policy and practice. The concern for CSR will be evidenced not only in a school's approach to the education of future managers, but also in its behaviour within its own environment. The latter is covered in the assessment criteria on (a) community outreach and external relations; (b) extra-curricular activities; and (c) services to education.

Evidence of the commitment to ethical and socially responsible business practice is requested in all of the other areas but the chapter on 'Contribution to the Community' also includes a section on CSR. A description of a school's policy in this area is required. The school should list the initiatives that it has taken in implementing this policy: does the school partner actively with companies and organizations in promoting ethical behaviour and CSR? How are issues relating to ethical behaviour and corporate responsibility integrated into a school's degree programmes, executive education activities and research? How does a school show practical concern for the environment in its operations?

Within the other assessment areas, there are criteria/questions specifically relating to CSR issues:

- Does a school's governance practice and strategy statement formally encompass the area of CSR?
- Does a school educate its students to act ethically in their professional lives? Values such as integrity, respect for others, socially responsible action and service to society should be an integral part of the personal development agenda. Schools should be able to describe the means by which issues relating to business ethics and CSR are integrated into personal development processes.
- Does the course design and content explicitly include aspects of corporate responsibility?
- Does a school have a code of ethics or related document?
- Do any research projects relate to CSR?

globally responsible leaders. The GRLI community today consists of more than sixty companies and business schools/learning institutions from five continents, reaching more than 300,000 students and a million employees.

The mission of GRLI is to be a catalyst to develop a generation of globally responsible leaders. As such, it is a pioneering select group of companies and business schools/learning institutions engaged 'hands on' in that mission. To do this it is challenging the issues facing the company in the twenty-first century, the mission of business schools/learning institutions and the process of cultural change in organizations.

The vision of GRLI is to build a world where leaders contribute to the creation of economic and societal progress in a globally responsible and sustainable way. Its goal is to do this by developing the next generation of globally responsible leaders through a worldwide alliance of companies and learning institutions, networking, acting and learning together to implement and promote globally responsible leadership. Specifically, it intends to build a body of knowledge on globally responsible leadership, develop globally responsible learning initiatives and promote the goals of the Initiative.

The challenges facing humankind are large, undeniable and global. Economic, social and environmental inequalities abound and are increasing. Businesses are among the most influential institutions worldwide. They have a tremendous opportunity to shape a better world for existing and future generations. Business schools and centres for leadership learning can play a pivotal role, alongside business, in developing the present and future leaders required to ensure that business is a force for good.

Decisions made by globally responsible leaders rely both on their awareness of principles and regulations and on the development of their inner dimension and their personal conscience. These characteristics can be informed and developed through dialogue and debate – and essentially through experiential and challenging confrontations. Guiding principles that establish a starting point for globally responsible leadership include: fairness; freedom; honesty; humanity; tolerance; transparency; responsibility and solidarity; and sustainability. These are not fixed ethical points but need to be constantly refined and developed.

All learning institutions need to make corporate global responsibility *their* responsibility. GRLI offers a foundation for how to develop

– in practice – the purpose of the institution, the curriculum, specific programmes, faculty, alumni and relations with the local community and society at large. Change can be driven by inspiring, involving, influencing and interconnecting with internal and external stakeholders. Globally responsible behaviour must be internalized within the conduct and activities of the people within the institution. Business education needs to be broadened to reflect the global business environment and the knowledge, skills and attributes required of the globally responsible business leader.

Last but not least, a range of innovative approaches to pedagogy and learning needs to be tested and utilized that engage more of the whole person in the learning experience. However, we should be clear that a commitment to CSR and responsible management, though essential, is not in some way a substitute for traditional sound management practices. Being a good corporate citizen does not automatically make for a good corporate performance at the balance sheet level. Damage is caused by mismanaging the core business not by a want of CSR focus. Creating a sustainable business must be the first priority of a business manager within the framework of broader CSR practices.

This means that in a dynamic and unstable world, sound management practice is more important than ever. This is why the role of management education, which alone can combine and inculcate both best practice in management skills and in CSR, is vital. Nor should we forget the role of management research and its dissemination through journals – and, perhaps just as importantly, via magazines and newspapers. The current crisis has done nothing if not show us that understanding and managing complexity in our interconnected world is a huge challenge.

Corporate responsbility and the role of management education

Rethinking the context of management education

Developing the competencies, capacities and attitudes required for a future generation of globally responsible leaders requires more than relying solely on the simple acquisition of knowledge. Experiential, presentational, propositional and practical ways of learning must be integrated into the curriculum. One of the problems of management education remains its continuing (though reduced) emphasis on the trappings of functional disciplines when in reality managers work in a cross-disciplinary, even multi-disciplinary, world. Many different elements interact to make managers capable of a broader view.

The top business schools of the future will have to train their students to meet the demands of an increasingly complex world and in doing so they will use challenging and innovative approaches to management education. They will implement substantial changes in the ways they prepare the next generation of leaders. In particular, they will, and should, put globally responsible leadership and corporate responsibility at the heart of the business school curriculum. This will also present the schools with an opportunity to expand and enrich their academic offering and to employ new pedagogical approaches.

While some schools are already employing multi-disciplinary approaches to learning, the topic of corporate global responsibility presents a further opportunity for integrated learning and for cooperation between traditional business school subject areas. Corporate global responsibility requires both the knowledge and application of learning to a diverse set of business topics. Studies in this area provide an avenue whereby business schools can move beyond functional boundaries to holistic practice.

The successful business schools of the future will offer to their students innovative programmes backed by the appropriate resources to guarantee an excellent faculty body, an international experience and a multicultural environment. The top business schools of the future will not only implement changes to remain competitive but they will seek accreditation and quality improvement programmes to prove to the market that they are committed to excellence and innovation. But as business schools struggle to increase funding and spending to achieve greater value propositions, they will also need to adopt strategies that will allow them to differentiate themselves from their competitors and prove that value.

Quality will become an ever-growing concern for business schools, in particular with regard to measures for determining and improving the quality of programmes. The most competitive schools are already looking for benchmarking opportunities as well as quality improvement programmes that will provide them with an opportunity to gain a thorough understanding of their strengths and weaknesses, to develop new and better programmes and to prove the level of their offerings to the market through accreditation. Students and faculty will also benefit greatly from having tools that aid them in their choice of institution and programme.

The link between the business and the academic worlds must also be strengthened and redesigned. It is clear that there is a need for a consultation process to discuss the definition of strategic objectives, the development of shared infrastructures and the production of competencies. This means that greater mutual understanding must be achieved, not just in general terms but also in specific areas such as recognition of the necessity of fundamental research and its connection to a productive economy.

Learning institutions are often criticized for a lack of focus on (individual and team) human resource management (HRM). In a context that has become increasingly international and multicultural, they tend to follow a functional and quantitative approach. Ethics and entrepreneurship also appear neglected. One study based on numerous in-depth interviews with top managers has corroborated these suspicions. According to the study, graduates, especially from MBA-type courses, are considered overly analytical and functionally specialized, crucially lacking in practical and decision-making aptitudes and in the ability to communicate and adapt to an international context. Many of these criticisms are aimed at business schools in North America but Europe has also encountered – and continues to face – similar problems. Institutions have, however, done some remarkable work, supported in this by international accreditation systems.

EQUIS, in particular, which mainly focuses on corporate and international relations, has been a strong change driver and has undoubtedly brought about an improvement in European management teaching and research. Changes in French Grande École business schools over the past decade are a particularly good illustration of this, with today's institutions having truly integrated the dimensions mentioned above into their daily regimes.

The role of an academic/corporate partnership
One main priority for businesses should be to fund their sources of future competitiveness via an educational system producing the best managers in the world. Nothing can be done without commitment from both academic institutions and corporations themselves, who need to rethink deeply their different roles and contributions to

society. Not paying attention to broader demands in an era of globalization would be downright suicidal.

Companies (and organizations in the broadest sense of the term) must be much more integrated into professors' teaching and research concerns, and not only as fields of investigation. This is a pre-requisite if we ever hope to see companies become important actors in institutional funding and governance. Europe and its further progress must also be at the centre of institutions' vision and communications. Last but not least, institutions, as opinion-makers and centres of thinking, must also contribute to certain societal debates, with corporate social and societal responsibility clearly being a key theme for institutions of management learning and research.

Management education in Europe already presents an excellent 'return on investment' in all of its dimensions. Despite this, adaptations will become increasingly necessary, especially since a homogeneous European higher education system will certainly attract new competitors. To face these challenges, our institutions must demonstrate sufficient creativity and inventiveness to evolve towards a new paradigm, one that is more in sync with the realities of today's and tomorrow's global competitive dynamics.

10 | NGOs and the United Nations Global Compact: the link between civil society and corporations

ODED GRAJEW

Introduction

The United Nations Global Compact gathers companies from all over the world around the commitment to respecting and complying with its principles towards a more sustainable and inclusive global economy. The Global Compact signatories include business organizations from varied cultures and from countries presenting different levels and models of economic and social development. Each of these countries has laws that set forth minimum parameters the companies must comply with as well as inspection mechanisms for compliance with such parameters and penalties for those trying to get away with behaving against the law. However, Global Compact signatory companies are expected to comply with the ten Principles even if the legal requirements of the countries in which they operate are lower than the commitments proposed by the pact.

The Global Compact Principles are guidelines for companies' responsible action. When we refer to 'social responsibility', it is important to make clear that we mean voluntary initiatives, adopted as a choice that goes beyond a legal obligation. After all, the social responsibility realm starts where legal requirements end and it is ruled by principles and values deemed fair and necessary. It is in this sphere that non-profit and non-governmental organizations (NGOs) act.

The Global Compact unites a significant number of NGOs under its umbrella. Currently, more than 75 global NGOs and almost 600 local NGOs from a variety of countries are participating in the initiative. Although NGOs and companies have not always had a peaceful relationship, the social responsibility field fosters a convergence of goals. More than that, NGOs can help companies move forward in their commitment to the Global Compact in three realms. The first one is the realm of *knowledge*. NGOs have shown worldwide their ability to raise important issues as well as generate and diffuse information, their expertise, analysis and problem-solving methodologies. Therefore, NGOs can help companies rethink their social and environmental practices and redefine them towards complying with the ten Principles.

The second realm where NGOs can help companies achieve the ten Principles of the Global Compact is the mobilization aimed at *creating an environment* that is favourable to achieving these principles and, at the same time, unfavourable to certain practices deemed socially and environmentally irresponsible and even criminal, which harm the social rights of more vulnerable populations or the environment. The creation of this favourable environment, as shown below in some processes underway in Brazil, can go far beyond mobilization and denunciation, taking the role of articulating major market segments in the creation of more sustainable production relations. Finally, the third contribution of NGOs is *setting examples*, becoming a model of how the ten Principles can be put into practice and setting the standard for companies and organizations as a whole in the principles' application. Next, these three realms will be discussed in more detail, with the presentation of real cases and exemplary results.

Pointing out routes

Every company tends to concentrate its energy and expertise on its business – that is its focus. It is challenging for companies, by themselves, to generate specific knowledge about good policies regarding human rights or the environment, or about how to offset the impact of their activities on the communities or, even, how to add value to all stakeholders, promoting the sustainable development of the surrounding communities. These are some examples of the application of the ten Principles of the Global Compact. Likewise, companies hardly invest in the development of concepts and management tools that include the ten Principles in their everyday management, or of stakeholder communication models that ensure transparency or stakeholder engagement. These are concrete areas where NGOs have a lot to contribute to companies.

There is a large number of civil society organizations working on deepening one or more of these themes – childhood protection, decent work, equity and diversity in work relations, mitigation of environ-mental damage and environmental conservation, communities' social development and capacity-building for employment and income gen-eration, food security, education and health programmes to employees and the community, etc. – developing key specific knowledge so that companies can move forward in the implementation of the Global Compact Principles and in communication with society.

In Brazil, a good example is the 'Ethos Institute for Business and Social Responsibility', a non-profit NGO that is working on the pro-duction and collation of knowledge that contributes to encouraging responsible action towards society as a whole, the environment and their stakeholders, as well as to developing a sustainability-orientated corporate culture. At its foundation in 1998, the Ethos Institute had only eleven associated companies and faced a situation in which the concept of corporate social responsibility (CSR) was practically unknown and companies' social actions were mistaken for philan-thropy. The institute currently encompasses around 1,350 companies accounting for 35 per cent of Brazilian gross domestic product (GDP). Social and environmental responsibility has become a permanent theme on the agenda of companies and Brazilian society.

Over the past ten years, Ethos' first major task was to disseminate among companies and Brazilian society the need for and feasibility of socially and environmentally responsible corporate behaviour. It was a phase of persuasion and guidance about what companies could do. With this in mind, Ethos promoted seminars and open debates, developed studies based on the idea that the business world can act pursuant to ethical principles and in a responsible manner regarding the environment and all its stakeholders. Many handbooks have been published to guide companies on how to behave in different situa-tions, consolidating the knowledge accumulated by civil society in its various organizations.

As part of its contribution to the development of a new business management vision based on social responsibility and sustainable development, Ethos also developed management and diagnostic tools following international standards, as well as tools for communicat-ing these new practices to society, such as the *Ethos Indicators on Corporate Social Responsibility* and the *Social and Sustainability Reporting Guide,* annually updated, and improved and enhanced from time to time.

Besides large companies, Ethos has also sought to disseminate social responsibility practices among micro and small enterprises which are the major employers in the country. For this purpose, it partnered with the Brazilian Micro and Small Business Support Service (Sebrae) to develop a specific dissemination programme for this segment, as well as versions of the Ethos Indicators adapted to this kind of business. Currently, the Brazilian business environment can count on a wide range of management tools to assist companies of all sizes, from early starters in social responsibility up to sustainability reporting according to the Global Reporting Initiative (GRI) Guidelines.

As a matter of fact, organizations from all over the world and of all sizes nowadays publish annual reports aimed at showing the advances achieved regarding a more sustainable economy. In order to increase the credibility of these instruments, companies can count on NGOs with acknowledged know-how and practices to audit the reports in their expertise areas. For the sake of transparency and credibility, companies operating in different parts of the world should publish reports specific to each country, audited by local NGOs. Financial reports are already prepared with a local focus, thus showing how viable this can be for social reports.

The Global Compact itself should not acknowledge reports of multinational companies (MNCs) made in a generic manner, with no details for each region where the company operates. Despite all the clear major differences among countries such as Kenya, Brazil and France, for instance, the approach to the ten Principles should be the same in each of the countries. As the realm of social responsibility starts where the realm of legislation ends, companies cannot hide themselves behind local legal differences to explain their different procedures in several parts of the world.

Creating a favourable environment

One way that NGOs can help companies put into practice the Global Compact Principles is by creating a favourable environment for this to occur and, at the same time, creating a highly unfavourable and restrictive environment for practices that harm the ten Principles. Historically, civil society organizations' reports of economic power abuses all over the world have been the starting point for defending those affected by such practices, and their review and replacement with friendlier stakeholder relations. Certainly, the articulation and mobilization power of NGOs can go far beyond denouncing and mobilizing public opinion, by creating more lasting and sustainable pacts and engaging business organizations, government and civil society organizations.

In Brazil, through its strategy of disseminating the CSR concept, the Ethos Institute has helped to create a favourable environment for the development of good management practices by opinion-makers, investors and consumers. For opinion-makers, it systematically carried out initiatives involving the media and academia – those accounting for the future staff of companies, as well as initiatives aimed at the professional people directly responsible for the daily management of companies. In this area, Ethos created the *Prêmio Ethos de Jornalismo* (Ethos Journalism Award) for news on corporate social responsibility practices published in different media. It established, in partnership with the *Valor Econômico* newspaper, the largest Brazilian daily business newspaper, the *Prêmio Ethos Valor Social* (Ethos-Valor Award), aimed at acknowledging the academic research made by undergraduate and graduate students focused on socially and environmentally responsible business management. In the field of media specialized on companies and business, the Institute contributed to the development of publications such as *Guia Exame da Boa Cidadania Corporativa* (Exame Guide on Good Business Citizenship), which in 2007 broadened its focus and became the *Guia Exame de Sustentabilidade* (Exame Guide on Sustainability), publishing a ranking of companies with outstanding sustainability practices. *Exame* magazine is the most important Brazilian business magazine.

The Ethos Institute also created the *Akatu Institute for Conscious Consumption* to value socially responsible practices among consumers. It is a non-profit, NGO focused on raising awareness of consumers both to demand more commitment from the companies and to value those who are socially responsible. One of the results of the work with investors was the promotion of the *Prêmio Balanço Social* (Social Report Award), a partnership among the Ethos Institute, the Association of Investment Analysts and Professionals of the Capital Market (APIMEC), the Brazilian Association of Business Communication (ABERJE), the Social and Business Development Institute Foundation (FIDES) and the Brazilian Institute of Social and Economic Analyses (IBASE).

The most significant work in this segment, though, was in the capital market, involving the São Paulo Stock Exchange (Bovespa) as well as several civil society and market organizations. It resulted in the creation, in 2005, of the São Paulo Stock Exchange Corporate Sustainability Index (ISE), a stock portfolio of companies that manage their business according to social and environmental responsibility criteria. To build the index, shares of around 30 companies are selected from among the 150 companies with the highest levels of liquidity at Bovespa and best sustainability practices according to the Ethos Indicators, among others. Through the ISE, the capital market now acknowledges and values the companies that integrate sustainability into their business strategies.

As important as, or even more important than, creating favourable conditions for corporate responsibility practices, NGOs are able to mobilize broad segments of civil society, public power and companies to halt or prevent practices harmful to the ten Principles of the Global Compact. Examples of such pacts include the corporate pacts against child labour and forced labour, the pact against corruption and the pacts to defend the Amazon, which include the soybean moratorium and, the recent timber, cattle-raising and soybean pacts that are already established.

Improving labour standards: case examples

The first experience of a pact involving NGOs, companies and the public power was the one aimed at fighting child labour, led by the Abrinq Foundation for the Rights of Children and Adolescents. The Abrinq Foundation is an NGO established in 1990 as an initiative of businesspeople from the toy sector (members of the Brazilian Association of Toy Manufacturers). It was founded in the same year that Brazil approved the Statute of Children and Adolescents (ECA), a legal instrument that sets forth parameters to defend and protect this vulnerable segment of the population. The Abrinq Foundation's performance played a key role in the dissemination of ECA and the inclusion of the elimination of child labour on Brazilian society's agenda. It became a landmark in the defence of rights and protection of children and adolescents in the country.

In 1995, the Abrinq Foundation created the Child-Friendly Company Program around fundamental principles, such as not exploiting child labour and not hiring adolescents in activities deemed unhealthy, hazardous and in night shifts. Companies also commit to demanding compliance and monitoring their production chains; contributing to raising clients', suppliers' and communities' awareness about the harmful effects of child labour; developing education and health actions to the benefit of children and adolescents, for both employees and the surrounding community. Companies who comply with these principles become Abrinq Foundation accredited and entitled to bear the Child-Friendly Company label on their products, an edge that adds value to the brand and provides recognition by consumers and the public opinion as a 'good' company.

The strategy used to build this pact was exemplary and became a model for other pacts. The first step is identifying a blameworthy and even criminal practice, such as child labour or forced labour along a production chain, and recording the data in an unequivocal manner. The second step is going public: presenting the information to the companies that belong to the production chain (especially the large ones), public agencies (such as the Public Prosecutor's Office and the Ministry of Labour), society as a whole, international organizations (such as the International Labour Organization ILO), and even governments of other countries. Usually, child labour and forced labour do not occur in companies at the end of the production chain, but in the intermediate links. When confronted, large companies usually deny their involvement or excuse themselves saying that they were not aware of the fact.

This occurred, for instance, with multinational car manufacturers operating in Brazil. One link of its production chain, the charcoal plants in the State of Mato Grosso do Sul – the charcoal feeds the iron and steel plants that produce raw material used to make the chassis – used child labour under extremely unhealthy and hazardous conditions. Although the companies stated that they did not employ children in the manufacturing of their cars, part of their production chain did so.

The idea of disclosing the production chain links in which child labour, or forced labour, is being used breaks this circle of ignorance and hypocrisy, making the leading companies formally aware of what is going on and making them commit to acting to prevent it from continuing. NGOs have carried out similar actions in the sugar cane, orange and charcoal sectors, among others. The performance of the

Abrinq Foundation and the Child-Friendly Company Program made it clear that the large companies, or those at the end of the chain, are responsible for what goes on in their production chains, and need not only to monitor their suppliers but also to contribute to their development, by having them commit to the Global Compact Principles. In order to change the situation, companies must also commit to working on child protection with employees and their families, their suppliers and other stakeholders, such as the surrounding communities and customers. Once again, the NGOs' contribution is paramount and indispensable.

The Brazilian National Pact for the Elimination of Slavery, signed in 2005 by companies, government, NGOs and the ILO, was born out of an investigative report published in the *Observatório Social* magazine, an NGO linked to the Unified Workers Confederation (CUT), which showed the use of forced labour in pig iron production in Carajás, the largest charcoal reserve in Brazil, from where Brazilian and international companies extract iron ore to be used in the Brazilian iron and steel industry, and from there in the car manufacturing, civil construction, machinery and equipment industries, being also exported to manufacturing plants all over the world.

The report proved to be correct and was widely publicized, including to the governments of the USA, Italy, Germany and Sweden, countries where the parent companies are based. The cars are manufactured in Brazil and exported to several parts of the world, including the countries where parent companies are located, making use of forced labour in their production chains. There were serious repercussions in the iron and steel sector and the reaction was positive: the large companies committed to fighting forced labour and seeking to change the conditions that allowed its occurrence.

Forced labour has also been identified in other sectors such as textile, meat and grains. During 2004, the NGO *Repórter Brasil* mapped the business relations of rural properties mentioned in the two first versions of a 'Forced Labour Blacklist', organized by public agencies, listing the companies where the presence of workers in a condition similar to slavery was tracked down. The NGO followed the production flow lines of these companies up to retail and exportation. The connections were checked and evidenced, resulting in the business profile of around 200 companies. Again, the companies at the end of the production chains, such as exporters, retailers and large companies, stated that they were unaware that their suppliers, whether direct or indirect, made use of slave labour at some stage of their production.

The Ethos Institute, besides articulating the pact, which involved companies, the Public Prosecutor's Office, unions, government and the ILO, has also prepared a draft describing the basic commitment made by all parties to eradicating forced labour, working to fight poverty in the production chain and promoting decent work. The pact was successful in the iron and steel sector. The Citizen Charcoal Institute (ICC) was established with the aim of inspecting suppliers, listing those having decent work relations and developing the work of social insertion of workers that have been freed from this production chain, offering legal openings for these workers with social and labour protection. The textile sector has signed a similar pact.

The government has played an important role in the good results achieved: both the Fernando Henrique Cardoso administration, which acknowledged the existence of forced labour, and the Lula administration, which increased four-fold the inspection and intervention of public agencies for combating this crime, took action. The official 'Forced Labour Blacklist' helped NGOs and governmental agencies map, inspect and denounce companies in both the country and in the international market, and also helped involve the financial sector. The government prohibited banks and development agencies from making loans to companies listed in the Forced Labour Blacklist, which made the Brazilian Federation of Bank Associations also commit to not making loans to these companies.

Defending the Amazon: case examples

The Amazon has one of the highest biodiversity levels on Earth and is the home of hundreds of indigenous peoples and other traditional communities, such as the riverside and extractivist populations. In addition, it is critical for the conservation of water resources, rain and wind cycles and for the climate balance of the planet as a whole. However, in recent decades the region has been harmed by the expansion of soybean and cattle-raising. Forests have been cut down and replaced by cultures and grazing through burning and the operations of illegal logging companies, which also extract commercially valued species and chop down the surrounding vegetation.

The pacts to defend the Amazon have been led by civil society organizations. The first one was the Soybean Production Moratorium – an agreement articulated by Greenpeace, involving the Brazilian Association of Vegetable Oil Industries and the National Association of Cereal Exporters. It was born out of a report published by Greenpeace in April 2006, following twelve months of investigation that denounced the Amazon's invasion by soybean farmers and detailed how the international demand for the grain feeds the forest devastation and encourages illegal deforestation, illegal land occupation and exploitation ('grilagem'), forced labour and violence against local communities.

The soybean planted in deforested Amazon areas are exported to feed animals in Europe that end up on supermarket shelves and fast-food networks. In May 2006, Greenpeace blocked Cargill's terminal in Santarém, State of Pará, halting for a few hours the unloading of soybean cultivated in deforested areas of the Amazon. International repercussion was immediate. McDonald's was the first to respond to the pressure by eliminating soybean from the Amazon from its supply chain. It was then followed by several European and Brazilian food companies that engaged in the initiative. Greenpeace articulated a Network of business organizations that started to require guarantees from their Brazilian suppliers that the soybean they sell does not cause Amazon deforestation and complies with the national laws in force.

In July 2006, the Brazilian Association of Vegetable Oil Industries and the National Association of Cereal Exporters, accounting for over 90 per cent of the Brazilian soybean production, and their respective associates, including the main international soybean traders, such as Cargill, Bunge, ADM, Dreyfus and the Brazilian group Maggi, announced a two-year moratorium on the purchase of soybean from deforested areas of the Amazon as of that date, and the exclusion of farms from their supply chain that use forced labour.

As with everything involving the Amazon, monitoring the pact is complex and expensive. Hindrances include land regulation, and measuring cultivated areas and their changes. The pact was renewed in June 2008, showing it is possible to ensure food production without cutting down one more single hectare of forest. Enhancing this pact by involving other production sectors operating in the Amazon was the purpose of the workshop 'Sustainable Connections: São Paulo–Amazon' which discussed the role of the city of São Paulo in both the devastation and the preservation of the Amazon. As the largest economic zone in the country, the city is also the largest and most important consumer of products from the Amazon Rainforest.

Promoted by the *Movimento Nossa São Paulo* (Our São Paulo Movement) and the Amazon Forum, the event gathered businesspeople, civil society and public power representatives who discussed a pioneer study, carried out by the NGO *Repórter Brasil* and by *Papel Social Comunicação* which showed who benefits from the Amazon deforestation and the social and environmental impacts on the forest caused by agriculture and animal husbandry and extractivism. The work identified companies that kept in their production chains land owners and rural investors caught by the public power committing environmental crimes and making use of forced labour. It also showed that at the end of these chains, large supermarket networks, developers, civil construction and agribusinesses companies benefitted from these crimes, which end up involving the residents of the largest consumer centre of the country – the city of São Paulo.

In order to halt deforestation and related environmental and social crimes, three business pacts and one governmental commitment were proposed, involving the timber, cattle-raising and soybean production chains, civil society organizations and government agencies. The draft documents demand that signatories commit to funding, distributing and selling only 'origin certified products' or those undergoing a regulation process that their suppliers are not on the Forced Labour Blacklist or do not have land with activities suspended by the Brazilian Institute of Environment and Renewable Natural Resources (IBAMA). The pact signatories also commit to carrying out awareness-raising campaigns aimed at their consumers and suppliers in order to engage more companies.

Large supermarket retail networks immediately engaged in the soybean and cattle-raising pact. Large cold-storage plants, accounting for 80 per cent of the meat supplied to São Paulo, also agreed to sign on. However, many producers are still reluctant. Just like soybean, cattle-raising has been one of the drivers of deforestation in the Amazon: the meat supplied for the São Paulo population has one link of its production chain in the Amazon region. Like in the other pacts, the main constraint on controlling the cattle is tax evasion. Cattle-raisers oppose ensuring traceability of their cattle, although they make it quite easy to comply with the legal sanitary requirements.

The soybean segment, though more organized and counting on its Soybean Production Moratorium experience, has resisted. The Ethos Institute, a member of the Amazon Forum, and the Sustainable São Paulo Institute, responsible for the executive secretariat of the Our São Paulo Movement, produced seventeen draft versions of the soybean pact, but until late 2008 the Brazilian Association of Vegetable Oil Industries, the representative of the large crushers of the grain, had not signed the document. The deadlock was the proposal that pact signatories should no longer sell soybean originated from farmers whose products are suspended by IBAMA, regardless of the location of the crop. In other words, if a farmer grows soybean in Paraná in a legal manner, but does the same in the Amazon in an illegal manner, then all soybean will be refused.

Nevertheless, since large supermarkets who have signed the pact may procure soybean-derived products from other more sustainable sources, and consumers are being mobilized to join this effort, the prospects are good. If we compare these three segments, the timber pact has the best chance to mobilize as the sector is already well organized. There are sustainable management areas of natural forests, a strong sector of planted forests with certified management, a consolidated experience of custody chains and a sufficient offer of certified wood to ensure prices at levels equivalent to the current ones – the forest species offered may be different, but it is a matter of adaptation. It is proposed that this pact move forward to certify the origin of all wood that is utilized.

The constraints on forest raw materials' traceability are related to legalizing the business and to tax evasion that affects a large part of this production chain. In order to face them, it is necessary to ensure inspection that prevents documentation forgery and the attempts to fill the management areas with woods sourced from deforestation. At the other end of the line, consumers must demand certification of the wood they buy, whether as furniture or for their houses. The São Paulo civil construction sector is the largest consumer of woods sourced from deforestation areas of the Amazon. To change this situation, the public power has to link the occupancy permit to evidence that the wood used in construction is not sourced from deforestation areas. However, if the Movement for the Defence of the Amazon manages to control the entry of wood into São Paulo, this will have an effect on the rest of the country.

Meanwhile, the local administration of São Paulo (a city with 11 million inhabitants), made the commitment to monitor its purchases so that no product acquired would be contaminated in any stage of its production chain by the illegal deforestation of the Amazon and with unacceptable labour practices like forced labour and child labour, and to improve the legislation so that the economic activities in the city will contribute to the sustainable development of the Amazon.

The power of example

The third realm in which NGOs can contribute so that companies comply with the Global Compact Principles is the power of example. Besides NGOs, the foundations and institutes connected to CSR, the churches, the pension funds, the United Nations itself and the various supranational sectoral organizations can show the way to become more transparent organizations, setting the example of how to put the ten Principles into practice.

All these organizations should, for instance, disclose the criteria used to choose the companies where they invest their funds. Currently, many of these organizations delegate these decisions to specialized financial agents. As a result, although they fight for human rights, they may be investing in very profitable companies whose production chains take advantage of forced labour or child labour, or disregard diversity or the rights of women and minorities, or have predatory environmental relations. To prevent this from happening, they should know in the first place where they are investing and should demand transparency from both companies and their value chains.

NGOs, foundations, churches and supranational organizations also have a wide range of suppliers of goods and services and should disclose the contractual requirements they impose on these suppliers, the degree of control they have over their production chains and how their agreements are inspected. Finally, these organizations should be transparent in their decision-making, hiring and HRM processes, setting an example of Global Compact Principles' application. The Principles of the Global Compact have all been developed, acknowledged and implemented thanks to the initiative, effort and commitment of countless civil society organizations. Only with the engagement of these organizations will it be possible to have these Principles implemented so that business and market can actually, and not only on paper, be socially responsible.

11 Financial markets and the United Nations Global Compact: the Principles for Responsible Investment

JAMES GIFFORD

Introduction

The Principles for Responsible Investment (PRI) are aspirational guidelines for institutional investors on integrating environmental, social and governance (ESG) issues into investment processes and ownership practices. Launched in April 2006, the PRI Initiative has grown to become the largest investor effort focused on addressing ESG issues. As of early 2010, the initiative has over 700 signatories representing assets of US$20 trillion, constituting close to 20 per cent of global capital markets. This chapter tells the story of where the PRI Initiative came from, where it is now, and where it is heading.

Origins of the PRI

In the 1990s and early 2000s, responsible investment in all its various forms experienced strong growth. Socially responsible investment (SRI) – primarily values-driven and retail investor-focused – had a small, but established foothold in many developed markets. Shareholder activism – particularly by US pension and SRI funds – was being conducted on a range of issues from ESG disclosure to corporate governance to labour standards, with increasing numbers of shareholder resolutions filed at US companies each year. In the early 2000s, a number of large UK fund managers began to engage in dialogue with companies on ESG issues and had established dedicated teams to conduct these engagements. Clean-tech and investment in renewable energy was taking off. Climate change was emerging as a major issue and a regulatory momentum was evident.

During this period, the debate around environmental and social issues started to shift from questions of ethics to questions of good governance, long-termism, risk management and emerging opportunities. Mainstream, financially focused institutions started for the first time to concentrate on the materiality of ESG issues to the long-term financial performance of companies, based on the premise that those companies that managed environmental risks and relationships with employees, stakeholders and regulators well would deliver higher returns at lower risk than their peers.

Many of the Social Investment Forums (SIFs) around the world had been operating for many years, promoting socially responsible and ethical investment. By 2003, some of them such as the Sustainable Investment and Finance Association (UKSIF), the Association for Sustainable & Responsible Investment in Asia (ASrIA) and the European Sustainable Investment Forum (EuroSIF), had started to engage the pension fund and mainstream fund management sectors.

A number of other investor initiatives focusing on ESG issues emerged during the early 2000s. In the USA, Ceres – a coalition of investors, companies and civil society groups – initiated the Investor Network on Climate Risk (INCR), a Network of mainly public pension funds. The Carbon Disclosure Project was established to use investor leverage to seek disclosure of carbon emissions by companies. The Pharmaceutical Shareowners Group (PSG) was in dialogue with global pharmaceutical companies on access to medicine in the developing world, the Extractive Industry Transparency Initiative (EITI) was addressing corruption and facilitation payments in the extractives sector in Africa, and the Institutional Investors Group on Climate Change (IIGCC) was bringing European investors together to promote public policies to address climate issues. The common theme with all of these developments was an increasing focus on the economic and financial implications of many issues that had previously only been viewed through a values or ethical lens.

Governments had also started to move on this agenda. A number of countries had introduced disclosure regulation requiring pension funds to disclose the extent to which they were integrating ESG issues into their processes. While these regulations did not prescribe specific responsible investment approaches, they were seen as a clear signal from the government that responsible investment by pension funds was indeed legal and generally supported by governments.

While there was strong growth in responsible investment, on the whole, it was still very much in its infancy. The paradigm of shareholder engagement and active ownership – whereby investors use their position of influence as owners of companies to improve performance in a range of areas – was limited to the few mainly English-speaking countries, as well as a few organizations in the Netherlands, Switzerland and Scandinavian countries. Within all these countries, this was still only at an early stage. The notion that ESG issues could be material to long-term investment performance and should be integrated into mainstream investment processes remained the view of a small minority of investors. There was also no framework bringing all these activities together. There were no global guidelines or principles to point investors in the right direction or to define what responsible investment is, particularly as it related to mainstream investors.

The United Nations recognized the potential for investors, particularly those with a long-term outlook such as pension funds, to contribute to sustainability and good governance, and began to explore how it could promote responsible investment. In 2002, the UN Environment Programme Finance Initiative (UNEP FI) established its Asset Management Working Group, made up of representatives from mainstream and SRI fund managers whose goal it was to mainstream the integration of ESG issues into investment management processes. In 2003, the Global Compact initiated a dialogue with the finance sector on the importance of ESG issues in financial analysis within the 'Who Cares Wins' initiative. In December 2003, the Institutional Investor Summit on Climate Risk, chaired by Kofi Annan and organized by Ceres, convened some of the largest North American institutional investors and fund managers to discuss the financial implications of climate change. In mid-2004, the United Nations launched a number of initiatives that paved the way for the emergence of the PRI. The UNEP FI Asset Management Working Group launched a fourteen-month study by mainstream analysts of the materiality of ESG issues to equity pricing. The Global Compact launched the 'Who Cares Wins' report (Global Compact 2004b), which included a series of recommendations on how to integrate environmental, social and governance issues into analysis, asset management and securities brokerage, endorsed by the CEOs of more than twenty global financial institutions.

These publications concluded that:

- ESG issues can be material to investors, especially over the long term. Investors who do not take these issues into account are putting the interests of their beneficiaries at risk and may be overlooking key opportunities.
- There is a need for better-quality and more comparable information on the ESG impacts of companies if investors are to assess the significance of these issues to their investments.
- While voluntary initiatives such as the Global Reporting Initiative (GRI) have been providing standardized reporting frameworks for companies, the overall level of disclosure remains limited, and not focused on investor needs. In addition, more investor resources need to be applied to the interpretation and evaluation of this information.
- Institutional investors, especially when working together, can have significant influence as owners and clients over companies, fund managers, consultants and brokers and can use this influence to encourage improvements in ESG performance by companies.
- Frameworks for collaboration among institutional investors are important in increasing the effectiveness of shareholder and policy-maker engagement, allowing the pooling of investor resources, reducing the 'free-rider' problem and facilitating the participation of the many smaller institutional investors that do not have the in-house expertise to research, evaluate and engage in dialogue with companies. These collaborative platforms are generally missing from most markets and on most issues.
- Capacity-building is required on a global basis. While there is significant experience with implementing responsible investment by some institutional investors in a small number of markets, the industry is generally at a very early stage. There is significant potential to leverage existing experience to form the basis of a global collaboration and capacity-building programme.

Based on these conclusions, UNEP FI and the Global Compact decided in mid-2004 to move ahead with a major UN initiative to promote responsible investment globally, the first step of which would be developing a set of principles for responsible investment. It was felt that the United Nations was well positioned to promote responsible investment within the mainstream investment sector, and in particular, promote collaborative shareholder engagement and integration of ESG issues among pension funds and their managers. Some of the justifications for initiating the PRI process at the time included:

- Investors need common frameworks that they can use to work together. In the case of pension funds, not all trustees will have the skills, time and resources to develop their own guidelines and UN-backed principles would provide a sound basis for investors to develop their own policies and approaches to addressing ESG issues.
- The PRI would be a natural extension of the Global Compact Principles, applicable for investors, and build on the work of UNEP FI with asset managers.
- The development of these principles would provide an ideal platform on which to build a global network of investors to work together on ESG issues, pool resources and share costs of activities such as collaborative shareholder engagement.
- An important outcome of such a network would be the internationalization of the debate on responsible investment through bringing developed, emerging and frontier market investors together to discuss opportunities and threats around cross-border investment.

It was also felt at the time that there was an urgent need for globally relevant, high-quality resources on best practice and tools for implementation of responsible investment. The proposal to develop the PRI was announced publicly in July 2004 by the Executive Director of the United Nations Environment Programme (UNEP), Dr Klaus Töpfer, joined by a number of leaders from the investment community.

Development of the principles

The PRI drafting process was undertaken over a one-year period from early 2005. An advisory group of thought leaders was set up to guide the process in the early days. This group felt strongly that the drafting process had to be led by the asset owners – primarily pension funds – that sat at the top of the investment chain. The idea was that if the asset owners really bought into this agenda they would ensure that the rest of the investment chain (asset managers, investment consultants, research providers, etc.) would follow. Conversely, if fund managers and service providers were driving the process, it was felt that the initiative could end up focusing on a commercial product and service orientation rather than on addressing systemic market failure, and that this would not result in the type of industrywide reform the UN agencies were seeking.

There were two groups set up to draft the Principles: a twenty-person investor group of mainly pension fund CIOs, CEOs and trustees, and a larger, seventy-person expert group, consisting of specialist and mainstream fund managers, NGOs, academics, consultants and other relevant stakeholders. The investor group was given the final say over the text. The process was undertaken over nine days of meetings. Participants were invited in their personal capacities. The stated goal was to develop principles that reflected best practice which, if implemented across the board, would improve financial returns as well as delivering ESG outcomes.

The first Expert Group meeting, where participants brainstormed structured questions in groups of ten, developed the key points that were seen to be core to a set of Principles for responsible investment. The output of the first Expert Group meeting set the tone for the PRI and sketched out what would ultimately become their key elements. The group recommended that the Principles should commit investors to:

- Integration of ESG issues in investment analysis (which became Principle 1)
- Active ownership: shareholder engagement and voting (which became Principle 2)
- Transparency of investor and investee company ESG performance (which became Principles 6 and 3, respectively)
- Sending signals throughout the investment chain that ESG issues need to be incorporated (which became Principle 4)
- Measures against 'short-termism' for long-term investors (touched on in Principle 4 but rejected as a principle of its own)
- Assessment of ESG impacts on: (1) investment performance, (2) corporate behaviour and (3) the environment and society (all touched on in Principle 6 but not thoroughly)
- Responsiveness to beneficiaries' needs and preferences (ultimately rejected)
- Incorporation of international norms such as the Global Compact, ILO Core Conventions, Universal Declaration of Human Rights (UDHR), etc. (ultimately rejected except in so far as Principle 3 seeks disclosure from companies on performance against such norms).

The clearest area of divergence and debate was, predictably, the degree to which investors have responsibilities to go beyond the exclusive *financial* interests of beneficiaries. Some argued that investors have an obligation to incorporate the broader interests of beneficiaries, society and the environment into their investment decisions. However, many of the large pension funds and mainstream fund managers argued that the Principles would only ever be adopted if they were firmly within the scope of fiduciary duty, and that it was therefore necessary to remain focused on financial risk/return objectives. It was clear that many of the mainstream funds would have great difficulty signing up to an explicitly normative or ethical approach. There was, however, agreement that even within the paradigm of the 'exclusive (financial) interests of beneficiaries', there was significant scope to integrate ESG issues into investment and active ownership processes. The paradigm that was adopted was that ESG issues are potentially material and are not being adequately incorporated into mainstream investment and ownership processes, and therefore, doing so should enhance risk-adjusted returns *and* deliver ESG outcomes over the long term.

Some also argued that the 'best interests of beneficiaries' should be interpreted more broadly, and that it made no sense for pension funds to deliver strong financial returns to their members while at the same time contributing to degrading the world into which those members would retire. While there was some sympathy for this view, it was felt by the more mainstream investors that going beyond financial interests of beneficiaries was not part of their responsibility, was difficult to operationalize and opened them up to accusations of political motivation.

One of the most difficult issues discussed during the drafting process was that of investor responsibility for investee company compliance with international agreements on human rights, labour and the environment. For example, to what extent should investors be accountable for the behaviour of their investee companies? If a company is found to be involved in egregious human rights violations, what are the obligations of its investors? There was a belief among many participants in the PRI consultation process that investor engagement to encourage corporate compliance with various global norms was a good thing, and might deliver not only social and environmental benefits – especially in the developing world – but also lay the groundwork for stable economic growth, enhancement of the rule of law and a more favourable investment climate over the long term. Others said that such 'international policing' by investors was beyond their fiduciary duty, that most of these international instruments were designed for countries, not companies, and that investors could not be expected to enforce international treaties. But there was certainly a strong normative thread running through the approaches of a number of mainstream funds involved in the discussions, including large government-related or public pension funds, who felt that the reputational damage or other harm attached to owning the 'worst corporate offenders' was significant enough that a negative screen should be applied.

Another idea that was discussed throughout the drafting process was the 'Universal Owner' hypothesis (Hawley and Williams 2000), which states that highly diversified investors own a slice of the economy, and therefore suffer from negative externalities imposed on the economy by irresponsible corporate behaviour. The financial interests of large investors are therefore more aligned with the economy as a whole than with any one company or sector within it and, as such, these investors have an incentive to push for the reduction of environmental and social externalities arising from corporate behaviour within their portfolios. Once this paradigm is adopted by investors, any corporate behaviour that is shown to impose negative externalities on the economy is potentially harmful to portfolio returns and therefore there is a rationale for investors to act, ideally collectively, to reduce the externality. This view adds another powerful argument for the consideration of ESG issues by large, diversified investors. It is also very much aligned with modern views of fiduciary duty, which hold that the health of the portfolio in its totality trumps the health of individual investments that might be in that portfolio. While the Universal Owner hypothesis was discussed at length during the consultation process, it was not included in the Principles themselves, but continues to be an important driver of the PRI's post-launch activities.

The first investor group meeting developed the key philosophies that would underpin the PRI.

- The Principles should be framed in terms of fulfilling the primary responsibilities of the fund (i.e. fiduciary duty)
- The Principles should be aspirational, but contain practical suggestions for implementation
- The Principles would represent a voluntary industry code, but contain a commitment to reporting

- The Principles should have a positive impact on investment performance *and* on the world in which we live.

The issue of fiduciary duty was the single biggest concern of the Investor Group, and it was made clear that they were 'fiduciaries first'. The fiduciary duty issue had to be addressed clearly within the PRI text or it would prevent many pension funds from signing the Principles.

Because of the importance of the fiduciary duty issue, both drafting groups heard presentations from global law firm Freshfields Bruckhaus Deringer on its legal review of fiduciary responsibility (UNEP FI 2005). This review had been commissioned by the UNEP FI Asset Management Working Group in 2005 because the fiduciary issue was clearly the most important perceived obstacle to responsible investment within the mainstream pension fund sector. The review explored the legal basis for the integration of ESG issues into institutional investment, and concluded that integrating ESG considerations in an appropriate manner should not raise any legal hurdles for investors and, where such consideration was financially relevant to investment decisions, it was arguably a *requirement* of fiduciary duty to consider such issues. This turned the fiduciary duty concern on its head by arguing that ESG issues were potentially material to corporate or portfolio performance and that 'traditional' fund management processes were overlooking key emerging issues. Therefore, consideration of such issues was firmly within the bounds of fiduciary duty. While the materiality of specific ESG issues to particular stocks or portfolios is always open to debate, the 'Freshfields Report' provided sufficient reassurance to investors to allow them to feel comfortable with the direction in which the PRI was heading.

There were some other interesting proposals raised within the process but ultimately rejected. These included the notion that investors should commit to seeking out investments or undertaking activities (such as shareholder engagement) that have positive ESG outcomes, as long as there are *no significant negative financial implications* for the fund. That is, if you can do good without losing any money, you should do so. A similar suggestion centred on the notion that, all other things being equal, investors should choose the investment with better ESG performance. It was felt that these ideas were too difficult to incorporate, that no two investments are ever equal and that, furthermore, this could fit within the scope of Principle 1 on the integration of ESG issues into investment decision-making.

The final meeting resolved to deal with the fiduciary duty issue head on, with the group including a caveat in the Preamble and concluding paragraph noting that the Principles should only be applied in ways that were consistent with fiduciary duty. While the final principles were, of course, a compromise, the goal was to create a set of principles that would bring the mainstream on board and develop a global community of investors. The building of this community, with the goal of catalysing a collaborative shareholder engagement culture among the world's largest investors, was the key purpose behind the development of the Principles, as discussed below (see also box 11.1).

The PRI were launched in April 2006 by the UN Secretary-General, Kofi Annan at the New York Stock Exchange (NYSE). The Secretary-General rang the bell to open the day's trading – the first time a UN Secretary-General had done so. Indeed, this was the first official visit by a UN Secretary-General to the NYSE – illustrating the increasing importance of the finance sector to the United Nations and the fulfilment of its goals. The organizations involved in the investor drafting group joined the Secretary-General on the podium above the trading floor and later took part in a signing ceremony. This event was followed a week later by the European launch at Palais Brongniart in Paris, the former Paris Bourse. Another thirty organizations signed the PRI at this event. After the two launches of the PRI, the initiative had fifty signatories, representing US$4 trillion in assets under management.

From words into action

The Principles themselves were originally designed to provide a framework around which to build an active community of investors sharing best practices and, ultimately, pooling resources and influence to seek improvements in the ESG performance of investee companies. It was felt that this community would only develop, and the initiative would only fulfil its potential, if the Principles were backed by a dedicated secretariat tasked to promote them, build the community and coordinate investor collaboration. As soon as the Principles were launched, the secretariat was established and got to work, with the strong support of the UN partner agencies. The initial financial model

Box 11.1: The Principles for Responsible Investment (PRI) and possible actions for implementation

---

As institutional investors, we have a duty to act in the best long-term interests of our beneficiaries. In this fiduciary role, we believe that environmental, social and corporate governance (ESG) issues can affect the performance of investment portfolios (to varying degrees across companies, sectors, regions, asset classes and through time). We also recognize that applying these Principles may better align investors with broader objectives of society. Therefore, where consistent with our fiduciary responsibilities, we commit to the following:

1. *We will incorporate ESG issues into investment analysis and decision-making processes.*

Possible actions:

- Address ESG issues in investment policy statements
- Support development of ESG-related tools, metrics and analyses
- Assess the capabilities of internal investment managers to incorporate ESG issues
- Assess the capabilities of external investment managers to incorporate ESG issues
- Ask investment service providers (such as financial analysts, consultants, brokers, research firms, or rating companies) to integrate ESG factors into evolving research and analysis
- Encourage academic and other research on this theme
- Advocate ESG training for investment professionals

2. *We will be active owners and incorporate ESG issues into our ownership policies and practices.*

Possible actions:

- Develop and disclose an active ownership policy consistent with the Principles
- Exercise voting rights or monitor compliance with voting policy (if outsourced)

- Develop an engagement capability (either directly or through outsourcing)
- Participate in the development of policy, regulation and standard setting (such as promoting and protecting shareholder rights)
- File shareholder resolutions consistent with long-term ESG considerations
- Engage with companies on ESG issues
- Participate in collaborative engagement initiatives
- Ask investment managers to undertake and report on ESG-related engagement

3. *We will seek appropriate disclosure on ESG issues by the entities in which we invest.*

Possible actions:

- Ask for standardized reporting on ESG issues (using tools such as the GRI)
- Ask for ESG issues to be integrated within annual financial reports
- Ask for information from companies regarding adoption of/ adherence to relevant norms, standards, codes of conduct, or international initiatives (such as the Global Compact)
- Support shareholder initiatives and resolutions promoting ESG disclosure

4. *We will promote acceptance and implementation of the Principles within the investment industry.*

Possible actions:

- Include Principles-related requirements in Requests for Proposals (RFPs)
- Align investment mandates, monitoring procedures, performance indicators and incentive structures accordingly (for example, ensure that investment management processes reflect long-term time horizons when appropriate)
- Communicate ESG expectations to investment service providers

- Revisit relationships with service providers that fail to meet ESG expectations
- Support the development of tools for benchmarking ESG integration
- Support regulatory or policy developments that enable implementation of the Principles

5. *We will work together to enhance our effectiveness in implementing the Principles.*

Possible actions:

- Support/participate in networks and information platforms to share tools, pool resources and make use of investor reporting as a source of learning
- Collectively address relevant emerging issues
- Develop or support appropriate collaborative initiatives

6. *We will each report on our activities and progress towards implementing the Principles.*

Possible actions:

- Disclose how ESG issues are integrated within investment practices
- Disclose active ownership activities (voting, engagement and/ or policy dialogue)
- Disclose what is required from service providers in relation to the Principles
- Communicate with beneficiaries about ESG issues and the Principles
- Report on progress and/or achievements relating to the Principles using a 'Comply or Explain' approach
- Seek to determine the impact of the Principles
- Make use of reporting to raise awareness among a broader group of stakeholders

The PRI were developed by an international group of institutional investors reflecting the increasing relevance of ESG issues to investment practices. The process was convened by the UN Secretary-General.

> In signing the Principles, we as investors publicly commit to adopt and implement them, where consistent with our fiduciary responsibilities. We also commit to evaluate the effectiveness and improve the content of the Principles over time. We believe this will improve our ability to meet commitments to beneficiaries as well as better align our investment activities with the broader interests of society.
>
> We encourage other investors to adopt the Principles.

of the PRI was based on voluntary contributions from signatories. This model allowed the PRI to grow from one to twenty staff from 2006 to 2009. However, by 2009 it was felt that the initiative needed to expand further to fulfil its objectives and the PRI Board resolved to move to mandatory fees from 2011.

Clearinghouse

The first priority was to stimulate collaboration among large investors on shareholder engagement with companies, in order to improve corporate ESG performance. Specifically, this involves bringing investors together to come up with shared positions on issues, and then putting direct pressure on investee companies to improve some aspect of their ESG performance. This project became the PRI Clearinghouse, and remains the most important strategic priority for the Initiative. Established in late 2006, the Clearinghouse provides an online forum where investors post proposals for collaboration with peers to seek changes in company behaviour, public policies or systemic conditions, or simply discuss issues of concerns. The Clearinghouse lowers the barriers of entry to active ownership and offers leverage to single institutions that may have a 'good point' that others may not have identified. The tool, starting as a simple online bulletin board, has become an active hub of investor collaboration hosted on a searchable IT platform and supported by a number of dedicated staff. Signatories also have the opportunity to present their proposals to their peers and explore emerging issues in monthly 'webinars' as well as at the PRI in Person annual event. The secretariat also works with signatories to come up with new ideas for collaboration, and ensures they are framed in ways that are likely to gain as much support as possible from peers.

The Clearinghouse, for the first time, has provided investors with a truly global forum for collaboration. As of mid-2009, there have been more than 170 collaborations undertaken within the Clearinghouse across many different regions on topics, including:

- Climate change disclosure and performance
- ESG disclosure in emerging markets using the GRI
- A range of corporate governance issues around board structure
- Executive compensation
- Access to medicine
- Shareholder rights
- Director elections
- Risks and opportunities around biodiversity and ecosystem services
- Encouraging communication on progress by Global Compact participants.

Activities conducted within the Clearinghouse are signatory-led, and with the exception of those promoting the Global Compact itself are not conducted in the name of the PRI or the UN partner agencies, but rather go out under the name of the investors themselves.

Some of the most vibrant collaborations have been based around the Global Compact and its Principles. In late 2008, a group of fifty-two PRI signatories representing US$5 trillion in assets wrote to 9,000 listed companies asking them to join the Global Compact. Within some months, over 100 companies had joined the Compact, and non-responsive companies were followed up throughout 2009. This was the largest mass recruitment effort undertaken on behalf of the Compact.

In 2008 and 2009, Aviva Investors led a PRI collaborative engagement focused on eighty Global Compact corporate participants that were not fulfilling their reporting obligations under the Compact. Working within the Clearinghouse, Aviva put together a coalition of twenty investors representing over US$2 trillion in assets to write to these companies. Around 20 per cent of the targeted companies agreed to fulfil their reporting requirements under the Compact. This engagement did not only focus on the poor reporters; twenty of the most notable reports were identified and these companies were congratulated. Some of the best feedback came from the staff at these companies. It sends a very powerful and positive signal to boards and CEOs when companies are publicly recognized by a large proportion of their investors for their sustainability reporting. Feedback from mid-level staff indicated that this type of positive reinforcement is incredibly helpful internally and is likely to result in increased resources being applied to such efforts.

Some other engagements highlighted in the PRI 2009 *Annual Report* (PRI 2009) include:

- A collaboration launched in December 2008 to encourage some of the world's largest companies to sign up to the CEO Water Mandate, a Global Compact water sustainability initiative.
- An engagement that encouraged major listed companies in Singapore and Hong Kong to improve their corporate governance and transparency in order to qualify for inclusion in the FTSE4Good index.
- A collaborative engagement to promote better and more systematic ESG disclosure by emerging market companies, focusing on South Africa, Brazil, South Korea and India.
- Letters from thirty-six PRI signatories, managing US$757 billion, to all S&P 100 companies asking for material information on how they protect and enhance labour rights for their US employees.
- An ongoing collaboration between ten investors from North America and Europe to engage with financial authorities regarding regulations on acting in concert (i.e. laws that prevent investors from communicating about and working together in their interactions with companies).

The Clearinghouse has been the most important area of the PRI support activity to date, and provides the only global collaborative investor forum on ESG issues. Yet, as of mid-2009, less than a quarter of PRI signatories are actively involved, and the engagements are mostly limited to letter writing. For the Clearinghouse to fulfil its potential, it will require a significant scaling up – in both coordination and intellectual resources – and a considerable increase in the intensity of engagements and the weight of assets backing them.

Other initiatives

The PRI also has a number of other initiatives to support implementation:

- An *Enhanced Research Portal* supports signatories in identifying leading ESG research and integrating it into mainstream fund management processes.
- The *Small Funds Initiative* assists those signatories with limited resources (typically those managing less than US$2 billion) to implement their responsible investment goals by bringing them together to pool resources and share knowledge.
- *PRI in Practice* provides a repository for implementation guidance on all aspects of implementing the six Principles across all asset classes, investor types, responsible investment approaches and regional contexts, with a number of concise and relevant articles and other resources posted every month.
- The *PRI in Emerging Markets and Developing Countries Project*, funded by the Swedish International Development Agency and coordinated by UNEP FI, has allowed a major expansion of PRI outreach and implementation support activities into a number of new markets. There is now considerable PRI momentum within key emerging markets, particularly in South Korea, South Africa and Brazil.
- The *PRI Academic Network* provides a global community of academics and interested practitioners around PRI-related research. It is developing a number of joint research programmes on responsible investment on areas such as engagement, integration and the 'Universal Owner' theory. It is also working to promote responsible investment education in business school curricula, and translating cutting-edge academic research into a practitioner-friendly format and disseminating it throughout the industry.
- The *PRI Private Equity Work Stream* has initiated a dialogue between leading asset owners and private equity firms, resulting in the US Private Equity Council announcing its own set of responsible investment guidelines. It has also published best practice case studies of responsible investment in private equity. This dialogue also led to significant numbers of private equity firms signing the PRI.
- The *PRI Public Policy Network* brings together policy-makers and investors to enhance investor participation in the public policy-making process and to promote public sector/investor collaboration to deliver mutual goals. There is strong interest from the public sector in participating in dialogue on how responsible investment can assist in public policy-making.

Accountability mechanisms

With any voluntary guidelines, one of the first questions that is asked is: 'What if an investor signs up and then does nothing? How does the PRI initiative intend to ensure that its signatories do what they commit to doing?' The main accountability mechanism for the PRI is the annual Reporting and Assessment process. This is based on an annual survey where signatories self-assess their progress against 100 indicators. This self-assessment is supported by hour-long verification calls, whereby around a third of signatories each year run through a selection of their responses with secretariat staff members.

The individual comparative results are not published, but signatories are notified of their quartile position on a per-principle basis, allowing a rough comparison with their peers. While there is an accountability aspect to this questionnaire, the most important function – at least for the first years of the initiative – is to provide a framework for signatories themselves to evaluate and monitor progress, and for the PRI secretariat to assess progress of the initiative overall. Another important purpose of this exercise is to identify leading organizations and best practices so that concrete examples can be disseminated to the signatory body as part of the secretariat's implementation support programme. Finally, the process also provides an off-the-shelf reporting framework for signatories to make disclosure to clients, beneficiaries and the public a simple exercise.

By 2009, the Reporting and Assessment process had been repeated for three years in a row and the data show considerable progress by signatories overall. This exercise is not without its challenges. Some signatories feel that it is too prescriptive and time-consuming, while others feel that signatories should be held more accountable for their progress, and that non-performing signatories should be delisted. With any voluntary initiative, the challenge is to strike a balance between the need to develop a useful accountability and learning tool, and the need to keep the reporting burden as efficient and manageable as possible. To date, the initiative has not sought to define a minimum set of indicators for public transparency, though the PRI Reporting and Assessment process does offer a comprehensive framework for disclosure, and indeed dozens of signatories have chosen to publish their responses to the survey as their public responsible investment report. However, in 2010, investor transparency guidelines will be developed and become part of the mandatory reporting and assessment process from 2011 onwards.

Looking forward: the need for global growth in responsible investment

The PRI Initiative has an ambitious agenda for growth, based on the vision of the PRI as the global, one-stop-shop for responsible investment collaboration and implementation guidance. It has become clear as the PRI expands that these ideas still remain very new in most countries. It is also clear that investors need significant support in implementing responsible investment strategies within their investment processes. The goal is for the initiative to become the leading global hub of investor collaboration, thought leadership and implementation support on responsible investment and a comprehensive range of ESG issues, across all markets and asset classes, working closely with our UN partners. An ESG think tank will be established, providing applied research in support of the Clearinghouse. Implementation support activities will be expanded to cover the full spectrum of asset classes and responsible investment approaches.

The Clearinghouse will remain the core collaborative forum, and grow beyond ad hoc engagements into a comprehensive, thematic collaborative platform, where support for each major theme (e.g. remuneration, climate change, corruption, labour standards, biodiversity, regulatory issues, etc.) is well resourced with dedicated staff and world-class research (through the PRI Think Tank and Academic Network), driving international investor collaboration across all major issues of importance to investors. The Clearinghouse should also develop the capacity to allow signatories to respond quickly to new issues – for example, the next crisis, when it inevitably emerges.

Another area of strategic interest is those investments that not only have attractive returns but also contribute in explicit ways to the goals of the United Nations. The PRI initiative has, to date, been focused on shareholder engagement, integration and transparency. It is now time to look more closely at investments that actually contribute to the development and sustainability agenda, and find ways to link the public and private sectors to invest directly in solving some of the world's largest problems, such as climate change, water and sanitation, poverty and the protection of forests and ecosystem services.

In summary, the PRI initiative has far exceeded expectations. It is an innovative public–private partnership, leveraging the convening power and legitimacy of the United Nations with the power and influence of long-term investors. It has sought out the synergies between the interests of the United Nations and those of investors, particularly over the long term. It has not only survived, but thrived, in a global financial crisis. But the initiative cannot stand still. Most investors have a long way to go before they can stand up and say that their activities represent a truly sustainable approach to investment which takes into account and addresses the challenges facing the world. Responsible investment is still very much in its early days.

12 | Learning from the Roundtables on the Sustainable Enterprise Economy: The United Nations Global Compact and the next ten years

MALCOLM MCINTOSH AND
SANDRA WADDOCK[1]

Introduction

This chapter is about research that we have been conducting about the *next* ten years, starting from three premises. First, given the last ten years and the development of the United Nations Global Compact, what has been learned? Second, what would the world look like if the ten Principles of the Compact were implemented (and the Millennium Development Goals (MDGs) delivered)? And, third, how can we engage with a wide range of thinkers and actors around the world to see if there is commonality across cultures, industrial sectors, professions and intellectual disciplines? Our inquiry started in the House of Lords in London in January 2007, where we held six meetings of Roundtables on Sustainable Enterprise (RSE), and up to January 2009 also engaged with different participants through Roundtables in Cape Town, Toronto, New York, Sydney and Beijing as well as two international conferences at the Eden Project in Cornwall, UK, and at the Headquarters of Wessex Water in Bath, UK.

If we start with the idea that the Global Compact was designed to operate as a learning system, then we can see that it is fascinating to examine it as a model of how the world might be managed this century. The state we find ourselves in as a *global* community, rather than an *international* community, is that states, companies and non-government and non-business organizations *all* have legitimacy, all have a voice, all command attention, all demand to be recognized

---

[1] This chapter draws on Waddock and McIntosh (forthcoming), a book which complements this volume.

and all claim rights and responsibilities. Since the collapse of the financial system in 2008 and the terrorist attacks in September 2001 in New York the state has been reinvented and reinvigorated. And since November 2007 we know that climate change adaptation and mitigation can happen only if the state acts, regulates and delivers the enabling mechanisms necessary to prevent absolute human catastrophe.

Let us also remember that the Compact is just one of a number of contributions to the business in society discourse and action. As such one of the architects of the Compact, John Ruggie put it simply in 2000: 'The issue is how they [companies] make their money.' It is worth quoting Ruggie's argument in full:

As markets are going global, so, too, must corporate social responsibility and citizenship. The Global Compact is one means to that end . . . But is this worthwhile? On that question, where you stand fundamentally depends on where you sit. If you want globalization to work for everyone, as we do, then it is worthwhile. But if you reject globalization, global corporations or even the system of capitalism itself, then you won't like what we're doing at all, any more than your predecessors liked Keynesianism or social democracy because such pragmatic innovations inevitably reduce the social rationale and political support for more polarized rejectionist postures. (Ruggie 2000)

Ruggie made his academic name writing about 'embedded liberalism'[2] which is best linked to the Global Compact in this statement:

The industrialized countries in the first half of the twentieth century slowly learned to embed market values in shared values, principles and institutional practices at the national level. The Global Compact seeks to weave universal values and principles into global corporate behaviour. (Ruggie 2000)

The Global Compact has operated as a significant convening, enabling and learning forum around the world and it is clear that many of the participants would not be discussing human rights, labour standards, environmental protection or anti-corruption without the ability of the United Nations, as the only legitimate international political organization to engage states, companies and civil society.

---

[2] 'The only way ahead was to construct the right blend of state, market, and democratic institutions to guarantee peace, inclusion, well-being, and stability' (Harvey 2005: 10).

In performing this role it continues to complement initiatives at other levels while arguing that it does not undermine those other initiatives, particularly those who would humanize globalization faster than it is at present.

On its tenth anniversary the Compact has remained true to its founding principles, continuing to argue that its legitimacy lies in contributing to a more sustainable and inclusive global economy because business is the primary agent driving globalization. But, in January 2009 UN Secretary-General Ban Ki-moon, following on his predecessor's support for the Compact, told a Davos World Economic Forum 'that the Global Compact provides an excellent platform' for tackling climate change. This reflected the growing realization that 'climate change threatens all our goals for development and social progress' and 'is the one true existential threat to the planet'. So the emphasis of the Compact, and indeed of the whole United Nations, is now on tackling a threat to human life on Earth. Echoing thinking around the world the Secretary-General called for an alignment of capitalism and caring, of humanizing globalization, of creating a capitalism that delivered both public goods and private wealth. The global economic crisis had, he said, provided 'a gilt-edged opportunity' – 'we are at a crossroads' (for all quotes, see United Nations 2009e).

If this is true, that we are at a crossroads, then what have we learned from the last ten years of the Compact's life, and how has the Compact engaged with multiple stakeholders around the world through various activities and initiatives? The most important thing we have learned is that it has been possible to establish an initiative that is based on a set of values, that is founded on a set of internationally agreed principles, that brings together state and non-state participants, that has increased significant debate about how we manage in this age of global trade, that has brought states, companies and people into the debate who might otherwise have not been included (particularly in emerging economies), and that has helped to put human rights, labour standards, environmental protection and anti-corruption on the boardroom agenda in a few companies around the world.

The small Compact team, based in the Secretary-General's Office, has been busy, led energetically by the Chief Executive, Georg Kell. There are some who have criticized the Compact for developing breadth at the expense of depth. These critics argue that there are too many initiatives, too little support, too little thinking through the implications of each of the principles, and too little understanding of how the Compact may have actually interrupted, rather than aided and abetted, progress towards a more inclusive world. The answer to these criticisms is that the Compact was never meant to replace other initiatives, even if at times some of its rhetoric may have seemed triumphalist. Its aim was always as a meeting place for business and the United Nations, and as a learning forum for all stakeholders on taming the beast that is unfettered capitalism.

When former UN Secretary-General Kofi Annan spoke in 1999 about business needing a new social compact with society, he obviously articulated something important to many observers of the world of business in society. Annan's words focused on creating 'a global compact of shared values and principles, which will give a human face to the global market' (United Nations 1999). The thousands of active participants have made it by far the largest corporate citizenship initiative in the world. It now classifies itself as the world's only truly global political forum, as an authoritative convener and facilitator, with the capacity to bring together actors from business, with governments, the United Nations itself, civil society actors, trade/labour unions and academia.

The Global Compact has been much lauded and promoted as an aspirational way of engaging businesses with other stakeholders in dialogue and learning forums, and upholding the ten Principles that are at the core of its work. It has provided forums for learning about how companies – and others – are implementing the ten Principles on human rights, labour rights, environmental sustainability and anti-corruption, and has developed and disseminated numerous tools, analytical frameworks and approaches that signatories can use to ensure that they are living up to their commitments. It has developed formal links with other voluntary multi-stakeholder initiatives on corporate responsibility, such as the Global Reporting Initiative (GRI), and paralleled other initiatives such as the Social Accountability International's (SAI) SA8000 labour standards, and the AccountAbility AA1000 standards, the Extractive Industry Transparency Initiative (EITI), and others.

In building its global and Local Networks, the Compact has fostered shared learning and dialogue among signatories, while finding leading companies to serve as role models for other businesses on the issues of concern. It has explored and raised important issues that were otherwise 'off the table' for many corporations, bringing these issues centre stage onto the tables of directors, managers and boardrooms for discussion – including human rights, participation of business in zones of violence and conflict, water scarcity, climate change, the stability and security of financial markets and their ability to incorporate environmental, social and governance (ESG) issues among numerous others. Through its various Networks and learning forums, it has fostered collaborative, multi-sector approaches to dealing with the numerous issues related to development that are facing humanity.

In 2007, the Global Compact released the Principles for Responsible Management Education (PRME) at its Leaders Summit, as a means of bringing the attention of business school leaders to the ESG issues and principles at the heart of the Compact. Earlier, the Compact had served as a model for what became the Principles for Responsible Investment (PRI), promulgated in 2006, which provide approaches for investment institutions to incorporate ESG issues into their investment decisions.

This chapter is not a descriptive piece. Rather we seek to stand back and provide an overview and some analysis as we reflect from the high ground of hindsight. From where we stand there are a large number of interesting issues that come to mind when looking back at the first ten years of the Compact that might help us guide this initiative for the next ten years. One of the questions that was asked in our earlier book, *Learning to Talk: Corporate Citizenship and the Development of the UN Global Compact* (McIntosh, Waddock and Kell 2004), was: 'What would the world look like if the Compact's principles were adopted and implemented?' In other words, we did not see the principles as utopian but as real, as a possible roadmap for the future evolution of global markets and social progress.

Ten years later there is much to be discussed in terms of the measurable impact that the Compact has had, but one clear message from our global research through the RSE is that the Compact is viewed very differently in different countries. For instance, US companies were slow to sign up partly because they saw the principles as binding them to certain obligations and legal necessities, and thereby making them accountable, and exposing them to possible litigation. In South Africa many of the Compact's Principles are enshrined not just in rhetoric but in the legal framework of the groundbreaking post-apartheid constitution. And in China the Compact is aspirational, a roadmap for the future, a guide as to how newly privatizing companies might see themselves *vis-à-vis* non-Chinese international corporations. The Global Compact is certainly not seen as a set of principles by which to be judged. In the USA, the Compact has been seen as giving corporations more responsibilities but in China it has freed them from some of the obligations that burden them as state-owned enterprises (SOEs) – and these are very real contrasts for the Compact moving forward. Elsewhere in the world the Compact is sometimes not seen as connected to local legal or political frameworks but as a public relations exercise or a leg-up into the world of global corporate operations. We are reminded, however, that according to the United Nations Conference on Trade and Development (UNCTAD) (UNCTAD 2009), there are 70,000 TNCs, of which only a small portion at this writing have joined the Compact.

Accountability – or rather lack of accountability – for signatories actually upholding the Principles of the Global Compact in practice is a serious issue for many Compact critics (Williams 2004). But, as Williams points out, these critics assume that the Compact is a code of conduct, which it is not, rather than the set of aspirational principles that it actually is. Other groups, particularly non-governmental organizations (NGOs), believe that without the enforcement powers that government can supply through mandate and regulation, the Compact can never be fully effective (Williams 2004). On the opposite side of the spectrum, for quite some time after its launch in 2001, US companies were hesitant to sign onto the Compact. Despite assurances to the contrary, it was not clear that litigation could be avoided if the company failed to live up the Compact's Principles, while European companies in a less litigious context were more apt to become signatories (Williams 2004).

Outside the USA people are much more naturally sympathetic to the United Nation's historic and moral mission, and, while acknowledging the organization's shortcomings there is not the aggressive antipathy shown towards its efforts that is displayed in what should be its natural home – the USA. This may be, as Martin Jacques has pointed out, because the United Nations resembles democracy – it speaks its mind – and in doing so challenges the status quo (Jacques 2009). In this respect the Compact speaks to the United Nations' moral foundations and considers international obligations that apply to all economic institutions – governments and businesses alike.

Striking a chord: what does it mean to be human in a globalized world?

Despite all of these and other criticisms, it is clear that the Global Compact struck a chord with many people. What was the chord that struck so deeply and generated so much forward momentum, despite the many critiques that have been levelled against it? We want to argue that it was the very fact that the ten Principles *are* aspirational (and perhaps voluntary) that captured – and still captures – the hearts and minds of so many stakeholders. It is these same types of aspiration – to have a better, more sustainable and more equitable world – that were consistently expressed in the series of RSE associated with the Global Compact held around the world. People are searching for meaning in the world – and particularly in the world of business – and the Global Compact has offered an aspirational hope that business, by living up to the Principles, can supply at least part of that meaning.

The RSE focused on the broader awareness and action items associated with humanizing globalization. Framed around defining the concept of sustainable enterprise, the RSE focused on issues associated with sustainability and climate change, the need to reconstruct multilateral institutions, and learning to live and conduct human affairs, including business, within the Earth's carrying capacity. Structured loosely around the concepts of appreciative inquiry (Cooperrider *et al.* 2001, Cooperrider and Sekerka 2003, Cooperrider and Srivastva 2001), the RSE were an exercise in conversational learning (Kolb 1984). Participants from all sectors – business, civil society, government and multilateral institutions – were invited to participate in a discovery process that focused on defining sustainable enterprise in the global context in which the UN Global Compact arose and is functioning today. RSE were held on all of the world's populated continents – in London, Cape Town, Toronto, New York, Sydney and Beijing with exploratory workshops and seminars held in Barcelona; Hamilton, New Zealand; Coventry, UK; Brussels, Belgium; Boston, USA; and Paris, France.

Polanyi (2001) discussed the great transformation that occurred when new institutional processes were put in place in the industrial revolution and after the two world wars. We believe that we may well be in the midst of the *next great transformation*, a transformation we are calling 'SEE Change' the change to a sustainable enterprise economy. In what follows we present a synthesis of some of the ideas brought out in the RSE, focused broadly around the concepts of the UN Global Compact and its potential to help heal the world. Though these ideas by no means represent a unified consensus, they do suggest important themes that ran through virtually all of the conversations, which were held under The Chatham House Rules, meaning that while ideas and quotations can be used, no attributions will be given.

Two themes, which will be developed in greater detail below, stand out from the RSE. First, there is a need, desire, even thirst, to rethink what it means to be human today, especially in light of climate change, globalization and the growing gap between rich and poor. Second, there are no easy or pat answers to the question of how to redefine being human today, because the situation facing humanity – apparent human-induced climate change, massive processes of industrialization, an established elite that has created an economic structure with obvious flaws but no simple solutions because of entrenched interests – is one that has never been faced by humankind before. Not business, nor government, nor civil society has the answer, so if answers are to be found it will be up to institutions and individuals in all of these sectors to come together and collectively find solutions.

Some of these answers can be found in the integrated systems thinking of the concept of 'human security', which is distinct from national or global security by its focus on individuals and communities. First described by the United Nations Development Programme (UNDP) in 1994 it has been described and refined by writers such as Nobel Economist Amartya Sen and is gaining greater prominence as governments try to make sense of the links between the five challenges to our survival: local and global governance, climate change, water, energy and population (McIntosh 2010, McIntosh and Hunter 2010).[3] The Applied Research Centre in Human Security at Coventry University, UK, describes human security in the following terms:

Human security is a new security framework that centres directly on people and recognises that lasting peace and social justice cannot be achieved unless people are protected from threats to basic needs and rights. Its essence is about protecting people as well as the state. Among the main threats to

---

[3] See also www3.griffith.edu.au/03/ertiki/tiki-read_article.php?articleId=20342 for more information on the perfect storm of the global economic crisis and the climate change prognosis.

people's security are climate change, an inequitable global economic system, bad governance, corruption, abuse of human rights and violence. (Applied Research Centre in Human Security 2009)

What does it mean to be human today?

One RSE participant summed up a sentiment that was richly present in the Roundtable conversations: 'My three and a half year old grand-daughter said, "I'm learning how to be a big girl" the other day. *We* need to learn how to live on this planet, as grown-ups.' We live, today, in a world of both large and small organizations and institutions that collectively create the infrastructure of societies. But the systemic issues facing the planet – from the economic meltdown of 2008 to peak oil and lack of suitable energy alternatives to support the nearly 7 billion people that now live on the planet to growing concern that issues of climate change will not be sufficiently addressed in a timely way – make 'growing up' and facing the reality of the world ever more imperative.

A 24/7 connected world

The problems of the world combine with technological shifts that have created new 'effective communities', things like Twitter, Facebook, MySpace, eBay, global action networks (see also www.scalingimpact. org), instant global communications and ubiquitous phone and elec-tronic technologies, which create a new form of connectivity among people. Voices from the RSE clearly called for a new sense of community and places and organizations that are founded on integrity and authen-ticity in the context of a world where spin, power and competitiveness have heretofore dominated. In a world where many organizations are actually quite dehumanizing places to work, driven by a frenetic energy based largely on cut-throat approaches to competition in a win-at-all-costs mentality, many people appear to be seeking more reflective spaces where human connections, even if virtual, can happen.

Connecting across physical and temporal space in a 24/7/365 economy using the global neural network that the worldwide web constitutes necessitates that individuals (and groups) be able to estab-lish their own boundaries or face burnout. The 'anything goes' men-tality that effectively resulted in the 2008 global economic collapse of

many major financial institutions and which necessitated their being
propped up or nationalized by governments, clearly suggests that
for many those boundaries are not already in place. One reason, we
believe, for the resonance of the Global Compact's ten Principles is
that, despite their aspirational quality, they help to provide a moral
grounding for businesses and individuals working in them. Effectively,
the principles, because they are derived from globally agreed documents, if even more broadly disseminated might provide a moral consensus around business practices that many people, seeking meaning
in their work, would find attractive.

The need for hope

When the conversation turned to what it is like to live in the world
we have constructed today, participants in the RSE agreed that there
is a need for optimism and positive thinking. As one individual stated,
'One of my great hopes for the future is my grandchildren. I love that
quote "Hope is a verb with its sleeves rolled up" . . . The Russians
define pessimists as optimists with information. In interviews for the
radio everyone had something bad to say, but at the end I asked each
of them about hope, and they all have it.'

Another person agreed that 'There is a need for us also to embrace
the positive, to be optimists with hope for change. So many of us are
thinking through "where does the problem lie? Where are the solutions?" We need to embrace the conversation's hope and optimism,
and think how to move that forward to create a critical mass, a different culture of living.' Today's fast-pace, a constant connectivity that
makes 'getting away from it all' virtually impossible for many people
in the developed world, and unceasing change and ambiguity create a
context of uncertainty. People in these conversations are clearly struggling to cope with this world – while simultaneously recognizing that
more than half of humanity faces significantly different and perhaps
even more dire problems associated with poverty, resource scarcity
and *not* being technologically connected in a developed culture.

Elders, technology and knowledge

In much of the Western world, at least, there is a significant orientation
toward valuing youth over age and experience. Young people are more

apt to adopt and use the technological resources that our societies have put at their disposal, while the knowledge that comes with experience, and the wisdom gained by communities' elders seem to be less valued. There is also a feeling that the relentless speed of now means that we do not have a sense of the past. One Roundtable participant raised doubts about whether real wisdom is being gained through all of the technological advances societies have promoted: 'We are technological adolescents. In societies where traditional knowledge is important, when there is a sudden infusion of technology that 'fixes things' there are changes in the structure. The elders normally are fonts of knowledge, but if a new culture brings skidoos and guns, all of [that] knowledge . . . is undermined. "We've improved things." But have we?'

Another participant worried, 'In sustainability, it is about us using tools more effectively/intelligently? Or is it that technology has outgrown us and we don't know what we're doing? If so, sustainability is a very different conversation.' Along this line, the thrust of many of the conversations was about a need for humanizing markets, and ensuring that the planet is actually livable for future generations, a goal that climate change, the poverty gap and the serious current economic flaws makes questionable. To accomplish these shifts, some RSE participants argued, means breaking down sector and other barriers. As one stated, '"I don't do research. There isn't time for it." We don't need to think of these as exclusive, but reinforcing. Dialogue, education, action, research. They all need to be on the same page.'

System and values change

These ideas speak to the need, to be discussed further below, for more collaborative approaches that are based in scale and scope on human considerations and needs. But as another participant pointed out, shifting values – indeed, a complete shift of mindset, or what Senge (1990, 2006) termed *metanoia*, is needed. One Roundtable participant put the dilemma quite boldly, stating, 'I think everyone in this room wants to effect positive change. Why we're all drawn here. I think everyone knows the direction of change but is less sure about how to bring about this change . . . Nothing changes till the values change, and they are implicit, so we can draw on deep-seated values to bring about change. So the discussion is one about which strategies bring about change.'

Conversations in the RSE tended to focus not as explicitly on the Global Compact as on the premise underlying Kofi Annan's initial call for a new social compact between business and society – one that could put a more 'human face' on the global market. It is exactly this need for humanization of markets, businesses, and societies that what we are now calling *SEE Change* deals with: change toward a SEE. In what follows, we will relate some of the ideas underlying SEE change as articulated by participants in the RSE.

What is SEE change?

Generally speaking, Roundtable participants saw an SEE as founded on the types of principles underpinning the Global Compact but with an emphasis on the values in the preamble:

Never before have the objectives of the international community and the business world been so aligned. Common goals, such as building markets, combating corruption, safeguarding the environment and ensuring social inclusion, have resulted in unprecedented partnerships and openness among business, government, civil society, labour and the United Nations. Many businesses recognize the need to collaborate with international actors in the current global context where social, political and economic challenges (and opportunities) – whether occurring at home or in other regions – affect companies as never before. (Global Compact 2009c)[4]

A clearly articulated set of values that frames sustainable enterprise seems to pick up on the very themes that Paul Hawken (2008) discovered in his work on what he calls 'blessed unrest' in his book focusing on ecological sustainability and social justice.

In addition, Roundtable participants tended to view sustainable enterprise as changing the responsibilities of business and the ways in which business can work with other actors, including governments, intergovernmental organizations and NGOs, to address some of the contemporary challenges noted earlier. There was recognition that old ways of organizing into silos, functions, disciplines, divisions, competitors and sectors, for example, are no longer workable in a world where boundaries are regularly broken and in a web 2.0 world where so much is visible.

---

[4] This was the preamble to the Global Compact in 2000 which has been superseded by new documents on the Compact.

Boundaries that used to be considered fairly secure are regularly breached today through technology, partnerships, alliances, collaborations, social entrepreneurship, privatization, nationalization and coopetition, among others. The Internet – whether through web 2.0 technologies like Twitter, Facebook, MySpace, and others, through the instantaneous nature of communications, or the ability of people to quickly access all sorts of information through media like Google and Amazon.com – has shifted things for enterprises in general so that, whether they like it or not, there is much more transparency about their activities today than ever before.

Taking all of this into consideration, participants saw one significant aspect of the SEE partly as a forum in which different cultures meet, across national and organizational boundaries, with friction over roles, motivations and identities but also great potential synergies. As evidenced by some of the RSE, which were held in developing nations, the participants, who come from all sectors, see sustainable enterprise as a vehicle for hope and aspiration, even in the most oppressed social contexts. Far from believing that the problems humanity faces are insoluble, many people believe that they know what they and their societies need, and further are articulate about what needs to change, and how. Some of the types of changes they proposed will be highlighted below.

System change and radical rethinking of companies

Design – redesign – of the systems and institutions currently in place is a core element of shifting toward an SEE. Although we all know how hard it is to change existing institutions, there are many new types of enterprises being created today with different design principles than those of the industrial era, which permeate many of today's existing organizations. As one participant stated, 'Design is one of the holy grails of sustainability thinking – product design, models of organizational structure, sustainable enterprise – the seeking of wealth creation and missing drivers, design has the power to dictate this kind of change.'

We can already see these principles of design being put into place in initiatives like that of Corporation 2020 (see www.corporation2020. org), which is all about redesigning the purpose of corporations to better suit the emerging needs of the twenty-first century. Other redesigns are apparent in the new types of enterprises that many participants in the RSE are involved with, enterprises that are public–private in nature, social enterprises (both independent and within larger companies), for-benefit corporations, enterprises coming from multilateral institutions that bridge into business territory, and many others. Many of these enterprises are already working, as one participant put it, to design infrastructure and products so we can be more light-footed.

Two examples of new enterprises come to mind from the wealth of material discussed at the RSE. The first comes from a communications company in London. 'We sell "good." We only work on sustainable development communications, and our clients include government, oil companies and NGOs.' The second comes from Canada and is an anecdote from a lone pioneer: 'I found that I had a talent for making jewelry and people were buying my stuff so I set up a business. I can guarantee certain things, for instance the conditions in which my people work, but I cannot guarantee the desire for speed from my customers. They buy our stuff because it is sustainable and ethical but then they demand it in five days, so I have to fly it to the US! So, in a global market I run into a brick wall.'

The shift to an SEE is partially based on technologies that already exist – and knowledge that already exists – but as some RSE participants pointed out, the economy is in some senses becoming de-materialized and creating wholly new contexts for humanity. The 'clouds' of information now available in the hyperspace that the global web of computers represents, through Google, eBay, Facebook and MySpace, are prime examples, represent something wholly new for humanity. Combined with the fact that information is not a scarce resource like traditional resources, because when shared, information expands and morphs, rather than being used up (Brown and Duguid 2000), the information and post-information economy is an essential element of an SEE.

In this context, there is a clear process of what Joseph Schumpeter (1975) called 'creative destruction' already underway. Many of the progressive companies that have signed onto the Global Compact have internal initiatives that involve them in social entrepreneurial ventures, some aimed at what Prahalad has called the 'bottom of the pyramid', and others dealing with issues in developed nations (Prahalad 2005, Prahalad and Hammond 2002). In many of these initiatives, companies verge onto territory that was once formerly reserved for government (e.g. Scherer and Palazzo 2008, Scherer, Palazzo and Baumann 2006, Matten and Crane 2005) – for instance, with involvement in educational activities or, in Africa, in dealing with issues associated with the HIV/AIDS crisis. Despite these initiatives, the difficulties of effecting significant organizational change – or change in the purpose of existing corporations – suggests that there are questions about the extent to which multinational corporations (MNCs) will completely transform themselves into sustainable enterprises or whether they will go the way of the dinosaurs.

Mission possible: entrepreneurs and boundary spanners

The SEE is inclusive and recognizes that solutions to local and global problems may come from innovation, creativity and entrepreneurship in all sorts of organizations – private, public, social, or individual. There is a significant focus on social entrepreneurship as a way in which participants believed that sustainable enterprise might evolve, but we found examples of positive social change agents in all organizations, at all levels. As one participant noted: 'Entrepreneurs are not necessarily the sustainable development "educated" – they use common sense, intuition, belief and follow their own paths.' Many times, they work inside large existing organizations; however, often they work outside in their communities. They tend to work below the radar for a period of time, while developing their ideas, and are clearly able to work across boundaries and counter-culturally, coping with not having all the answers, and working in a context of uncertainty, outside of normal comfort zones.

Similarly, pioneers who have been able to work across traditional sector boundaries, or collaboratively across entities that typically compete with each other, have a tendency to believe in the impossible. They are somehow able to create new opportunities for learning and change in their organizations that others have not been able to conceive. In one Roundtable we heard from a senior academic in a civil engineering department at a very high-minded university explaining how she had introduced sustainability to the teaching faculty. This had meant crossing intellectual boundaries, dealing with the sometimes intangibility and changing perspectives of new eco-systems science while also dealing with the hard science of highway construction and dam building.

Because the problems facing the world today are what Ackoff (1975) once termed 'messes' (i.e. intractable, unbounded, difficult problems), they have not been readily resolvable by entities operating with the mindset of a single sector. Indeed, participants tended to agree that, in many cases, dealing with the intractable problems of the world, like human rights, climate change and other issues of sustainability, requires multi-sector approaches. Even in parts of the world where governments have traditionally been expected to solve problems and have all the answers, this view was common in the RSE.

A role for governments

Despite the fact that many intractable issues facing the world require multi-sector solutions, there is, according to participants, a clear role for government and regulation. In a world where progressive corporations attempting to align their practices with stated values, like those expressed in the Global Compact, are already going beyond existing regulation and norms of compliance, it is companies that are sometimes setting the standards.

To make the playing field level in these circumstances requires that all players eventually live up to the standards, and accomplishing that may well require new regulation demanding more sustainable and rights-orientated practices. Governments, after all, were the original signatories to the treaties from which the Global Compact's Principles derive, and they probably eventually will need to take a stronger role in enforcing these types of standards, particularly to deal with the numerous laggards who are not already up to speed with the types of changes needed.

Leadership of a different sort

One of the topics most discussed in the Roundtables was the type of leadership needed to effect changes towards an SEE – to ensure that principles like those of the Global Compact are lived in practice. But it is a different sort of leadership than the world is used to. Participants tended to agree that leaders needed to be systems thinkers, who are also concerned about the social impacts of their (business and other) activities, who are not only values-driven but also able to articulate those values clearly.

One participant described an exercise undertaken with business leaders, in which they were asked to deal with the statement that '"Leaders know what is important to them," by spending five minutes writing down what is important to them. What comes back are not kick-ass strategies to drive their competitors out of the marketplace, but family, community, mentoring. Not what you'd expect from hard-nosed businessmen and women.' Another participant stated that 'We need to design a space within business where it is not illegal to bring in values.'

For many, it seemed that awakening to the need for sustainable enterprise happened as a result of a wide range of personal experiences. One individual noted: 'If you really ask a business leader what was the cause of the change, it was a personal experience. For example, Lee Scott's [retired CEO of the retail giant Wal-Mart, who turned the company toward sustainability] experience with Katrina . . . There is deference to the emotional bond. We pursue the rational learning gap, but the real learning is the emotional learning path. What really drives you when you're alone?'

The type of leader described by Roundtable participants is potentially able to deal with issues related to sustainability, social justice and equity, along with climate change and values-driven management. This leader has a number of qualities: an ability to work with ambiguity, develop vision, link business *to* society, a capacity to harness internal resources – employees' knowledge and skills – for the betterment of society as well as better business. Most important is a capacity for systems thinking and the ability to deal effectively with complexity, and a strong foundation of vision and core values that are held with passion.

The capacity for systems thinking – understanding the broad implications of the enterprise and its activity for stakeholders, and for societies, and the need for an integrated approach to sustainability, vision and values – is a difficult capacity to develop. One participant pointed out that only a small percentage of the population currently has this capacity (and research suggests that this is, in fact, true (Torbert 2004)), yet arguably it can be developed in future leaders by exposing them to problem-finding in new ways, to systems problems and their implications, and by actually asking them to deal with complex, real-world, ambiguous and messy problems in their education and beyond, rather than more neatly structured problems.

Change and its obstacles

One person suggested in a Roundtable conversation that 'Change happens in ordinary institutions when individuals sit up and realize that something has to happen and that they can drive change.' More people need to have these epiphanies. Another suggested that 'severe learning disabilities' are preventing us from seeing the problems and potential solutions, all of which is complicated by the fast pace of many of today's largest institutions and most developed societies, that makes lack of time for reflection particularly problematic.

Other obstacles to change have to do with more mundane aspects of the change process such as educational systems – e.g. in business education, around sustainability, human rights, equity, labour rights, corruption, values and the need for vision, not much of which is actually taught today in many management or management development programmes. A further obstacle is the difficulty of generating adequate metrics that could measure progress or performance on some of these issues.

The potential leverage points that could actually generate change discussed by various participants, however, generates some hope. Based on inside knowledge of the system they work within and hope to change, participants identified points of leverage, mechanisms of influence and different (multiple) points of entry. Leverage points include policy, accreditation, education and training and regulation. Mechanisms to influence change could be advocacy, education, research, collaboration, facilitation and mobilization. Entry points for system change include attracting the interest, attention and support of leaders, educating future and current actors, and lobbying government, industry and community bodies in order to change the framework conditions.

Concluding thoughts

There is a clear and present need for solutions to the interconnected challenges of poverty, globalization and terrorism; peak oil, water neutrality and a zero-carbon economy. Yet we already know enough about economics, about ourselves and about technology to be able to find these solutions now. The Global Compact with its ten Principles outlines a set of values that might (must, even) be incorporated into any SEE as a basic set of foundational values. Yet the participants in the RSE on Sustainable Enterprise ask for something more: they want human-scaled, humanized organizations, embedded with values that make life worth living for both themselves and future generations.

In looking forward there is a vision, a hope and even a myth of a sustainable future. Here we mean 'myth' in the sense of story-telling, of envisioning change and a different world and creating a new narrative about what we are doing here in this world. Story-telling is a powerful vehicle for social change and the Roundtable's participants' comments suggest that there are many ways in which this new story might be developed and told. These conversations called into question what it means to be human, what choices we make everyday as human beings and in societies and what choices we can make as a species to save ourselves and our planet home.

13 | The United Nations Global Compact as a learning approach

GUIDO PALAZZO AND
ANDREAS GEORG SCHERER

Globalization as the new context of global business firms

Globalization can be defined as a process of intensification of social and economic relations across national borders (Beck 2000, Giddens 1990). The causes of this process are manifold and have been discussed intensively in the literature (for an overview, see Held *et al.* 1999, Scherer and Palazzo 2008): political decisions on reducing barriers to trade and opening borders for the transfer of goods, capital and people; technological developments that lead to a decline in the costs of cross-national transportation (e.g. air cargo, container shipping) and coordination (e.g. telephone, Internet); social developments (migration, individualization, erosion of traditions); and emerging transnational risks (global environmental problems, global diseases, global security and terrorism, etc.).

Today, global business firms can take advantage of blurring borders and expand their possibilities of choice for economic exchange processes by shifting their value chain activities to locations that offer lower costs or higher returns. At the same time nation-state institutions are often inadequate for the regulation of transnational businesses, providing global public goods or reducing or compensating negative externalities (Beck 2000, Kaul *et al.* 1999, Kaul, Grunberg and Stern 2003). In addition, a growing part of world production is being shifted to locations where there is no rule of law, where human rights are not protected, where social and environmental standards are not enforced, or where governments and public authorities are corrupt (Palan 2003). Under these conditions neither the institutions of nation-state governance nor international governmental institutions such as the United Nations, the Organization for Economic Cooperation and Development (OECD), or the International Labour Organization (ILO) are capable of influencing the prevailing conditions and dealing with negative externalities such as social distress or environmental disasters (Scherer and Smid 2000).

As a result, businesses operate in increasingly complex environments with gaps in regulation and growing activities of non-governmental organizations (NGOs), such as human rights, or labour rights groups, or environmental groups (Doh and Teegen 2004). Today these civil society groups not only target public authorities but are directly challenging corporations outside the political arena through activism, such as civil disobedience, strikes, protest marches, political campaigning, lobbying, media and Internet activism, boycotts and disinvestments. Such activism can lead to a loss of corporate reputation, decline in sales and profits and diminishing confidence of citizens in the legitimacy of the economic capitalist system and of the corporations and their managers as its main protagonists (Palazzo and Scherer 2006).

The United Nations Global Compact was established in response to this situation (United Nations 1999). The target is to use the resources and capabilities of business firms in order to address global public goods issues, such as human rights, social and environmental standards and the fight against corruption. The idea of the Global Compact is that private business firms should voluntarily deliver these public goods where state agencies are failing and international organizations are not capable of influencing conditions (Williams 2004).

It is our intention here to discuss the consequences of these global developments for corporate responsibility and global governance. We shall highlight the role of the Global Compact and its goals and describe Corporate Social Responsibility (CSR) as a corporate learning process. We shall then discuss the challenges in this learning process by pointing out what corporations must learn, and conclude with some recommendations for what the Global Compact can do in order to improve the learning process.

Corporate responsibility and global governance

The erosion of governmental regulatory influence on corporate behaviour has triggered two reactions: first, the legal pressure of governments is partly replaced by the moral pressure of civil society. Second, as a reaction to that new form of pressure, corporations have started to behave as political actors themselves (Scherer and Palazzo 2007). They provide public goods by engaging in public health or education. They protect and promote human rights (Kinley and Tadaki 2004, Matten and Crane 2005). They fight for peace or against poverty, corruption and AIDS (Fort and Schipani 2004, Margolis and Walsh 2003, Misangyi, Weaver and Elms 2008) or engage in corporate citizenship initiatives, such as the Forest Stewardship Council, the Global Reporting Initiative (GRI), or the Global Compact, in order to co-develop global standards for their own operations (Scherer and Palazzo 2007). Especially through the latter form of engagement, corporations become actors in global governance initiatives that try to fill the regulatory gap through self-regulation. This form of engagement has become a widespread phenomenon: 'That corporations do sometimes act as social change agents is not in dispute; indeed it is an empirical reality around the world. Moreover it is becoming a political reality as well' (Bies *et al.* 2007: 788). In the past, the production of public goods and the protection of citizenship rights have been the exclusive responsibility of governments (Matten and Crane 2005). Today not just state agencies, but also civil society actors and private business firms engage in new forms of global governance that have become a key element in the discourse on corporate responsibility.

Global governance can be defined as a 'nexus of systems of rule-making, political coordination and problem-solving which transcend[s] states and societies. It is particularly relevant to describing the structures and processes of governing beyond the state where there exists no supreme or singular political authority' (Held and McGrew 2002: 8). Global regulation in this sense can be understood as *governance with and without government* (Rosenau and Czempiel 1992). It includes private actors, such as NGOs and corporations in the process of setting and enforcing rules, and it unfolds in a broad variety of institutional formats. While national regulation is mainly manifested in the formulation of 'hard law', global governance initiatives such as the Kimberley Process, the GRI or the Forest Stewardship Council rather produce standards in the form of 'soft law' (Gilbert and Rasche 2008, Shelton 2000). In contrast to hard law, soft law is characterized by the imprecision of rules, weak or even non-existent enforcement mechanisms and delegation of authority to third parties such as NGOs or private business firms (Abbott *et al.* 2000).

Compliance with hard law is enforced through judicial sanctions. Depending on the level of competition, soft law standards of global governance can be supported by the pressure of market mechanisms as far as the demand side (e.g. customers) values the definition and implementation of these standards (Hale 2008, United Nations Human Rights Council 2008b). Corporations that comply with particular standards can, for instance, use labels in order to signal their responsibility to customers and investors, thereby developing reputational capital (Gardberg and Fombrun 2006). In turn, companies that ignore those standards can be targeted by NGO campaigns that 'may raise consumer awareness of poor corporate . . . practices, tarnish public image, reduce goodwill, and pressure firms, even if [they] occur in overseas locations' (Gardberg and Fombrun 2006: 334). The emphasis on the market mechanism, however, must not conceal the broad range of possible motivations individual actors may have for the engagement in the formulation and implementation of soft law standards: individual benefit, altruism, virtues, imitation, or others.

Global governance initiatives are often institutionalized as multi-stakeholder forums in which corporations, NGOs, transnational institutions, humanitarian organizations and even governments cooperate (Scholte 2005). Global governance is manifested in various interrelated steps. Governance initiatives may include one or more of the following elements:

1. *Provision for arenas for deliberation and learning:* Through discourses, corporations and civil society actors learn to develop shared interests and a common understanding of problems and potential solutions. Deliberation helps them to move from conflict to collaboration. Companies can learn from each other's existing policies, programmes, strategies and mistakes, and they can avoid typical pitfalls of misunderstanding, especially between managers and activists through mutual learning (Rowley and Moldoveanu 2003).

2. *Development of CSR standards:* In reaction to a lack of regulation and gaps in global governance, multi-stakeholder initiatives develop standards in order to tackle specific behavioural challenges (e.g. avoiding the link between civil war and diamond mining, defining environmental and social criteria for sustainable forest management or sustainable fishing) or specific communication challenges (e.g. reporting on CSR performance).

3. *Development of standards and procedures of auditing and compliance enforcement:* Soft law mechanisms do not dispose of the sanction power of hard law. It is, however, important to hold those corporations that participate in the initiative accountable to the standards. In order to avoid opportunistic behaviour and 'greenwashing' (Laufer 2006), multi-stakeholder initiatives have to develop credible and transparent control mechanisms for standard compliance.

4. *Marketing of labels and certifications:* Finally, multi-stakeholder initiatives must create incentives for companies to join and to comply with their standards. Labels such as those of the Rainforest Alliance, the Marine Stewardship Council, and the Forest Stewardship Council, or certifications on the degree of compliance, such as in the case of the GRI, help corporations to signal their responsibility to their stakeholders and to reap advantages from their efforts.

Situating the Global Compact in the emerging global governance landscape

When Kofi Annan introduced the idea of a Global Compact at the 1999 World Economic Forum, he invited corporations to become partners in the development of global governance (Fritsch 2008). While previously multinational corporations (MNCs) and the United Nations had had a rather hostile relationship (Thérien and Pouliot 2006), Annan's initiative helped to reframe that relationship into one of cooperation on the basis of a shared interest in the creation of a sustainable and stable world order (Williams 2004). The Global Compact invites corporations 'to embrace, support and enact . . . a set of core values in the area of human rights, labour standards, the environment, and anti-corruption' (Global Compact 2004c: 4). The Global Compact network brings together corporations and civil society actors in specific regions, countries, or industrial sectors in order to trigger an 'incremental process of learning and improvement' (Williams 2004: 761).

Three levers are used to promote the internalization of UN principles in corporate behaviour: learning events, dialogues and concrete partnership projects in which the principles are enacted (Rasche 2009a). Rasche (2009a) has also emphasized that the core idea of the initiative is to create a 'long-term learning experience' by fostering dialogue. In this sense, the Global Compact is a 'first pragmatic response to government governance failures' and thus constitutes a supplement to other 'more regulative' efforts in the landscape of global governance. On a macro level, the Global Compact helps to understand the regulatory challenges on the transnational playing field, and on a micro level it provides learning opportunities for the implementation of ten globally shared Principles (Rasche 2009a).

The Global Compact has been criticized by various scholars and civil society activists. The critique holds that it promotes misuse of the United Nations, it helps corporations to 'bluewash' their image, it does not hold corporations accountable and it does not possess mechanisms to control for compliance (e.g. Bigge 2004, Laufer 2006, Sethi 2003, Thérien and Pouliot 2006). As Rasche (2009a) has argued, these critics somehow miss the point of the Global Compact because they criticize it on the basis of mistaken expectations. Given the varied dimensions of global governance described above, it is important to evaluate the Global Compact as to how it performs within the dimension it claims to promote – the promotion of CSR deliberation and learning.

Global governance mechanisms have the same legitimacy and efficiency challenges as governmental regulatory regimes (Zürn 2004). However, since they are not embedded in comparable democratic processes, they must be evaluated in a different way. It is important to understand that legitimacy and efficiency challenges exist within all dimensions of global governance initiatives. However, those initiatives that develop standards or those that provide mechanisms for controlling compliance may face different challenges than those that focus on the promotion of learning and growing awareness through deliberation. In our view, the performance of the Global Compact must be evaluated against the following set of questions:

- Does it promote open and fair deliberation?
- Does it promote learning?
- Do corporations that participate in the Global Compact perform better with respect to the ten Principles than companies that are not members of the Compact?
- Does the Global Compact create the awareness that corporate responsibility on the global playing field is broadening?
- Are there mechanisms in place that prevent window-dressing?

How do corporations learn to manage CSR?

In order to evaluate the contribution of the Global Compact to raise the awareness of the social and environmental duties that come with the globalization of business operations and to support a learning process on the implementation of those duties into corporate policies and strategies, it is important to take a closer look at how corporations progress on the CSR learning curve in general. The literature on social and environmental responsibility suggests that corporations go through a learning process that in the ideal case leads them from a very low to a high level of CSR performance (Mirvis and Googins 2006). Hunt and Auster (1990) have argued that corporations move through five stages, moving from being a beginner to fire fighting, civic concern, pragmatism, to a proactive stance. It seems that many CSR activities are triggered by pressure from civil society (Scherer and Palazzo 2007), and companies react in various ways. Roome (1992) argues that those reactions to external pressures go from 'non-compliance' through various stages to 'environmental excellence'. In his analysis of more than a decade of CSR activities at Nike, Zadek (2004) proposes an organizational learning model that starts with a stage of denial and ends with a civil and proactive approach to CSR, where CSR is embedded in corporate strategy and the corporation acts as a first mover when new CSR challenges come up.

These models are based on a similar evolutionary logic (see e.g. Scherer 2003, Zadek 2004): they all start with the assumption that corporations at the beginning refuse to accept broader societal responsibilities. Through pressure from civil society they learn that ignorance of social and environmental issues can create risks, and they react with some superficial CSR activities in order to avoid further sanctions. These superficial activities range from donations to good causes to the formulation of a code of conduct for suppliers. However, those activities are subsequently criticized for being ineffective and the criticized problems, such as labour conditions, remain unsolved. As a result, the pressure grows and the corporation finally accepts the fact that society expects them to solve problems they did not previously perceive as their responsibility, as can be seen from the reaction of Nike in the early 1990s ('We don't own the factories', see, e.g., Katz 1994). In order to comply with changing societal demands concerning social and environmental standards, they start to control their suppliers by sending auditors or allowing for third-party control. And again, it turns out that these measures are not sufficient. As long as the CSR activities are disconnected from core business operations and corporate strategy, they have no sustainable effect. For instance, procurement managers whose incentives solely depend on successful price negotiations will have no motivation to commit to CSR objectives. Suppliers who do not know whether they will get contracts in the future have no incentive to invest in the implementation of CSR in their factories. The further evolution of CSR is thus driven by the growing understanding that CSR must be managed strategically. Finally, if corporations start to manage CSR strategically, they will probably start to scan their environment for emerging issues and sooner or later will manage those issues proactively and in cooperation with civil society partners (Zadek 2004). Responsible corporations at this final stage (which Zadek calls the 'civil' stage) will begin to engage in multi-stakeholder initiatives. They move from including stakeholders in their own decision-making to becoming a partner in processes and institutions of global governance. They become political actors (Scherer and Palazzo 2007).

The problem of these evolutionary models of CSR learning is that they 'imply a linear, one-dimensional progression on all fronts' (Schaefer and Harvey 1998: 116, see also Stubbart and Smalley 1999). Learning is described as an almost automatic and predictable process. There is a lot of anecdotal evidence for the assumption that CSR learning is mainly triggered by external shocks and pressure (e.g. Scherer 2003, Zadek 2004). There is also some evidence for the assumption that insufficient reactions to social and environmental problems provoke more pressure and push the corporate learning process. However, it can be doubted whether stage models really describe the process of learning or, rather, deliver a typology of various approaches to CSR which do not necessarily combine in an upward spiral of positive learning. It is possible that corporations move from being a high performer to being a low performer in CSR. It is also possible, or even desirable, that corporations, after a first knee-jerk reaction of denial and resistance, start to engage in a serious dialogue with their critics and a subsequent transformation of their core business operations – as, for instance, in the case for Chiquita (Were 2003). In fact, it can be assumed that learning processes are even fuelled by serious dialogue with stakeholders (Calton and Payne 2003, Heugens *et al.* 2002). Starting those dialogues early might thus help the corporation avoid certain stages or misleading types of CSR.

Three types of learning can be differentiated. A learning process in which corporations learn through trial and error without questioning their fundamental assumptions about the world has been called *single-loop learning* (Argyris and Schön 1978). As single-loop learner, a corporation learns how to improve what it is already doing. In the context of CSR this can mean that a company reacts to external pressure through a sophisticated PR campaign. CSR is just another topic that must be sold to key stakeholders who have to be convinced that any critique from NGOs is not justified. The company understands that it is important to be seen as a good corporate citizen and their learning simply consists in a new and enlarged understanding of stakeholder communication. External pressure triggers 'processes that promote incremental change within an established set of operating principles that are not altered' (Post and Altman 1992: 13). *Double-loop learning* means that a corporation develops new capabilities that broaden their behavioural options (Argyris and Schön 1978). Radical changes in the environment trigger a process of adaptation that can change the objectives and the policies of the corporation. A corporation that was good in monitoring product quality within their supply chain might learn that it is also important to monitor the CSR performance of their business partners. They engage or develop the expertise to audit factories. Finally, *triple-loop learning* describes a process of meta-learning in which 'philosophies, structures, and operating principles are put in place to facilitate ongoing transformation, following a radical organizational transformation or frame-breaking experience' (Post and Altman 1992: 15).

It has been argued that corporations, especially if they are successful, pursue an architecture of simplicity, which consists of strong routines and 'increasingly homogeneous managerial 'lenses' or world views' (Miller 1993: 117). Those routines can inhibit or even block learning (Argyris and Schön 1978). Routines tend to reinforce existing assumptions about the order of things. While routines can contribute to the success of corporations under the condition of changing environmental constellations, they can transform core capabilities into core rigidities (Leonard-Barton 1992) and silence dissenting voices (Morrison and Milliken 2000).

As much as strategic control systems must reflect these management problems in order to sustain competitive advantage (Kaplan and Norton 1996, Schreyögg and Steinmann 1987, Simons 1995), CSR management systems have to be open and sensitive to emerging new challenges. Interestingly, the organizational implications of both strategic control and CSR management systems are much the same (Steinmann and Kustermann 1998, Scherer 2003: 442–5).

CSR activities in the above-described political sense go beyond the minimum set of responsibilities that the orthodox economic theory of the firm imposes on corporations (e.g. Sundaram and Inkpen 2004). Corporations should comply with laws and maximize profits. In a globalized world, however, multinational business firms manage workers rights, avoid complicity with dictators, promote freedom, or fight against AIDS (Matten and Crane 2005). They should, as Kofi Annan intended with the Global Compact, become partners in the promotion of UN principles. Such a demanding concept of corporate responsibility has not yet appeared on the radar screen of management theory and practice (Walsh 2005). It is thus no surprise that under the pressure of growing demands, corporations tend to stick to their routines and the traditional division of labour between politics and business. In order to fuel corporate learning in the domain of CSR, it is necessary to break their rigid frame of established routines.

What must corporations learn?

When dealing with the social and environmental problems of a globalized world and the growing demands from societies, corporations have to resolve organizational challenges in order to foster learning processes and implement CSR. The five key challenges are as follows.

Understanding growing and changing societal expectations

Business firms have to understand the growing societal expectations and have to adequately respond to such changes. Societal expectations often emerge as weak signals that are difficult to detect when organizations and their members are deeply embedded in their day-to-day routines. However, as Zadek (2004) has explained, societal issues can develop in maturity from latent to emergent to consolidating, and corporations have to find the appropriate level of response. Likewise, corporations have to understand what the main issues in their particular industries are and how they relate to the firm's value activities and supply chain. For example, it does not make sense for a pharmaceutical firm to engage in CSR projects on living wages, when living wages are not an important issue in the pharmaceutical industry and when the same firm does not respond to growing societal demands in other areas – such as, for example, access to medical care in developing countries. Therefore, the big challenge for CSR management is to adapt the level of CSR response to the maturity of the societal issues and expectations. In the case of multinational firms this may be even more challenging when these firms operate in heterogeneous environments with complex and even contradictory societal demands

Understanding corporations' own social and environmental issues along their supply chain

This is a difficult task especially in the case of diversified big MNCs operating in various countries and businesses. Under these conditions it is very difficult to oversee the complex value chain activities and the social and environmental problems within the corporation's own operations and its upstream and downstream supply chains. Here the corporation must achieve an adequate balance between the centralization of CSR principles and policies in the corporate headquarters and the decentralized knowledge on CSR issues and possible solutions. For example, in an MNC operating with more than 100,000 employees in over 100 countries, it is very difficult to analyse what human rights issues in the various parts of the organization and its suppliers or customers are prevalent. Here the problem is to motivate the various country managers to share their information on human rights issues and to implement the corporate CSR policies in a way that is suitable to the local demands as well as to the expectations of consumers and the public in the headquarters of their home country.

Understanding how to implement CSR

The organizational implementation of CSR is a major challenge. The US Sentencing Commission Guidelines for Organizations require companies to take formal and organizational measures such as codes of conduct, use of compliance officers and formal training for employees in order to avoid costly legal sanctions in case of misconduct by the organizational members, committed on behalf of the firm (Dalton, Metzger and Hill 1994). As a consequence, many corporations have implemented these formal mechanisms and follow a compliance approach to CSR (Paine 1994). However, CSR cannot be managed by *ex ante* defined formal rules and sanctions alone (Stansbury and Barry 2007). Rather, in complex and dynamic environments the successful implementation of CSR also relies on the integrity of organizational members and their ethical judgement that cannot be completely regulated in advance. This is because organizational regulators cannot fully understand the complexity of conditions and cannot anticipate emerging CSR issues in the entire organization. As a consequence, the response to ethical challenges cannot be managed by formal rules and sanctions alone. Students of Business Ethics and Organization Theory therefore suggest an integrity approach that relies on values instead of formal rules, on voluntary action instead of enforcement, and on integrity instead of compliance (Paine 1994). However, for successful CSR implementation both elements, compliance and integrity – formal rules and values – have to be combined in a balanced way.

Ability to create dialogue with critical stakeholders

Business firms must respond to the concerns of their various stakeholders and constituencies. However, the challenge is (1) how to identify the most important stakeholders and (2) how to respond to their concerns in an appropriate way. In the literature on stakeholder theory it is suggested that the following three factors are important in the selection of stakeholders (Agle, Mitchell and Sonnenfeld 1999): stakeholders' power, the urgency, and the legitimacy of their demands. Agle, Mitchell and Sonnenfeld (1999) suggest that business firms focus on the concerns of the most powerful stakeholder groups. However, conditions may change and so may alter factors such as power, urgency and legitimacy. In addition, other authors maintain that legitimacy has become a crucial condition for the survival and sustained competitive success of business firms (Palazzo and Scherer 2006). Companies that lose their legitimacy will have difficulties in finding the necessary resources for their continued existence. Organizational legitimacy is based on social acceptance and is subjectively perceived and ascribed to organizations and their behaviour in processes of social construction. Suchman (1995) suggests that there are three ways of creating of legitimacy – i.e. a fit between the perception of organizational practices and the expectations of stakeholders: (1) organizations can influence the perceptions of their constituencies through strategic means of marketing and PR, (2) organizations can also adapt their practices to the expectations of their constituencies, or (3) organizations can engage in a dialogue with their stakeholders in which the legitimacy of organizational behaviour and the social expectations are analysed by way of argumentation. Palazzo and Scherer (2006) suggest that in a globalized world the manipulation of expectations or the adaptation to social demands often no longer work so that argument has become a necessary option in the management of organizational legitimacy.

Transparency on CSR engagement

In order to gain credibility of their stakeholders and constituencies corporations have to be transparent in their CSR policies and actual engagements. A company that is making public claims about its CSR codes of conduct and policies but does not modify its operations according to its own maxims is in danger of losing credibility and thus legitimacy. Today a more and more active civil society with human and labour rights groups and environmental groups is analysing corporate activities and is often making cases public where companies fail to live up to their own standards. The history of the Nike case is instructive in this respect. Therefore, the implementation of CSR is not just a task for corporate communications to define standards and inform the public about what corporate image the organization wants to create. Instead, it is also a task of continuously analysing the operations and supply chains in order to detect and to report on policies, problems and achievements in a transparent manner.

What can the Global Compact do (and what does it do) in order to improve CSR learning?

The Global Compact can support the corporate learning process in a number of ways:

1. *Create platforms for the exchange of experience with problems and for best practices:* The Global Compact can help to establish regional or industry forums where corporations from certain regions or industries can exchange their views on social or environmental issues and can exchange best practices in CSR. This may help business firms to establish a level playing field within their industries and to define common standards of business conduct so that those firms that engage in the implementation of the Compact's principles will have no competitive disadvantage due to the higher costs of applying these principles.
2. *Create platforms for dialogue between corporations and NGOs:* The United Nations is respected by both private firms and NGOs. The Global Compact can create arenas where corporations and NGOs regularly meet to discuss issues of general concern in the areas of human rights, social and environmental standards and fighting corruption, and thus can help to establish a basis of mutual trust. These forums can also be helpful in responding to situations of crisis when, for example, a solution needs to be developed quickly.
3. *Help business firms to achieve an acceptable level of transparency in their CSR activities:* As members of the Compact, business firms must regularly report on their CSR projects. Although the reports are quite informal today, business firms may be motivated to develop their CSR reporting further with the help of the GRI or other standards of social and environmental reporting.

Corporations operate in a globalizing geopolitical context. As a consequence, the stable nation-state order of the twentieth century, with its clear division of labour between politics and business, is gone and the role of corporations in society is about to be redefined. The Global Compact, initiated by Kofi Annan and taken up and strongly promoted by his successor Ban Ki-moon, offers a unique opportunity to learn and enact those broader responsibilities that corporations must assume in the future.

PART III

Governance and Communication on Progress

14 | *The United Nations Global Compact's governance framework and integrity measures*

URSULA WYNHOVEN AND
MATTHIAS STAUSBERG

Introduction

The Global Compact's governance framework, including the integrity measures, has evolved significantly during the initiative's ten years of operations. Much of this evolution is due to the multi-stakeholder nature of the Global Compact and the initiative's character as a public–private platform with both global and local components.[1] Shifting stakeholder expectations and the rapid growth of the Global Compact throughout the years have further contributed.

The journey to the current governance framework has been marked by a series of milestones, including:

- The emergence of Global Compact Local Networks (GCLNs) around the world, with their own evolving governance and relationship with the Global Compact Office
- The establishment of the Global Compact Advisory Council (GCAC) in January 2003
- The introduction of the Global Compact's integrity measures
- The introduction of the current governance framework in the third quarter of 2005 following a one-year governance review
- The formalization of the role of donor governments in the framework.

[1] This chapter does not discuss in detail the governance of the Global Compact Office, which has remained largely unchanged since the inception of the initiative. The Executive Director of the Global Compact Office reports to the Secretary-General and the Global Compact Trust Fund is administered in accordance with UN Financial Rules and Regulations.

Global Compact governance continues to evolve as the entities that are part of this framework grow further in their roles. Two important elements of this narrative merit their own chapter: GCLNs, including their governance (chapter 18), and the initiative's key integrity measure – the Communication on Progress (COP) (chapter 15) requiring participants to disclose progress made in the implementation of the Global Compact's Principles annually to their own stakeholders. The remaining elements are described in greater detail in this chapter, with a particular focus on the Global Compact's other integrity measures and the concept of social vetting, which is key to the initiative's emphasis on transparency and public accountability.

Global Compact Advisory Council

The GCAC was formed in January 2002 to focus attention on questions of governance and strategy for the initiative. Its twenty members, who were drawn from business, civil society and labour, met on several occasions over a two-year period to discuss and address critical issues geared towards protecting and strengthening the initiative. One of the key tasks was to propose more robust standards of participation in order to improve the Compact's effectiveness and to safeguard its integrity.[2]

One of the most important achievements of the GCAC was its proposal to introduce a set of integrity measures to address allegations of systematic and egregious abuse of the Global Compact Principles. The proposal to introduce a new issue area and 10th Principle on anti-corruption to the Global Compact, following the adoption of the United Nations Convention Against Corruption (UNCAC) in 2003, also emerged from the GCAC (see also chapter 6 by Huguette Labelle).

As the Global Compact continued to expand around the world, the issue of governance and how to ensure adequate participation by the different stakeholders gained increasing relevance. Consequently, then-Secretary-General Kofi Annan decided to request a review of the

---

[2] Advisory Council members also served as champions of the Compact, advised the Secretary-General and his staff on key issues of strategy and policy and on how to improve the initiative's reach and effectiveness in their respective country, region, or segment of society.

Global Compact's governance, expressed in his closing remarks at the 2004 Global Compact Leaders Summit in 2004:

We also need to devise a new governance structure for the Compact. To put it in corporate terms, the primary mission of the Global Compact Office should become brand management and quality assurance. We must avoid bureaucratization. And ownership and the power of initiative must be much more broadly shared among all participants, including businesses, labour and civil society; the UN agencies that are the guardians of the principles; and the rapidly expanding family of national Networks that have sprung up, almost spontaneously. (United Nations 2004)

Governance review (2004–5) and governance framework

Georg Kell, Executive Director of the Global Compact, and Professor John Ruggie, then Special Adviser to the Secretary-General on the Global Compact, were given the task of conducting the review, which took place over a one-year period, concluding at the end of Summer 2005 with a set of concrete recommendations on a new governance framework for the initiative. The comprehensive review included briefings and consultations with participant and stakeholder groups, seeking their input on the right constellation of entities to serve the goals outlined by the Secretary-General.

The review was carried out on the premise that an initiative with the ambitious mission of helping to bring about sustainable and inclusive global markets and fostering organizational change the world over has a keen need for high-quality strategic advice and direction, and for finding effective and scalable ways to engage those whose organizations are to change. The quality of participants' engagement in the initiative was seen as crucial, especially considering that corporate commitment could be diminished significantly if a substantial number of participants did not strive for continuous improvement. Given that much of the larger public was still unfamiliar with many corporate responsibility initiatives, it was felt that special attention needed to be paid to the ways in which participation in the Global Compact, as well as its emerging brand, were being used.

The new governance framework proposed thus aimed at achieving a wide range of objectives, including:

1. Building commitment to and ownership of the initiative among its diverse participants and stakeholders by giving them a voice in the overall direction of the initiative.
2. Establishing authoritative, legitimate bodies for critical decision-making and policy guidance on issues affecting participants' engagement in the initiative.
3. Finding means consistent with the mandate of the initiative by which further improvements in the quality of participants' engagement could be achieved.
4. Having a standing high-level Expert Group that followed the progress of the initiative closely and that could be relied on for strategic advice and guidance.
5. Protecting the United Nations and the good efforts made by participants that were serious about their commitment from efforts by some to 'bluewash' their reputations through their association with the Global Compact.

The new governance framework was adopted by the Secretary-General in August 2005 and implementation began almost immediately. In keeping with the Global Compact's voluntary and network-based character, the governance framework was intended to be light, non-bureaucratic and to foster greater involvement and ownership by participants and other stakeholders. The new framework also underscored the multi-stakeholder nature of the Global Compact, engaging business, civil society, labour, employer organizations, governments and the United Nations at various levels. Following from the new framework, Global Compact governance functions are now shared by seven entities, each with differentiated tasks within a multi-centric framework: Global Compact Leaders Summit, Global Compact Board, Local Networks, Annual Local Networks Forum (ALNF), Global Compact Office, Inter-Agency Team (IAT), and Global Compact Donor Group. The role of each entity in the governance framework is defined and explained in the following sections.

Global Compact Leaders Summit

The Leaders Summit is a triennial gathering of the top executives of all Global Compact participants and other stakeholders. As the largest gathering of its kind, the Summit represents a unique opportunity for

Global Compact participants to discuss the Compact and corporate citizenship at the highest level, and to produce strategic recommendations and action imperatives related to the future evolution of the initiative. More broadly, the Leaders Summit aims to deepen the commitment of participating leaders from business, labour and civil society to the Global Compact and its Principles; to build and scale up momentum within the business sector; and to foster enabling environments and collective action. The first Leaders Summit was held at UN Headquarters in New York on 24 June 2004.[3] The second took place at UN Headquarters in Geneva on 5–6 July 2007.[4] The next Leaders Summit, celebrating the initiative's tenth anniversary, will take place at the UN Headquarters in New York on 24–25 June 2010.

Global Compact Board

As the successor entity to the GCAC, the Global Compact Board was established in 2006 as a multi-stakeholder advisory body chaired by the Secretary-General. The Board meets at least once per year (usually twice) to provide ongoing strategic and policy advice for the initiative as a whole and issue recommendations to the Global Compact Office, participants and other stakeholders. The body comprises four constituency groups – business, civil society, labour and the United Nations – with differentiated roles and responsibilities apart from their overall advisory function. In addition to formal Board meetings, the constituency groups are expected to interact with the Global Compact Office on an ongoing basis. The Secretary-General, the Chair of the Foundation for the Global Compact and the Executive Director of the Global Compact Office are *ex officio* members of the Board.

The currently twenty-four Board members are champions willing and able to advance the Global Compact's mission. They are appointed by the Secretary-General and serve in a personal and honorary function; Board members are not UN officials. Drawing in particular on the expertise and recommendations of its business members, the Board is also expected to play a role in the implementation of the Global Compact's integrity measures. The

---

[3] For a summary of the 2004 Leaders Summit, visit www.unglobalcompact.org/NewsAndEvents/event_archives/global_compact_leaders_summit.html.

[4] For a summary of the 2007 Leaders Summit, visit www.unglobalcompact.org/NewsAndEvents/event_archives/Leaders_Summit_2007.html.

integrity measures, and the progress of the Global Compact Office in implementing them, is a regular agenda item at each of their meetings. In addition to their overall Board responsibilities, the civil society and labour constituency groups are expected to provide close liaison to their communities and share with the Board as a whole, and the Global Compact Office and IAT in particular, insights on current trends and best practices in corporate responsibility in their respective domains.

Local Networks

Local Networks are regional or, more usually, national groups of participants that come together to advance the Global Compact and its principles within a particular country or geographic region. They perform increasingly important roles in rooting the Global Compact within different national, cultural and linguistic contexts, and also in helping to manage the organizational consequences of rapid expansion. Their role is to facilitate the progress of companies (both local firms and subsidiaries of foreign corporations) engaged in the Compact with respect to implementation of the ten Principles, while also creating opportunities for multi-stakeholder engagement and collective action. There are currently more than eighty Local Networks around the world. Chapter 18 in this volume explains their role, including in the governance of the initiative, in more detail.

Apart from acting in accordance with the Global Compact's principles and objectives, Local Networks are self-governing. They have the opportunity to nominate members for election to the Global Compact Board, provide input on major activities undertaken by the Global Compact Office and convene the ALNF. Their input is also sought on the agenda for the triennial Leaders Summit. Furthermore, Local Networks play an important role in support of the communications on progress and integrity measures.

Annual Local Networks Forum

The ALNF is the main occasion for Local Networks from around the world to share experiences, review and compare progress, identify best practices and adopt recommendations intended to enhance the effectiveness of Local Networks.

Global Compact Office

The Global Compact Office is the UN entity formally entrusted with the support and overall management of the Global Compact. It has received the endorsement of the UN General Assembly on several occasions (a full list of such references can be found on the Global Compact website)[5] and has been given UN system-wide responsibilities for promoting the sharing of best practices. The Global Compact Office also has responsibilities with regard to advocacy and issue leadership, fostering network development and maintaining the Global Compact communications infrastructure. Furthermore, the Office plays a central role in advancing the partnership agenda across the UN system and has overall responsibility for brand management and implementation of the integrity measures. The Global Compact Office represents itself and the other members of the IAT on the Board. It also supports and services the Leaders Summit, the Global Compact Board and the ALNF.

Inter-Agency Team

Within the governance framework and daily operations of the initiative, the IAT is responsible for ensuring coherent support for the internalization of the principles within the United Nations and among all participants. The agencies most closely associated with the ten Principles also have an advisory role with respect to the management of the integrity measures complaints procedure. As of October 2009, six UN entities are represented in the IAT: the Office of the UN High Commissioner for Human Rights (OHCHR), the International Labour Organization (ILO), the United Nations Environment Programme (UNEP), the United Nations Office on Drugs and Crime (UNODC), the United Nations Development Programme (UNDP) and the United Nations Industrial Development Organization (UNIDO). It is anticipated that over time other UN agencies will elect to join the IAT.

The IAT is represented on the Global Compact Board through the Global Compact Office's Executive Director. The six core UN agencies participate in the Leaders Summit and the ALNF. UN agencies, funds and programmes, in particular UNDP through its global

[5] See www.unglobalcompact.org/AboutTheGC/Government_Support.html.

presence, also play a critical role in many GCLNs around the world
(see, for instance, the reflections in chapter 21 by Flavio Fuertes and
Nicolás Liarte-Vejrup).

Global Compact Donor Group

The Global Compact Office is funded by voluntary contributions
from Governments to a UN Trust Fund. Contributions from any
Government are welcome. Current (2009) donors include the People's
Republic of China, Colombia, Denmark, Finland, France, Germany,
Italy, the Republic of Korea, Norway, Spain, Sweden, Switzerland
and the UK. The Donor Group, which adopted its own Terms of
Reference in November 2008, meets twice annually at capital level to
review progress made and ensure the effective and efficient use of the
contributions that Donor Governments have provided to the Global
Compact Trust Fund. Donors and other interested Governments
are also welcome to participate in a Friends Group that meets more
frequently in New York to be kept informed of developments in the
initiative.

The Global Compact integrity measures

The purpose of the Global Compact's integrity measures, first introduced in 2005, is to safeguard the integrity and good efforts of the
United Nations, the Global Compact, participants and stakeholders. Owing to the Global Compact's explicit emphasis on learning,
dialogue and partnerships, the initiative wishes to engage only those
businesses that have a genuine interest in continuous performance
improvement.

Contrary to occasional misperceptions about the Global Compact's
mission and mandate, the chief purpose of the integrity measures is
not providing a remedy for alleged instances of corporate social or
environmental abuse. By design, this role does not lie within the
Global Compact's mandate, and neither does the initiative have
resources for such an undertaking. This is not to diminish the importance of the availability of effective remedies. Rather, the Global
Compact Office's limited resources are concentrated on fostering
effective learning, dialogue and partnerships as a complementary
contribution to – not a substitute for – other approaches aimed at

enhancing business' contribution to sustainable development and other UN goals.[6]

Social vetting and screening of new participants

Introduced in 2007, new applications for participation in the Global Compact are checked against various global databases to see if the company concerned is the subject of a sanction or other measure by the UN or international financial institutions. Such companies are excluded from participation for the duration of the sanction or other measure. Any other information found in the database is also shared with Local Network focal points, where a Network exists, of the country concerned. As standard procedure, the Global Compact Office also reaches out to Local Network focal points prior to admission to see if other reasons exist that could preclude a company from joining the initiative. These screening measures are performed promptly and normally allow the Global Compact Office to respond to the applicant within two weeks of submitting an application (box 14.1).

Evaluation and monitoring

Due to its nature as a voluntary platform, the Global Compact is not a performance measurement or assessment tool and does not issue judgements about the performance of business participants (see also Rasche 2009a). It is for this reason that the Global Compact Office does not and cannot routinely track or monitor companies' activities. The initiative does, however, seek high quality and integrity in the contributions of its participants, and since 2005 all participating businesses have been required to publish an annual COP, to be shared openly and publicly and to be made available for peer review and stakeholder comment. While the main purpose of the COP policy as a disclosure framework is to promote transparency and accountability in the spirit of the Global Compact Principles, it also is seen

---

[6] See, for instance, the dispute resolution mechanism, which describes the procedure of the OECD Guidelines for Multinational Enterprises, and/or the interpretation procedure under the ILO Tripartite Declaration of Principles concerning Multinational Enterprises and Social Policy (please see the corresponding websites, www.oecd.org/daf/investment/guidelines and www.iloorg/public/english/employment/multi/download/english.pdf, for more information).

Box 14.1: The Global Compact and social vetting

From its inception, the Global Compact has emphasized the importance of public disclosure of company activities as crucial to its commitment to accountability and transparency. The implementation of the Global Compact's integrity measures in 2005 and the strict enforcement of the annual COP requirement were practical expressions of this approach and have since significantly increased public awareness of business practice in meeting the commitment to the Global Compact's Principles.

In this respect, the Global Compact has long relied on the notion of 'social vetting', built around the premise that civil society, media and the public at large will continuously follow and examine information on the engagement of companies in the Global Compact and (i) recognize and encourage good business practices or (ii) stimulate a constructive public debate in situations where business practices are felt to be inconsistent with a company's commitment. Given that reputation management, risk minimization and social legitimacy are increasingly understood as material to overall business performance, social vetting has thus become a significant driver of organizational change.

Against this background, the Global Compact's disclosure approach underlines the role of the initiative as a neutral facilitator, or platform, of dialogue and learning. In fact, it opens the critical debate effectively to the public sphere, where corporate activities are vetted against the interests and concerns of different stakeholders. This has led to a sharp increase in media coverage and civil society activism around corporate operations in the context of the Global Compact. While civil society groups and activist Networks have been critical observers of the Global Compact (and, more broadly, the United Nations' collaboration with the private sector) from the very beginning,[1] some efforts to advance social vetting were initiated by the Global Compact Office itself. One example is a pilot project launched in 2003–4 in collaboration with Net Impact chapters at the NYU Stern School of Business and Brigham Young University's Marriott

---

[1] Early examples include the Alliance for a Corporate-Free UN under the auspices of CorpWatch.

School of Management. Several groups of MBA students critically reviewed and commented on case studies and practice examples submitted by Global Compact participants, leading to more than fifty responses and clarifications from business.[2] More recently, in 2009, the Global Compact Office began exploring the use of social media as vetting tools, launching a blog (http:// unglobalcompact.wordpress.com) and a Twitter feed to broaden the reach and awareness of its activities and to invite commentary from the wider public.

Naturally, civil society organizations and media (with boundaries often blurring due to the rise of citizen journalism on the Internet) account for most vetting activities. More recently, in 2007, a coalition of organizations and individuals launched Global Compact Critics (www.globalcompactcritcs.net), a weblog entirely devoted to the Global Compact's operations and participant activities. Certainly, disagreements between the Critics and the Global Compact over individual issues raised are often significant. Nevertheless, the Global Compact Office has welcomed this effort in principle, as it underscores the critical role of civil society organizations in the spirit of the Global Compact's mandate and mission and serves to open the debate effectively to the public sphere, where corporate activities are vetted against the interests and concerns of different stakeholders.

On a broader level, critical public coverage of the Global Compact has over time oscillated between questions around the Global Compact's legitimacy *vis-à-vis* calls for binding global regulatory frameworks for corporate conduct and more serious allegations about specific business practices. The former was particularly evident in the initiative's earlier years, when different actors expressed vocal scepticism over its voluntary nature, fearing that corporations were 'bluewashing' their reputation through association with the United Nations. However, in recent years, the tone of coverage and commentary has become more conciliatory and constructive, reflective of what appears to be a better understanding of the purpose (and limitations) of the initiative as a neutral facilitator, or platform, of dialogue and learning.

[2] See http://w4.stern.nyu.edu/news/releases/UN%20GC%20project020504. pdf for details.

It remains to be seen if and how the global financial crisis and subsequent economic downturn of 2008–9 will have a lasting effect on patterns and focus of social vetting, particularly in light of renewed calls for stricter global regulatory frameworks. The Global Compact Office will continue to monitor media and civil society activity in order to develop a better understanding of this process.

One notable development is the refinement of the Global Compact's COP policies and the ongoing effort to encourage the integration of clear indicators of environmental, social and governance (ESG) performance into the disclosure framework mandated by the Global Compact. The latter has opened opportunities for a new type of vetting by financial markets and regulators alike, rooted in an understanding of the materiality of ESG performance to the long-term sustainability (and success) of business. Joint efforts by the investor and asset manager signatories to the UN-backed Principles for Responsible Investment (PRI) may prove to be a powerful complement to the existing vetting efforts.

as a valuable tool to advance knowledge exchange, sharing of good practices and to promote continuous performance improvement.

The dialogue facilitation mechanism

The Global Compact is not an adjudicative body, but rather exists to facilitate adherence to the principles through transparency and enhanced communication. To this end, and in coordination with the Global Compact Board, a dialogue facilitation mechanism was introduced in 2007 (and further refined in 2009). In the event that the Global Compact Office receives information suggesting that a business participant's actions are inconsistent with its commitment to the Global Compact Principles and suggest a lack of commitment to continuous improvement, the Global Compact will endeavour to encourage dialogue between companies and those who have raised concerns. As a matter of policy, only issues related to a participant company's conduct and overall implementation of the Global Compact's Principles should be raised under the integrity measures.

The issues raised should rise to the level of systematic or egregious abuse of the Global Compact's Principles. Examples include substantiated allegations of company involvement in:

- Murder, torture, deprivation of liberty, forced labour, the worst forms of child labour and other child exploitation
- Serious violations of individuals' rights in situations of war or conflict
- Severe environmental damage
- Gross corruption
- Any other particularly serious violations of fundamental ethical norms.

Generally, the Global Compact Office will not entertain matters that are better suited to being handled by another entity, such as a court of law, local administrative agency, or other adjudicatory, governmental, or dispute resolution entity. Thus, for example, the Global Compact does not get involved in disputes by individual employees about their employment or in industrial relations disputes between a trade union and a company where other mechanisms exist to effectively handle such matters. In the latter case, the matters will be referred to the ILO.

In circumstances where the company concerned fails or refuses to respond in writing to the person or organization that raised the matter, the Global Compact Office may choose to mark the company as 'non-communicating' on the Global Compact website. However, if the company provides a plausible rationale for its refusal, the Global Compact Office may seek advice on the matter from any one or more of the entities referred to in the integrity measures (such as from Local Networks or relevant UN agencies). The Global Compact Office may then decide, as appropriate, either to list the company as 'non-communicating' until the responses are provided or not to do so if the rationale is reasonable. Generally speaking, though, in the spirit of the Global Compact's emphasis on dialogue, the Global Compact Office encourages a company to be willing to engage in dialogue with those who raise concerns about its conduct.

In addition to failure to prepare and post a COP and matters raised under the dialogue facilitation process, the integrity measures also deal with the issue of misuse of a Global Compact logo or of association with the Global Compact. In the latter case, the Global Compact

Office reserves the right to take appropriate action. Possible actions may include revoking participant status, requesting the assistance of the relevant Global Compact governance entities and/or instituting legal proceedings.

15 | The United Nations Global Compact Communication on Progress policy: origins, trends and challenges

UZMA HAMID AND OLIVER JOHNER

Introduction

The Communication on Progress (COP) requirement was introduced in 2003 and has, since then, become the most important integrity measure of the Global Compact. It obligates all business participants to publicly report on the progress they have made in implementing their commitments to the twin goals of the Global Compact, embracing and enacting the ten Principles and undertaking projects in the pursuit of wider UN goals (see box 15.1). Many observers see the COP as an effective mechanism of public disclosure that holds companies accountable regarding their commitment to the Global Compact; others criticize the same COP for being too flexible a model, vague and lacking rigour. This chapter aims to set out the rationale for the need to have a public disclosure requirement, its assumptions and limitations, how the policy has evolved over time, trends in COP reporting and finally what the current challenges are, and how they can be overcome.

Need for accountability and transparency: origins and rationale

From its inception, the Global Compact was criticized for being a voluntary initiative with no binding rules or accountability. Allegations ranged from 'bluewashing' – that is to say, using the blue from the UN brand to create a positive spin, to cover over the real issues – to pre-empting more rigorous normative regulations on companies' responsibilities in a globalized economy: in short, there was widespread scepticism. Against this backdrop in early 2003, in an attempt to hold

Box 15.1: What is a 'Communication on Progress'?

'The Communication on Progress (COP) is an annual disclosure through which a business informs stakeholders about its efforts in implementing the United Nations Global Compact and its principles . . . Every COP must meet minimum requirements in form and substance: . . . To avoid duplication of efforts, a COP should be fully integrated in existing stakeholder communications, such as annual, corporate responsibility or sustainability reports . . . COPs should be written in the language(s) of the majority of stakeholders . . . Making a COP widely available to internal and external stakeholders is an essential component of communicating progress. Participants are encouraged to use the established methods of stakeholder communication . . . Business participants that fail to meet the COP deadline will be marked as 'non-communicating' on the Global Compact website. Business participants that fail to submit a COP after having been 'non-communicating' for one year, will be delisted from the Global Compact.'

Source: Global Compact (2009d: 1).

companies accountable to their commitment to the Global Compact, the then Advisory Council of the Global Compact discussed ideas to ask companies 'to use their annual financial reports or other prominent public corporate reports to describe the actions they are taking in support of the Global Compact and all of its [back-then] nine principles' (Global Compact 2003). The idea of a COP was born and its aim was to achieve transparency in how companies implemented the Global Compact Principles. This requirement was encapsulated as a policy. The Global Compact Office was urged to actively communicate with participating companies to ensure that they understood the expectation related to public reporting.

Interestingly, at this early stage, the Advisory Council also discussed issues such as: the scope of the COPs (e.g. should business be required to report on selected or all principles); the need for guidance on reporting to avoid inconsistency; and the special needs of small and medium-sized enterprises (SMEs). These issues will be discussed later in this chapter, as they have proved to be increasingly relevant and challenging over the years.

A perfect model?: Assumptions and limitations

As a voluntary initiative the Global Compact does not monitor its participants for compliance with the Principles, as this is not its mandate and would require a huge amount of (local) knowledge and human resources. Therefore, the main objective of the COP is to protect the integrity of the Global Compact by requiring transparency in the public domain. The COP thereby allows stakeholders to learn and judge how companies live up to the commitments they have made as signatories. The Global Compact is the only voluntary global initiative focusing on corporate responsibility with a disclosure requirement.

The COP was intended to serve multiple goals, such as: (1) Strengthen the credibility of the Global Compact commitment; (2) Drive performance of implementing Global Compact Principles; (3) Foster learning among participants; (4) Enhance opportunities for social vetting of participating companies; and (5) Safeguard the integrity of the Global Compact as a voluntary initiative.

The COP mechanism is based on three basic assumptions that deserve some critical reflection:

1. *COP will create public accountability:* The assumption is that the general public or interested stakeholder groups such as consumers, employees, civil society, investors, media, or academia will read COPs and hold companies accountable for the claims they make within them. Further, the COP will serve as an active mechanism for stakeholders to give feedback and engage with businesses in relation to their commitment to the Global Compact. This model is called 'social vetting'.

   However in contradiction to this assumption, it is unclear to what extent 'stakeholders' currently use COPs or non-financial reports in general as sources of information. For example, it is questionable that the general public is informed about corporate practices related to the Global Compact Principles, or care to know. Non-governmental organizations (NGOs) with an interest in the Global Compact tend to focus on individual well-known companies, rather than assessing all companies, including small ones. The media are interested in the high-level stories associated with big brand names, rather than reporting on the nuts and bolts of a corporate strategy. It is widely acknowledged that only a small group of people read non-financial reports such as COPs, and this is usually within a professional capacity – i.e. reading is part of their work as investors, academics, or consultants. Reading such reports requires resources, as does engagement with companies, and there is little evidence that many stakeholders do this.

2. *Transparency fosters a race to the top:* By publicly disclosing information on non-financial issues, through COP, it is assumed that businesses will see this as an opportunity to differentiate themselves from their competitors, and will prioritize better performance, in order to show their innovation or leading position on issues specific to their business. This will drive better implementation of the ten Principles, and facilitate a 'race to the top'. However, this approach is hard to prove; while it is clear that leading companies see value in maintaining a competitive advantage through continuous improvement, and are influenced by peer pressure, other companies are less ambitious in further implementing and reporting on the Global Compact, beyond the basics. They seem less concerned about the perception of their progress and are happy to simply maintain the status quo. Also, in the absence of a generally agreed and accepted standard for measuring progress in corporate responsibility, comparing companies' COPs, even within an industry, is difficult. While the Global Reporting Initiative's (GRI) Sustainability Reporting Guidelines are generally seen as the world's *de facto* standard in non-financial reporting, studies found that very few GRI-based reports live up to the level of comparability that are known from financial reports (WestLB 2007).

3. *Reporting is proxy for implementation:* While it is generally agreed that reporting is a reflection of how businesses implement the Global Compact Principles, some questions remain, for example, 'What information must be disclosed to fully reflect a company's status of implementation?' and 'How is progress or performance defined?' A report can never reflect a company's activities in detail, it can only give a flavour and usually focuses on the positives. Also many impacts depend on the local context, which can change

dynamically over time, and so reports can become quickly out of date. To date the Global Compact has not specified exactly how businesses need to implement the principles, and what information companies must disclose on different issues and in what level of detail the information should be presented. It is therefore difficult to accept that reporting is a proxy for implementation, as it is easy for companies to report only on their achievements, and remain silent on their dilemmas or challenges. Not only in the nascent fields of business and human rights or corruption is more clarification and guidance on what companies are expected to report on needed.

Moving with the times: evolution of the COP policy

Consistent with the nature of the Global Compact, the COP policy was designed to be flexible and inclusive, which has also been a factor of its evolution over time. Only three basic elements – statement of continued support for the Global Compact, description of activities and measurement of outcomes – were required to be included to constitute a document a COP. The idea was that the COP requirement should not become an administrative burden for businesses and that they should be given time to improve in reporting and implementation, ensuring that there was room for 'beginner' or small and medium companies to manoeuvre.

Once the policy was introduced, it was communicated to all participating companies and the growing number of Global Compact Local Networks (GCLNs) was asked to support companies in meeting the COP requirement. However no suggestions were made on which format to follow or how to integrate COP-required information into existing reporting structures. While some businesses integrated the COP requirement into their formal reporting process, others – many of whom were approaching non-financial reporting for the first time – took advantage of the flexibility to 'tell their story' in a way that was particular to them, rather than trying to communicate through a rigid structure.

Also as a result of the lack of clarity around the COP, GCLNs each had a different understanding and interpretation of what a COP should look like, and developed diverging approaches on COP, both of which affected the advice given to businesses and the quality of what was being produced. For example in Spain, there is an online template with a set of questions, the completion of which constitutes a valid COP. The Local Network assesses the answers provided and then helps businesses in their areas of improvement. In France the 'bonnes pratiques' (good practices) were promoted as completions of the COP requirement. This meant that a business had to submit a case story of good practice on any one principle of the Global Compact, which resulted in many stand-alone documents that did not make reference to the other principles or the business context in which the company was operating.

The flexibility of the COP policy resulted in many innovative approaches and reporting formats. Yet, the quality of COPs was generally considered as low by many stakeholders, given the disparate variety with regard to content, level of detail and structure/format. It became obvious that clarification and simplification of the COP policy was needed, and that this may help streamline the different approaches taken in the past years.

In May 2008, the Global Compact Board asked the Global Compact Office to take stock of the experiences with COP so far and to explore the development of a minimum standard for COP. At this time the Global Compact Office worked together with KPMG International to agree and execute a partnership project, which aimed at evolving the COP process to ensure that it continues to be effective and delivers value to its stakeholders. A crucial stage of the project was to conduct extensive consultation with key stakeholder groups including businesses, Local Networks, financial analysts, NGOs, academia and UN agencies. The project resulted in a number of key findings and recommendations:

- The need for clearer minimum standards in COP
- The need for clearer and simpler guidance on how to implement and report on the Global Compact, especially for small and medium enterprises
- The need to identify leading corporate behaviours and leaders in implementation and reporting
- The need to create a system for companies to compare progress and performance, through COPs
- The need to involve Local Networks in educating stakeholders on COP and facilitating multi-stakeholder feedback to companies.

The stock-taking exercise resulted in a refined COP policy that simplified the COP process, clarified the minimum requirements that could be enforced and improved the searchability of the COP database. The major changes of the revised COP policy are:

- New business participants are given one year (instead of two) from the date of joining to prepare and submit their first COP.
- As a minimum, during the first five years of participation, a COP must address at least two of the Global Compact's four principal issue areas, while all must be addressed after five years.
- The COP submission form on the Global Compact website requires additional information, to improve searchability.
- The 'inactive' participant status will be eliminated. Business participants that have been 'non-communicating' for more than one year will be delisted and removed from the Global Compact website.

The updated COP policy was communicated to all Global Compact participants, Local Networks and stakeholders in April 2009. It became effective on 1 July 2009 for all business participants.

Past and current trends in Communication on Progress

Despite the efforts made by Local Networks, the Global Compact Office and many others, the number of COPs that were submitted and published on the Global Compact website in the early years was quite low. Many companies did not know about, did not understand, or simply did not want to do a COP. Therefore, activities focused on 'keeping the pipeline flowing', i.e. increase the number of companies that submitted COPs. Communication on the COP requirement was intensified, Local Networks were asked to support companies even more, the IT platform that administers the COPs was improved and training for business was organized.

While the absolute number of COPs has grown significantly in recent years, this overlooks the fact that still only half of all participants that are required to submit a COP actually do so. As can be seen in table 15.1, the probability that a participant submits a COP is related to the size of the company. Almost all *Fortune* 500 companies submit COPs, while only around one out of three SMEs do so.

Table 15.1 *Evolution of COP Reports, 2004–2009*

Year	2004	2005	2006	2007	2008	2009[1]
Number of COPs	167	648	881	1386	1733	2071
COP ratio of all business participants (%)	26	62	57	73	53	48
COP ratio of FT500 (%)	72	77	85	95	95	94
COP ratio of businesses (more than 249 employees) (%)	15	61	58	76	65	59
COP ratio of SMEs (with 10–249 employees) (%)	9	54	42	61	35	31

Note:
[1] Estimate for 2009 based on percentage of COPs submitted by July in previous years; COP ratios (%) as of 20 July 2009.

There are significant geographical variations in the percentage of reporting participants that can mainly be explained by the strength of and efforts undertaken by Local Networks. Local Networks that provide extensive support to companies on COP such as Argentina, France, or Spain have higher COP capture rates than other Networks (see also chapter 21 by Flavio Fuertes and Nicolás Liarte-Vejrup). The efforts undertaken by these Networks partly explain the increase in the capture rate in 2007 (the peak was also due to the removal of a large number of participants for failure to submit a COP). On the other side of the spectrum are countries where either no Local Networks have been established so far or where the Local Network could not successfully manage the fast growth of participants. As a result many of the companies were delisted from the Global Compact for failure to submit their COPs.

In the early years, the Global Compact Office did not systematically measure the quality and comprehensiveness of COPs that could facilitate a demonstration of general businesses progress over time. The Notable COP programme was introduced in 2004 to attempt to do this and to highlight and recognize outstanding COPs that represented illustrative and inspirational examples of communicating progress. It was not until 2007 that all COPs were subject to this assessment, based on a set of robust, transparent criteria. These COP assessments are now able to give some insight with regard to the format and quality of the COPs (data from COPs submitted between August 2007 and June 2009):

- 45 per cent of COPs are integrated into formal reports such as an annual financial, corporate responsibility or sustainability report; 55 per cent are stand-alone COPs
- Around 30 per cent of COPs are using the GRI reporting framework
- Around 20 per cent of COPs are externally verified/assured
- Around 30 per cent of COPs address all ten Principles of the Global Compact.

The Swiss-based Guilé Foundation, an organization that focuses its activities on entrepreneurial responsibility in the process of economic globalization, conducted and published a COP study in 2009 that sheds some light on the state of COP.[1] COPs from forty large companies, made up of twenty from developed economies and twenty from emerging economies, across four industries were analysed in detail. A criteria-based methodology evaluated COPs in two dimensions: quality and comprehensiveness of information. The main findings of the COP study were:

- Leading businesses (those who are advanced in terms of reporting) from both developed and emerging economies have strong reporting practices and provide relevant information about how they implement the ten Principles of the Global Compact within their sphere of influence.
- There are large differences in the reporting practices of businesses. COPs differ in their comprehensiveness and quality across and also within the analysed sectors.
- Only few businesses report on the ten Global Compact Principles in a balanced manner. Most companies put emphasis on some principles and neglect others. Comprehensiveness of information also varies between the four issues areas of the Global Compact. Businesses disclose more information on environmental issues or anti-corruption than on human rights or labour issues.

---

[1] The Guilé Foundation has entrusted a team of leading experts in corporate responsibility to engage with companies of two investment funds based on their commitment to the Global Compact (see Guilé Foundation 2009).

- While most businesses report on their commitment to the Global Compact Principles, information about the relevance (materiality) of the Principles for their business was found to be relatively vague. As effective implementation of the Principles relies on a sound analysis of their relevance for a business and its value chain, one would expect to find a deeper reflection why and how a principle affects or will affect the company in a positive or negative way.
- Companies tend to disclose information on their achievements rather than on dilemmas and contested issues. The report concludes that more transparency on challenges would add credibility to companies' efforts to find practical solutions.

While many efforts were made to communicate and support participants in preparing COPs, a dual challenge remains: first, the percentage of reporting companies must be increased over time to avoid an imbalance with those signatories that will be delisted for failure to communicate on progress. Second, the quality of COPs must be improved to achieve the multiple goals of the COP mechanism.

Keeping up: challenges and ways to overcome them

Context of the current challenges

This leads us to consider the key challenges that face the COP mechanism and explore potential ways to overcome them. Before we do this it is useful to highlight the ways in which non-financial reporting is evolving and how practitioners view this, in order to provide a context for current challenges. The majority of businesses consulted in the Global Compact Office–KPMG partnership project believed that the importance of non-financial reporting will grow strongly in the future five–ten years, despite and as a direct result of the global recession. Investors and markets will continue to be more interested in non-financial issues which may drive inclusion in a wider global regulatory framework. It is possible that non-financial reporting will become mandatory through domestic regulation, as it has to some degree in Denmark, France and Norway.

Currently there are many corporate responsibility initiatives, programmes and standards open to businesses and involvement with them can be time-consuming, especially if a business has multiple relationships. It can be confusing to know how they link together and which reporting standard or model is the best. The corporate responsibility marketplace could benefit from forming strategic partnerships to streamline the number of initiatives or explain better how they link together to avoid the 'reporting fatigue' that businesses complain of.

Non-financial reporting as a process has many barriers and challenges, as identified by the practitioners who prepare this information:

- Defining 'materiality' in corporate responsibility is an ongoing challenge. What and how much to disclose is problematic, as stakeholders ask how and what issues are being addressed in the context of the business' strategy and operations.
- The importance of identifying and engaging with stakeholders increases, as they need to be consulted and involved in defining what is strategically important and relevant for the business.
- Corporate responsibility reports are becoming increasingly important and overlooked at the same time. They are too long, the data within them is hard to access and they are not aimed at targeted audiences. As there are growing multiple audiences, companies need to focus on the key ones to provide relevant data and in different formats.
- There needs to be more inclusion of governance and strategy information and less photos and philanthropy. There is a need for increased verification of data.

Quality of the COP: the need for consistency

The quality of COPs should improve or remain high to demonstrate the seriousness of the commitment of businesses to the Global Compact and this remains an ongoing challenge. As explained earlier, the quality of current COPs varies with each participant. It is hoped that the updated COP policy will clarify expectations, but another challenge still remains, mainly ensuring that the policy and changes are successfully implemented.

One way to improve the quality of COPs is to ensure that there is global consistency on what constitutes a COP and the potential role of Local Networks facilitating this cannot be underestimated. As part of their mandate to incentivize businesses to be more involved with the Global Compact and the ten Principles, they can promote the publication of high-quality COPs that are consistent with what the policy dictates. Their value is in their knowledge of local issues and can extend to how best to measure and communicate progress against the Principles in regional contexts in a way that allows global consistency. Practically, they can screen COPs and offer guidance to a business before they publish their document. Ensuring that minimum agreed standards are applied globally will further strengthen the COP and raise the quality of what is produced, and can also introduce a form of standardization which increases the value of COP reporting to wider stakeholder groups. Minimum standards must also be enforced by the Global Compact Office to keep quality levels high.

Guidance on reporting and implementation

The Global Compact has always maintained that it is a philosophy, a vehicle for facilitating the acceptance of universally declared values, rights and responsibilities by the private sector. Its role is not to prescribe what actions should be taken, but to suggest and share best practice. However, the complex relationship between reporting and implementation raises issues for the COP, against the backdrop of this perspective. There are criticisms from the business world that the Principles themselves are difficult to understand in a corporate context, as the terminology is alien and they are too vague. This is seen as a barrier and challenge to reporting: if they do not know what they are trying to implement, what are they expected to report on? They argue that reporting guidance would at least show what the aims of each Principle are in the business context, for example, through indicators or best practices, so that they can aspire to implement based on these guidelines. Also as non-financial reporting becomes more sophisticated, there is a growing number of reporting standards that focus on numerical data, key performance indicators (KPIs) and quantitative information. This has led the lack of indicators in COP guidance to become more visible and critics say that the Global Compact Office should be more directive on how it expects businesses to measure their outputs, and provide Principle and sector-specific guidance and recommend indicators.

Currently the Global Compact Office advocates the use of any standard that allows a business to show year-on-year progress in a transparent fashion against the ten Principles. But this is not considered to be enough by many businesses who say that the Global Compact should go further and be more definitive; they argue that something such as providing numerical evidence of progress on anti-corruption or human rights is not simple and since it is the Global Compact Office that asks for this information, they should provide some direction on what form it should take. Stepping back from this criticism, consideration should be made of the fact that non-financial reporting itself as a movement is still in development and that there is not yet one standard agreed framework that businesses use worldwide to measure their non-financial impacts.

Against this backdrop it makes sense for the Global Compact Office to promote many models that allow businesses to express, in methods most suitable for them, the progress they are making. The Global Compact Office is also a key player in working groups that focus on reporting on anti-corruption (with Transparency International, TI) and on human rights (with the GRI and Realizing Rights – The Ethical Globalization Initiative) to explore and define indicators that help businesses to report in these areas. Similar efforts are underway with regard to water and carbon disclosure. Also, the Global Compact Office or Local Networks could put more emphasis on identifying good practices in both implementing and reporting on the Global Compact Principles. The sharing of good practices would not only be an incentive for businesses but also an effective way for other participants to learn and replicate from real examples.

Comparability/benchmarking of COPs

Comparability is strongly linked to value creation for wider stakeholders of both business participants and also the Global Compact itself. If the Global Compact, through COPs, can provide information to the market and consumers about the relative performance of a given business against the ten Principles, within sector categorization, this would strengthen its position as an international value platform. The Global Compact Office–KPMG International project revealed that financial analysts, rating agencies, NGOs, Local Networks, businesses and academics all agreed that there was potential to create more value from COPs as a source of information if they could be compared using agreed standards, which would allow readers to assess how well and in what areas businesses were active and progressing.

There is currently no empirical way to compare or benchmark COPs, as there is an absence of mechanisms that support comparability. Benchmarking has been suggested within the Global Compact–KPMG International project by various stakeholders as a method by which public comparisons of COPs can be made. The argument is that benchmarking will more effectively drive competition between companies to perform better, creating the desired 'race to the top', allowing wider audiences to see transparently the leading companies and progressive sectors. A benchmarking system can also be used as a tool for businesses to self-assess their performance and by financial analysts to access clearer, objective data. This kind of evaluation may even encourage more reading of the information within non-financial reports and COPs.

The Global Compact Office does not conduct benchmarking as it considers it to be outside of the original agreement of its mandate with businesses, and it would be unfair to change the terms and conditions. However, it does understand that such a system has benefits and is exploring the creation of benchmarks with different parties such as the investor community and academic institutions (through the Principles for Responsible Investment, PRI and the Principles for Responsible Management Education, PRME, respectively).

Alternatively, another way to drive the quality and improve the comparability of COPs is to introduce different reporting levels. Such a system of clearly defined reporting levels would allow businesses to self-categorize their progress based on the information in their COP and to differentiate themselves from other participants. This would also help businesses understand how they are performing in line with others, motivate them to perform better and outline what they need to do to progress.

Each reporting level would clearly describe what constitutes progress at different stages of participation, relating to the engagement and implementation of the ten Principles, thereby giving companies clear aims and a defined path for continuous improvement. It is assumed that current leaders would 'up their game' in order to reach higher levels and become role models, motivate companies that have been participants for a number of years to evolve and guide new participants on what first steps they can take.

Specific needs of SMEs

Small and medium-sized enterprises (SMEs) make up approximately 50 per cent of GDP in any given country and generate significant employment opportunities. They also make up slightly more than 50 per cent of Global Compact business participants (Global Compact 2008), but disproportionately only around one-third of them produce COPs. It is important to engage with this group on implementing and reporting on the Global Compact as they promote growth and make up a substantial proportion of Global Compact participants.

Some considerations to bear in mind about this group include the fact that resources and timing are big issues, as there is usually only one person tasked with implementation and reporting on corporate responsibility and this is not always a business priority. Working through how to implement commitments and which indicators to use in reporting requires a lot of thinking and implementing time. In order to engage with this group perhaps a simple step-by-step guidance approach would be valuable, to maximize their limited resources. Some guidance has been developed for SMEs that needs to be piloted and then shared more widely.

Conclusion

We have explored the drivers for the introduction of the COP requirement, how it has developed over six years, the challenges and demands that it faces and some possible solutions. This discourse has shown that the COP is not a perfect model for public disclosure, but it does provide benefits to companies as it offers a framework to begin a dialogue on how a business is behaving responsibly, around policy-driven issues that are universally recognized. It has proved to be especially useful for those businesses that are starting out on their journey in corporate responsibility, or are tackling some form of non-financial reporting for the first time.

The COP model itself has also been on a journey, being tweaked and changed along the way to suit the context of the time and better serve its stakeholders. The authors suggest that the COP should continue on that same journey, and that it should listen and anticipate the changes of its time, to ensure that it continues to deliver more value to businesses, NGOs, consumers, academia, the media and governments. It should strive to understand the needs of those who could and can find most value in it and leverage its benefits to build a stronger model – one that can be easily integrated into all non-financial reporting frameworks – for wider global application and recognition.

16 COP *reporting in action: the case of Petrobras*

ANA PAULA GRETHER CARVALHO

Introduction

This chapter provides a practitioner's perspective on how Petrobras builds and manages its Communication on Progress (COP) reporting. It is not possible to write about the COP experience of Petrobras without telling the story of the progress of the company regarding social and environmental corporate responsibility during recent years. Petrobras is an integrated oil and gas company, the largest corporation in Brazil, and one of the major companies in the international oil sector. As such, Petrobras acknowledges its prime responsibility for the environment where it operates and striving for sustainable development is a historical commitment of the company. Recently, these efforts have shown important improvements being integrated in its corporate governance.

In 2007, Social Responsibility became a corporate function at Petrobras. Therefore, in the '2020 Petrobras Strategic Plan' the mission of the company is to '[o]perate in a safe and profitable manner in Brazil and abroad, with social and environmental responsibility, providing products and services that meet client needs and that contribute to the development of Brazil and of the countries where we operate'. The company vision for 2020 is 'We will be one of the five largest integrated energy companies in the world and the preferred choice among our stakeholders'. Two characteristics of this vision are that Petrobras' operations should be a benchmark in social and environmental responsibility and committed to sustainable development. For this management challenge, a strategic goal for 2020 was also set: 'To be a world class reference for social responsibility, contributing to the development of sustainable business models.'

With this goal, Petrobras has established a social responsibility policy with eight specific guidelines (see box 16.1). Certainly, a milestone of Petrobras' commitment to social responsibility was becoming

Box 16.1: Petrobras' social responsibility policy

To Petrobras, social responsibility is the integrated, ethical, and transparent management of its business interests and activities and of its relationships with all of its stakeholders, furthering human rights and the full exercise of citizenship, respecting human and cultural diversity, working to eradicate discrimination, degrading work, child and forced labour, and contributing to sustainable development and reduction of social inequality.

1. Corporate performance: Assure that the Petrobras System's corporate governance is committed to ethics and transparency in its relationship with its stakeholders.
2. Integrated management: Guarantee integrated social responsibility management throughout the Petrobras System.
3. Sustainable development: Carry out the Petrobras System's business interests and activities with social responsibility, meeting its commitments pursuant to the principles set forth by the UN's Global Compact, and contributing to sustainable development.
4. Human rights: Respect and support internationally acknowledged human rights, basing the Petrobras System's actions on furthering the principles of decent, non-discriminatory labour.
5. Diversity: Respect the human and cultural diversity of its workforce and of the countries where it operates.
6. Labour principles: Support the eradication of child, forced, and degrading labour in the Petrobras System's supply chain.
7. Sustainable social investment: Seek social investment sustainability to drive social development at the communities.
8. Workforce commitment: Assure workforce commitment to the Petrobras System's Social Responsibility Policy.

Source: Petrobras (2009: 3).

a signatory of the United Nations Global Compact in 2003. Since then, the company has been committed to the ten Global Compact Principles. As a transparency commitment to its stakeholders, the company has annually published a COP report which covers each Principle of the Global Compact.

Petrobras: a brief company profile

Petrobras was established in 1953 as a state-ruled company after it was allowed by National Law to be incorporated to undertake oil sector activities in Brazil on behalf of the Federal Government. This decree was a result of a civil society movement for domestic exploration of oil and gas in Brazil. Oil exploration and production operations, as well as the remaining activities connected to oil, natural gas and the derivative sector were the monopoly of Petrobras from 1954 to 1997. In 1997, Brazil, via Petrobras, entered the group of sixteen countries that produced more than a million barrels of oil per day. During the same year a new law opened oil industry activities in Brazil to other private actors.

In 2003, coinciding with the celebration of its fiftieth anniversary, Petrobras doubled its daily oil and natural gas production, passing the 2 million barrel per day mark in Brazil and abroad. In 2006, it then started the operations at platform P-50, in Campos Basin, which enabled Brazil to reach self-sufficiency in oil production. Petrobras today is an internationally acknowledged oil and gas company with proprietary technology for ultradeep waters. CENPES, the Petrobras research centre, has one of the most advanced technologies in the world and is internationally renowned for its high proficiency. Petrobras operates in the following sectors: refining, trading and transportation, petrochemicals, distribution, biofuels, as well as natural gas and electricity. It is present in twenty-seven countries in the Americas, Europe, Africa and Asia. In December 2008, the company had 112 production platforms and seventeen refineries with a processing capacity of 2.2 million barrels per day and more than 344,000 shareholders. The company also had around 7,300 service stations in Brazil and abroad.

In addition to its holding activities, the Petrobras System includes a number of subsidiaries, which are independent companies with their own executive boards that are associated to the head office.

Petrobras' Social and Environmental Report

Since 2004, Petrobras' Social and Environmental Report has been structured as a COP. It is considered a disclosure of information and rendering of accounts to the society, covering actions that express social and environmental responsibility. Also, it is a basis for dialogue and engagement with stakeholders as well as a management tool for improvement in social and environmental responsibility practice. However, Petrobras has gone a long way to arrive at the present model of reporting. Even before reporting according to the COP structure, Petrobras had published Social and Environmental Reports.

The first Brazilian Social and Environmental Report was published in 1984 by Nitrofertil, a subsidiary of the Petrobras System; Petrobras Holding published its first Social and Environmental Report in 1998. At that moment, the report was a paper of corporate information about the social and environmental actions of the company. In 1999, the company adopted the IBASE Model to publish its social and environmental information. IBASE is a non-governmental organization (NGO) dedicated to democratizing information about the economic, political and social reality in Brazil. Started in 1997, the IBASE Model establishes indexes for economic, social and environmental performance, covering workforce aspects as well as corporate citizenship. The report, based on the IBASE Model, has become part of the set of accounting data sent to the Security and Exchange Commission (SEC) in Brazil.

The process of adopting social and environmental indexes as a guideline for social and environmental reporting began in 2001, when Petrobras started to partially follow the GRI framework (also including data on its main subsidiaries). Since then, the company progressively started to report a diversity of quantitative and qualitative indexes on economic, environmental and social aspects provided by the Global Reporting Initiative (GRI), the IBASE Model and others.

Building the Petrobras reporting model

The landmark year in the process of using social and environmental indexes for the report was 2003. The Petrobras' report expanded its list of social and environmental indexes, addressing GRI, the IBASE Model and the Dow Jones Sustainability Index (DJSI) questionnaire. To integrate the various questions of the different indexes into similar themes, we prepared an index matrix addressing more than 150 items. The main items of the matrix were: strategy and vision, company profile, governance and management system, economic performance and environmental as well as social information. The main items for economic performance were: sales and geographic distribution of markets, cost of inputs, salaries, profit distribution as well as taxes and subsidies. The items about environmental performance focused on data about: raw materials, energy and water consumption, biodiversity, waste and emissions. The social items were related to: labour practices, health and safety, training and education, diversity and opportunity, human rights, society and product responsibility.

During the same year, the company became a signatory of the Global Compact. Hence, the Social and Environmental Report was edited in accordance with the ten Principles of the Global Compact to become the company's COP. In practical terms, the report was structured around the Compact areas: human rights, environment, labour and anti-corruption, all of which became editorial chapters in the report. This newly established framework was an innovation because it allowed Petrobras to relate the already existing social and environmental indexes to the COP reporting structure. Petrobras was an early mover in this regard, as a specific guidance on how to associate COP reporting with the GRI Guidelines was not issued until 2006.

A method of participative preparation of the COP was implemented for collecting all the information for this large index matrix. A Network of internal collaborators was configured representing the main corporate areas. In 2003, external third-party verification of the COP was established as a part of the process. Ernst & Young (from 2003 to 2005) and then KPMG (from 2006 to 2008) were responsible for carrying out the verification in compliance with the standards provided by the American Institute of Certified Public Accountants. Third-party verification of the COP included the following activities:

- Interviewing Petrobras staff
- Analysing the computer records that provided the information included in the Social and Environmental Report
- Revising the external information sources that provided the information included in the Social and Environmental Report
- Revising the contracts, agreements and other documents supporting certain information included in the Social and Environmental Report
- Analysing the main processes and revising the internal control structure for these processes that generated the information included in the Social and Environmental Report

- Checking the accounting information included in the Social and
  Environmental Report against the financial statements for the same
  year, which are audited by the same company.

Petrobras was one of the first companies in Brazil to hire an external
company to check and revise the information of its progress reports,
even before the requirement by the Federal Accounting Council.

The goal of reporting quantitative and qualitative data and results
in the index matrix represented a big challenge. This reporting model
also allowed including data from the Petrobras System (i.e. holding,
subsidiaries and business units). Aiming to address this challenge,
the COP process included a Network of internal collaborators
and also consolidated an electronic database system for social and
environmental indexes.

Improving socially responsible corporate management

The creation of the Social Responsibility Management Committee in
2004 represented a significant corporate governance improvement.
The Management Committees at Petrobras are part of the overall gov-
ernance structure as forums for discussion of strategic issues among
top-level executives. Currently, there are the following Management
Committees: Technology, Health Safety and Environment, Human
Resources, Downstream, E&P, Gas and Energy, Analysis of Corporate
Structure and Management, Information Technology, Internal
Control, Information Security, Risk, Marketing and Brands, and Social
Responsibility. All the recommendations of these Committees are for-
warded to the Business Committees to be approved by the Executive
Board. The Social Responsibility Management Committee is responsible for creating, planning, developing and following the corporate
guidelines, management policies, and strategies for environmental
and social responsibility of the Petrobras System. This Management
Committee also monitors the related activities and projects of the
company in the area of social responsibility and proposes actions for
further alignment and integration (for the decision process underlying
the Social Responsibility Management Committee, see figure 16.1).

At the end of 2005, the Institutional Communication Area within
Petrobras was restructured to improve company governance. A result of
this restructuring was the creation of the Corporate Social Responsibility

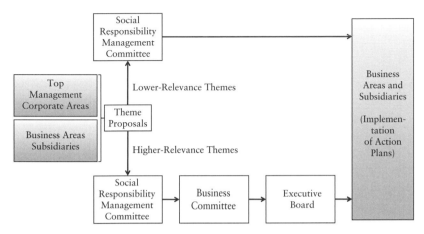

Figure 16.1 Social Responsibility Management Committee: outflow of decisions

area, sub-divided into three sectors – Social Programs, Environmental Programs, and Guidelines and Practices for Social Responsibility. During the same year, the Social Responsibility Management Committee established a specific commission for preparing and assessing the company's Social and Environmental Reports (the SER Commission). Coordinated by the Corporate Social Responsibility area, this Commission is responsible for all the reports concerning Social and Environmental Responsibility, including the COP.

The SER Commission currently includes twenty-nine focal points from the main corporate areas (Institutional Communications, Management System Development, Business Strategy and Performance, Human Resources, Investor Relations, HSE, I&T, Exploration and Production, Downstream, Gas & Energy, International, Finance, Accounting, Shared Services, Materials, Engineering, Research and Development, Ombudsman office) as well as the two main subsidiaries of the Petrobras System: Petrobras Distribuidora and Transpetro. These focal points are responsible for collecting, providing data and evidence for all the information reported in the COP. Hence, another objective is also to establish an ongoing communication channel between the corporate areas and subsidiaries, aligning them with the overall reporting principles and identifying opportunities for improving the management practices of the company.

In 2005, the corporate data system for social and environmental indexes was established. The objective was to consolidate all the

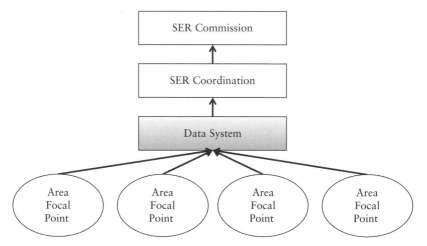

Figure 16.2 Petrobras Social and Environmental Report Commission

electronic data provided by the main areas of the company which are part of the SER Commission (see figure 16.2). Each area focal point is responsible for its final electronic questionnaire. The focal points are also responsible for the area Network of collaborators and the division of the questionnaires among these collaborators. The idea of the system is to create an ongoing dynamic electronic database for the social and environmental responsibility indexes of the entire Petrobras System.

The COP as a management tool

In 2004, the COP was used as a corporate management tool for the first time. A vulnerability map was prepared based upon the index matrix (including over 200 items for that year). This map was a critical study of Petrobras' position evidenced in the answers to social and environmental reporting indexes. This process of assessing the company's social responsibility performance turned into being a fixed part of the overall COP process. Every year, a critical analysis of the social and environmental reporting indexes assesses existing gaps and looks for opportunities for improving the management of social and environmental responsibility. The vulnerability map is analysed by the Social Responsibility Management Committee and is used as a base for the actions and strategies with regard to social and environmental matters. The decisions and actions of the Social Responsibility Management Committee are fundamental for making the workforce aware of Petrobras' social and environmental values. This, of course, reflects a continuous learning process.

The vulnerability map assessment has resulted in a variety of action plans, working groups and even specific commissions under the scope of the Social Responsibility Management Committee. For instance, based upon the first vulnerability map, the Management Committee created the SER Commission in 2005 and also the Index and Certification working group, the DJSI Challenge working group and the Gender Commission. The purpose of the Index and Certification working group is studying, analysing and proposing parameters for certification and references on social and environmental indexes in order to define the requirements of excellence for social and environmental responsibility to be followed by Petrobras. The DJSI Challenge working group was established to analyse the DJSI index and to improve Petrobras' performance to be finally considered as part of the DJSI (this happened during the following year, 2006).

The Gender Commission was guided by Global Compact Principles to comply with the third UN Millennium Development Goal (MDG): 'Promote gender equity and empower women.' Also as a result of the vulnerability map process, the Social Responsibility Management Committee expanded the scope of the Gender Commission in 2006, which was then renamed the Diversity Commission. This change increased the Commission's role, in line with Petrobras' commitments for acknowledging the principles of non-discrimination and promoting equality, regardless of race; religion; social, cultural, language, political and aesthetic factors; age; physical, mental and psychic conditions; gender; and sexual orientation. Another fundamental result of the vulnerability map process was the formulation of Petrobras' Social Responsibility Policy (see above). Issued in 2007, the policy was prepared during the second half of 2006 with direct participation of the top executives of the company and members of the Management Committee for Social Responsibility.

Searching for continuous improvement of the COP Report

A first survey of stakeholders (government, media, NGOs, customers and suppliers) was conducted in 2005 about the 2004 COP. As a result, summary versions of the 2005 COP were issued to four different parties: employees, the media, investors and the general public – following the Global Compact's idea of multi-stakeholder collaboration. This process of external analysis of the report by a survey of the stakeholders became part of the COP process as well.

For the 2006 COP, Petrobras adopted the third generation of GRI indicators (G3) launched in October 2006. The result was a complete report addressing the updated social and environmental GRI framework. The Petrobras report was rated A+ by GRI – meaning that all essential indicators were addressed (A) and that the report has undergone an external verification (+).

As recommended in the GRI Sustainability Report Guidelines, Petrobras has been performing a 'materiality test' since 2007. The test consists of a stakeholder survey addressing the following parties: clients and resellers, scientific and academic community, communities, consumers, suppliers, the media, investors, partners (institutions and associations), public authorities, employees and the third sector. These stakeholders are asked to answer a questionnaire about sustainability-related topics and also to rate topics according to their relevance. Of course, the stakeholders are also free to suggest other topics not included in the questionnaire. In addition to meetings with stakeholders, members of the SER Commission – representing the areas of the Petrobras System – are also consulted in order to classify the items according to their expectations.

This process helped to identify the most important ('material') topics to be addressed by Petrobras. In 2007, sixty stakeholders took part in the process during two workshops in Rio de Janeiro and São Paulo and telephone interviews. The main topics identified were: environment, corporate governance, health and safety, human rights, engagement with suppliers, strategic planning and engagement with customers and with communities. In 2008, the process was expanded, comprising 103 participants in two workshops in Rio de Janeiro and São Paulo as well as telephone interviews. Newly identified topics included: use of water, transparency, prevention of environmental impacts, impacts on the surrounding communities, renewable energy, consumption and energy use, R&D, emission and waste, pre-salt production, child and forced/degrading labour, promotion of equality and non-discrimination, accident rates, biodiversity, ethics code, corruption, profits, sustainability index participation, public policy commitment, social and environmental impact of contractors and suppliers, and indigenous people.

The materiality test process allows Petrobras to identify stakeholder expectations in order to create a more objective and suitable content of the report. As a result, since 2007, the scope of the report has consisted of GRI G3 indexes and the IBASE Model. The number of items addressed was reduced if compared with previous publications. This fact, however, has not jeopardized the overall social and environmental assessment. First, G3 represents an upgraded framework including the main social and environmental indicators that are internationally assessed. Second, other important references (such as the DJSI and the Goldman Sachs Energy Report) were still addressed by the Petrobras report or have been added to the vulnerability map analysis process.

Final remarks

The commitment of Petrobras to social and environmental responsibility is being acknowledged by distinguished institutions. Petrobras' 2005, 2006 and 2007 COPs were considered 'Notable' by the Global Compact. From 2006, José Sergio Gabrielli de Azevedo, the CEO of Petrobras, was invited to become a member of the Global Compact Board. Petrobras has also been an active member of the Brazilian Global Compact Network since 2005 and is currently co-chairing the human rights and labour commission of this Network. In a competition organized by the GRI – the GRI Readers' Choice Award – the 2006 Petrobras Social and Environmental Report was elected by the readers as the best report in the category of 'All Stakeholders Group' and also in the category of 'Civil Society'. In order to select the awards, GRI asked the readers of the sustainability reports to vote on the Internet for the best reports based upon their needs and preferences. More than 1,700 readers in 70 countries participated in the voting process.

Petrobras has been listed in the DJSI since 2006. In 2009, the company had remarkable scores for the oil and gas industry in: Corporate Citizenship, Brand Management, Transparency, Human Capital Development and Environmental Reporting. Since 2006, the Goldman Sachs Energy Report has ranked Petrobras as one of the top five companies in the oil and gas industry regarding environmental governance quality, capital return and industry position. In 2008, the Goldman Sachs Report listed the company as a benchmark in its industry sector with regard to the following categories: Sustainability Report, Gas Flaring versus Production, Oil Spills versus Production, Employee Training and Health Management, and Community Investments. During the same year, Petrobras was acknowledged by a Management & Excellence survey as the world's most sustainable oil company. Ranked first, the company is the global reference in ethics and sustainability (based upon 387 international indexes assessing areas such as pollutant emissions and oil leaks, power consumption and a transparent supplier service system).

To achieve its goal of being an international reference in social responsibility in 2020, Petrobras is continuously searching for improvement. Since 2007, short-, medium-, and long-term performance goals were set up to enable monitoring of strategic, social and environmental actions. Such performance goals also allow assessing results with management methods such as the Balanced Scorecard (which is also applied to the entire strategic business plan of the company). In 2008, the Executive Board approved the essential requirements for excellence in social responsibility management. The next big challenge will be to implement the social responsibility self-declaration process for the entire Petrobras System.

17 | The United Nations Global Compact and the Global Reporting Initiative

PAUL HOHNEN[1]

> The same types of governance gaps and failures that produced
> the current economic crisis also constitute what the Special
> Representative has called the permissive environment for
> corporate wrongdoing in relation to human rights. The necessary
> solutions for both similarly point in the same direction:
> Governments adopting policies that induce greater corporate
> responsibility, and companies adopting strategies reflecting the
> now inescapable fact that their own long-term prospects are
> tightly coupled with the well-being of society as a whole.
>
> (Ruggie 2008, extract from paragraph 19)

Introduction

In the decade following their launch, the United Nations Global
Compact and Global Reporting Initiative (GRI) have developed into
two of the most widely used global instruments to promote more
responsible business practices in the field of sustainable development.
Despite their different histories and organizational structures, their
strategic positioning as a mutually reinforcing 'value platform' appears
to have been successful. Separately, they have achieved pre-eminence
in their respective fields. Together, they are increasingly widely used
by companies to report their corporate responsibility goals, policies
and performance.

Looking ahead over the next decade, however, it is clear they will
not achieve their respective missions without directly addressing a

---

[1] Paul Hohnen is an associate fellow of the Royal Institute for International
Affairs (Chatham House), London. A consulting Special Adviser to the Global
Reporting Initiative (GRI) and former Senior Adviser to the UN Global
Compact, this chapter reflects his personal views and does not necessarily reflect
those of either GRI or the Global Compact.

range of criticisms. These include that they are neither broad enough in terms of users, nor deep enough in terms of measurable impacts and accountability. There are also issues about the sustainability of their respective business models. In many respects, however, their shortfalls are not of their own making.

Governments and other actors have not yet accorded them the support necessary to take them to scale. In the absence, however, of any foreseeable other initiatives which could realistically take their place as the 'go to' instruments to define internationally accepted global principles and to provide a framework for reporting related performance, the better public policy course would be to fast-track their further improvement and uptake. Mandating reporting and an UN-driven enquiry into how to scale up the two frameworks should now be on the agenda.

A short history of Corporate Social Responsibility

When the history of corporate responsibility in the early twenty-first century is written, a few dominant features seem likely to merit attention.

The first will probably be the factual note that it was a time of great creativity. In every region, and in every sector, it seemed that voluntary initiatives emerged which sought to define what constituted responsible business practice – popularly referred to as 'Corporate Social Responsibility' (CSR). For the most part, these CSR initiatives were produced by the for-profit sector, sometimes in partnership with non-profit organizations.[2] In a rapidly globalizing world, with a powerful private sector, a common motive was a desire to define the role and responsibilities of the business sector in relation to increasingly pressing social and environmental issues. The goal was to increase the positive contributions of business and reduce the negative impacts. During much of the development process, it may be noted, governments mainly stood on the sidelines, not discouraging this burgeoning private trend, but neither taking the opportunity to actively promote

---

[2] Examples of some of the many codes in existence can be found in 'Overview of Selected Initiatives and Instruments Relevant to Corporate Social Responsibility' (OECD 2008b).

particular instruments nor helping address shortcomings identified with existing instruments.

The second feature likely to be remarked on will be that this process consisted largely of independent CSR initiatives, each with their own mission, governance structure and methodology. This evolutionary approach was informally described at the time as the 'Let 1,000 flowers bloom' strategy. The adoption of multiple, parallel or even sometimes overlapping initiatives reflected an assessment that there was no 'one size fits all' CSR instrument for a world comprising so many different types of company operating across nearly 200 countries. The result was predictably mixed. While the menu of CSR offerings was rich and diverse, there was a lack of awareness about the relevance of CSR and a high level of confusion as to what instrument to use. For most potential users, it was impossible to keep track of all the initiatives, how they related and what their benefits were. As a result, there was a mixed pattern of usage, but with some instruments proving more popular than others. Overall, however, the vast majority of companies around the world did not appear to make any formal use of CSR tools. Where understood, CSR was often seen as irrelevant, too expensive or premature.

The third point of historical interest will probably be the emergence of CSR or 'sustainability' reporting. After nearly a century of financial reporting, 'non-financial' reporting on a company's CSR policies, objectives and performance suddenly became commonplace, in particular among multinational companies (MNCs). While in the early 1990s only a handful of companies supplemented their financial reports with information on their social and environmental performance, the practice quickly became mainstream in a little over a decade. As figure 17.1 shows, there was a rapid rise in the number of corporate responsibility reports beginning after the 1992 UN 'Earth Summit' held in Rio de Janeiro. The largest diplomatic gathering of its kind in history at the time, this conference issued the first specific call by governments to the business sector to report its environmental performance,[3] and prompted fresh thinking about the role of business in sustainable development. This was reinforced by the 2002 World

---

[3] Chapter 30 of *Agenda 21* notes that 'Business and industry, including transnational corporations, should be encouraged: (a) To report annually on their environmental records, as well as on their use of energy and natural resources' (United Nations 2009c).

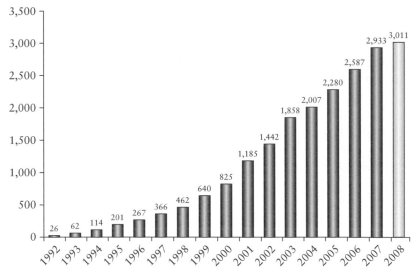

Source: Data Courtesy of www.corporateregister.com

Figure 17.1 Rise in corporate responsibility reporting, 1992–2008

Summit on Sustainable Development (WSSD) which also encouraged wider reporting by the business sector.[4]

The current context

It also seems likely that historians will identify two initiatives – the Global Compact and the GRI – as being central to these developments. A few facts illustrate their current significance for the phenomenon of expanded business interest in CSR and in non-financial reporting:

- With over 6,000 participants, the Global Compact is now the largest and most popular global responsible business initiative. The Global Compact website lists over 5,000 Communications on Progress (COPs), meaning reports on progress in advancing the ten Global Compact Principles. It characterizes a tenth of these as 'Notable',

---

[4] Paragraph 18 of the WSSD 'Plan of Implementation' spoke of the need to 'encourage industry to improve social and environmental performance through voluntary initiatives, including environmental management systems, codes of conduct, certification and public reporting on environmental and social issues' (United Nations 2009f).

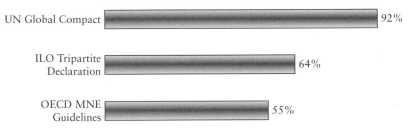

UN Global Compact 92%

ILO Tripartite Declaration 64%

OECD MNE Guidelines 55%

Source: Data Courtesy of Vigeo (2008).

Figure 17.2 Is your CSR approach based on or inspired by international instruments?

meaning that they contain a 'strong statement of continued support for the Global Compact'.[5]

- The advent of CSR reporting has enabled (and, it might be argued, encouraged) companies to disclose the principles and standards they use in shaping their business practices. Such reports increasingly reference the Global Compact, the majority using GRI. One survey conducted in 2008 showed that the Global Compact was the most widely referenced international instrument used by European businesses in this context (see figure 17.2; see also Vigeo 2008).

- According to GRI data, at least 956 non-financial reports were published and formally registered in 2008 by organizations using the G3 – the GRI reporting framework – most being companies, though the actual figure will likely be higher as GRI makes the Guidelines freely available and there is thus no requirement for companies using them to register their reports with GRI. On past growth rates, the annual number published in 2009 should exceed one thousand (see figure 17.3).[6] Another data source identifies at least 1877 GRI-based reports issued since the release of GRI's 2006 (or third)

[5] Notable COPs are defined by the Global Compact as those that contain a 'clear and detailed description of practical actions taken in implementing the Global Compact Principles and/or in undertaking partnership projects in support of broader UN goals; measurement of outcomes that allows for checking progress; reporting process that ensures reliability, clarity and timeliness of information and includes stakeholder dialogue' (Global Compact 2009e).

[6] GRI data on sustainability reporting can be found on the GRI website, www.globalreporting.org.

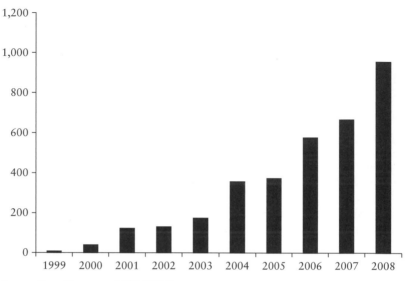

Source: Data Courtesy of GRI (2009).

Figure 17.3 GRI reports, by publication year, 1999–2008

version of its Guidelines (referred to as 'G3'), with a cumulative total of 3,790 reports being issued using the GRI framework.[7]
- A survey by the consultancy firm KPMG International in 2008 indicated that 75 per cent of the *Fortune* Global 250 used GRI in their reports (KPMG 2008, see also UNEP and KPMG 2007). While the majority of reporting companies are based in the OECD area, other regions of the world are also seeing a rise in reporting. Asian Global Compact participants are responsible for some 773 COPs, the Americas 896 COPs and Africa 177 COPs.

There are various possible explanations for the individual and combined success of the Global Compact and GRI in the marketplace. While sharing with many other initiatives and instruments a voluntary character and flexibility of use designed to appeal both to first time or experienced users, their distinguishing features include:

- *Sustainable development focus:* While many initiatives and instruments address one aspect of sustainable development, the Global Compact and GRI address all three dimensions: the so-called

---

[7] See http://www.corporateregister.com.

'people, planet, profit' aspects, also characterized as the social, environmental and economic elements of sustainability.

- *Governmental recognition:* Both the Global Compact and GRI enjoy a high level of support by governments and intergovernmental organizations. The Global Compact has been referenced in a series of UN General Assembly and World Summit resolutions and statements and by the G8 Summit. The GRI, a co-initiative of the United Nations Environment Programme (UNEP), has also won a high level of governmental endorsement, including that of the WSSD and G8. Both are commonly referenced in national government CSR policies or guidance documents.

- *Multi-stakeholder approach:* The two instruments both encourage a partnership-based approach. While the Global Compact Principles were developed by the UN Secretariat, the Global Compact Governing Board comprises representatives of business, labour and civil society organizations and the Global Compact encourages and attracts participation by organizations from all sectors of society. The GRI is even more deeply multi-stakeholder in character, in both the nature of its governance and users, and the fact that the GRI framework and its ongoing development are the product of a global process involving inputs by the business, labour, governmental and civil society sectors. These characteristics set them apart from CSR initiatives that, for example, were developed solely by business organizations.

- *Compatibility:* While emerging from separate processes, from an early point in their histories the Global Compact and GRI have as far as possible complemented each other. The rationale for this was both philosophical and strategic in nature. Philosophical in the sense that they shared a common mission (i.e. the advancement of sustainable development and internationally agreed principles, with business as a central part) and approach (global, multi-stakeholder, 'learn-by-doing'). Strategic in the sense that, for many potential users, their value was stronger when combined than used separately: one gave guidance on what the main principles were, and the other a framework for reporting on corresponding policies and performance.

Initially, the functional aspects of this strategic relationship consisted in the main of executive-level mutual statements of support, cross-links on their respective websites and regular consultations on user feed-back. There were also joint seminars, in particular in the process leading up to the development of the G3 version of the Guidelines. An important additional link was made when the Global Compact intro-duced the requirement for COPs, and recognized (although not exclu-sively) the GRI as an appropriate mechanism for this purpose. A high point was reached in 2006 when the two organizations announced a 'strategic alliance' aimed at 'providing the global private sector with an opportunity to embrace a responsible business strategy that is at once comprehensive, organizing, integrated and enjoys near or total universal acceptance' (Global Compact 2006b).

In the same year, the ongoing strategic discussion between the Global Compact and GRI, together with other closely related interna-tional CSR initiatives, evolved a concept referred to as the 'Big Bet'. The core proposition of the 'Big Bet' was that, in the longer term, the global market would not be able to support the large number of inde-pendent instruments. Given the choice, users would increasingly look for a small set of complementary tools that provided recognition, flex-ibility and functionality. The 'Big Bet' was basically a statement that the Global Compact and GRI should and would be at the heart of this convergence process, and – while retaining their separate governance and organizational structures – work together ever more closely.

In many respects the evolving 'strategic alliance' formalized and gave additional profile to a process that had been in train for some time. It sought to recognize the market demand for a reputable 'one-stop-shop' for guidance on the fundamental principles of CSR and a mechanism for implementing them in an effective and recognized manner. The alliance highlighted the synergistic potential of using the two platforms in combination: the Global Compact with respect to its ten universal Principles in the areas of human rights, labour stand-ards, the environment and anti-corruption; and GRI in relation to its G3 guidelines, based on the major UN agreements, which provided transparency and guidance on how to report on performance results, with an inbuilt materiality test, enabling companies to select with their stakeholders the most relevant issues.

A further step in this direction was taken with a 'call to action' by the two organizations. On the release of the GRI G3 Guidelines in October 2006, there was a 'call to action' by Global Compact Executive Director Georg Kell and GRI Chief Executive Ernst Ligteringen, who urged leaders in government, business and civil society to mainstream the use of the Global Compact and GRI. As a contribution in this respect, and as further evidence of their organizations' determination to provide a 'value platform for sustainability', they launched a joint paper, entitled 'Making the Connection: Using GRI's G3 Reporting Guidelines for the UN Global Compact's Communication on Progress' (Global Compact and Global Reporting Initiative 2007). The paper (which was also made available as a web-based tool) was designed to serve as a 'user guide', providing an explanation on the Global Compact Principles and the corresponding GRI performance indicators.

It is not possible to determine the impact of the Global Compact/ GRI strategy with any accuracy. As will be discussed below, in the absence of mechanisms to track and assess voluntary CSR instruments systematically, it is often not clear what instruments are being used, with what effect, and by whom. There are reasons to believe, however, that the strategy has influenced company behaviour. There has been a marked trend in recent years for companies to make specific reference to the international principles, standards and instruments they use in guiding their operations. An increasing number of companies now refer to both the Global Compact and the GRI on their websites or in CSR reports:

- The Indian MNC Acelor, for example, not only printed the full text of the Global Compact Principles in its 2007 CSR report, but also showed which of the GRI performance indicators it had used to report on its activities in relation to the Global Compact Principles it was seeking to advance (Acelor Mittal 2007).
- SAB Miller, an international brewing company, referenced the Global Compact in a joint statement by the Chief Executive and the Chairman of the Corporate Accountability and Risk Assurance Committee, published at the introduction of its 2008 *Sustainable Development Report*, which also used the GRI framework.
- Not surprisingly, this trend is most marked among companies listed on 'sustainability' or related indexes, such as the Dow Jones Sustainability Index (DJSI) and the FTSE4Good Index series, where references to the Global Compact and the GRI are increasingly commonplace in non-financial reports. The Global Compact is mentioned by over half the companies on their respective 2007

indices, with GRI showing an even higher reference rate (Hohnen 2009a).

Brickbats and bouquets

The positive contribution of the Global Compact and GRI to advancing awareness about CSR issues has been expressed in various ways.

As noted above, this is evident in the level of uptake by multinational enterprises (MNEs) in particular, and by their reference in government CSR policies and guidance. For example, a 2009 white paper on CSR published by the Norwegian government gives priority attention to a few instruments, including the Global Compact and GRI. The Norwegian Pension Fund uses the Compact to help provide its ethical investment framework. Going a step further, the Danish government has actually mandated CSR reporting, using a 'comply or explain' approach. Companies can choose their own reporting framework, but the government recommends GRI or Global Compact COP reporting. Companies that have acceded to the Compact and which publish COPs are considered as complying with the law. They are, however, required to identify where their reports can be found.

The level of government, business and NGO participation in the Global Compact and GRI conferences is also testimony to their perceived value. Both organizations manage to attract ministerial and CEO-level speakers and attendees at their flagship events, such as the 2007 Global Compact Global Leaders Summit and the GRI's biennial Amsterdam Global Conference on Sustainability. In this respect, they are clearly ahead of other comparable initiatives.[8]

The emergence of the Global Compact and GRI, individually and together, as the dominant initiatives in the CSR space, however, has not been without its problems and critics.

As two independent organizations seeking expanded uptake of their platforms, there has been a level of understandable competitive tension. While working harmoniously together, one cannot help observe that neither framework makes a high-profile reference to the

---

[8] The World Economic Forum (WEF) and the Clinton Global Initiative, which attract a larger number and higher level of participants on average, are not included here as they are not CSR frameworks *stricto sensu*. Their success, nonetheless, is noteworthy here.

other. The 2006 GRI G3 Guidelines mention the Global Compact in passing in the context of its Labour 'Indicator Protocols'. Similarly, the Global Compact confines its reference to the GRI in guidance on issuing COPs.[9] No joint international conferences have been held. In large part, the sensitivity to being seen to be 'too close' to the other is driven by concerns expressed by their respective supporter bases. From the Global Compact side, some users have reportedly expressed discomfort with the detail of the GRI and a wish to preserve a high degree of flexibility as to their communication framework. On the GRI side, other users have raised questions about the generality of the Global Compact Principles.

In functional terms, however, these aspects appear to have had little impact on their day-to-day working relations, which seem close and collegial, and remain consistent with the agreed strategy.

As the first decade of the twenty-first Millennium closes, a number of generic external criticisms of the two organizations can be identified. By and large these are not unique to either the Global Compact or GRI, but form part of a wider critique of the efficacy and appropriateness of CSR instruments. Among the concerns expressed about the voluntary approach to corporate accountability include the related assertions that voluntary initiatives:

- Can *prevent or slow progress* towards mandatory measures. They do this by giving the impression of a greater level of business activity on CSR issues than is actually the case.
- Can *oversimplify and misstate agreed international principles* and commitments, thereby undermining government policies and programmes.
- *Lack adequate assurance and impact assessment mechanisms* by which claims can be substantiated. As a result, it is possible for an

---

[9] The new Global Compact policy, decided in April 2009, came into effect on 1 July 2009 for new business participants joining from this date. It will be applicable to all business participants as of 1 July 2011. It provides that (1) New business participants will be given one year from the date of joining to prepare and submit their first COP; (2) During the first five years of participation, a COP must address at least two of the Global Compact's four principal issue areas, while all must be addressed after five years; (3) The COP submission form on the Global Compact website will require additional information to improve searchability; (4) The 'inactive' participant status currently in use will be eliminated. Business participants that have been 'non-communicating' for one year or more will be delisted and removed from the Global Compact website.

organization to use these tools without in fact changing its behaviour or impacts.

- Can *overstate their importance and impact* in the competition for market share and uptake.
- *Rely excessively on the 'watchdog' role of civil society*, without recognizing or respecting the capacity limits and missions of NGOs.

In the case of the Global Compact, its association with the United Nations has prompted concerns about what is seen as the 'corporatization' of the UN agenda by business. Some NGOs have raised questions about the private sector having privileged access to the UN and other international policy processes. They have also pointed to the risk of 'bluewash' – the notion that Global Compact participants from the business sector have the publicity benefits of association with the United Nations (and its blue logo), while providing little or nothing measurable in return.[10]

These critiques cannot be dismissed lightly and, as noted below, need to be addressed comprehensively if the two organizations are to make the further progress that they and their supporters seek.

The proposed release in 2010 of a new voluntary global instrument, the ISO 26000 'Social Responsibility' Standard, can be expected to further sharpen debate around these issues. While the contents of the Standard are still being finalized, the draft available at the time of writing is both detailed and comprehensive in addressing social and environmental issues. Major unanswered questions surrounding the ISO Standard include how far it will be taken up in the marketplace and how it relates to existing CSR frameworks.

The next decade

Science clearly shows that anthropogenic greenhouse gas emissions – mainly produced by the use of fossil fuels – are provoking dangerous climate change, putting at risk not only the environment and ecosystem services but the very basis of our present and future prosperity. The costs of inaction far outweigh the costs of moving towards low-carbon societies.

G8 Leaders' Statement, L'Aquila Summit, 8 July 2009 (see Group of Eight 2009: paragraph 61)

---

[10] Examples of current critiques of the Global Compact can be found at http://globalcompactcritics.blogspot.com.

The sustainable development challenges facing the world seem likely to become even more urgent in the coming decade. However, as the current financial crisis evolves, at the level of the planet's biophysical systems issues such as climate change, fresh water availability, depletion of marine fisheries and deforestation and their impacts all seem set to become more acute.[11] In turn, these and other changes in economic and ecosystems will sharpen the policy challenges facing governments at both the national and international levels. If governments are to make more rapid progress towards agreed global goals such as preventing dangerous climate change and achieving the UN Millennium Development Goals (MDGs) by 2015, while at the same time promoting economic growth, peace and human rights, it seems evident that a new level of commitment, creativity and resources will be necessary to address the scale and urgency of the problems faced.

By most assessments, the rate of progress currently being made is not enough. The reasons are mixed, and include such factors as the failure of current market policies to accurately price human rights and environmental services and provide incentives for new technologies; the inability of nation-states to agree on appropriate response measures in meaningful time scales; and the lack of broad-based public support for many proposed changes (e.g. a carbon tax).

Against this background, a central challenge for governments, business and civil society organizations this decade will be to find more effective decision-making processes to address sustainable development. Here, a series of governance issues arises. These include whether:

- Existing intergovernmental organizations are 'fit for purpose', and how they might be made more responsive to emerging issues.
- The current mix and balance of regulatory and voluntary instruments to promote sustainable development are effective, and how they might be improved.
- The current range of voluntary instruments is 'fit for purpose', and how they might be improved to ensure a greater level of dissemination, uptake and impact.

---

[11] See, for example, the *Millennium Ecosystem Assessment* and *State of the World 2009 Report* (Worldwatch Institute 2009).

In addressing these and other global challenges, it seems likely that governments will need to work ever more closely with the private sector and civil society. This will be necessary both to help define effective response strategies and secure support for their implementation. To achieve this, however, governments (and business) will need to respond to the concerns raised by a range of stakeholders regarding the perceived failure of voluntary mechanisms to deliver on their promises.

While the Global Compact and GRI have enjoyed a comparatively high level of success in the CSR space, it can be argued that they have failed to realize the level of support necessary to fully achieve their separate and shared missions:

- While they are the most popular instruments in their fields, *the level of uptake is far from universal.* The majority of companies in the world are still not using them, nor showing signs of doing so.
- While their adoption by many of the largest companies in the world is impressive, there is *no consistent or clear research demonstrating the beneficial impacts* on company performance. Users of the two frameworks continue to be targeted by NGOs for alleged breaches of principles, or reporting that is considered incomplete, inaccurate, or irrelevant.
- Non-users point to their *vagueness (Global Compact) or excessive detail (GRI)* as among the reasons not to use them, and suggest that a greater attention to relevant sectoral issues is required to ensure greater user value.
- Their *business models have not succeeded in generating the resources needed* to scale up their activities and provide effective, on-the-ground support around the world.
- They have *not succeeded in persuading the wider NGO community to engage* at the level that would be necessary to achieve their outreach, uptake and assurance objectives.

Their relative failures in these respects, however, are not entirely of their own making. In almost all the above cases, work is underway to address the identified weaknesses. (For example, both organizations are actively pursuing a strategy of developing sector-focused initiatives and instruments. GRI has fourteen separate 'sector supplements' launched or under development.)

In the first place, governments themselves must take a large share of responsibility. In many respects, they are the primary beneficiaries of effective CSR instruments. These offer a relatively low-cost means of advancing policy, raising awareness and social partnerships and complementing regulatory measures:

- *Policy support:* At the current time the majority of countries do not have clear public policies on their expectations of 'responsible' or 'sustainable' business. (Of the dozen or so that do, however, most reference one or both frameworks.) As a result, many business organizations have no idea of what the Global Compact and sustainability reporting are, nor do they consider them important. By contrast, the evidence strongly suggests that where governments do have a clear public policy of promoting CSR, and specific initiatives such as the Compact and GRI, levels of uptake by the business sector are high. In Denmark, for example, it is estimated that the majority of large companies report publicly on their social responsibility activities (Danish Minister for Economic and Business Affairs 2008). Governmental support can take many forms, and does not always involve high cost or regulation. It can include awareness-raising, high-level encouragement for business sector engagement, promoting private–public relationships, supporting research and ensuring policy consistency (Hohnen 2007).
- *Funding support:* In a field where there are various proprietary CSR standards and consulting service providers, both the Global Compact and GRI provide free public goods which are consistent with internationally agreed policies. On this basis, it might be assumed that both initiatives would enjoy broad-based government financial support. While the details of their governmental donor base and specific contributions are not readily available to the public, it is understood that only a small number of governments provides any form of consistent financial support for their respective operations. Rather than spend their efforts on building a wider and deeper support base, there is evidence that fund-raising occupies a high proportion of staff time. While the Global Compact has established a 'Foundation for the Global Compact' to enable funding from the business sector, the absence of a clear sign of broad-based government support has hampered the establishment of a sustainable and robust funding base.

The civil society and business communities might also take some responsibility for the failure of the Global Compact and GRI to acquire greater traction.

In dismissing the potential of voluntary instruments to help effect change, NGOs risk creating a self-fulfilling situation. Not all human behaviour can or should be regulated. Indeed, many of the largest international NGOs have chosen voluntary instruments to guide their own external accountability, recognizing the need for flexibility and learning.[12] It might be argued that by adopting a strategy based largely on extended regulation of corporate accountability, some of the NGO sector has ignored the opportunity to fully assess and build on the changes that CSR approaches have effected, and increase the impact of their advocacy. Better leveraging of the CSR commitments made by companies, more consistent challenges on perceived performance shortfalls, or greater pressure for more evidence of positive impacts are examples of activities that could be pursued, as is increased participation with the Global Compact and GRI processes where direct dialogue with the business sector can be maintained. Equally, the case for a stronger regulatory approach cannot fully be made without better evidence that voluntary instruments are not working. Put another way, the Global Compact and GRI have provided the most comprehensive platform in history for encouraging and enabling business and other organizations to report publicly on their activities. Unless NGOs are in a position to maintain a focused, fact-based and sustained dialogue on COPs and GRI reports, or their absence, they miss an opportunity to advance their advocacy.

For its part, the business sector must also share a level of responsibility. While the business sector has generally taken the lead in driving the development of most CSR instruments, and played a critical role in the development of both the Global Compact and GRI, the support has not been uniform across the sector. Although, as noted above, there is growing evidence that corporate policies are being reshaped by concerns to 'do better by doing good', there is still evidence that most companies are not taking up the opportunities offered by the Global Compact and GRI. Worse, some have adopted them and are yet to show clearly how their business practices and impacts might

---

[12] See, for example, the 'International NGO Accountability Charter', at www. ingo-accountability-charter.org/cmsfiles/ingo-accountability-charter-eng.pdf.

have changed for the better. In the wake of the current financial crisis, it will be interesting to see how far the business sector uses the potential of sustainable development and ethical considerations to improve their risk management, stakeholder outreach and product offerings to build competitive advantage. Leaders in the business sector recognize that there can be 'no sustainable business without sustainable societies'; the challenges of the coming decades seem set to put this assessment to the test.

Conclusion and recommendations

Given the utmost urgency of addressing sustainable development at the global level, the current approach will not be sufficient. The present mix of international conventions and declarations, national regulations, and voluntary mechanisms is not driving organizational change that is deep, wide, or rapid enough. On the brighter side, however, it should be recognized that the level of concern and attention across human society is now unprecedented. More people than ever in human history are engaged in efforts to build awareness and promote more just and sustainable development. This presents a unique and not-to-be-missed opportunity to harness, focus and amplify these disparate efforts. Time is of the essence.

While recognizing that there are many creative ideas and initiatives on the table, this chapter concludes with two practical proposals that relate specifically to the Global Compact and GRI. If implemented, they could take the sustainability debate to new levels of outreach and effectiveness.

A bird in the hand?

The first concerns the *mandating of CSR reporting*. Given the magnitude and urgency of the sustainability challenges ahead, it is increasingly hard to defend the case for organizations not to be measuring and reporting on their contributions to sustainable development, and to do so in relation to internationally agreed principles. Regulators, investors, employees, consumers and communities have a shared interest in knowing how well every business organization – especially the larger ones – is addressing key questions such as its greenhouse gas (GHG) emissions, use of water and respect for human rights. By offering a mechanism for this, the Global Compact COP, and the use of the GRI Guidelines, provides a ready-made framework for all businesses to go down this path.

Two valuable pointers in this direction have recently emerged. The first was the decision by the Danish government to mandate CSR reporting. While the format and content of the reports remain flexible, all large companies are legally required to report annually on their CSR policies, or explain why they are not doing so (Hohnen 2009b). This is smart regulation. It retains much of the voluntary character of CSR, but at the same time raises awareness and encourages increased competition in the marketplace. If governments are serious about ensuring that the private sector makes its full contribution to sustainable development, but without resort to regulation, this is a model which could be quickly replicated in other countries. Sweden, it may be noted, has also regulated sustainability reporting – using GRI – but the current government has limited this to state-owned companies. This precedent should also be available for other states to follow.

The second was the issue by the Board of GRI of 'The Amsterdam Declaration on Transparency and Reporting' in March 2009.[13] Addressed in part to the G20 Summit held in London on 2 April 2009 on the global economic crisis, the Declaration represented a major shift in GRI's position. By calling on governments to introduce a 'report or explain' approach, GRI signalled the need for a new sense of urgency in relation to the routine provision of non-financial information, including ESG aspects. In this regard, the GRI Board appears to have been reflecting a growing recognition that the provision of financial information alone is now insufficient, whether as a basis for assessing the value of a company, the quality of its management, or how well it is meeting its social responsibilities (UNEP FI 2005).

At this point in history, governments have three broad options with respect to promoting responsible business practices. These are: to continue a 'business-as-usual' approach; to recognize the potential

---

[13] 'The Board of GRI calls on governments to take leadership by: 1. Introducing policy requiring companies to report on ESG [environmental, social and governance] factors or publicly explain why they have not done so. 2. Requiring ESG reporting by their public bodies – in particular: state-owned companies, government pension funds and public investment agencies. 3. Integrating sustainability reporting within the emerging global financial regulatory framework being developed by leaders of the G20' (GRI 2009).

(and limitations) of voluntary instruments and select a small number to improve and popularize; or to introduce legislation. The first carries huge risks, to both long-term public trust in business and to worsening sustainability conditions. The second involves a degree of 'picking winners' – however, it can be argued that this has already occurred. Governments have already identified a few instruments that they would like to see developed, and the market appears to share this assessment. The third option may be used for general reporting, or might be used for some specific issues (e.g. CO_2 reporting), but will still encounter wide differences in approach between jurisdictions.

While it might be contended that the weaknesses identified above might point in the direction of a fourth option – the development of an entirely new global ethical and reporting framework – the better course would seem to be to improve and build on the existing Global Compact/GRI frameworks. These offer a familiar and widely used approach that stands ready to be taken to scale. By contrast, it seems unclear where and how an alternate framework might be developed within a meaningful time scale. For example, the draft ISO 26000 Standard has already been five years in the making, and does not provide any guidance on sustainability reporting comparable to GRI. No other large-scale initiatives, moreover, are known to be under development.

In policy terms, this is a classic 'bird in the hand is worth two in the bush' situation. Governments, business and civil society need to ask themselves whether there is either a clearer and better alternate vision of a global framework than the Global Compact/GRI platform for advancing responsible business practices, and whether there is time to develop such a framework. If not, then the time has come for a new level of commitment to improving and advancing these existing initiatives, possibly in combination with other instruments that may add value.

A CSR Ruggie?

Which leads to the second and final proposal. This is that it is time for a new and concerted level of UN engagement on responsible business issues. The UN/Bretton Woods institutions have a formal responsibility for advancing development that is rights-based and sustainable. While set up as governmental organizations, they all now recognize that progress cannot be made without the engagement of business and civil society. At the present time, most UN bodies and agencies have some form of business engagement capacity. To a large extent, however, this is not well known, defined, or coordinated. It is often also not highly respected, being seen as excessively formal and inflexible. Apart from the Global Compact's high-level 'Leaders Summit' meetings, there is no place in the UN system equivalent to, say, the World Economic Forum or the Clinton Global Initiative where senior ministers, CEOs and leaders from civil society can meet in a relatively informal 'decision-finding' mode to explore how they might work better together on sustainable development issues. This gap might well be judged by history as a leadership failure on the part of the UN system, and is one that should be addressed. While sustainability policy implementation has elements that can be privatized, the process of policy-making remains the responsibility of government.

Given, however, the likely difficulty of securing quick General Assembly agreement on the creation of a new forum or on the extension of the mandate of an existing body to address CSR issues, two other options might be considered.

One would be to create an Eminent Persons Group (EPG) with a mandate to explore the issue of how to 'fast-track' the uptake of the Global Compact Principles and their reporting, and to make recommendations to the Secretary-General. This approach would have the advantage of offering diverse, balanced and expert advice from around the world in a relatively short timeframe.[14]

Another option would be to appoint a UN Special Representative with the mandate to explore these issues. As the work of Professor John Ruggie, the Secretary-General's Special Representative (SGSR) on Human Rights, has demonstrated, a high-level and sustained enquiry by a well qualified and respected individual with the proper resources can play a crucial role in raising interest, the quality of debate and new ideas (Ruggie 2008). Parallel work, closely linked to and complementing the work of Professor Ruggie, would play an invaluable role in adding the impetus and attention needed in relation to the rapid globalization of the Global Compact's ten Principles and detailed reporting on progress.

---

[14] EPGs have been formed to address issues such as UN Reform (2003–4), United Nations–Civil Society Relations (2003) and trafficking in small arms (2002).

The mandate of a SGSR on responsible business practice could include such elements as:

- How the Global Compact and GRI are currently being used, and how they might be improved to ensure faster global uptake and deeper integration into business strategies and everyday operations.
- How to promote coherence between the Global Compact COPs and the GRI Guidelines, as well as with other governmentally developed frameworks (e.g. the OECD Guidelines for Multinational Enterprises).
- The case for mandating COPs/GRI reporting and how to address related monitoring and assurance issues.
- How the improved performance by companies on ESG issues could contribute to a more robust and sustainable business sector emerging out of the current financial crisis.
- Whether and how the Global Compact might play a more formal central role within the UN system.

The issue of climate change has underlined both the value of engaging business fully in the sustainable development challenge and also the limitations of reliance on a purely voluntary approach. In the absence of more rapid change in consumer and business practices, regulations and even product bans (e.g. incandescent lighting) are becoming more acceptable approaches. In 2009, governments still have the option of utilizing both regulatory and voluntary instruments. Any further deterioration of global systems in this century, however, could progressively weaken support for voluntary approaches. If the flexibility and creativity of voluntary approaches are to be retained, it will be important for governments, as well as all other stakeholders, to work together on improving their uptake, value, rigour and transparency. In these respects, the Global Compact and GRI have an invaluable role to play.

PART IV

Local Networks: the emerging global–local link

18 | *Building the United Nations Global Compact Local Network model: history and highlights*

NESSA WHELAN

Introduction

Almost as soon as the United Nations Global Compact was launched in 2000, participants recognized a value in engaging locally in an effort to better understand the practical meaning of the Compact and its ten Principles. Without any clear direction from the Global Compact Office in New York, these early 'networks' emerged in a diverse and uncoordinated manner, responding to the needs, interests and capacity of their participants. Some saw their role as simply to gather committed stakeholders together at the national level in order to promote the ten Principles and to exchange experience with each other. Others, in contrast, quickly established themselves as formal entities ready to support and facilitate, in more practical terms, (through tool provision, learning events, etc.) the implementation process. In many cases, the creation of a Global Compact Local Network (GCLN) was the direct result of a committed individual or organization seeking to promote the agenda among their peers. In some cases however, GCLNs were established to tackle a specific issue or need. For example, one GCLN was created in an effort to re-establish trust between the public and the business sector in post-crisis Argentina. As the initiative grew during these early years, the Global Compact soon began to realize that GCLNs would become a key element in its success, in terms of both its growth and sustainability.

Ten years on, the Global Compact has approximately ninety established and emerging GCLNs, located in all regions of the world. GCLNs are perfectly positioned to support the Global Compact's objective of mainstreaming the ten Principles in business activities everywhere. Through outreach and awareness-raising, GCLNs can involve stakeholders who – operating locally – would otherwise be excluded from the corporate citizenship agenda at the global level. However, as the review of activities in this chapter shows, most GCLNs have moved beyond outreach as well as awareness-raising activities and also emphasize the role of learning and policy dialogues in an effort to support their stakeholders in a more meaningful way.

The growth in the number of GCLNs over the years has presented governance challenges, in terms of both the GCLNs themselves and how they link into the governance framework of the Global Compact initiative overall. As outlined in this chapter, these challenges have been addressed incrementally and in a manner which appreciates and respects the need for diverse approaches. From a loose network of self-appointed entities, GCLNs have now developed into an internetworking group who, in addition to the Annual Local Networks Forum (ALNF), form two of the seven entities with differentiated tasks within the Global Compact's multi-centric governance framework (see chapter 14 by Ursula Wynhoven and Matthias Stausberg). GCLNs are now expected to meet a set of minimum criteria, which have been developed over time and through consensus, in order to protect the integrity of the Global Compact initiative and its brand. In this chapter, the history of Local Networks will be reviewed, highlighting how governance structures within and between Networks were created. The last section discusses some current trends (e.g., regarding the set-up of regional Network meetings) and challenges facing GCLNs moving forward.

Defining Local Networks

GCLNs are clusters of participants who come together voluntarily to advance the Global Compact and its Principles at the local level, while emerging Networks are groups of participants who are making progress towards the establishment of a GCLN. By providing on-the-ground support and capacity-building tied to distinct cultural, economic and linguistic needs GCLNs perform increasingly important roles in rooting the Global Compact within different national and cultural contexts. Their knowledge of the local business environment and their familiarity with social, cultural and political factors are positive drivers for the implementation of the Principles and for collaborative problem-solving.

The main role of GCLNs is to support companies in their efforts to implement the Global Compact (both local firms and subsidiaries of foreign corporations), while also creating opportunities for multi-stakeholder engagement and collective action. They undertake a variety of activities to support their participants – including identifying local priorities, organizing learning and dialogue events, producing learning materials in local languages and motivating participating companies to develop partnership projects to contribute to the UN Millennium Development Goals (MDGs). Additionally, as the capacity and accountability of GCLNs has developed over the years, they have increasingly assumed responsibilities with respect to the overall integrity of the Global Compact. Such work includes facilitation of participant Communication on Progress (COP), screening of new signatories from their respective countries and promotion of dialogue facilitation in cases where concerns are raised about a company's engagement.

Over time, it has become clear that GCLNs are the vehicle for increasing and intensifying the impact of the initiative on the ground. Early on, an impact assessment carried out by McKinsey & Co. in 2004 identified the proliferation of GCLNs as crucial, highlighting the fact that participants identified locally driven initiatives as having the most impact of the Global Compact's activities (McKinsey & Company 2004). It indicated that the primary assets of GCLNs are their local presence, focus on implementation and flexibility. As the initiative has grown from forty companies in 2000 to more than 6,500 companies in 2009, GCLNs have become integral – acting as the main liaison between the Global Compact Office and participating companies spread around the world.

The Global Compact has witnessed a gradual but steady growth in the number of GCLNs, with a significantly higher uptake in Europe. The growth of GCLNs has in many ways kept up with the pace and nature of the initiative's overall growth. For example, the Global Compact has established a strong presence in developing countries with more than half of participants headquartered outside OECD countries. Similarly, roughly three-quarters of the established GCLNs are located in non-OECD countries.

With respect to geographic distribution, the number of GCLNs has increased steadily in all regions of the world but has witnessed

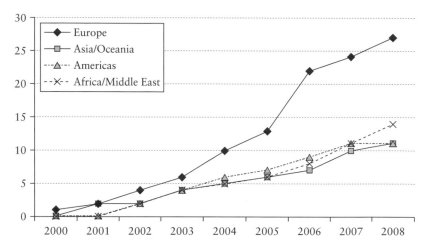

Figure 18.1 Growth of Global Compact Local Networks, according to geographic region, 2000–8

somewhat higher uptake in Europe (see figure 18.1).[1] Countries with the largest number of Global Compact participants also tend to have the largest GCLNs. In fact, the twenty largest GCLNs work with approximately 80 per cent of the overall number of participants engaged in GCLNs. However, the presence of Networks in dozens of countries that have comparatively few participants suggests that companies find value in GCLNs regardless of the overall level of awareness of the Global Compact in a country.

Why and How do Companies Engage in Local Networks?

Reasons for engagement and types of activities

Increasingly, participating companies look to GCLNs for support – with 60 per cent of respondents to the 2008 Global Compact Implementation Survey reporting local engagement (see figure 18.2). As figure 18.3 indicates, the top reasons for engagement cited

---

[1] This is in large part due to the work of United Nations Development Programme (UNDP) country offices in Eastern Europe and the Commonwealth of Independent States (CIS). Early on, UNDP recognized the value of a Global Compact platform at the local level in an effort to engage the private sector in its development agenda through partnership projects and policy dialogues.

Source: Global Compact (2008).

Figure 18.2 Is your company engaged in a Global Compact Local Network?

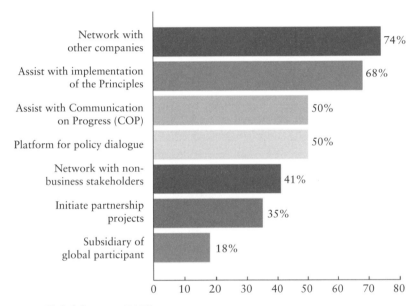

Source: Global Compact (2008).

Figure 18.3 Why is your company engaged in a Global Compact Local Network?

by participating companies are: networking with other companies, receiving assistance with implementation of the principles and developing COPs. Through the GCLNs, participants have the opportunity to share information and exchange experience with their peers, mainly at the local level but also at the regional and global levels through events and publications.

Of course, reasons for engagement vary. For example, in some Networks, companies use the platform to showcase best practices, in others to engage in peer review on reporting. Increasingly, Networks are seen as a good platform for facilitating policy dialogues to improve the enabling environment for business sustainability and responsibility. In some emerging economies, domestic companies are focused on entering and then excelling in the field of responsible corporate citizenship. The engagement of multinational subsidiaries in GCLNs can facilitate such shared learning and has proven to be a draw for local companies. Furthermore, in some instances suppliers have been encouraged by large companies to actively engage in GCLNs in order to improve their performance and adherence to principled business practices. Finally, the award and recognition schemes undertaken by some GCLNs have served to attract and motivate Global Compact participants to engage locally. Because all GCLNs are established and sustained by local interest and enthusiasm, activities are based on local priorities and needs.

After nearly a decade of Network growth and development, there is now a wide portfolio of activities underway. Overall, Network activities fall into the following categories: outreach events and awareness-raising, tool provision (often related to developing publications or translating existing publications), learning events (e.g. workshops and training sessions), policy dialogue (providing a platform for dialogue between public and private actors), COP facilitation and partnership facilitation. Learning and outreach were the two most frequent activities reported by GCLNs in 2008 (see figure 18.4). Asia and Europe have also reported a significant number of policy dialogue activities. The following sections will take a closer look at the different types of activities and present case examples.

Outreach activities

During the early years of the Global Compact, the main focus of activities was on awareness-raising and the recruitment of companies. Global Compact Office staff travelled extensively promoting this new initiative to the business community around the world. It was during these outreach events that the idea of gathering a cluster of participants together to form a Network in order to exchange experience and learn from each other at the local level emerged. Usually one committed individual or organization would volunteer to coordinate efforts. These 'efforts' would generally be awareness-raising and outreach events.

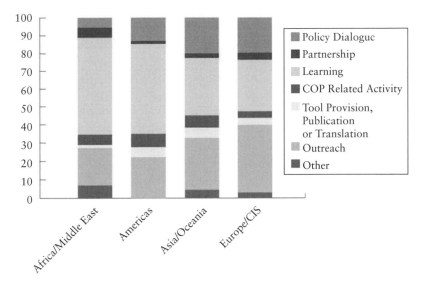

Source: Global Compact (2009f).

Figure 18.4 Relative distribution of Local Network activities, by type of activity, 2008

The purpose of this activity is to spread the word about corporate responsibility and the Global Compact among companies and non-business actors in a country. Particularly in, but not limited to, the early phase of development GCLNs typically organize conferences, workshops and media campaigns to initiate discussion on how global responsibility trends can be applied to specific countries, and consequently what value the GCLN can bring to companies and society. These events help recruit new companies by sending public messages about the potential value of corporate responsibility and providing tangible options for action. Once enough interest in the initiative has been generated, and a critical mass of stakeholders who recognizes the value in engaging locally has been assembled, a launch of the GCLN will take place.

GCLNs continually conduct outreach and awareness-raising activities for recruitment and profiling purposes, and such activities remain one of the main aims of a GCLN moving forward (box 18.1). This continued need is underscored by the fact that 55 per cent of Global Compact participants not engaged in a Local Network cite lack of awareness of a GCLN in their country as the reason.

Box 18.1: Outreach and awareness-raising examples of Local
Networks

---

*South Africa: seventeen South African companies sign on to the
Global Compact*

On 10 April 2008, CEOs and senior executives from seventeen
leading South African companies gathered at the AngloGold
Ashanti Offices in Johannesburg to sign on to the Global
Compact. The signing ceremony marked the closing of 'The
Global Compact in Africa' conference, co-hosted by the National
Business Initiative and the Stellenbosch University Unit for
Corporate Governance in Africa. The one-day conference
explored the meaning of the Global Compact in Africa, particularly the unique role that companies operating on the continent
could play by implementing the ten Global Compact Principles.
A wide range of topics was discussed, including the role of South
Africa as a dominant regional economy, the influence of China
and India on Africa, regional water issues, the state of corruption,
responsible management education and case studies on practical
implementation.

*Albania: business convenes to discuss the Global Compact and
Corporate Social Responsibility*

In December 2008, forty Albanian companies, members and
non-members of the Global Compact, gathered together to
discuss and promote responsible business practice in Albania.
Discussions focused on promoting employment and the environment through the ten Principles. The event was organized by
the United Nations in Albania and the Global Compact Office
in New York in cooperation with the Ministry of Economy,
Trade and Energy. Representatives from the business community,
government, United Nations and media attended the event.

In addition to general awareness-raising and outreach for the
purpose of increasing the level of participation at the local level,
GCLNs also conduct awareness-raising campaigns related to specific
priority areas of the UN Global Compact. For example, to celebrate

the Sixtieth anniversary of the Universal Declaration of Human Rights (UDHR), many GCLNs put human rights issues on their agenda in 2008, through workshops, collective statements by business and lecture series. On 10 December, Local Networks in South Africa, Japan and Bulgaria held meetings to celebrate the Declaration, and in Canada and Ukraine companies issued collective statements of commitment. Earlier in the year, workshops were held in Colombia, the United States and Zambia. The German Network hosted a series of lectures on human rights and business. In Brazil the Local Network organized a high-level conference with President Luiz Inácio Lula da Silva in attendance, while in Spain, participants were encouraged by the Network to report on human rights practices (see box 18.2 for case examples on other issue-specific activities).

Learning activities and tool provision

The *Global Compact Annual Review* 2008 indicated that assistance with the implementation of the principles is one of the main reasons that companies engage in GCLNs (Global Compact 2008). Workshops, training or study tours provide valuable learning platforms where Global Compact stakeholders can gain a better understanding of the ten Principles, as well as the more general concept of corporate responsibility. Learning platforms also provide a method for stakeholders to share experiences and lessons learned. While the Global Compact has developed a valuable set of globally designed and generic tools, materials and training are successful only if they are a source for practical action and inspiration in a local context. GCLNs add value by adjusting and redeveloping them to the local context and language (see box 18.3).

Policy dialogues and partnership facilitation

In recent years, some GCLNs have begun to promote public–private dialogues related to the business–society agenda. Increasingly, political or public issues are seen by the business community as relevant to their commercial future – for example, in areas related to improving the business climate such as anti-corruption, as well as the role of the private sector in supporting development. It is anticipated that more companies will be interested in participating in public discourse in the

Box 18.2: Examples of issue-specific awareness-raising activities by Local Networks

---

USA: business and human rights conference

In recognition of the Sixtieth anniversary of the UDHR, the US Global Compact Network convened its first working symposium of 2008 on 28 April 2008 at the Harvard Business School in Boston. Jointly convened with the Harvard Business School, the event drew approximately 100 corporate executives, civil society representatives, academics and other human rights experts. The meeting also featured the US launch of 'Embedding Human Rights in Business Practices II', a compendium of case studies developed by the Global Compact Office and the Office of the UN High Commissioner for Human Rights. Also attending the meeting were members of the Global Compact's Human Rights Working Group, which held a related meeting on 29 April in Boston. On 5 May, the UN Global Compact Office and the Harvard Business School released the report and summaries of the presentations.

Mexico: national campaign to end child sexual exploitation

With the goals of educating the population and ending child sexual exploitation, the GCLN in Mexico launched a multi-stakeholder campaign in Cancún. Each stakeholder provided unique value, with NGOs providing local and topical expertise, the government developing an anonymous hotline and the private sector establishing an agreement among international tour operators. Local actors and popular football players assisted in promotional efforts.

---

future and that this activity will become more widespread among the GCLNs.

Another important area of GCLN activity is the facilitation of partnerships with UN Global Compact stakeholders, as GCLNs often provide a unique convening platform for cross-sector engagement. GCLNs play an important role in helping to identify pertinent partnering themes and engaging relevant actors in concrete projects where their comparative advantages are utilized (box 18.4). Half of

Box 18.3: Examples of Local Networks' learning activities and tool provision

---

Poland: new book on discrimination in the workforce

UNDP Poland has published a book entitled *Equal Opportunities Company: Good Practice Guide* (UNDP Poland 2007). Based on the Global Compact's Principle 6 on the elimination of discrimination in the workplace, the book was conceived as a practical tool for the implementation of equal opportunities. Compiled by Global Compact Focal Point Paulina Kaczmarek, the book presents examples of measures, procedures, projects and initiatives implemented by employers striving to create equal opportunities for women and men.

Nordic Network: learning and discussion platform for members

The Global Compact Nordic Network was launched in 2001 and membership is open to all Global Compact participating companies and business organizations from Denmark, Finland, Iceland, Norway and Sweden. There are currently approximately 110 members of the Global Compact Nordic Network. With the primary goal of increasing members' insight and understanding of the principles and the challenges involved in successfully implementing and sustaining them, the Nordic Network has met twice annually for the past seven years, rotating between the five nations since 2001. The Network membership has been restricted to business, but NGOs, government officials and trade union representatives have been invited to discuss selected principles at the meetings. With each meeting focusing on a few selected principles, the Nordic Network acts as a learning and discussion platform for members and invited contributors. By sharing experiences, success stories and failures, and through input from other participants, the aim is to inspire participants to implement the ten Principles in their daily operations.

Box 18.4: Examples of policy dialogues and partnerships facilitated by Local Networks

---

Kenya: Public–private platform to advance the business environment

With a founding objective to serve as a public–private platform to advance Kenya's business environment, the Network was involved in two Prime Minister roundtables on the national business agenda. In addition, the Network held meetings linked to national business policies on climate change and poverty.

Bolivia: Forum on sustainable development and the rights of children

Representatives from public and private institutions participated in the Forum on Corporate Social Responsibility, 'Sustainable Development and Children's Rights in Bolivia', which was jointly organized by the Vice-Ministry of Medium and Large Enterprise and Industry, the Bolivian Social Responsibility Corporation and the United Nations Children's Fund (UNICEF). The forum focused on the need for CSR projects and programmes to seek mutual coordination and to be in line with national public policies.

Moldova: 'Green Day'

During April 2008, around 170 employees representing eleven companies – members of the Global Compact Network Moldova – decided to spend one Saturday together in 'Valea Trandafirilor' public garden in the Botanica district of Chişinău municipality. For three hours, volunteer teams planted lindens, painted benches, raked lawns and picked up leaves, dug tree beds and swept alleys. The initiative displays the ability of local businesses to unify their efforts for achieving a worthy purpose, and their capacity to get together and jointly implement projects promoting actual global values, such as environmental protection.

companies surveyed in 2008 are engaging in cross-sector projects to address development gaps. Many of them are doing so through GCLNs (Global Compact 2008: 42).

COP facilitation

As the role of COPs has evolved and increased in importance, so have the role and relevance of GCLNs in the COP process. COP facilitation is the most frequent activity of GCLNs, with more than 80 per cent of Networks in all regions involved. Three out of four Networks conduct COP training and awareness-raising events and about half of them have some kind of mentoring process. One-quarter of GCLNs are involved in peer review processes. Around one-third of Networks engage others, including non-business stakeholders, in some kind of social vetting process. More and more Networks see the COP as an important way of discovering what other companies are doing (Global Compact 2009f). Equally important is the role of the COP as an integrity measure, where brand protection and integrity increasingly are being guarded as a joint effort between the UN Global Compact Office and GCLNs.

Evolution of Network Governance and Management

The 'early days' of Local Networks

The Global Compact was initially surprised to observe the formation of 'local clusters' of committed participants, now referred to as GCLNs. The first example of this was the Nordic Network in 2001. Having been introduced to the Global Compact at an outreach event, the business community in the region was eager to create a platform where they would share experiences and learn from each other. As the Global Compact's initial outreach efforts continued, a similar motivation would be felt by interested stakeholders in other countries and regions of the world. It was not long before some thirty countries were indicating a move in this direction.

The organic and self-appointed nature of these clusters resulted in widely diverse approaches with respect to how they organized themselves. As they emerged, it became increasingly clear that these local hubs could bring enormous value to the initiative. It was also clear that a flexible approach to the organization of these entities was required, one that would take into account the local context in which they were operating. As the Global Compact continued to expand, it became increasingly apparent that a certain amount of accountability and brand protection would be necessary in order to ensure the overall integrity of the initiative. It was also necessary to gain a greater understanding of how these satellite hubs would feed into, and relate to the work of the Global Compact at the global level.

2003: first gathering of Networks

It was in this context that an international workshop on 'The UN Global Compact Networks and Outreach', hosted by the Swiss Ministry of Foreign Affairs,[2] was held in Berne, Switzerland, in June 2003. This was the first international gathering of country representatives, which would later be referred to as the Annual Local Networks Forum (ALNF).

The purpose of the workshop was to discuss and agree on the strategy, mechanisms, tools and activities to impart focus and coherence to what had become an evolving global network of Local Networks (see also chapter 19 by Dirk Ulrich Gilbert). Representatives from over thirty countries shared their experiences in an effort to obtain better clarity on the diversity of approaches. It heard the perspectives of representatives from some of the earliest established Local Networks – for example, Spain, India, Panama and Zambia. They discussed the roles and responsibilities of the Global Compact Office and the growing number of Local Networks. It was clear from the discussions in Berne that the comparative advantage of the Global Compact is its engagement of companies in both developing and developed countries.

Not surprisingly however, this meant that different approaches would be adopted in order to suit the local context. Therefore it was clear that, moving forward, there would be a need to address and

---

[2] It should be noted that the Swiss Government provided invaluable support for the development of Local Networks from the very start of the process. In addition to supporting the first Network Meeting, they provided financial support by way of seed funding to a number of developing country Networks. Most importantly, however, they seconded to the Global Compact Office, a senior representative to act as Head of Networks. Anton Stadler played a key role in coordinating and guiding the development of Local Networks during this critical early stage.

agree on the best way to manage, motivate and sustain decentralized Networks, and to organize effectively both vertical communication between Local Networks and the Global Compact Office and horizontal communication between and among the Local Networks. It was agreed that the Global Compact Office should provide the necessary guidance, information and tools on matters of common concern, while allowing governance and organization methods to emerge based on local circumstances.

2004: consensus on minimum requirements for Networks

By 2004, the Global Compact had grown to become the largest corporate responsibility initiative in the world, with over 1,700 participating companies. The number of Local Networks had increased from approximately thirty in 2003 to over forty-five in 2004. With this success came new and complex organizational and branding challenges. In order to address these challenges, UN Secretary-General Kofi Annan called for a revised governance model for the initiative to be presented in 2005. This new governance structure would be designed to foster greater involvement in and ownership of the initiative by participants and other stakeholders. It was in this context that the second Global Compact Networks Conference was held in London in November 2004, hosted by the UK Government and the Global Compact UK Network.

The discussions in London highlighted the challenge facing the Global Compact initiative in formulating an appropriate governance framework – that of protecting and building the 'Global Compact' brand, improving the quality of engagement and achieving greater positive impact on the ground while respecting diversity in the approaches taken at the local level and recognizing that there would be no one-size-fits-all model. The tense and often difficult discussions during the conference emphasized that the Local Networks differed from each other in many important ways, including:

- Framework conditions in the home countries
- The number and size of participating companies
- The level of formality of the governance systems (ranging from highly informal Networks to those with formally constituted legal entities).

It was noted that this diversity was an important source of innovation and strength, and that any approach to Network governance would need to have a high degree of flexibility. While several Network representatives said that they thought increased formality was a useful way of improving and clarifying such governance, others said that they felt it was unnecessarily bureaucratic. In a dramatic ending, which almost resulted in the rejection of any aspect related to Network governance, the London meeting came to be considered a milestone in the evolution of GCLNs, in that consensus was reached on a set of minimum governance requirements:

1. Each Network has to be committed to the principles and practices of the Global Compact. This includes the ten Principles themselves, the practices of learning-by-doing, dialogue, partnerships and striving to bring together other stakeholders.
2. Each Network, for management purposes, should establish a Focal Point authorized by the Network to interact with the Global Compact Office and the wider Global Compact network.
3. Each Network should produce an annual activities report, describing the activities and initiatives undertaken in the previous year. Each Network is expected to run a minimum number of events/ activities annually.
4. Each Network should display a willingness to actively support efforts by participants to develop COPs, and help find solutions to situations related to integrity measures.

2005: Networks develop first policy document linked to governance

When the new governance framework of the Global Compact was introduced in 2005 two new elements were included, the Local Networks and the ALNF. Under the terms of the new governance framework Local Networks were granted the opportunity to nominate members for election to the Global Compact Board,[3] provide input on major activities undertaken by the Global Compact Office and convene an ALNF. The framework also specified that Local

---

[3] In July 2009, six new Global Compact Board members from the private sector were appointed based on recommendations by Local Networks.

Networks would play an important role in support of the COP policy and integrity measures (Global Compact 2005a).

Local Networks met for a third time at the ALNF in Barcelona in September 2005. This meeting was hosted with the support of the newly established Fundació Fòrum – the Barcelona Center for the Support of the Global Compact. Local Network representatives continued the discussions on recommendations for enhancing their effectiveness. Inputs received during these discussions resulted in the development of the first policy document related to Local Network governance entitled 'What is a Local Network?' (for the most recent version of this document, see Global Compact 2009h). While the document stressed that 'Local Networks determine their own internal governance arrangements and activities', it also outlined basic requirements which such Networks are expected to meet.

It was evident from the discussions held in Barcelona that while aspects related to the early stages of Network development were still of great importance, an increasing number of Local Networks were moving away from an emerging 'outreach and awareness-raising phase' to a more mature and established phase allowing them to focus on more substantive issues related to continuous quality improvement. Using input received by Local Networks during the discussions in Barcelona, the Global Compact Office prepared a guidance document aimed at helping Local Networks in their efforts to advance the Compact at the local level. Supplementing the 'What is a Local Network?' document, 'Guidance for Local Networks' (Global Compact 2005b) updated previously existing guidance and reflected best practices concerning the development of a Local Network, as well as a clear set of procedures to guide the relation between Local Networks and the Global Compact Office.

2006: role of ALNF in Global Compact governance solidified

The fourth ALNF in September 2006 was held for the second time in Barcelona with the support of the Fundació Fòrum. Continuing the trend of growing in size with each passing year, the meeting gathered together over 180 participants representing emerging and existing Local Networks from over sixty countries. The Fòrum witnessed a key step in the implementation of the Global Compact's governance framework with the adoption of the 'Annual Local Networks Forum

Terms of Reference'. The Terms of Reference outline the Forum's role in the initiative's overall governance framework and clarify the relationship between the Forum and other entities in the framework. The key role of Local Networks in meeting the challenge faced by the Global Compact in ensuring the submission of COPs by participating companies was highlighted. Consequently, Local Networks agreed to include the facilitation of the COP process as part of their work plans.

2008: *formalizing relations with Networks through the Annual Memorandum of Understanding (MoU)*

The next big step forward with respect to Network governance occurred at the sixth ALNF 2008 in Bonn. Convened by the Fundació Fòrum and the Global Compact Office with the collaboration of Deutsche Gesellschaft für Technische Zusammenarbeit (German Technical Cooperation, GTZ), with over 220 participants representing seventy Local Networks, the Forum took important decisions aimed at strengthening the governance and capacity of local operations. Key among them was the decision to insert into the ALNF's Terms of Reference additional language to clarify the Forum's decision-making processes. Going forward, a quorum of two-thirds of the GCLNs would be necessary to conduct ALNF business.

In addition, while every attempt would be made to achieve consensus around Global Compact governance issues, it was agreed that a simple majority vote would be considered sufficient to adopt decisions. Further to this, and more importantly particularly with respect to the integrity and brand management of the Global Compact, it was agreed that GCLNs would be required to sign an annual Memorandum of Understanding (MoU) with the Global Compact Office confirming, for the coming year, authorization to use the name 'Global Compact' as part of the Network's name and to use the Global Compact Network logo in connection with the Network's activities.

2009: *strengthening Networks' roles and responsibilities*

At the 2009 ALNF held in Istanbul in June, Network representatives gathered at the largest-ever Forum, which was attended by 320 participants from seventy-seven Networks. At the Forum, Networks worked to further define and strengthen their role. Notably, they agreed on a set of recommendations concerning their role in facilitating companies' COPs, the engagement of micro-enterprises and civil society organizations and the governance of Networks. Despite their wide differences, over time the Global Compact has managed to introduce key policies helping to increase the quality of Local Networks, albeit in an incremental way. Network governance will continue to evolve in a 'problem-orientated' fashion, meaning that it will evolve to overcome challenges faced by the Global Compact and its Networks.

Trends in Network Management

Formalizing organizational structures

Many GCLNs have gone beyond simply meeting the minimum criteria when creating their organizational structure. Increasingly, GCLNs have recognized the need for a strong institutional framework in order to support their activities, while others have preferred a less formalized approach, preferring rather to act as an ad hoc and event-driven local initiative. Examples of light and informal structures can be found in the Nordic and Swiss Networks among others. Created more as a platform for organizing one or two events per year to allow for awareness-raising and shared learning, the participants do not perceive an added value in establishing robust structures. Others, however, have opted for a stronger institutional framework, for example in Spain and Ukraine. Overall, the Global Compact has observed a trend towards the more formal approach for the following key reasons: greater involvement in the initiative on the part of members and partners, strengthening the decision-making mechanism and supporting a sustainable financing structure.

As outlined in the annual MoU between GCLNs and the Global Compact Office, all GCLNs have to identify a person to liaise with the Global Compact Office on day-to-day issues related to the running of a GCLN and nominate a person authorized by the GCLN to act on behalf of the Local Network at the ALNF and in the management of the Network logo. Over half of the Networks have gone further, by creating steering committees, appointing GCLN Chairpersons, establishing secretariats and forming working groups to focus on specific priority areas (see also chapter 20 by Constanze J. Helmchen).

Some GCLNs have registered their association as legal entities at the national level. The most recent case of this occurred in
China in April 2009 at a ceremony attended by a large number of
business leaders, as well as senior government officials and civil
society representatives. In another positive development from the
same region, the GCLN in Japan took measures to strengthen its
operations in 2008 when it transitioned its secretariat functions
from the United Nations Information Centre to a full-time, private
sector-led secretariat. More important, however, was the decision
to initiate a CEO-led board which the Network hopes will not only
build strength for the Global Compact in Japan, but also invigorate
Networks in other countries.

Additionally, in some cases GCLNs have even developed processes
in order to handle complaints against Network participants. The
primary way GCLNs have dealt with complaints is by initiating dialogue between the parties or referring the case to the Global Compact
Office in order to initiate the dialogue. Others, such as the GCLN in
Germany have referred to the arbitration mechanism of the German
National Contact Point for the OECD Guidelines for Multinational
Enterprises in order to mediate conflicts concerning violations of the
ten Principles. As the Global Compact continues to grow, GCLNs
will be increasingly relied upon to manage and support such integrity
measures.

Regional Network gatherings

In addition to the regular networking opportunity in the context of
the ALNF, Networks have also experienced a high degree of interaction at the regional levels. Since 2006, regional meetings for Local
Networks have been convened to provide Global Compact Focal
Points and other members of the Network Steering Committees with
an opportunity to learn from the achievements of other Networks and
to share experiences on the processes and issues relevant within the
regional context. Set apart from the learning exchange that occurs at
the ALNF, these more informal regional meetings provide opportunities to discuss regional challenges and opportunities as well as to identify potential regional approaches and joint activities. These annual
regional meetings are also used to seek input from Local Networks on
the agenda for the ALNF.

Over the years, a number of regional support centres have been established to support the development of GCLNs. The earliest example is the Global Compact Bratislava Hub based within the UNDP Regional Bureau for Europe and the CIS. The hub was established after it became apparent that the Global Compact-related activities of UNDP in the region had been growing constantly and rapidly since 2003. Since 2007, the United Nations Economic and Social Commission for Asia and the Pacific (ESCAP) has hosted a project that supports the formation and development of GCLNs in Asia and the Pacific region in particular. The project not only aims at supporting existing and developing GCLNs and coordinating exchange between them, but it also has fostered the establishment of new GCLNs in the Asia Pacific region. A regional sub-Saharan office in support of the Global Compact was established based on a joint agreement between the Global Compact Office and the GTZ. While the work of this support office ended in 2007, efforts are currently underway to create a new regional approach in Africa which hopes to continue these efforts. Plans for a regional centre for the support of GCLNs in Latin America and the Caribbean were announced in late 2008 and the Regional Support Centre Latin America and the Caribbean, based in Bogotá, Colombia, was established in late 2009. The Support Centre's objective is to increase awareness of the private sector's contribution to sustainable development and of the Global Compact in particular. The Support Centre works closely with existing and new GCLNs in the region and provides support to ongoing Local Network activities and coordinates regional activities.

Conclusion

As indicated above, the emergence and development of GCLNs was unexpected when the Global Compact initiative was originally launched. The fact that they emerged in highly diverse contexts and settings resulted in their lack of uniformity. This diversity is in part produced by the necessity of the GCLNs to adapt to the contingencies of their local contexts. However, one could also argue that one of the main reasons was a lack of clear direction and guidance from the Global Compact. Often, GCLNs were left to themselves to develop solutions to the challenges they faced in establishing strong and vibrant networks. Not all were successful. Some GCLNs were created only to fall dormant once the 'committed individual/organization' who had taken the lead in driving the agenda moved on. Others suffered the fate of being 'captured' by the interests of one organization to the detriment of the GCLN as a whole. Over the years, the Global Compact has attempted to develop guidance and share the experience of others in order to assist GCLNs in avoiding such problems. The representative model currently enforced through the GCLN MoU is the best way to ensure that participants are engaged not only in the GCLN's activities but in its governing and sustainability over time. The recently launched 'Knowledge-Sharing System'[4] has been created to assist GCLNs in sharing and accessing information regarding the management and activities of all other GCLNs. It is hoped that this tool will improve interaction between Networks, allow for the sharing of best practice and ultimately improve the development of engagement mechanisms at the local level.

In order for GCLNs to survive, they must be capable of adapting their actions and focus over time in order to remain relevant and to continuously add value to their participants. Aside from ensuring that their participants meet the COP requirements and demonstrate progress with respect to the ten Principles, GCLNs will have to do more in the area of incentive-creation in order to keep participants motivated and to provide recognition to those who demonstrate leadership; as such, the value of award and recognition schemes is becoming increasingly apparent. Additionally, GCLNs will have to make every effort to remain on top of the current trends and challenges facing the corporate citizenship agenda, particularly in light of recent events. For example, the recent economic crisis has meant that many small and medium size enterprises (SMEs) are finding it harder then ever to live up to their commitment. Given that SMEs make up almost half of the Global Compact's participant base, and their engagement is almost entirely at the local level, GCLNs will have to meet the challenge of responding to the demands of this important constituency. The challenge for the Global Compact will be to ensure that we build the capacity of the GCLNs to enable them to do so.

---

[4] The 'Knowledge-Sharing System', developed by the Global Compact Office and launched in October 2009 is an online information-sharing tool which allows GCLNs to update each other on all issues related to Network management, governance and activities. It will also allow for the systematic collection and analysis of GCLN information at the aggregate level.

Probably the most important area that the Global Compact will increasingly rely on the GCLNs to support moving forward is with respect to integrity measures. As already discussed, GCLNs are already actively engaged in the COP process through facilitation, trainings, peer-reviews, etc. Most non-English-speaking GCLNs also assist with translation in order to ensure that a COP meets the minimum criteria. In addition, GCLNs are also asked to screen new participants from their country to ensure that the Global Compact does not accept the participation of an organization who for some reason may pose problems to the initiative's reputation. The final way in which GCLNs are involved in the Global Compact's integrity measures is as part of the dialogue-facilitation mechanism in cases where an allegation of systematic or egregious abuse has been brought against a GCLN participant. In such a case, the Global Compact may ask the relevant GCLN to assist with the resolution of the matter. As described above, some GCLNs have developed their own processes to handle such situations.

Witnessing the growth and development of GCLNs over the last decade has been a remarkable and exciting experience. While the process has not been without its challenges, the Global Compact can be proud of what it has achieved. The GCLNs have come a long way from a handful of committed individuals operating in various locations across the globe to an internetworking group of organizations whose diverse approaches to similar challenges is part of the UN Global Compact's strength. The resourcefulness and vitality demonstrated at any ALNF is testament to the fact that the Global Compact's message of responsibility has gained traction around the world and has become a truly global phenomenon. GCLNs will continue to face obstacles along the way, but it is also clear that we have a lot to look forward to in the coming years and it will be interesting to see how far they have progressed on the occasion of the Global Compact's second Anniversary.

19 | *The United Nations Global Compact as a Network of Networks*

DIRK ULRICH GILBERT

Introduction

The United Nations Global Compact reflects a Global Public Policy Network bringing together UN agencies, corporations, civil society actors, non-governmental organizations (NGOs) and labour representatives from all over the world. Today, the Global Compact provides the most far-reaching initiative worldwide to catalyse a voluntary participation of multinational corporations (MNCs) in corporate social responsibility activities (Arevalo and Fallon 2008, Kell and Levin 2003, Kell and Ruggie 1999, Leisinger 2007). The Compact offers a platform for businesses to advance ten Principles in the areas of human rights, labour, the environment and anti-corruption (Kell 2005, Williams 2004). The core tasks of the Global Compact are to mainstream these principles in global business activities and to facilitate cooperation among those constituents who are willing to create multi-stakeholder engagement.

Unlike certification-based initiatives (e.g. SA 8000), the Compact has no intention to enforce or even measure the behaviour of firms participating in the initiative. The Global Compact rather intends to bring together a variety of different actors to discuss, learn about and advance its underlying principles (Kell 2005, Kell and Levin 2003, Rasche 2009b, Ruggie 2001, 2003, Williams 2004). Against this background the Global Compact can be considered as a strategic policy initiative for business focusing on the implementation of its ten Principles and the promotion of broader UN goals (Rasche 2009a).

We are particularly interested in the collaborative dimension of the Global Compact which is represented by the idea of fostering Local Networks as clusters of participating firms who try to collaborate and to further advance the initiative and its Principles within different

340

natural, cultural and language contexts. In their role to help companies to implement the ten Principles Local Networks define their own internal governance structures and activities to manage the collaboration of different stakeholders. The question we are going to investigate in this chapter is *how* Local Networks are actually being managed and *how* the Network partners coordinate their different activities. While most work on the Global Compact deals with questions of whether a participation of firms actually helps to expand corporate citizenship activities and whether more effective mechanisms are needed to ensure that companies in fact comply with the ten Principles (Arevalo and Fallon 2008, Rasche 2009a), only limited attention has been given to the question of how Local Networks are and should be organized to increase the legitimation of the Global Compact.

The chapter is organized as follows. We will first discuss the creation and design of Local Networks and outline important guidelines and recommendations for Global Compact Networks on the local level. We will then turn our attention to Network Theory. The management of Networks has been one of the core subjects in the area of strategic management and organization theory over the last few years (Dyer and Singh 1998, Granovetter 1985, Jones, Hesterly and Borgatti 1997, Miles and Snow 1986, Rowley 1997). We argue that insights from Network Theory can help us to better understand and, even more important, further advance the discussion on how to manage Local Networks. By using Network analysis we can derive recommendations on how the collaboration between multiple, interdependent stakeholders can be enhanced and governance structures should be designed to safeguard the implementation of the Global Compact. We will also show that trust between different Network partners plays a particularly important role as it is the basis for a sound collaboration between constituents on the global and the local level.

Creation and Design of Local Networks

Local Networks play a crucial role and are an integral part of the overall governance of the Compact. They are defined as a 'cluster of participants who come together to advance the Global Compact and its principles within a particular geographic context' (Global Compact 2009g). Local Networks not only help to root the Compact within different national and cultural contexts but also deepen the learning experience of all participants through their own activities and events which promote action in support of broader UN goals (Ruggie 2001). The Global Compact is a genuinely global initiative because Local Networks have been set up all around the globe. Numbers of Local Networks are gradually increasing and today there are sixty-two established Networks and twenty-seven so-called 'emerging Networks'. To be considered as a Local Network by the United Nations each of the Local Networks is required to sign an annual Memorandum of Understanding (MoU) with the Global Compact Office. The MoU confirms the authorization to use the name 'Global Compact' as part of the Network's name and to use the Global Compact Network logo in connection with its activities. The annual reconfirmation is based on the understanding that the Local Network will continue to engage in activities that are in line with the objectives of the Global Compact.

Minimum requirements for Local Networks

To be regarded as an established 'Local Network' a Network has to fulfil the following minimum requirements, whereas an 'emerging network' is a group of participants who are making progress towards the actual establishment of a Local Network (Global Compact 2009g):

- Commit to the Principles and practices of the Global Compact. This includes the ten Principles themselves, the practice of learning-by-doing, dialogue, partnership and striving to bring together other stakeholders.
- Hold a minimum number of events and activities annually.
- Display a willingness to actively support efforts by participants to develop a Communication on Progress (COP).
- Proactively manage and protect the integrity of the Global Compact and develop a capacity to find solutions to dilemma situations involving participants in the Network.
- Produce an annual activities report.
- Identify a person to liaise with the Global Compact Office on day-to-day issues related to the running of a Local Network, and nominate a person authorized by the Local Network to act on behalf of the Network at the Annual Local Networks Forum (ALNF) and in the management of the Network logo.

Local Networks are encouraged to establish some form of governance structure and find their own sources of funding to support their manifold activities. To sustain a steady level of ongoing activities on the local level, funding is crucial. This is why Local Networks typically start to raise funding by asking the core group of companies that founded it to spend some money. Sustainable funding is important and likely to be reached when both specific funding (e.g. sponsoring specific collective actions) and structural funding (e.g. an annual contribution) occur. Another important step in setting up a Local Network is usually to nominate a Focal Point and a Steering Committee with a majority of company representatives (Global Compact 2007c: 21). Local Networks should include other organizations than companies and often appoint a well-regarded leader to chair the steering committee. When members of a Local Network are well connected and have good access to local business leaders, the government, labour organizations and civil society, this will help to ensure the effectiveness of the Global Compact.

Activities of Local Networks

One of the core objectives of the Global Compact is to become an initiative which is on the one hand truly global in reach and on the other hand capable of dealing with local differences in terms of culture, language and governance. Local Networks are key to reaching these objectives by organizing manifold activities related to the ten Principles of the Compact and the eight UN Millennium Development Goals (MDGs) (Global Compact 2008). Activities that Local Networks typically undertake are the following (Global Compact 2009g, Global Compact 2007c):

- Local Networks are often a forum for dialogue and emerging issues related to the Global Compact and act as a platform for learning. By organizing national, regional, or sectoral learning events in Local Networks participating companies assist each other with the implementation of the ten Principles.
- Local Networks take responsibility in mobilizing joint efforts involving multiple stakeholders in the form of collective action. Based on this, Local Networks develop partnership projects to contribute to the achievement of the ten Principles and the MDGs.

- Individual companies can become mentors on the local level and volunteer to support other firms who are interested in pushing their activities related to the Compact further.
- An important task of Local Networks is to act as an access point for government entities dealing with human rights, labour, environment and anti-corruption.
- On a very operational level, Local Networks can help in translating documents, tools and learning materials into local languages. This function should be undertaken with the help of the Global Compact Office.

Communication on Progress (COP) and Local Networks

Based on the above-mentioned activities another core objective of Local Networks is to foster continuous quality improvement and integrity by helping companies in the preparation of their annual COP. Every COP has to meet three minimum standards proposed by the United Nations (Global Compact 2009d) and must include:

- A statement by the CEO (or equivalent) expressing continued support for the Global Compact and renewing the participant's ongoing commitment to the initiative and its Principles.
- A description of practical actions the company has taken to implement the Compact's ten Principles.
- A measurement of outcomes (e.g. identify targets, define performance indicators, or measure outcomes).

The annual COP represents a crucial requirement for participation in the Global Compact and serves several important purposes (see also chapters 14–17 in part III of this volume). First, COP helps to drive continuous improvement of activities associated with implementing the ten Principles. Second, COP helps to achieve accountability and safeguard the integrity of the Compact as a whole. And, third, COP by participating firms helps to create a database of corporate practices. In the recent past more and more MNCs have started to create and publish Corporate Social Responsibility (CSR) reports and the COP policy reflects this trend towards greater transparency and accountability. COP reports are publicly available and provide stakeholders with timely information regarding the actions of a participant toward the ten Principles (Rasche 2009b).

Although Local Networks have leeway regarding the structure and content of the COP, this policy helps to foster the implementation of the Global Compact's Principles and allows for an evaluation of a firm's actions by external and internal stakeholders on the local as well as on the global level. In 2008 a record number of 1,732 COPs were posted, representing a 25 per cent increase from 2007 and an almost 100 per cent increase from 2006 (Global Compact 2008: 53). In total approximately 5,000 COPs are available on the Compact's website for public review, representing one of the largest global repositories of corporate disclosure on environmental, social and governance (ESG) work. In total 76 per cent of the companies have an 'active' status in the Global Compact and 404 firms were delisted in 2008 because of failure to communicate on progress (Global Compact 2008: 53).

Local Networks play an important role in assisting participants of all sizes in the process of preparing a COP by using learning activities and sharing case examples. A recent survey reveals that 50 per cent of the companies engage in a Local Network to receive assistance with creating a COP Report (Global Compact 2008: 20). Local Networks should also strive to provide feedback to the companies and introduce a peer review system. In many of the Local Networks COP acts as a tool to motivate participants to deepen their engagement in the Compact (Global Compact 2009g). Local Networks should also make subsidiaries of large MNCs aware of the option to prepare their own COP on the local level, or to make reference to the COP of their parent company.

Challenges for Local Networks

The United Nations is aware of the problem that it can be challenging to protect the multi-stakeholder character of the Compact because Local Networks are often business-led. In the end a Local Network is primarily a gathering of companies where they learn from each other, engage in dialogue or partnerships with each other and coordinate their communication with the Global Compact Office. Therefore, it seems crucial for the success of Local Networks to promote collective learning and action by also inviting non-business actors to take part in the meetings, projects, partnerships and, maybe most important, the steering committee. By doing so the inclusive and open nature of the

Global Compact can be respected on the local level (Global Compact 2009g).

In a collaborative effort, affected stakeholders should also work on improving communication between Local Networks and the Global Compact Office, among different Local Networks and within the Local Network itself. As a part of this strategy the Global Compact Office attempts to provide Local Networks with tools, publications and any other material that has been developed to foster the implementation of the ten Principles. Last but not least, the Global Compact Office once a year summarizes best practices in learning, dialogue and collective action of all Local Networks and publishes a 'Local Network Report' (Global Compact 2009f). The report shows that the Local Networks are constantly changing and while some grow stronger, others recede. It also takes a deeper look at the Local Networks' efforts to facilitate COP and the initiatives set up to involve civil society organizations in Network activities (Global Compact 2008: 5).

Each of the Local Networks is unique but all share one goal: to work together and form a global Network of Networks to advance the ten Principles of the Global Compact by providing local and global opportunities for dialogue and collaboration on critical issues between businesses, NGOs, labour and government. Local Networks create a platform to exchange good practices and experiences to help find practical solutions to challenging problems associated with the Global Compact. Local Networks also represent access points to the United Nations' broad knowledge and can help companies to increase their legitimacy. Via participation in the Compact and its Local Networks opportunities to take part in processes of public deliberation have increased in the recent past. By providing an institutional infrastructure around corporate responsibility, firms have the opportunity to discuss and change the 'rules of the game' in multi-stakeholder dialogues and to retain what some call their 'license to operate' (Gilbert and Behnam 2009).

A Brief Introduction to Network Theory

Over the last two decades we have witnessed a rapid increase of publications and approaches to a new form of governance in business, the so-called 'network organization'. Many authors like Granovetter (1985), Jones, Hesterly and Borgatti (1997), or Williamson (1985) consider networks as a governance structure somewhere between market and hierarchy which has distinct features and requires a special kind of 'management' to work efficiently. A network thereby represents a connection of different stakeholders by a certain type of relationship where *'economic action and outcomes, like all social action and outcomes, are affected by actors' dyadic (pairwise) relations* and *by the structure of the overall network of relations'* (Granovetter 1992: 33, emphasis added). The relationships between the actors in a network are not only characterized by economic transactions but also by social ties. Granovetter (1985: 501) highlights that often *'social relations between firms are more important . . . in bringing order to economic life than is supposed in the markets and hierarchies line of thought'* (1985: 501, emphasis added). Against this background the main focus of network analysis is the interdependence of actors and how their respective positions in the network influence their behaviour, opportunities and strategies to achieve their objectives (Rowley 1997).

Network analysis mostly focuses on the design of governance structures in networks and tries to identify ways to more effectively manage how interdependent parties can work together. The management of a network is much more complicated and calls for a different approach than the management of a firm. In other words, the key features of governance (Williamson 1995) differ and focal actors in a network have to be careful when making management decisions. Whereas in a hierarchy (firm) administrative power is the appropriate means to coordinate activities, the key feature of governance on markets are differential incentive systems (e.g. prices). A network, on the other hand, is a compromise mode that is located somewhere between market and hierarchy, and this is why both attributes (power and price) work well, plus a third form of governance, a trust and contract law regime (Kale, Singh and Perlmutter 2000, Williamson 1995). Trust in particular seems to be important to manage network relations. For Jarillo trust is *'the essential glue that holds networks together'* (1990: 498, emphasis added) and without trust networks probably would quickly disintegrate and not achieve their objectives.

From a Network Theory perspective there are at least four potential ways in which firms could manage their relationships to be better able to allocate people and resources to projects and problems in a decentralized manner and to gain competitive advantage (Dyer and Singh 1998):

1. *Relation-specific assets*: Network partners should invest a certain amount of resources in relation-specific assets to increase performance. Williamson (1985) mainly identifies three different kinds of asset specificity: (1) site specificity, (2) physical asset specificity and (3) human asset specificity.
2. *Knowledge-sharing routines*: As interorganizational learning is critical to gain competitive advantage, superior knowledge transfer is a key to success in networks. Thus, network partners can generate rents by developing superior knowledge-sharing routines as regular patterns of interfirm interaction.
3. *Complementary resources*: Another way in which firms can create relational rents is by leveraging the complementary resources of a network partner. Often only utilizing a firm's own resources in conjunction with the complementary resources of another network partner can create competitive advantage and greater rents than those obtained by the individual firm.
4. *Effective governance system*: Last but not least, an effective governance system (e.g. trust and contracts) in a network can generate relational rents, by (1) reducing transaction costs, (2) providing incentives for the network actors to make greater investments in specialized assets, because of the lower cost of safeguarding them, or (3) reducing opportunistic behaviour.

In summary, Network Theory comes to the conclusion that one of the main reasons why firms enter networks is to learn from their network partners and to gain competitive advantage, while at the same time they want to protect themselves from opportunistic behaviour to retain their core competencies and proprietary assets (Kale, Singh and Perlmutter 2000).

A Critical Analysis of Local Networks from a Network Theory Perspective

We can learn a lot from Network Theory for the management of the Global Compact as a 'Network of Networks'. The Global Compact can also be considered as a 'governance structure' between market and hierarchy and the outcomes of its efforts to further push the acceptance of the ten Principles are heavily affected by the actors' dyadic relations as well as by the structure of the overall global network of relations. One of the most important stakeholder groups taking part in the Compact are businesses and this is why relationships between the actors are often of economic nature. However, in line with Granovetter (1985) the Global Compact highlights the fact that social relations between firms and their stakeholders are also important to bring order to the economic system and make markets work effectively.

In the following we draw on Network Theory to derive some recommendations on how the collaboration between multiple, interdependent stakeholders in Local Networks can be enhanced and governance structures be designed to safeguard the implementation of the Global Compact. We will also show that *trust* plays a particularly important role in Local Networks as it is the basis for a sound collaboration between constituents on both the global and the local level. As indicated above, there are at least four ways to manage the relationships in a network and to create trust between the partners (see Dyer and Singh 1998).

Relation-specific assets in Local Networks

Partners in Local Networks should think about investing a certain amount of resources in relation-specific investments. Such investments can be physical assets (e.g. investing in a network secretariat and employing full-time staff) or human assets. Because many Local Networks may lack the financial resources to pay for a secretariat human asset specificity seems to be the most promising way to further advance the Global Compact. Human asset specificity refers to know-how accumulated by the network partners through long-standing relationships. Experience and a willingness to cooperate are also prerequisites on the personal level for such a human co-specialization. From a Local Network perspective this means the firms should only appoint people to liaise with the Global Compact and the other Local Network partners who have a long-lasting experience in questions of human rights, labour standards, environmental issues and/or the fight against corruption.

Knowledge-sharing routines in Local Networks

One of the most important lessons that one can learn from Network Theory for designing the Global Compact as a Network of Networks is that knowledge-sharing routines are key to success when managing interfirm relations. Local Networks should try to facilitate learning about the implementation of the Global Compact by defining regular patterns of interfirm action on the local level that permit the transfer, creation and recombination of specialized local knowledge (e.g. regular meetings, an email newsletter). Empirical research reveals that the opportunity to network with other organizations and the option to acquire practical know-how associated with the Compact are among the top reasons to join the Initiative (Cetindamar and Husoy 2007, McKinsey & Company 2004, Runhaar and Lafferty 2009).

The steering committee on the local level must also ensure that other actors like civil society organizations, unions and governments are included when making a decision on knowledge-sharing routines. For Local Networks this often is a major challenge. A study by McKinsey & Company (2004) reveals that only 5 per cent of Local Networks engage the full range of non-UN stakeholders (e.g. NGOs, labour, governments and companies), 58 per cent of Local Networks include only one or two stakeholder groups in their ongoing activities, meaning that companies are most likely to be the single party involved. This exclusion has led to a lot of criticism and shows the need to not only include a broader set of stakeholders in Local Networks but also to back up their interaction by knowledge sharing routines.

The COP by the members of a Local Network and an annual meeting of all local network partners can also be considered as knowledge-sharing routines. In sum the likelihood to increase trust increases when knowledge-sharing routines lead to a high level of transparency and openness between Local Network partners (Kale, Singh and Perlmutter 2000: 221). Firms and other stakeholders must also learn and become willing to reveal critical information in terms of human rights, social and environmental issues and corruption. Without an open discussion of conflicts on the local level trust is unlikely to emerge, which then hampers the implementation of the Compact's Principles. Knowledge-sharing can thereby be enhanced in a Local Network by aligning incentives that encourage the actors to be transparent and to transfer knowledge. In the context of the Global Compact, an incentive can be based on the informal norm of reciprocity, meaning that the participants of a Local Network should respond to each other in kind.

Complementary resources in Local Networks

As indicated above, another way to ensure effectiveness in a network of actors is to leverage the complementary resources of the network partners. Theory suggests that complementary resources *'are resources of network partners that collectively generate greater rents than the sum of those obtained from the individual endowment of each partner'* (Dyer and Singh 1998: 666–7, emphasis added). Networks, which are able to exploit synergies, usually produce stronger competitive positions than those achievable by the firms operating individually.

The most valuable resource in the context of Local Networks is their local presence and the knowledge of all participating stakeholders about the particular cultural circumstances. Being 'on the ground' enables Local Networks to solve problems in a decentralized manner and to find solutions which fit with the local environment. Research shows that this contributes to implementing the ten Principles more successfully (McKinsey & Company 2004). It is, however, often very costly and difficult to identify potential partners who possess relevant knowledge. This is why partners in Local Networks should create a 'knowledge management' function, responsible for the ongoing collection and distribution of Local Network-specific knowledge. The role of such a 'knowledge manager' is to identify and evaluate potential partners, screen the knowledge available and establish trust on the personal level between the different participants of a local network.

Effective governance system in Local Networks

An effective governance system plays a key role in the Global Compact and its Local Networks and is a crucial prerequisite to achieving the overall objectives of the initiative. As mentioned above, governance in a network helps to avoid opportunistic behaviour and reduces transaction costs – both important objectives for Global Compact Local Networks (GCLNs). If we take a look at the key features of governance we also learn from Network Theory that both a contract law regime (third-party enforcement) and trust (self-enforcing agreements) are crucial to manage network relations successfully.

Because of its voluntary nature the Global Compact actually does not aim at 'forcing' companies to participate in the initiative and to sign binding 'contracts'. The Compact is not designed as a certification process or an initiative to sanction its participants. Hence, the Compact deliberately does not enforce or measure the behaviour or action of companies; it rather relies on public accountability, transparency and the enlightened self-interest of relevant stakeholders to join the initiative (Rasche 2009a). This is why there are only very few binding 'contracts' to be signed to take part in the Global Compact. One is the 'Letter of Commitment' from the Chief Executive Officer (CEO) firms have to send to the UN Secretary-General expressing support for the Global Compact and its Principles. In this letter, firms express their intent to advance the Principles within their sphere of influence. They also commit themselves to making the Global Compact and its Principles part of the strategy, culture and day-to-day operations of the company.

Approaches to establish a formal and binding governance structure also occur on the Local Network level (e.g. steering committees, COP). Only recently, at the sixth Annual Local Networks Forum (ALNF) in Bonn, Germany, the Local Networks strengthened their governance system significantly. Despite their diverse nature they agreed on a set of minimum requirements necessary to ensure the integrity of local operations. Every Network is obliged to produce an annual activity report and should be willing to support participants in their efforts to create and further develop COP. Moreover, every Local Network has to appoint an individual to formally represent the Network at the ALNF and in the management of the Network logo (Global Compact 2009f: 7).

Because there are only very few sanctioning mechanisms when firms actually fail to keep their promises associated with the Compact, it becomes obvious that self-enforcing agreements are also important to help to further develop the initiative (Thérien and Pouliot 2006). Self-enforcing agreements may rely on trust relations or also reputation. The more the participants of a Local Network trust each other the more willing they will be to share relevant knowledge about a proper implementation of the ten Principles. Research shows that trust between network partners increases not only the quantity of knowledge being shared but also its quality (Kale, Singh and Perlmutter 2000). Communication between trusting parties is much more open and fosters learning in the Network. Hence, in a trusting environment it is easier to implement knowledge-sharing routines and generate complementary resources.

Research also indicates that strong interpersonal ties between two or more organizations and a certain level of personal trust provides channels through which partners in a network can learn about other firms' reliability and competences (Kale, Singh and Perlmutter 2000: 218). From this perspective successful learning rests upon close *interpersonal* ties; first, at the dyadic level but second, also, on a Network level. For Local Networks it follows that the creation of personal relationships and a careful selection of managers responsible for running network-related activities is at least as important as formal governance structures (e.g. the Steering Committee). An analysis of the Global Compact shows that besides trust relations on the local level mutual trust between Local Networks and the United Nations is also important and reduces the need to agree on formal safeguards (e.g. contracts) when collaborating on issues related to the Global Compact.

Conclusion

The Global Compact is by far the most prominent corporate responsibility initiative, with more than 6,500 participants. It is designed as a multi-stakeholder initiative which engages all kinds of societal actors – including firms, labour, academia and civil society. This chapter shows that Local Networks can play an increasingly important role in rooting the Compact within different national contexts and that Networks also foster the rapid progress of companies engaging in the initiative. We have shown that Local Networks are key to the Compact's success as they facilitate learning activities and create opportunities for multi-stakeholder engagement and collective action. The Global Compact can be seen and conceptualized as a 'Network of (local) Networks'. The design of the Compact as a 'Network of (local) Networks' helps to better adapt and adopt the ten Principles at the local and regional level. There is a broad consensus in theory and practice that the decentralization of the Global Compact via Local Networks and the establishment of regional offices are important tools to make the initiative more effective (Rieth *et al.* 2007).

By drawing on Network Theory, we have derived some insights on how to actually 'manage' Local Networks and have shown that relation-specific investments, knowledge-sharing routines, complementary resources and an effective governance system are important to further develop the Compact in general and Local Networks in particular. The Global Compact is very dynamic in nature and future research should put a particular focus on how to further develop the governance structure of the initiative to leverage the United Nation's global reach and convening power to include a full range of stakeholders in the initiative. The Global Compact is a 'Network of Networks', and only collective action on the global as well as on the local level can help to realize its vision to create a more sustainable and inclusive economy.

20 Running a Global Compact Local Network: insights from the experience in Germany

CONSTANZE J. HELMCHEN

Introduction

Some eighty Global Compact Networks are on the ground locally, usually organized as national Networks. Spread across regions and entire continents, the various Global Compact Networks offer each other support, exchange and a link between the central Global Compact Office in New York, at UN Headquarters, and the individual company committed to the Global Compact's ten Principles.

When Kofi Annan envisioned it, the Global Compact started as an initiative without long-term plans concerning its operational structure. As it gained momentum, it became clear that the Global Compact Office in New York could hardly cater to all the different participants worldwide. Companies were joined by hybrid and civil society organizations in their effort to promote the ten Principles; characteristics differed starkly between the different business participants. Locality, sector, size and ownership structure create a variety of challenges; at times the only real connecting component was the commitment to the Global Compact itself. Thus, local support structures started to develop. Some were initiated by the United Nations itself, some grew from self-organized groups of signatories to the Global Compact, and others joined existing initiatives in the field of corporate responsibility. Over the last five years, these Local Networks started communicating and comparing their respective organizational structure and related problems, their output and assumed impact. With the Annual Local Networks Forum (ALNF) bringing together representatives from networks around the world – so-called *Focal Points* – a platform was created to streamline and coordinate these new structures and ensure their connection to other Global Compact entities. Each network's individual circumstance is different and worth looking at. In the following look at the German

Global Compact Network, we aim to shed light on some of the lessons learned by offering insight into issues we identified, problems we faced and niches we found in our search for best practices when running a Local Network. Obviously, we are still searching – and still learning.

Developing the German Global Compact Network to date

German friends of the Global Compact

Six major German companies were among the first signatories of the Global Compact: BASF, Bayer, Daimler, Deutsche Bank, Deutsche Telekom and a formerly prominent insurance company. Company representatives met regularly as a group of 'German Friends of the Global Compact' to exchange thoughts and practices. Accompanied by the German section of the International Chamber of Commerce (ICC), these companies grew into a small but vocal group of advocates for the Global Compact in German business circles.

Building a Network and Global Compact brand in Germany

Before long, German politics acknowledged the potential of this new philosophy. In 2001 the Federal Ministry for Economic Development and Cooperation (BMZ in its German abbreviation) decided to support Kofi Annan's initiative. Similar to global development policy discourse turning to the private sector for creative and resourceful leverage in order to reach the UN Millennium Development Goals (MDGs), the BMZ had initiated a development programme for public–private partnerships (PPPs) a few years earlier. The Global Compact therefore fitted nicely into the new policy direction of cooperating with the private sector. As a UN initiative providing learning and guidance opportunities for businesses, the Global Compact offered a prominent new framework. Hence, the BMZ decided to offer core funding to the New York office, the Global Compact Office, and – moreover – started building the coordination structure for German Global Compact signatories, which later turned into the German Global Compact Network. As with most of the BMZ's work, one of its implementation organizations oversaw this new coordination task. The German Technical Cooperation's (GTZ in its German abbreviation) Centre for collaboration with the private sector was a good match, keeping in mind opportunities for capitalizing on synergies with their public–private partnership programme.

With a clearly identified contact point – i.e. the Focal Point – the number of German signatories increased, steadily forming a growing network of like-minded organizations. Interestingly, not only business but soon also civil society organizations joined the Network, e.g. Transparency International (TI), based in Germany and critical in establishing the Compact's 10th Principle (see chapter 6 by Huguette Labelle). The fact that coordination lay in the hands of the GTZ proved to be important to the overall genesis and character of the Network. Owned by the Federal Government of Germany, GTZ itself joined the Global Compact in 2004. Yet to most, the GTZ is a semi-governmental institution, often perceived as a hybrid, politically and structurally located somewhere between the government and non-governmental organizations (NGOs). This hybrid character, however, secured the Global Compact Focal Point a high level of credibility early on in its work, as it was recognized as non-partisan; civil society identified with GTZ's mission to advance development in the South, state actors realized its proximity to the Federal Ministry and companies acknowledged its understanding of the business sector in developing countries. To this day, this mixed character plays an important role in securing the Network's structure – especially in its distinctly multi-stakeholder form, as will be elaborated further below.

Once a critical number of German participants had joined the Global Compact, the Focal Point, together with these committed organizations, established a Network with a distinct method of operation, in particular a certain type of event: based on the Global Compact's idea of the learning platform, controversial and frank discussions were regularly fostered in a Chatham House rule-based conference at the GTZ in Berlin. With these 'working conferences' ('Arbeitstreffen'), a regular structured meeting place for German Global Compact participants was created, enriched by external experts and topical inputs, but defined by an in-group feeling of trust, mutual respect and common purpose.

Professionalizing our work

In 2007, the German Network still had a relatively small number of companies compared to other Global Compact networks in Europe. However, this Network could boast almost two-thirds of the big

DAX 30 companies, and a certain dynamic was tangible. Participating companies started debating whether to contribute financially to the German Focal Point's work to accelerate its professionalization; a trend that shortly thereafter was reflected in the worldwide discussion on how to structure Global Compact Local Networks (GCLNs) and appropriate decisions in the ALNF, representing all Networks.

The informal group of business representatives that had been functioning as a close sounding board for the Focal Point was exchanged for a formally appointed and thus mandated Steering Group for the German Global Compact Network. In order to reflect the German Network's nature as a business driven multi-stakeholder network, the Network's plenary decided that the Steering Group's members should be elected from three constituencies: business, civil society and state institutions (in our case, the relevant Federal German Ministries). Moreover, each sector chose its respective mode of election, reflecting the group's interests and characteristics. At its constitutional meeting in the summer of 2007, the Steering Group was made up of four business representatives (plus two standing deputies), two governmental representatives (plus one deputy) and two NGO representatives.

This resulted in some structural adjustment and a content-related shift in our work. First, the discussion on financial responsibility for the Network's costs was concluded with the decision to form a foundation and ask businesses to contribute in form of voluntary contributions. While it is crucial to leave the donation to the voluntary decision of each participating company, in the long-term the Network can only survive on the basis of a mixed funding structure. As a business-driven multi-stakeholder initiative, the German Global Compact Network must involve both public *and* private commitment and funding. Secondly, the traditionally flexible search for suitable content and topics of exchange for the regular working conferences – often in reaction to politics of the day – became more structured, covering selected Global Compact Principles and their related underlying issues.

What we do and how we do it

Define the target group: struggling change agents

Observing whether representatives, specifically from business, would appreciate the newly more focused design of the Focal Point's events and conferences coincided with a reflection on the character of the *individuals* that come together in the Network. When defining our work, it became important to consider that not 'a company', but rather a specific individual comes to our events, reads our publications and, ideally, benefits from our work in supporting his/her company's respective commitment to foster the ten Principles. These individuals are usually those in charge of corporate responsibility, sustainability, or similar subjects. Depending on the company's structure and set-up, the relevant issues may be located in the communications or PR departments, as was quite common some years ago. They may, however, also lie in the hands of the human resource department, or the Chief Compliance Officer may handle them. In some cases, especially in more industrial production-focused companies, corporate responsibility, and hence the Global Compact, might be grouped with topics of environmental responsibility.

Wherever located within the internal structure of a company, those in charge of Global Compact implementation never come with in-depth expertise in all four issue areas (i.e. human rights, labour standards, environmental issues and what would today include climate change and adaptation, and anti-corruption). Instead, we consider such people *change agents*: groups or individuals who use their skills and relationships to implement change in an organization. Of course, some are more intrinsically motivated for the cause and for infusing the company with knowledge and instruments in order to strengthen the ten Principles than others. Nevertheless, most change agents struggle, because they want to change something, but lack the expertise their respective colleagues present, against whom they try to instal new perspectives and – ideally – new business practices.

These corporate representatives are then joined in the GCLN by members of civil society, of state institutions (e.g. ministries) and by academic observers. They are mostly interested in offering their thoughts, often constructive, sometimes critical on whether participating companies are doing enough to strengthen the ten Principles and whether their chosen path is promising. In some instances their own organizations have joined the Compact and these individuals play a dual role, as change agents themselves and critical companions to others.

Infusing ideas and proposing tools

The German Global Compact Network is a business-led multi-stakeholder initiative. This defines how we work as a Focal Point, what we attempt to offer to our participants and how we do it. A certain type of events has proven to be useful for those business representatives responsible for their company's corporate responsibility or sustainability portfolio, including the Global Compact. Wherever located in the company structure, participating individuals are usually *universalists* – i.e. no experts on one or two of the Compact's principles but rather equipped with a solid overview of the ten Principles and understanding their relevance to their company. Usually, these individuals function as a contact node within the company regarding Global Compact implementation. The German Focal Point learned that these individuals were looking for support in their effort to move the company towards more Global Compact action, i.e. equip them as change agents.

With all our formats, be it working conferences or more intense coaching sessions, we try to offer the appropriate content to enter a constructive debate on implementation through changing business practices. Our work is geared towards the following:

- Offer topics general enough that most can relate to them in their daily work.
- Offer topics specific enough that they offer concrete implementation instruments.
- Be ahead of the mainstream corporate responsibility debate.
- Design formats that foster discussions among company representatives, ideally among those with varying experience on the topic, and other critical stakeholders.
- Approach participants to present case studies from a context that many other participating companies will benefit from, not utilizing a company's unique selling proposition (USP) as a focus for a case study.
- Avoid uninspiring corporate responsibility-pitches.
- Find a tone and format that facilitate workshops and presentation, allowing for 'stupid questions' and controversial debates while avoiding stigmatization or teacher-like evaluation.

The principal aim of our work is to infuse companies and organizations participating in the Global Compact with new ideas in relation to the ten Principles. Concretely, this means exposing participants to new insights from the academic world, shedding light on newly or more strongly articulated demands from stakeholders and delivering new perspectives from case studies from within the industry. Often these triggers are translated from work done at the Global Compact Office, while at other times they derive directly from work conducted by the German corporate responsibility community.

The next step, then, must be to translate these discussions into possible and realistic action. For years, specialized working groups have elaborated on a variety of tools and instruments for designing an internal change process, for establishing and utilizing relevant data, for ensuring the necessary buy-in of management and for finding the best solutions. The Global Compact itself offers working groups on specific topics to exchange views and experiences. In the German Global Compact Network, we benefit from their work and offer results to our participants in order for 'our' company representatives to take home insights with which they can infuse their own institution.

Focus on selected topics

It is not always necessary to start from scratch concerning these issues. In many instances, company representatives come to the Global Compact with a heightened awareness of the importance of a topic. However, it is often difficult to convey all information and manage controversy with NGOs and others in a single Network meeting, be it a plenary debate or more in-depth workshops. To accommodate more detailed attention to the relevance, urgency, related expectations and the tools and strategies of certain issues, the German Network's Steering Group identifies two focus topics to be discussed throughout a year during various conferences, workshops, lectures and, in one case, a coaching format. While retaining some flexibility to include news of the day into the Network's exchanges, this has created the – generally appreciated – possibility of more in-depth and continuous work on one set of challenges.

For this more focused approach, the feedback from our constituency is positive. We still attempt to reflect discussions, events and news from outside the Network at our working conferences, in order to avoid excessively inflexible and 'academic' work. While the advantages of this more concentrated topical approach are obvious, the difficulty lies in convincing a critical mass of participants of our work's quality and relevance for their own questions. This challenge increases as we have further differentiated our formats (see below). Indeed, there must remain a balance between benefiting from a concentration on specific issues and retaining the wide variety of Global Compact topics.

Offering additional formats

Inspire: the Global Compact Yearbook

Apart from conferences with topical workshops and discussions, a central product of the German Global Compact Network is its *Global Compact Yearbook*, a publication filled with participating companies' examples of how to approach the ten Principles. Edited and organized by the German media company Macondo, a Compact participant, this *Yearbook* is now in its sixth edition and exemplifies the Compact's philosophy; a corporate initiative that offers real-life evidence on how to bring the ten Principles to life.

Inform: publications/background papers in German

Starting with the identification of yearly focus topics for the German Global Compact Network, the Focal Point has compiled and published complementary background papers for each of these topics. Each written in close coordination with expert institutions and published early in the year, these papers offer an introduction to the topic as well as sketching out the issues to be discussed throughout the year's programme.

Coach: in-depth sessions among business representatives

To delve even deeper into the issues and – specifically – solutions for companies, the German Network has decided to offer in-depth coaching sessions for a small number of business representatives. They are joined by an expert who looks into their specific challenges. The goal is to create ideas to move forward. In late 2008 the first session took place on 'human rights and business' with a positive reaction; business representatives welcomed the forum for in-depth and expert-led discussions on concrete implementation tools for their idiosyncratic problems and the chance to voice confidential questions and doubts. In late 2009, another session on human rights and one on climate adaptation strategies were successfully run. Business participants from these coaching sessions still meet regularly to foster the peer learning exchange initiated here. With the economic crisis cutting into companies' travel budgets, the Network must consider how many of the offered interaction formats can be sustained.

Communicate: German Global Compact website

On the German Global Compact website (www.globalcompact.de), more data is available concerning German Global Compact signatories and Compact-associated topics, news from relevant actors and more in-depth information on and links to interesting initiatives, publications, events, experiences and case studies. Launched in the fall of 2008, this website is evolving and will slowly grow into the principal information source and communication device for and from the German Global Compact Network. Depending on participants' demands and support this website could develop into the primary source for information related to corporate responsibility in Germany, ideally including a well-used internal login section to exchange information and know-how complementing personal face-to-face exchanges.

Reaching out: raising awareness in the interested public

Ten years after its launch, the Global Compact continues to face criticism and no doubt always will. Some of this is due to well-founded, deficit-orientated and thought-provoking critique; other criticism, however, is based on false information or ignorance of what the Global Compact is and aspires to be. By raising awareness of the Compact's basic ideas, rules and results, a national Network can increase the knowledge among the interested public. It is especially important for us to consider critics as stakeholders for our work, and where possible, their vocal and challenging nature on a local level should be capitalized on. In contrast to our bread-and-butter work, however, the interested public cannot be successfully addressed through a learning forum or background papers. Other activities are needed. These include holding lectures in student and academic circles, participating in Global Compact companies' stakeholder debates and speaking at conferences on the topic. Moreover, in 2008 the German Network ran a lecture series specifically for the interested public on one of the two focus topics 'human rights and business'. With prominent speakers from business, academia and politics it became apparent that not only Global Compact participants, but also members of what is labelled 'political Berlin' attended in substantial numbers.

However, among Global Compact participants the debate continues as to what the Network should primarily aim to achieve. Informing the interested, sceptical public clearly is not central to our mandate; as there is a spectrum of work to do, the Network – both its Steering Group and its Focal Point – continuously needs to reinvent and reaffirm its role and output.

Surviving in a crowded market

Looking for niches

Corporate responsibility, sustainability, sustainable development, corporate citizenship, responsible business practice and many other terms (a comparable number of additional expressions are in use in the German language) all denote a similar body of theories and – mostly – activities aspiring to offer a contribution from the business world to solving globally critical problems. The Global Compact is one of many initiatives offering companies both guidance and a forum, especially in Germany. With the discussion on environmentally responsible business conduct predating the corporate responsibility debates by decades, a large number of initiatives on these issues are active and indeed vying for members and attention. The German Global Compact Network needed to consider, identify and establish very clearly what niche it would address.

Considering the flipside of this, it is important to note, though obvious, that the Global Compact is not equally suited for every company, nor could the Compact's structure accommodate all businesses, were they all interested in joining. The same is true on the national level. Imagine 300,000 enterprises, ranging from small to multinational companies aspiring to join the Compact in Germany, committing to its principles and demanding support from us. Surely, formats would be found and structures established.

In the meantime, however, the German Global Compact Network has identified a number of aspects it considers its USP through trial and error, learning-by-doing, internal reflection and simply benchmarking its activities against others. Some are derived from the Compact's global role and aspiration, others are specific to the German landscape of similar initiatives; not all are shared equally by all interested parties, but for now these parameters guide the GTZ's work as a Focal Point in designing the network's activities.

Spotlight: large enterprises

Germany alone counts several million companies in total; more than 90 per cent of these fall into the category micro, small and medium enterprises (SMEs): the local bakery, service providers at every city street corner and medium-sized firms. These firms span a variety of sectors, from service to IT to automobile, trade, textile and specialized services. Thus, a more precise grouping becomes problematic. Also, it is difficult to generalize solutions without denying their global reach. Some specialized manufacturers are, although small in size, interlocked in the global marketplace, regarding both their supply chain and customer structure. Nevertheless, for the Global Compact in Germany, we have identified the big enterprises, that are large in size and global in reach, as our prime target group. This is to focus not only on the international character of their business practices, a condition that would not suffice as distinctive, but also on firms which are international in business reach (especially in their sourcing activities) *and* large enough to ideally benefit from the Global Compact. The reach and size of these corporations is central to the Global Compact and its ten Principles, which embrace important aspects of corporate responsibility in today's understanding.

What will be elaborated as a potential USP of the German Network below is to be viewed critically in connection with the size and thus capacity of participating companies. Time and capacity are needed in order to benefit from what the German Global Compact Network has to offer; it is (almost) as simple as that. Of course, the Compact as an idea, as a framework and as a guiding principle into the responsibility of companies is useful *not* only for large companies; quite the opposite. However, in order to profit from the *work in the Network*, a business needs the availability of sufficient employee time and energy. This ensures that activities are not merely participated in, but also that the issues heard and discussed are *translated* into specific business practices. Furthermore, it is essential to transmit new perspectives and instruments to colleagues in order to infuse the company with new ideas and trigger change.

Moreover, discussions among Global Compact participants during Network events touch on all four Compact topical segments. For smaller companies selecting one or two specific issues relevant to their particular business model will lead to more visible results. In Germany, for instance, a large number of single-issue initiatives work to strengthen know-how and implementation on one particular topic, such as preventing climate change or fostering anti-corruption legislation. With limited capacity and time, smaller businesses can benefit more immediately from joining these discussions and focusing their efforts on one issue, rather than spreading their effort on all four issue areas of the Global Compact. This, however, does *not* mean that the German Network does not welcome SMEs at its events and discussions. In fact, we value their insight and experience. Nevertheless, when identifying how to address issues and how to handle challenges, the Network benefits most from the input of the corporate responsibility manager of a large enterprise (i.e. the abovementioned change agent struggling to infuse a large company with new perspectives).

The fact that the Global Compact is a UN initiative, brought to life by Kofi Annan and today linked directly to the Secretary-General Ban Ki-moon, offers the Network legitimacy and upfront credibility. While we have to prove our value every time business representatives join our activities and spend time and money on doing so, the overall UN framework is a strong USP in the German context. Mandated by and closely connected to the Global Compact Office in New York, businesses view us as the tangible addition to this worldwide UN initiative. However, some large business actors approach the United Nations directly if they require information. So indeed the UN connection means legitimacy in terms of quality assumption by virtue of the close connection – no less and no more.

The mix is crucial: The Global Compact in Germany is a multi-stakeholder forum

Our second differentiating feature is the multi-stakeholder character of the German Global Compact Network. Based on the framework of the Global Compact as a business-led multi-stakeholder initiative, the German Network is among the Global Compact entities reflecting this idea best. In all its work, events and activities as well as in the Network's decision-making processes and outreach portfolio, the mix between business representatives, civil society members, state authorities and academic voices is crucial to foster critical reflection on the Compact's issue areas. To discuss sustainability issues on their own, business representatives have alternative forums.

The added value of the German Global Compact Network, instead, lies in the exchange of perspectives beyond business circles: critical demands from civil society, new perspectives from NGOs, paired with the opportunity for direct dialogue with government officials and NGO representatives. Apart from interesting case studies and implementation tools, this assembly makes the Network interesting and unique. Should this multi-stakeholder aspect be lost, the Network would lose its appeal to many of its current participants. This is no mere speculation, but became evident when a couple of years ago a German business association expressed interest in taking over the Network's Focal Point. A closed-shop business initiative would not attract any of the regular NGO representatives to the Network. We are neither running a management consultancy nor merely offering businesses a platform for describing their activities. Real exchange of differing opinions and perspectives is what makes up the added value of the Network activities.

Opportunity-driven: the Global Compact as a framework brand

The Global Compact offers interested parties and participants a broad range of topics, covering four issue areas: human rights, labour and social standards, environmental issues and anti-corruption. In Germany, a whole range of initiatives offer forums to deal with these specific topics in detail. However, the Global Compact offers a more comprehensive take on its range of topics than most other initiatives and only here do business representatives gain access to worldwide experience and expertise in each of these subject areas. At the German Global Compact Focal Point we feel we can be the broker to facilitate this access.

The difficulty we try to diffuse by identifying focus topics is, in fact, also an opportunity: The breadth of relevant subjects provides the Network with an umbrella of material that can encompass much more than all the individual special interest initiatives can address (this is also true for the work of Local Networks in many other, especially industrialized, countries). The Global Compact serves as a framework brand, if the topics selected are precise yet conclusively broad. To get this balance right is not easy when considering the stark competition from other initiatives, but the United Nations is an unrivalled brand not to be underestimated. While often associated with overall bureaucracy and overcomplicated decision-making processes, for most Germans, the United Nations carries positive connotations of supranational, non-partisan legitimacy, global reach and worldwide applicability.

The German Global Compact Network emphasizes not only its broad range but also its global reach of topics. Human rights, for example, is not only an issue of anti-discrimination policies in Germany; it is also important in terms of security issues for workers in developing countries. As the Focal Point is located at the GTZ's centre for cooperation with the private sector, we are naturally especially interested in what happens in developing and emerging countries. Businesses and other Global Compact participants in Germany welcome this development angle, founded on expertise, experience and collaboration with a global network of partners. It serves as one more differentiating feature of our work compared to other corporate responsibility circles in Germany, most of which clearly focus on what happens or should happen in Germany. Regarding the four Global Compact issue areas, however, most of these are regulated by law in Germany. To improve things here and in most other OECD countries might mean rewriting regulations or improving their enforcement. By contrast, in many developing and emerging countries the situation can be improved in the short term by counting on what drives the Global Compact; voluntary commitment by business itself.

Concluding remarks

To run a Global Compact Local Network is a distinct challenge and creates very different opportunities in every country. These depend on many factors, including the nature of participating entities and their spectrum of interests, the landscape of similar and rival initiatives, the standing and legacy of the United Nations and the characteristics and motivation of the coordinating Focal Point and its interaction with other relevant actors. In Germany all of these have been – on the whole – favourable for a continuously successful Global Compact Network with its specific style. However, this progress has not come easily and the task is certainly not done. Demands will change as the Network grows challenging the character of collaboration, the Network's funding structure and existing organizational routines. As a result, the portfolio of activities will have to be adapted accordingly. Most importantly, it must be remembered that neither the Global Compact Office nor the situation on the ground singularly defines what a Network can and will do. Rather, the joint impact of these two facets defines what is possible.

21 | Building corporate citizenship through the United Nations Global Compact: contributions and lessons learned from the Argentinean Local Network

FLAVIO FUERTES AND
NICOLÁS LIARTE-VEJRUP[1]

The United Nations Global Compact and Networks' Communication on Progress

The purpose of the Global Compact is to promote social dialogue with a view to creating global corporate citizenship to reconcile business interests with UN values and mandates demanded by civil society, trade unions and governments. These values translate into Principles related to the defence of human rights, labour standards, the environment and the fight against corruption. This Compact (based on the voluntary adherence of the world's businesses) consists of ten universal Principles that, in time and through learning, are supposed to become embedded in firms' strategic management and their value chain.

The Global Compact is not an instrument that businesses must compulsorily adopt nor does it pursue the objective of imposing a new regulatory framework. On the contrary, the Global Compact is a set of values and Principles proposed by the United Nations that businesses must voluntarily decide to impose upon themselves. In this

[1] The evidence shown in this chapter is based on the Communication on Progress (COP) Reports submitted by the Argentinean Global Compact members in 2007. The authors would like to express their thanks to: UNDP, especially Mr Carlos Felipe Martínez (Resident Coordinator) for his support, ECLAC in the name of Bernardo Kosacoff (Director) for his inspirations and reflections and to the Governance Body of the Global Compact Local Network in Argentina for their openness to discuss the results of the research done. Special thanks to María José, Rocío, Natalia and Vera for their daily support, enthusiasm and happiness brought to our lives.

manner, the Global Compact calls for the gradual incorporation of the ten Principles into a company's business practices. This entails great challenges for the management of any organization and even more so for a business which is, by definition, dynamic and innovative. Given the criticism targeted at the Global Compact (it does not control, it does not impose, it does not assess company behaviour), in 2004 the United Nations Global Compact Office installed integrity measures to protect the initiative's credibility. The main measure is known as Communication on Progress (COP). From then on, Global Compact participants were asked to prepare an annual report (at the end of each fiscal year) to reflect any progress made in the implementation of the ten Global Compact Principles.

This chapter discusses the current status of the Argentinean Global Compact Local Network (GCLN). Our analysis is based on an in-depth analysis of members' COP Reports and discusses a variety of issues related to them (e.g. which of the ten Principles companies address most often and how firms share COP Reports with interested stakeholders).

The Argentinean Global Compact Network: Local characteristics, composition and members.

In Argentina, the Global Compact lagged behind due to the prevailing economic and social conditions after the major crisis in 2001. This crisis hindered the process of promoting Global Compact Principles and the creation of the Local Network. Nonetheless, the Compact was finally launched and adhered to in April 2004, experiencing strong receptiveness among the different business and social leaders. This triggered the proposal to start building a GCLN in Argentina.[2] A promoter group was composed of seventeen organizations (companies, business associations, universities and NGOs) with the guidance and leadership of three UN agencies – the United Nations Development Programme (UNDP), the Economic Commission for Latin America and the Caribbean (ECLAC) and the International Labour Organization (ILO).

---

[2] For additional information please refer to the document '*Base de Adhesión del Sector Privado Argentino*' (Basis for Support of the Argentine Private Sector) and the working document '*Evaluando el Pacto Global en Argentina, el perfil de las empresas adheridas*' (Assessing the Global Compact in Argentina: Profiles of Adhering Businesses), both available at www.pactoglobal.org.ar.

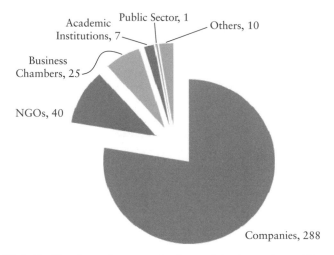

Figure 21.1 Profile of member organizations of the Argentinean Network

Since 2004, 369 Argentinean organizations have signed their commitment to the Global Compact Principles. The Argentinean Network is composed mostly of organizations that characterize themselves as businesses (almost 80 per cent; see figure 21.1).[3]

Taking into account the number of participants, the Global Compact Network in Argentina has raised interest among a great number and variety of organizations. At the international level it is in fact one of the biggest Networks (ranked eighth in the world according to the last report submitted by the Global Compact Office; see Global Compact 2007c). As depicted in figure 21.2, most members joined the Network in 2004 when the Global Compact was launched in the country. Since then membership has grown slowly but constantly. The year 2006 was the 'exception to the rule'; the Local Network started the transition from a UN-led Network to a business-led Network. The Network has a governance body composed of twenty members (eleven companies, three business associations, two universities, two NGOs and two other stakeholders) elected democratically during the National Assembly every two years. It is the only local network in the region with this kind of process in place.

---

[3] The information may vary from the available data at www.unglobalcompact. org because the Global Compact Office does not list companies with fewer than ten employees (micro enterprises).

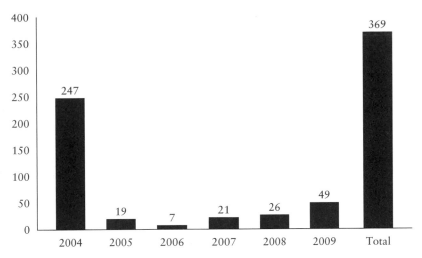

Figure 21.2 Members joining the Argentinean Global Compact Local Network, 2004–9

An analysis of COP Reports submitted by Argentinean businesses

Number of COP Reports in Argentina

With regard to COP Reports, at the end of 2004 53 had been submitted. This number increased to 64 at the end of 2005; dropped slightly to 63 in 2006, rose to 105 in 2007 and fell to 89 in 2008. So far, over 50 Reports have been submitted at the time of writing in 2009. Members of the Argentinean Network have submitted 431 COP Reports in total; essentially representing a unique, public, online reservoir of Corporate Social Responsibility (CSR) practices in the country. There are some facts worth highlighting. First, as depicted in figure 21.3, there has been a gradual increase in the submission of COP Reports, which reflects a learning process in their drafting. In this sense, there are at least six Argentinean companies that could be considered champions in submitting COPs (they submitted COPs between 2004 and 2008)[4] as well as ten companies that have

---

[4] The list includes: Manpower Argentina, Paolini SAIC, Tersuave – Disal SA, Torresolar SRL, Transba SA and Transener SA.

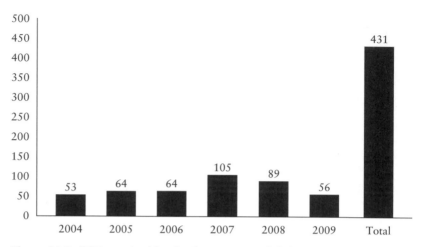

Figure 21.3 COPs received by the Argentinean Global Compact Local
Network, 2004–9

submitted 'Notable COPs' (for a further discussion of Notable COPs
see chapter 15 by Uzma Hamid and Oliver Johner).[5]

Secondly, 90 per cent of the COPs received in 2006 came from
organizations that consider themselves as 'businesses', while the
remaining 10 per cent were submitted by 'civil society organizations'
(including organizations such as non-profits, non-governmental organizations (NGOs), business associations and universities). This shows
the level of commitment towards the initiative among all involved
organizations and also reflects the multi-stakeholder character of the
Argentinean Network.

Argentinean COPs and their geographical distribution

As to the geographical distribution of submitted COPs, most of
them are from Buenos Aires City and Buenos Aires Province, followed to a lesser extent by Mendoza and Córdoba Provinces. At
first sight, it could be assumed that the geographic proximity of
the communicating companies and the Focal Point Office (UNDP)

[5] The list includes: Mastellone Hermanos SA, Banco Galicia, Telefónica de
Argentina SA, Grupo Los Grobo SA, Central Costanera SA, Central Dock Sud
SA, Hidroeléctrica El Chocón, Masisa Argentina, Tecnovo SA and Gas Natural
Ban.

in Argentina fosters a close relationship between these entities: the majority of COPs comes from Buenos Aires City where the UNDP Office is located. In many cases, however, we find that though the commercial offices of participating businesses are located in Buenos Aires City, their productive processes take place in other provinces of the country.

On the other hand, it was also noted that those businesses that carry out productive and/or commercial activities in more than one province report as a corporation on the activities that take place in only one of these places/provinces. Since the objective of COPs is to protect the Compact's credibility and businesses' reputation, this finding raises the question of whether it is sufficient to report on selected operations in a COP. Although the answer is not simple, this dilemma also appears within the global context; companies with a strong commitment to reporting do so from their home offices yet exclude their actions in foreign markets.

Size and sector of communicating businesses

Many specialists consider the COP to be a barrier for small and medium-sized enterprises (SMEs) to participate in the Global Compact. Theoretically, there are no reasons to think that a company (no matter the size) should not be able to submit a COP each year. In order to analyse whether there is a link between the size of businesses and the submission of reports, a three-category scale was set up. The categories are: Business Corporations (companies having over 501 employees), Big Businesses (between 151 and 500 employees), and SMEs (between 1 and 150 employees). Table 21.1 depicts the submission rate of COPs related to the size of business.[6]

The data indicate that almost half of the submitted COPs came from Business Corporations. This is understandable since they are used to preparing social and environmental reports (many of them draft reports following the main national and/or international methodologies as laid out by the Global Reporting Initiative, GRI), and

---

[6] It must be highlighted that companies are normally classified according to their structure or size, taking into account the relationship between the variables of headcount and annual invoicing. For the purpose of this study no information was available on businesses' invoicing since it is not an indicator required by the Global Compact.

Table 21.1 *Submitted COPs related to business size, per cent*

Number of employees	Type of business	COP distribution (%)
0 – 150 employees	SMEs	20
151 – 500 employees	Big business	37
> 501 employees	Business corporation	43

have the necessary technical and professional skills and resources to this effect. It must be highlighted, however, that SMEs also make an important contribution which, in our sample, accounts for one-fifth of Argentinean COPs submitted in 2006.

The analysis of COPs in terms of industries and respective economic activity identified most reports (32 per cent) as submitted by the Manufacturing industry, while Utilities (Energy, Garbage Collection, Telephony) accounted for 25 per cent. This is followed by Private Services (such as Bank Services, Consulting and Professional Services) with 23 per cent and the Extractive industries (Hydrocarbon Exploitation, Production and Mining) accounting for 11 per cent. Ranked fifth is the Commercial sector (with 8 per) cent and finally, agro-industries with only 1 per cent.

Areas of action reported by the businesses

We analysed all COPs according to the Global Compact Principles previously or currently implemented by the businesses. As can be seen in figure 21.4, the distribution is almost even: 28 per cent of the businesses report having worked on the human rights principles; 28 per cent on the environmental principles; 26 per cent on the labour principles; and 17 per cent on fighting corruption (within and outside the business).

Considering the working paper prepared by UNDP in 2004, the 2006 sample highlights significant developments made regarding the fulfilment of the 10th Principle by the signatories of the Compact.[7] This

---

[7] In 2004, UNDP published a document based on the COPs submitted that year by Argentinean Global Compact participants. The document stated that more efforts could be made by companies to implement the labour and the anti-corruption principles. The document is available at www.pactoglobal.org.ar. The Ministry of Employment then created the CSR and Decent Work Network

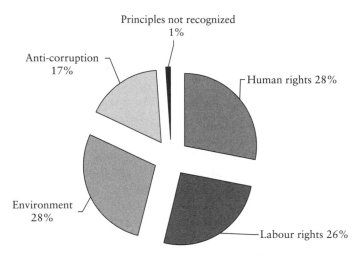

Figure 21.4 Global Compact Principles implemented by Argentinean businesses, 2006

is not a minor detail as it seemingly reflects a greater integrity of the reports, i.e., the Global Compact's Principles are well integrated into CSR programmes, actions and policies. The COP Reports indicate that important contributions are being made to work towards providing environments which protect against corruption (e.g. by setting up virtuous management habits). This is also visible when looking at existing Codes of Ethics or Conduct as well as Confidentiality Policies. As recognized in various UN documents, corruption is one of the most important hindrances for country development and other social actors should replicate any progress in this regard (see also chapter 6 by Huguette Labelle).

If we consider the size of the reporting companies and the contributions made according to the fields of action, a few trends can be recognized. First, we find that Argentinean companies with over 500 employees make a greater effort to combat corruption than SMEs. This trend signals the importance that is attached to protecting reputation and promoting management practices which favour

in Argentina under the leadership of the Government, with the support of UNDP and ILO. The collaboration between the Government and the UN Agencies was consolidated when a joint programme was signed in 2008. More information is available at www.undp.org.ar/nov41.html.

transparency – particularly given the damage that corrupt practices known worldwide have caused to big businesses (Enron and Parmalat, among others). Secondly, an increase in staff results in companies evenly distributing their personnel among the four issue areas of the Global Compact.

Regarding the difficulty to strictly match the principles with the actions carried out, businesses often report activities that are correlated to more than one principle or issue area of the Global Compact. For instance, actions that have an effect on environmental management are, directly or indirectly, related to labour conditions, and are thus presented as contributions to or 'fulfilment of' Global Compact Principles 5 and 8.

A close analysis of the Global Compact Principles

The Global Compact Principles addressed by Argentinean businesses in their progress reports were examined in a disaggregate manner. First of all, they recognize working on Principle 1 (in 14 per cent of the cases); secondly on Principle 8 (12 per cent), and thirdly on Principles 7 and 6 (11 per cent).

These findings, as mentioned before, appear because of the broadness and scope assigned to Principle 1 (to support and respect the protection of internationally proclaimed human rights), which embodies an overarching purpose that in many cases includes more than one principle. We can identify certain peculiarities if we consider the reporting organizations with regard to their economic activity and their contributions according to each issue area (human rights, labour rights, environmental standards and the fight against corruption):

- Manufacturing industries recognize that they work firstly on environmental principles and secondly on labour rights.
- In Utility companies, labour rights and human rights have first and second priority, respectively.
- In Private Services, greater efforts are made on human rights and secondly with regard to the environment.
- Extractive industries prioritize the environment and secondly human rights.
- Finally, the Commercial Sector prioritizes human rights and secondly labour rights and the environment on an equal basis.

Based on these results, it can be concluded that joining the Global Compact is a commitment which presupposes the need to contextualize the ten Principles. In fact, it is a particular strength of the Global Compact to allow for a variety of, often innovative, approaches to implement them. In addition, it is also valid to assume that the efforts in support of the ten Principles are closely related to the sector in which Corporate Social Responsibility (CSR) programmes are implemented. To summarize the main actions undertaken in support of the Global Compact Principles in Argentina, table 21.2 lists the most-reported activities.

Integrated or independent COP reporting?

The Global Compact offers its participants the possibility to disseminate COPs based on two reporting models: integrated reports or independent reports. Integrated reporting requires businesses to integrate the progress of Global Compact implementation into their existing sustainability report/social report/corporate citizenship report. This model is recommended to big businesses that have experience in preparing reports on socially and environmentally responsible practices. Independent reports are those that are mainly recommended for SMEs or businesses that do not have the technical or economic resources to prepare a stand-alone sustainability report. Independent reporting means that businesses draft a COP Report which is not based on any existing documents.

In all cases, the Global Compact Office recommends reports to include the following elements so as to facilitate, standardize and systematize the information submitted by businesses: (1) A description of the business' *Commitment* to the described Principle, (2) detail of the company's *Systems or Policies* used to manage such commitment, (3) narration of *Actions* carried out and (4) *Performance* (*Outcomes*) achieved. When analysing the communications submitted by members of the Argentinean Local Network, we found that 93 per cent of the businesses drafted independent reports and the remaining 7 per cent submitted integrated reports. With regard to the latter, a growing trend is evident in the preparation of sustainability reports under internationally supported methodologies and indicators (such as the Global Reporting Initiative, GRI).

Table 21.2 *Main actions taken to address the Global Compact Principles in Argentina*

Principles	Main actions reported
Human rights principles	<ul><li>Training and funding of community projects</li><li>Community training centres</li><li>Art competitions</li><li>Product donation and/or services to schools and/or soup kitchens</li><li>Public heritage recovery</li><li>Programme for training in safety and first aid</li><li>Community education in energy use and security</li><li>Funding NGO projects</li><li>Building houses</li><li>Secondary school programmes for adults</li><li>Rural orchard programmes</li><li>Community education programmes</li><li>Participation in seminars and conferences (Global Compact dissemination)</li><li>Value communication to customers.</li><li>Scholarship and traineeship programmes</li><li>Community development programmes</li></ul>
Labour principles	<ul><li>Scholarship programmes</li><li>Recreational activities</li><li>Nutrition programmes for employees</li><li>Aid fund for employees</li><li>Hiring of disabled persons</li><li>Occupational Health and Safety Standard (OHSAS) programmes</li><li>Employees' children programmes</li><li>In-house training</li><li>Enhancing work–life balance</li><li>Reducing occupational and household accidents</li><li>Hygiene and safety programmes</li><li>Internal health campaign</li><li>Smoke-free working environment</li><li>Donation of toys and school pencils, pens, rulers, etc. provided to employees' children</li></ul>
Environmental principles	<ul><li>Paper recycling</li><li>Saving of energy</li><li>Emission reduction</li></ul>

Table 21.2 *(cont.)*

Principles	Main actions reported
	• Selective garbage collection
	• ISO 9000, 14000 and other standards
	• Elimination of polychlorinated biphenyl (PCB) (electricity companies)
	• Forestation campaigns
	• Reduce consumption of water, oil and thermal loads
	• Environmental training for suppliers
Anti-corruption principle	• Code of Conduct or Ethics
	• Set-up of Ethics Office
	• Code of Bank Practices and Money Laundering Control and Prevention Committee (financial industry)
	• Visit to plants

Sharing the Report with stakeholders

With the purpose of providing greater credibility and transparency to reports, Global Compact members must share COPs with their stakeholders. In this manner, reporting helps to build confidence between businesses and the community as well as having other companies learn from the successful CSR practices (locally or globally). It must be recalled that the Global Compact has the life-long learning gene in its DNA and, therefore, Local Networks must be strengthened to foster the exchange of experiences and best practices.

Once the Compact's Guidelines have been fulfilled in preparing the COP, businesses must post it on the Global Compact's website. When possible, a link to the webpage containing the COP must be provided on the businesses' webpage (consequently, the COP should be available on at least two websites). Finally, Global Compact signatories must also provide a brief description of the means used by the company to facilitate stakeholders' access to this document – e.g. through stakeholder consultations, meetings at Chambers of Commerce, the Intranet and other means available to the company.

According to the COPs submitted by Argentinean companies, most of the businesses (54 per cent) recognize that they use their own webpage to communicate progress in the implementation of the

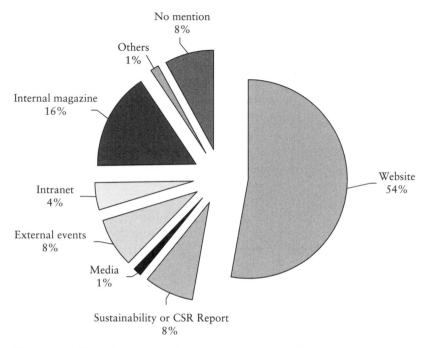

Figure 21.5 How Argentinean businesses share their COP Report with stakeholders

Global Compact Principles (see figure 21.5). Other possibilities are also identified, such as in-house magazines (16 per cent), institutional events (8 per cent) and the company's Intranet (4 per cent). An alarming fact is that 8 per cent of the companies do not state in their COP how they communicate their actions. In this regard, we think there are two possibilities: either they are not aware of the need to specify their communication strategy or they are simply not doing so. It is also striking that the mass media is not recognized as a vehicle to communicate progress on the Compact's Principles.

A responsible corporate citizenship agenda: a proposal for debate

Only five years after the Global Compact launch in Argentina there has been a remarkable increase in the submission of COP Reports. The timing of this launch, April 2004, was a key factor in the higher rate of submissions. It was a time of dynamism and challenges for the country's development. The 2001–02 crisis had left many wounds in Argentinean society. As UNDP pointed out in its 2005 *Human Development Report*, Argentina was 'facing a time of opportunities in which the country's citizens had to make decisions to allow the recovery of trust in the institutions and retrieval of the lost development path' (UNDP 2005: 4). One of them, no doubt, was the group set up to disseminate (together with UNDP, ECLAC and ILO) the Principles of the Global Compact in the country. Its impact was not immediately noted, but became decisive in transforming guidelines, principles and values based on which economic interactions currently take place. Key to achieving this objective was rebuilding (lost) trust in the relationship between society and the private sector. To that effect, it was essential to exert a positive influence on stakeholders and periodically report on progress achieved (and any regression experienced) in internalizing the Global Compact Principles.

There are, however, some aspects which should be highlighted to reinforce the implementation of the Compact's Principles in companies supporting the initiative. The following actions could produce larger benefits for the corporate citizenship movement that was developed in Argentina through the launch of the Global Compact:

1. It is necessary to strengthen the debate on the Compact within the business community by increasing the number of corporate responsibility managers in each company and enhancing the training of different internal referees.
2. It is worth highlighting that a wealth of business cases in CSR is available to the public at large on the Global Compact website, and visiting the site would help, for instance, to plan joint actions among the different supporters. This would also promote social capital generation in society and value chains. Collective action is one of the dimensions proposed by the Global Compact that has not been fully explored by Argentinean companies and that could bring about an almost immediate positive impact to consolidate a new business development model in the country.
3. When reading COPs it can be noted that there has been a greater conceptual development translating into different actions and programmes. This progress, however, is unequally distributed

across various industries (and will probably continue to be so in the future). This stems from some companies being innovative and designing new projects, while others merely reproduce their CSR programmes without exploring alternative paths to support the Principles and values proposed by the Global Compact.

4. Regardless of the size of the businesses, it can be observed that many of the submitted actions are not fully integrated into the company's business practices. Consequently, it is essential to review the mission, vision and values of the business to ensure a correct incorporation of CSR strategies into day-to-day activities.

5. Although some COPs are being 'integrated' into the proposed GRI methodology, Argentina does not account for a significant amount of GRI users.

6. The fundamental business activity of many Argentinean companies is training (to improve employability) and education (to facilitate entry into the labour market), through support of either non-profits, non-governmental organizations (NGOs) and/or schools (elementary and technical). These actions translate into scholarship support to tertiary-level institutes but also the creation of technical careers and refurbishment of educational institutions. Once again it is worth highlighting the importance of achieving greater impact by developing collective actions among companies in the same activity sector, or even in different areas that are grouped under the Global Compact umbrella.

7. As a result of the above, COPs recognize a low level of partnership in the actions carried out by the companies. It would be interesting to explore stronger alliances between NGOs and businesses as well as among businesses themselves. The climate change challenge or human rights advocacy seem to offer an excellent platform in this regard.

8. It is necessary to reinforce the debate *with* stakeholders (and not *to* them) on the importance of communicating annual performance as a tool to generate value for the whole of society. This would not only pave the way to alliances, but also find innovative formulae to create value for all the parties involved.

We believe that CSR in general (and the Global Compact in particular) must be considered as an opportunity for process innovations, market differentiation and social legitimization of Argentinean businesses operating in complex and very dynamic social and political contexts. CSR fosters understanding regarding the role of business in society and, at the same time, contributes to setting up a country with greater stability and social inclusion. That should be the aim of all CSR strategies. The Global Compact Principles as well as the Millennium Development Goals (MDGs), are an excellent source of inspiration in this regard.

22 | Concluding remarks: from alleviating the negative impacts of globalization to transforming markets

ERNST A. BRUGGER AND PETER MAURER

Looking back at more than six decades of UN history, the words 'indifference' and 'tension' would best characterize the relationship between the global organization of states and the business community as key actors in the global marketplace.

A widely held opinion – that the United Nations was a 'political' organization, far removed from the concerns of 'business' – nurtured the image of two distinct and often hostile universes. Controversial issues on the United Nations' agenda (like the New Economic Order, Human Rights Guidelines for Multinational Companies and calls for boycott and sanctions) contributed to the divide between seemingly divergent actors, as did the debate on various economic models. This last was a flashpoint in conflictual East–West relations and the widening poverty gap between North and South, and has dominated the United Nations' political agenda for over two decades.

Despite early and positive examples of private–public partnerships in development cooperation and on environmental, social and labour issues, only the Global Compact would, in 2000, reframe the relationship more fundamentally and lay the groundwork for a different type of cooperation between the United Nations and the global business community. Through the Compact, the United Nations would recognize the strategic importance of the private sector as a key stakeholder of globalization and, indirectly, the significance of open markets and global norms for economic development. It was in the United Nations' interest, as an enabler of development and a key actor in terms of peace, security and human rights, to open a largely Member State-driven organization to a very different partnership, and to offer a platform for engaging the global business community. The private sector, for its part, would recognize the importance of committing

386

itself to the United Nations' policy objectives within its sphere of influence, in view of both improving risk management and seizing business opportunities. Support for the nine original Principles, and action in support of broader UN goals such as the Millennium Development Goals (MDGs) or CO_2 reduction targets, would offer legitimacy and value to the private sector.

Those who still remember the twentieth-century relationship between the United Nations and the private sector cannot underestimate the strategic significance of the Global Compact, which launched a new area of shifting mindsets, coordination and cooperation. Its model of engagement, focusing on voluntarism, business leadership and Board commitments (mainstreaming Compact Principles into companies' strategies and operations, concrete actions in support of UN goals and public disclosure of progress on a yearly basis) has proven successful over the years. In looking beyond philanthropy and promoting the business case for corporate responsibility the Global Compact has drawn powerful partners closer to the United Nations' core objectives.

The previous chapters have provided ample illustration of the Global Compact's origins and evolution, of the expansion of its membership, the addition of a 10th Principle, refined tools for implementing commitments, measures of integrity, the creation and strengthening of Local Networks and the value of strong branding. Important tools for learning and engagement on key issues like human rights, peace-building, environment and climate change created a rich body of experience. Sector-specific initiatives like the 'Principles for Responsible Investment (PRI)' and 'Who Cares Wins' brought the financial sector into the equation. Also, the Compact managed to galvanize stakeholders around key issues like water or climate change.

The Compact's evolution over the past ten years has been strongly driven by the demand of its members, the leadership of the Secretaries-General and the Global Compact Office, which were all instrumental in transforming the Compact from its modest beginnings to the biggest corporate responsibility initiative worldwide. The Compact has managed a fine balance between seizing opportunities, responding to day-to-day pressures and business interests on the one hand, and the need to integrate multiple initiatives into a strategy which would pass the scrutiny of the Secretariat and Member States and their often divergent interests.

Over the years, the Global Compact has found its recognized place in the UN system. With strong institutional independence and a 'licence to operate' endorsed by Heads of State and Government at the 2005 Summit, by G8 and African Union statements, national and regional governmental meetings and in General Assembly resolutions, the Compact managed to become an entity *'sui generis'* in the UN system. At the same time, it has found its place in the Secretary-General's core objectives, reflected in his 2008 *Annual Report* to the General Assembly: The Secretary-General, offering strategic direction on core objectives like protecting people in need and promoting global public goods through a strong and reformed organization, also highlights the importance of partnerships like the Global Compact for achieving such objectives more effectively and efficiently.

Over the last ten years, the United Nations has witnessed important changes relevant to the Compact. The United Nations has substantially increased its field activities and focuses on implementing norms and standards and, in doing so, invited the scrutiny of its business operations. With 400,000 people in 156 countries under some form of contractual arrangement with the United Nations, and a (conservative) estimate of $40–50 billion in operational activities overall, the United Nations increasingly found itself having to ensure its operations' compliance with key corporate responsibility principles and face the challenges of revising its internal procurement guidelines, as well as the UN Pension Fund's compliance with PRI guidelines.

At intergovernmental and Secretariat levels, the UN organizational set-up addressing human rights, peace and environmental issues underwent important changes with the creation of the Human Rights Council, the Peace-Building Commission, the Mediation and the Rule of Law Unit which reflected on the evolving approaches of governments to key corporate responsibility issues: the Human Rights Council created its own Special Rapporteur on the Human Rights of Transnational Companies, and other entities were looking for private sector engagement in post-conflict peace-building. The Security Council increasingly focused on the economic drivers of conflict by holding thematic debates and taking concrete action, like establishing panels to investigate the links between business operations and conflict patterns ('blood diamonds').

In the context of climate change, the Convention became the international focal point for efforts to set emission targets and timelines, provide resources for adapting and facilitating transfer of clean technology. A stronger focus on values and the scrutiny of partnerships with business were accompanied by controversies with regard to the public and private sectors' responsibilities. Also, the focus concentrated on the difference of values in addressing Western versus Islamic, Northern versus Southern perspectives, affecting the Compact as a platform for global norms and standards.

Taking a step back and looking at broader trends, one can recognize that circumstances existing 'at creation' have heavily influenced the first decade of the Compact's history. Founded at a time of economic growth, expanding globalization and private sector confidence, the Compact, in the past ten years, was able to boost voluntary commitments and direct them towards the creation of global public goods (such as peace and stability) enshrined in the United Nations' core activities. The private sector could, in exchange, add value and legitimacy to serious corporate responsibility efforts and shield itself from civil society and non-governmental organization (NGO) criticism.

With the unfolding of deep economic crises in 2008, the dwindling confidence in markets and a policy debate increasingly shaped by controversies on macroeconomic stabilization, government regulation of and interventions in markets as well as transformation of global governance, the Compact is now confronted with a new environment. Not that the key concept and basic features have lost their significance and relevance over time, but rather that new circumstances demanded a critical analysis on how to recast the Compact in such new climate. With the coincidence of multiple crises – economic, financial, food and climate change – the Compact would have to refine its future orientation. While the first decade was characterized more by its focus on alleviating the negative impacts of globalization, the second would have to place the transformation of markets towards greater sustainability and inclusion centre stage.

As a reaction to the global economic crisis, the UN Secretary-General, businesses and governments supporting the Global Compact have developed strong arguments and a coherent narrative in favour of a renewed and re-invigorated commitment:

- While corporate irresponsibility has played an important part in the implosion of trust, restoring confidence and trust in the private sector will become a priority in light of the global economic crisis.

Incorporating social, environmental and human rights perspectives into business operations through regulatory and voluntary means could be crucial in rebuilding trust. Integration of long-term considerations into market expectations could become key to more sustainable business operations.

- Environmental, social, human rights and anti-corruption issues are real factors in the long-term viability and success of business, and should therefore predicate the strategic action of companies everywhere. The business case for corporate responsibility seemed clear but has become more obvious in the light of the economic downturn. The Global Compact provides a framework for incorporating such values into corporate strategy. The attention imparted to issues like climate change and corruption will not diminish as a result of economic decline. Moreover, environmentally, socially and governance-conscious investments will become crucial in returning the economy to a more sustainable growth path. Business has to provide solutions such as clean technology, renewable energy and sustainable food production. Furthermore, the 'Principles for Responsible Investment' (PRI) should serve as a guide for operations of financial actors and thus pave the way to a renewed avenue for growth and productivity.

- Decades of experience demonstrate that a commitment to a level trade and investment playing field based on multilateral rules, offers the best hope *vis-à-vis* wealth creation, development and peaceful economic integration. However, markets on their own cannot deliver prosperity, let alone justice. A renewed call is needed for ethical globalization comprising a shared responsibility for addressing global issues.

- Credible corporate responsibility approaches undertaken by companies require stakeholder engagement. And often, a group of companies that works collectively has more impact than individual companies. The Global Compact is both a platform to discuss current and emerging issues among different stakeholder groups as well as a launching pad for collective action within the private sector.

- Voluntary efforts that surpass expectations set out by rules can deliver value in terms of innovation and solutions. As a complement to government regulation of markets, companies should be encouraged by governments, international organizations and global leaders to promote responsible business. Good corporate citizenship should be rewarded and partnerships be promoted on key issues like climate change, corruption, health, etc. as both motivation and to affirm that the private sector is indeed a necessary partner in solving today's complex issues.

Such arguments seem compelling at first sight. Nonetheless, corporate responsibility as a concept or the Global Compact as a specific engagement platform are rarely mentioned as a factor or a response to the financial and economic crisis. References to the Compact and corporate responsibility in the *Financial Times*' editorials, for example, are incidental. The economic and financial crisis as well as public and political outcry against the irresponsibility of business leaders, their benefits and salaries, has widely discredited private initiatives and volunteerism as organizational principles of the economy. The seriousness of the economic crisis also highlights the importance of large scale, macroeconomic action rather than a corporate-level response. This has helped shape the international debate essentially along the lines of government responses to the crisis, which is understandable given the dimensions of the downturn. On the long road to recovery, responsible, ethical business behaviour which creates sustainable, shared value for shareholders and society alike is strategically significant. The Global Compact as a key corporate responsibility initiative has a crucial role to play in this endeavour in the years to come.

The existing institutional set-up of the Global Compact and the processes for implementing its commitments have well served the stakeholders of the initiative in the past. In order to strengthen the Compact for future challenges, existing tools should be further developed, refined and consolidated. Local Networks have developed significantly over the past decade; their potential for future growth is considerable. The recently refined Communication on Progress (COP) has proven a good measure in addressing the implementation gap and building minimal compliance pressure; further COP refinement and development are certainly key to establishing the Compact's future credibility.

Initiatives based on strategic issues like climate change, water, investment, etc. have grown significantly; such initiatives need to expand, to reach tipping-point numbers of participants and impact on real situations. Increasingly, such initiatives are taking on a profile, significance and life of their own. Their link to the Compact sets a series of challenges in terms of governance and branding. As the public sector becomes more deeply involved in markets due to the economic crisis, and with increasing numbers of business participants in the Compact and expanding initiatives, there will be renewed discussion on how to accommodate governments and their different functions, as UN stakeholders and as participants in corporate responsibility initiatives, and how to manage the further growth of the Compact.

Though the logic of the Global Compact remains compelling and its medium-term political significance obvious, questions arise with regard to possible future challenges. Six are foremost in relevance, from our perspective.

Changing context

The Global Compact will probably see some of its basic assumptions at creation questioned, particularly those orientated towards business' voluntarism. With voluntarism meeting public scepticism, the question arises of whether the future will not see very different interactions on corporate responsibility unfold. Governments may increasingly not limit themselves – neither as beholders of the common interest nor as market participants – to being distant observers of corporate responsibility. Increasingly, legislators may wish to set precise framework legislation for corporate responsibility, including distinct reporting and accountability procedures. This may change the whole environment in which the Global Compact will operate, and have an impact on new needs in terms of experience-sharing, best practices and support for responsible engagement.

Role of governments and stakeholders

With the state's role in the marketplace changing, the Global Compact may have to revisit the way it consults with key stakeholders. It is difficult to imagine that the Compact can remain and develop as an alliance of global business with the UN Secretary-General and its Secretariat in the future. Governments, civil society and labour (both trade unions and employers) will ask for more prominent roles either in shaping corporate responsibility policies or in scrutinizing such policies. While non-business organizations can join the Global Compact, it has not yet been defined how different stakeholder groups should engage with business participants (excluding investors who have an opportunity through the PRI). Also, more ambitious thresholds for companies who wish to get UN legitimacy and support for their endeavours may emerge.

Quantitative and qualitative growth

The impressive number of over 5,000 participating companies is a clear indication of success in the past ten years. However, the Compact will face serious challenges in scaling up and expanding in terms of number of companies and stock market capitalization, while endeavouring to deepen the relevance of its involvement. If the Compact wants to be more than just the biggest platform of *avant-garde* engagement, namely a serious factor in transforming markets and businesses to a more sustainable future, efforts to enlarge and deepen the Compact will be necessary (e.g. more issue specific engagement, extension of implementation efforts to supply chains, or activities in the area of public policy). If successful, this might again elicit a new quality of demands in terms of tools, reporting requirements and advice, which the Global Compact Office will then have to deliver.

What kind of growth path will the Compact follow and what will it mean to the Secretariat's backstopping services? Will there be more members or better members (and how will the more become better)? Managing relations between a growing Compact and multiplying thematic initiatives may represent an additional challenge: how can the Compact be broadened and deepened, and at the same time keep some sense of a unity of purpose?

For future growth, the initiative has to evaluate its organizational structure and identify bottlenecks. Institutional, procedural, or resource-related measures – e.g. decentralization or outsourcing of certain tasks to specialized organizations – may be appropriate to strengthen the Global Compact's Network structure and to make the initiative more efficient and effective in the future. The Global Compact is a network with various actors, many issues, different languages and activities on the global as well as on the local level. Scalable solutions must be implemented to make the Compact a self-sustained platform where good practices can be shared, discussed and improved, where stakeholders interact, synergies can be found and collective actions initiated.

Inclusiveness and differentiation

As the Global Compact may evolve as a tool for market transformation towards sustainable value generation, offering support to the multiple needs of companies will become even more important. As a UN initiative, the Compact cannot cater to only the most advanced global players – it must be, and be seen to be, a home to companies in different parts of the world, of all sizes, addressing different levels of ambition and institutional maturity. There will be not one single standard for compliance, but different levels of ambition to cater to. The Compact will have to offer incentives as recognition for high performers, such as special clubs, leadership platforms and incubators for innovative approaches, while at the same time remaining a credible entry point for smaller companies and newcomers from the Global South in particular.

One way to allow for differentiation would be to define different levels of implementation and disclosure. Companies could then commit to a specific level within a given period of time, which would increase peer pressure whilst maintaining the inclusive nature of the Compact. Also, such clearly defined levels would allow stakeholders to better assess the progress that companies have made over time. Ultimately, this would also improve the credibility of individual company commitments and the Compact overall.

Brand value

At the origin of the Global Compact there was a deal through which the United Nations offered legitimacy to the private sector in exchange for support in achieving UN objectives. Positioning the Compact as a high-value corporate responsibility brand, offering public legitimacy to private sector efforts, will remain crucial for the Compact's future. UN legitimacy was comparatively cheap in the first decade of the Compact; with the economic crisis unfolding and questions on private sector practice lingering, here again scrutiny on how Compact participants implement their commitments will increase and, with it, the price tag for the brand. A new deal on the branding and the use of the

Compact will have to be struck. One approach to strengthening the brand of the initiative would be to make the COP process more rigid, e.g. by introducing measures to chart progress in implementing the Principles. Also, the existing grievance mechanism for allegations of egregious and systematic abuses of Global Compact Principles could be extended and clarified. Currently, the mechanism is entirely based on dialogue between companies and stakeholders. As an idea, the Global Compact Office – or other entities in the initiative's network, such as the Expert Working Groups – could mediate the process and seek to define conditions to be met by companies in order to remain a Compact participant.

Governance framework

The Global Compact Board, the Office, the Inter-Agency Team (IAT), the Local Networks and their Annual Forum (ALNF), the Leaders Summit and donor relations have proven effective in successfully steering the Compact through its first decade. Depending on growth paths and overall strategies, on government–public sector relations, on voluntarism and regulations, on financial deals to promote and develop the Compact, the governance framework will have to be revisited. Depending on future roles of the Secretary-General, Member States and other stakeholders more centralized or decentralized paths of development will be possible: the Compact will have to navigate between a focus on more specific needs or on greater coherence. The Compact may become a loose corporate responsibility orbit or a coherent network for engagement.

The governance of the Compact will require a dispassionate look from all interested parties and sober needs analysis. There is no point in reorganizing just for the sake of it. At the same time, flexibility must exist to develop and change a successful initiative in the future. The Compact's growth should not be stunted by our unwillingness or inability to provide an adequate governance framework. Nor should the governance framework be changed if it is not really necessary in terms of delivering services to the initiative's stakeholders.

The past has clearly shown that one size does not fit all; subsidiary approaches to governance are more successful than top-down. Problem-orientated governance, which addresses issues as they arise, has its advantages over rigid, design-orientated solutions that act on the basis of an ideal architecture. In network development and management, flexible structures and evolutionary approaches to governance are key when defining membership and club rules, financing/ funding strategies, accountability architecture, risk assessment and branding. The strength of the Global Compact is and will be in its Network structure.

Glossary

Note:

The definitions listed in this glossary are based on various publications by the Global Compact Office as well as the Global Compact website (www.unglobalcompact.org). The terms do not reflect officially endorsed definitions and should not be treated in this way.

Annual Local Networks Forum (ALNF): As a critical element of the Global Compact's governance framework, the ALNF is a meeting aimed at bringing Local Network Focal Points and company representatives together to share experiences, review and discuss progress and to show-case best practices. This annual meeting also provides the opportunity to seek the input of Local Networks on key governance issues relating to them and, more broadly, to the Global Compact as a whole.

Caring for Climate: Launched in 2007, 'Caring for Climate' is a voluntary and complementary engagement platform for Global Compact participants who seek to demonstrate leadership on the issue of climate change. It provides a framework for business leaders to advance practical solutions and help shape public policy as well as public attitudes.

CEO Water Mandate: The 'CEO Water Mandate' is a unique public–private initiative designed to assist companies in the development, implementation and disclosure of water sustainability policies and practices. Open to all business participants of the Global Compact, the 'CEO Water Mandate' is a voluntary and complementary action platform to make water-resources management a priority, and to work with governments, UN agencies, non-governmental organizations (NGOs) and other stakeholders to address this global water challenge.

Communication on Progress (COP): A COP is an annual mandatory disclosure to stakeholders (e.g., investors, consumers, civil society, governments, etc.) required of all business participants in the Global Compact. The COP is expected to detail progress made in the implementation of the Global Compact's ten Principles. The COP policy was first introduced in October 2005 and has since been clarified and expanded on several occasions. As of July 2009, all new business participants are expected to submit an annual COP within one year of joining the Global Compact. If a participant fails to communicate its progress by the deadline, the company will be listed as 'non-communicating' on the Global Compact website. Where a participant fails to communicate on progress for two consecutive years, the company will be delisted entirely. While delisted companies are removed from the Global Compact's public database, the initiative allows companies to return to active status. To rejoin, companies must provide a new Letter of Commitment signed by the chief executive officer (CEO) and also submit a COP.

Foundation for the Global Compact: The Foundation for the Global Compact was established in 2006 as a non-profit entity to support the work of the Global Compact Office and other related activities. The Foundation is authorized to raise funds on behalf of the Global Compact Office. Contributions to the Foundation are voluntary, but will help the Global Compact Office raise awareness of the initiative, its Principles and how to implement them.

Global Compact Board: The Global Compact Board, appointed and chaired by the UN Secretary-General, is designed as a multi-stakeholder body, providing ongoing strategic and policy advice for the initiative as a whole and making recommendations to the Global Compact Office, participants and other stakeholders. The twenty-four-member body comprises representatives from four constituency groups – business, civil society, labour and the United Nations.

Global Compact Leaders Summit: First held in 2004, the Leaders Summit is a triennial gathering of the top executives of all Global Compact participants and other stakeholders. The Leaders Summit represents a unique opportunity for Global Compact participants to discuss the Global Compact and corporate citizenship at the highest level, and to produce strategic recommendations and action imperatives related to the future evolution of the initiative.

Global Compact Office: The Global Compact Office is the UN entity formally entrusted with the support and overall management of the Global Compact. It has received the endorsement of the UN General Assembly (A/RES/60/215) and has been given UN systemwide responsibilities for promoting the sharing of best practices. The Global Compact Office also has responsibilities with regard to advocacy and issue leadership, fostering network development and maintaining the Global Compact communications infrastructure.

Integrity measures: As a voluntary initiative that seeks to advance universal Principles on human rights, labour, environment and anti-corruption through the active engagement of the corporate community, the Global Compact is not designed, nor does it have the mandate or resources, to monitor or measure participants' performance. Nevertheless, in order to safeguard the integrity of the Global Compact and of the United Nations, a set of integrity measures was first introduced in 2005. These integrity measures govern cases of misuse of association with the Global Compact and/or the United Nations, failure to communicate on progress, and allegations of systematic or egregious abuses seen as inconsistent with the corporate commitment to the Global Compact principles. A variety of procedures and rules have been put into place to address these scenarios.

Inter-Agency Team: Within the governance framework and daily operations of the Global Compact, the Inter-Agency Team (IAT) is responsible for ensuring coherent support for the internalization of the Principles within the United Nations and among all participants. The agencies most closely associated with the ten Principles also have an advisory role with respect to the management of the integrity measures' complaints procedure. Six UN agencies are represented in the Inter-Agency Team. They are: the Office of the UN High Commissioner for Human Rights (OHCHR), the International Labour Organization (ILO), the United Nations Environment Programme (UNEP), the United Nations Office on Drugs and Crime (UNODC), the United Nations Development Programme (UNDP) and the United Nations Industrial Development Organization (UNIDO). Any UN Fund,

Agency or Programme is now welcome to become part of the IAT if it fulfils the following criteria:

1. The senior leadership of the UN entity should make a formal commitment to supporting the implementation of the Global Compact and its ten Principles and send a letter to the Secretary-General indicating this support.
2. The ongoing activities of the UN entity are of direct relevance to the implementation of the Global Compact and good corporate citizenship.
3. The agency agrees to the IAT Terms of Reference.

Local Network: Local Networks are formal or informal associations of participants who come together to advance the Global Compact and its Principles at the national or regional level. They perform increasingly important roles in rooting the Global Compact within different national, cultural and language contexts, and also in helping to manage the organizational consequences of the Compact's rapid expansion.

Notable COPs: The Global Compact Office introduced the Notable COP programme in 2004 to highlight and recognize outstanding COPs. COPs featured in the Notable COP programme are selected because of their adherence to the COP policy and because they represent illustrative and inspirational examples of communicating progress. In order to be considered notable, a COP must meet all the basic requirements as specified in the COP policy as well as additional qualitative and quantitative criteria.

Partnerships for Development: As a complementary objective to the internalization of the ten Principles, the Global Compact asks participants to 'take action and engage in partnerships to advance the broader UN goals, such as the Millennium Development Goals [MDGs]'. Partnerships for Development are rooted in the idea that there is much common ground between the private and the public sector and that a more effective response to many global challenges requires combining the skills and expertise of the private sector with the public sector's legitimacy and knowledge of development issues. Focus areas of partnerships include poverty reduction, health, education and community development.

Principles for Responsible Management Education (PRME): First introduced in 2007, the PRME represent a set of voluntary standards to which management schools and programmes agree to adhere in the interest of developing future leaders with the necessary insights, skills and competencies to deal with the issues that businesses and other institutions are facing in the twenty-first century. The PRME initiative provides an engagement framework to advance corporate responsibility through the incorporation of universal values into curricula and research.

Principles for Responsible Investment (PRI): Financial markets have witnessed the development and growth of the PRI, an initiative led by the Global Compact and the UNEP Finance Initiative (UNEP FI). Launched in April 2006 at the New York Stock Exchange (NYSE), the PRI initiative invites both asset owners (e.g. pension funds, foundations, endowments) and asset managers to commit to a set of six principles designed to put environmental, social and governance (ESG) issues into the core of investment decision-making. In addition to a number of issue-specific work streams and engagement opportunities, the PRI initiative has created the PRI Engagement Clearinghouse – the first platform of its kind – providing signatories with a forum to share information about engagement activities, to pool their resources and influence and seek changes in company behaviour, policy or systematic conditions.

Social Vetting: As a neutral facilitator and a platform for dialogue and learning, the Global Compact relies on civil society organizations, media and the wider public to critically examine the information provided by companies on their engagement in the Global Compact. This 'social vetting' is critical to the efficacy of the Global Compact's mission and is a key driver of the initiative's strong emphasis on transparency, disclosure and accountability. Constructive public debate is especially encouraged in cases where business practices are felt to be inconsistent with a company's disclosure or commitment.

United Nations Global Compact: Formally launched on 26 July 2000, the Global Compact is a strategic policy initiative for businesses that are committed to aligning their operations and strategies with ten universally accepted Principles in the areas of human rights, labour, the environment and anti-corruption. By doing so, business, as a primary agent driving globalization, can help ensure that markets, commerce, technology and finance advance in ways that benefit economies and societies everywhere. With more than 7,000 participants in over 135 countries (as of October 2009), the Global Compact is the world's largest voluntary corporate responsibility initiative.

Bibliography

Abbott, K. W., Keohane, R. O., Moravcik, A., Slaughter, A.-M. and Snidal, D., 2000. 'The concept of legalization'. *International Organization* 54 (3): 17–35

Acelor Mittal, 2007. *Taking Responsibility for Transforming Tomorrow: Corporate Responsibility Report 2007*. London: Acelor Mittal.

Ackoff, R., 1975. *Redesigning the Future*. New York: Wiley.

Agle, B. R., Mitchell, R. K. and Sonnenfeld, J. A., 1999. 'Who matters to CEOs? An investigation of stakeholder attributes and salience, corporate performance, and CEO values'. *Academy of Management Journal* 42: 507–25.

Akhurst, M., Morgheim, J. and Lewis, R., 2003. 'Greenhouse gas emissions trading in BP'. *Energy Policy* 31 (7): 657–63.

Allenby, B. 1999. *Industrial Ecology: Policy Framework and Implementation*. Englewood Cliffs, NJ: Prentice Hall.

Amnesty International and The Prince of Wales Business Leaders Forum, 2000. *Human Rights: Is it Any of your Business?* London: Amnesty International UK.

Anderson, M., 1997. *European Environmental Policy: The Pioneers*. Manchester: Manchester University Press.

Applied Research Centre in Human Security, 2009. *About Us: Human Security Research*. published online at: www.coventry.ac.uk/researchnet/d/592 [Retrieved 21 May 2009].

Arevalo, J. A. and Fallon, F. T., 2008. 'Assessing corporate responsibility as a contribution to global governance: the case of the UN Global Compact,' *The International Journal of Effective Board Performance* 8 (4): 456–70.

Argyris, C. and Schön, D. A., 1978. *Organizational Learning: A Theory of Action Perspective*. Reading: Addison-Wesley.

Avery, C.L., 2000. *Business and Human Rights in a Time of Change*. London: Amnesty International UK

Bailis, R., 2009. *Emission Reductions and Lower Carbon Intensity: Are we Making Progress?* (UN Global Compact Caring for Climate Series). New York: United Nations Global Compact Office.

Baker, J., 2007. *The Future of the Global Compact*, published online at: www.unglobalcompact.org/docs/news_events/9.6/The_Future_of_the_Global_Compact.pdf [Retrieved 27 July 2009].

Barkawi, A., 2009. *Sam and Dow Jones Indexes Launch Dow Jones Sustainability Asia Pacific Indexes*, published online at: www.sustainability-indexes.com/djsi_pdf/news/PressReleases/SAM_PressReleases_090303_DJSI_AsiaPacific.pdf [Retrieved 20 April 2009].

Bartunek, J. M., 2002. 'The proper place for organizational scholarship: a comment on Hinings and Greenwood', *Administrative Science Quarterly* 47 (3): 422–7.

Beck, U., 2000. *What is Globalization?* Cambridge: Polity Press.

Benedick, R., 1991. *Ozone Diplomacy: New Directions in Safeguarding the Planet*. Cambridge, MA: Harvard University Press.

Bies, R. J., Bartunek, J. M., Fort, T. L. and Zald, M. N., 2007. 'Corporations as social change agents: individual, interpersonal, institutional, and environmental dynamics', *Academy of Management Review* 32: 788–93.

Bigge, D. M., 2004. 'Bring on the bluewash: a social constructivist argument against using Nike vs. Kasky to attack the Global Compact', *International Legal Perspectives* 14: 6–21.

Birkinshaw, J. and Piramal, G. (eds.), 2005. *Sumantra Ghosal on Management: A Force for Good*. London/New York: Financial Times/Prentice Hall.

Black, B., 2000. *Petrolia: The Landscape of America's First Oil Boom*. Baltimore, MD: Johns Hopkins University Press.

Bowler, C. and Brimblecombe, P., 2000. 'Control of air pollution in Manchester prior to the Public Health Act, 1875', *Environment and History* 6: 71–98.

Brimblecombe, P., 1987. *The Big Smoke: A History of Air Pollution in London since Medieval Times*. London: Methuen.

British Petroleum (BP), 2009. *Energy and Environment 10 Years On*, published online at: www.bp.com/genericarticle.do?categoryId=98&contentId=7032698 [Retrieved 5 April 2009].

Brown, J. and Duguid, P., 2000. *The Social Life of Information*. Boston, MA: Harvard Business School Press.

Business Leaders Initiative on Human Rights, UN Global Compact and Office of the High Commissioner for Human Rights, 2006. *A Guide for Integrating Human Rights into Business Management*. New York: United Nations.

Calton, J. M. and Payne, S. L., 2003. 'Coping with paradox', *Business & Society* 42 (1): 7–42.

Carbon Disclosure Project, 2009. *About the Carbon Disclosure Project,* published online at: www.cdproject.net [Retrieved 13 April 2009].

Carson, R., 1962. *Silent Spring.* Boston, MA: Houghton Mifflin.

Cerny, P. G., 1994. 'The dynamics of financial globalization: technology, market structure, and policy response', *Policy Sciences* 27 (4): 319–42.

Cetindamar, D. and Husoy, K., 2007. 'Corporate social responsibility practices and environmentally responsible behaviour: the case of the United Nations Global Compact', *Journal of Business Ethics* 76 (2): 163–76.

Clark, J. H., 1999. 'Green chemistry: challenges and opportunities', *Green Chemistry* 1: 1–8.

Coen, D., 1999. 'The impact of US lobbying practice on the European business–government relationship', *California Management Review* 41 (4): 27–44.

Commission on the Private Sector and Development, 2004. *Unleashing Entrepreneurship: Making Business Work for the Poor* (Report to the Secretary-General of the United Nations). New York: United Nations.

Cooperrider, D. L. and Sekerka, L. E., 2003. 'Toward a theory of positive organizational change', in K. S. Cameron, J. E. Dutton and R. E. Quinn (eds.), *Positive Organizational Scholarship: Foundations of a New Discipline.* San Francisco: Berrett–Koehler: 225–40.

Cooperrider, D. L., Sorensen, P. F., Jr., Yaeger, T. F. and Whitney, D. (eds.), 2001. *Appreciative Inquiry: An Emerging Direction for Organization Development.* Champaign, IL: Stipes Publishing.

Cooperrider, D. L. and Srivastva, S., 2001. 'Appreciative inquiry in organizational life', in D. L. Cooperrider, P. F. Sorensen, Jr., T. F. Yaeger and D. Whitney (eds.), *Appreciative Inquiry: An Emerging Direction for Organization Development.* Champaign, IL: Stipes Publishing: 77–100.

Crane, A., 1998. 'Culture clash and mediation: exploring the cultural dynamics of business–NGO collaboration', *Greener Management International* 24: 61–76.

Daily, G. C., 1997. 'What are ecosystem services?', Proceedings of the *AAAS Annual Meeting & Science Innovation Exposition* 163(0): A6.

Dalton, D. R., Metzger, M. B. and Hill, J. W., 1994. 'The "new" US Sentencing Commission Guidelines: a wake-up call for corporate America', *Academy of Management Executive* 8: 7–13.

Danish Minister for Economic and Business Affairs, 2008. *Act Amending the Danish Financial Statements Act (Report on Social Responsibility for Large Businesses),* published online at: www.eogs.dk/graphics/ Samfundsansvar.dk/Dokumenter/ Proposal_Report_On_Social_Resp. pdf [Retrieved 22 May 2009].

Doh, J. P. and Teegen, H., 2004. *Globalization and NGOs: Transforming Business, Governments, and Society*. Westport, CT: Praeger.

Drucker, P., 1993. *Post-Capitalist Society*. New York: Harper Business.

Dunlap, R. E. and Mertig, A.G. (eds.), 1992. *American Environmentalism: The US Environmental Movement, 1970–1990*. New York: Taylor & Francis.

Dyer, J. H. and Singh, H., 1998. 'The relational view: cooperative strategy and sources of interorganizational competitive advantage', *Academy of Management Review* 23: 660–79.

Edelman., 2009. *Edelman Trust Barometer (Executive Summary)*. New York: Edelman.

Ehrlich, P., 1968. *The Population Bomb*. New York: Ballantine Books.

Flink, J.J., 1975. *The Car Culture*. Cambridge, MA: MIT Press

Fort, T. L. and Schipani, C. A., 2004. *The Role of Business in Fostering Peaceful Societies*. Cambridge: Cambridge University Press.

Freeman, E., 1984. *Strategic Management: A Stakeholder Approach*. Boston, MA: Pitman.

Friedman, M., 1970. *New York Times Magazine*, 13 December

Friedman, T., 2006. *The World is Flat*. New York: Farrar, Straus & Giroux.

Fritsch, S., 2008. 'The UN Global Compact and the global governance of corporate social responsibility: complex multilateralism for a more human globalization?', *Global Society* 22: 1–26.

Fussler, C., Cramer, A. and van der Vegt, S., 2004. *Raising the Bar: Creating Value with the United Nations Global Compact*. Sheffield: Greenleaf.

Gardberg, N. A. and Fombrun, C. J., 2006. 'Corporate citizenship: creating intangible assets across institutional environments', *Academy of Management Review* 31: 329–46.

Ghoshal, S., 2005. 'Bad management theories are destroying good management practices', *Academy of Management Learning and Education* 4: 75–91.

Giddens, A., 1990. *Consequences of Modernity*. Cambridge: Polity Press.

Gilbert, D. U. and Behnam, M., 2009. 'Advancing integrative social contracts theory: a Habermasian perspective', *Journal of Business Ethics* 89 (2): 215–34.

Gilbert, D. U. and Rasche, A., 2008. 'Opportunities and problems of standardized ethics initiatives: a stakeholder theory perspective', *Journal of Business Ethics* 83: 755–73.

Global Compact. 2003. *Reports on the Third and Fourth Advisory Council Meeting of the Global Compact*. New York: United Nations Global Compact Office.

2004a. *Embedding Human Rights in Business Practices*. New York: United Nations Global Compact Office.

2004b. '*Who Cares Wins': Connecting Financial Markets to a Changing World*. New York: United Nations Global Compact Office.

2004c. *The Global Compact: Corporate Citizenship in the World Economy*. New York: United Nations Global Compact Office.

2004d. *Transparency and the Fight Against Corruption*, published online at: www.unglobalcompact.org/docs/issues_doc/7.7/7.7.5/rep_transcor. pdf [Retrieved 9 March 2010].

2005a. *The Global Compact's Next Phase*, published online at: www.unglobalcompact.org/docs/news_events/9.1_news_archives/2005_05_04b/ govern_dispap.pdf [Retrieved 1 September 2009].

2005b. *Guidance for Local Networks*. New York: United Nations Global Compact Office

2006a. *Business against Corruption: Case Stories and Examples*. New York: United Nations Global Compact Office.

2006b. *Global Compact and Global Reporting Initiative Form Strategic Alliance*, published online at: www.unglobalcompact.org/ NewsandEvents/news_archives/2006_10_06.html [Retrieved 10th December 2008].

2007a. *UN Global Compact Leaders Summit 2007*, published online at: www.unglobalcompact.org/newsandevents/event_archives/Leaders_ Summit_2007.html [Retrieved 5 July 2009].

2007b. *Caring for Climate: The Business Leadership Platform. A Statement by the Business Leaders of the UN Global Compact*, published online at: www.unglobalcompact.org/docs/issues_doc/ Environment/CLIMATESTATEMENT_revised_postsummit.pdf [Retrieved 15 January 2009].

2007c. *UN Global Compact Annual Review*. New York: United Nations Global Compact Office.

2007d. *The Principles for Responsible Management Education*. New York: United Nations Global Compact Office.

2008. *UN Global Compact Annual Review*. New York: United Nations Global Compact Office.

2009a. *Pilot Reporting Guidance on Corruption*. New York: United Nations Global Compact Office.

2009b. *UN General Assembly Supports Global Compact*, published online at: www.unglobalcompact.org/docs/news_events/9.1_news_ archives/ 2004_01_20/gc_governments.pdf [Retrieved 23 May 2009].

2009c. *About the Global Compact*, published online at: www.unglobalcompact.org/AbouttheGC [Retrieved 21 April 2009].

2009d. *Communication on Progress (COP) Policy Document,* published online at: www.unglobalcompact.org/docs/communication_on_ progress/ COP_Policy.pdf [Retrieved 25 February 2009].

2009e. *Notable COPs,* published online at: www.unglobalcompact.org/ COP/notable_cops.html [Retrieved 25 July 2009].

2009f. *Local Network Report 2008.* New York: United Nations Global Compact Office.

2009g. *Local Networks,* published online at: www.unglobalcompact.org/ NetworksAroundTheWorld [Retrieved 20 June 2009].

2009h. *What is a Local Network?,* published online at: www.unglobalcompact.org/docs/networks_around_world_doc/What_is_a_Local_ Network.pdf [Retrieved 15 August 2009].

Global Compact and Global Reporting Initiative, 2007. *Making the Connection: Using GRI's G3 Reporting Guidelines for the UN Global Compact's Communication on Progress.* New York: United Nations Global Compact Office.

Global Compact, International Business Leaders Forum and Transparency International, 2005. *Business Against Corruption. A Framework for Action.* New York: Global Compact Office

Global Humanitarian Forum, (GHF) 2009. *The Anatomy of a Silent Crisis.* Geneva: Global Humanitarian Forum.

Global Reporting Initiative (GRI), 2010. *A Resource Guide to Corporate Human Rights Reporting,* published online at www.globalreporting. org/currentpriorities/humanrights [Retrieved 9 March 2010].

Global Reporting Initiative (GRI), 2009. *The Amsterdam Declaration on Transparency and Reporting,* published online at: www.global reporting.org/CurrentPriorities/AmsterdamDeclaration [Retrieved 12 May 2009].

Goldman Sachs, 2007. *GS Sustain.* New York: Goldman Sachs International.

Granovetter, M., 1985. 'Economic action and social structure: the problem of embeddedness', *American Journal of Sociology* 91 (3): 481–510.

1992. 'Problems of explanation in economic sociology', in N. Nohria and R. Eccles (eds.), *Networks and Organizations: Structure, Form, and Action.* Boston, MA: Harvard Business School Press: 25–56.

Greiner, T., Rossi, M., Thorpe, T. and Kerr, B., 2006. *Healthy Business Strategies for Transforming the Toxic Chemical Economy.* Spring Brook, NY: Clean Production Action.

Gross, L., 1948. 'The peace of Westphalia, 1648–1948', *The American Journal of International Law* 42 (1): 20–41.

Group of Eight (G8), 2009. *Responsible Leadership for a Sustainable Future (G8 Leaders' Statement, L'Aquila Summit, July 8, 2009),* published online at: www.g8italia2009.it/static/G8_Allegato/G8_ Declaration_08_07_09_final,0.pdf [Retrieved 15 July 2009].

Guilé Foundation., 2009. *Taking Stock of Disclosure on the UN Global Compact: The 2009 Guilé Communication on Progress Survey.* Zurich: Guilé Fondation

Haas, P., 1990. *Saving the Mediterranean: The Politics of International Environmental Cooperation.* New York: Columbia University Press.

Hackman, J. R. and Wageman, R., 1995. 'Total Quality Management: empirical, conceptual, and practical issues', *Administrative Science Quarterly* 40 (2): 309–42.

Hale, T. N., 2008. 'Transparency, accountability and global governance', *Global Governance* 14: 73–94.

Harvey, D., 2005. *A Brief History of Neoliberalism.* Oxford: Oxford University Press.

Hawken, P., 2008. *Blessed Unrest: How the Largest Movement in History is Restoring Grace, Justice, and Beauty to the World.* New York: Viking Press.

Hawley, J.P. and Williams, A.T., 2000. *The Rise of Fiduciary Capitalism: How Institutional Investors can make Corporate America more Democratic.* Philadelphia: University of Pennsylvania Press.

Hedberg, C.-J. and von Malmborg, F., 2003. 'The Global Reporting Initiative and corporate sustainability reporting in Swedish companies', *Corporate Social Responsibility and Environmental Management* 10 (3): 153–64.

Held, D. and McGrew, A., 2002. 'Introduction', in D. Held and A. McGrew (eds.), *Governing Globalization.* Cambridge: Polity Press: 1–21.

Held, D., McGrew, A., Goldblatt, D. and Perraton, J., 1999. *Global Transformations: Politics, Economics and Culture.* Stanford: Stanford University Press.

Hennes and Mauritz (H&M), 2003. *Corporate Social Responsibility Report*, published online at: www.hm.com/filearea/corporate/fileobjects/pdf/ common/COMMON_CSRREPORT_2002_PDF_1124204589850.pdf [Retrieved 15 July 2009].

Henson R., 2008. *The Rough Guide to Climate Change.* London: Penguin Books

Heugens, P., van den Bosch, F. A. J. and Riel, C. B. M., 2002. 'Stakeholder integration: building mutually enforcing relationships', *Business & Society* 41 (1): 36–60.

Hinings, C. R. and Greenwood, R., 2002. 'Disconnects and consequences in organization theory?', *Administrative Science Quarterly* 47 (3): 411–421.

Hird, J. A., 1993. 'Environmental policy and equity: the case of superfund', *Journal of Policy Analysis and Management* 12 (20): 323–43.

Hix, S., 2005. *The Political System of the European Union*. New York: Palgrave Macmillan.

Hohnen, P., 2007. *Governmental 'Soft Power' Options: How Governments can use the 'Soft Power' Art of Encouragement and Persuasion to Advance Corporate Engagement on Social And Environmental Issues*, published online at: www.hohnen.net/articles/2007_july_6_hohnen_ soft_power_discussion_paper.pdf [Retrieved 15 September 2009].

    2009a. *OECD MNE Guidelines: A Responsible Business Choice*, published online at: www.oecdobserver.org/news/fullstory.php/aid/2772/ OECD_MNE_Guideline:_A_responsible_business_choice.html [Retrieved 20 August 2009].

    2009b. *Non-Financial Reporting: Denmark ups the Ante*, published online at: www.ethicalcorp.com/content.asp?contentid=6280 [Retrieved 22 July 2009].

Holland, K., 2009. 'Is it time to retrain B-schools?', *New York Times*, 15 March, 2009, section 3: 15.

Hudon, M., 2009. 'Should access to credit be a right?', *Journal of Business Ethics* 84: 17–28.

Hunt, C. B. and Auster, E. R., 1990. 'Pro-active environmental management: avoiding the toxic trap', *Sloan Management Review* 31 (2): 7–18.

Intergovernmental Panel on Climate Change (IPCC), 2007a. *Climate Change 2007: Synthesis Report*. Geneva: IPCC.

    2007b. *Climate Change 2007: Synthesis Report (Summary for Policymakers)*. Geneva: IPCC.

International Chamber of Commerce, United Nations Global Compact, Transparency International and World Economic Forum, 2009. *Resisting Extortion and Solicitation in International Transactions: A Company Tool for Employee Training*, published online at: www. transparency.org/global_priorities/private_sector [Retrieved 15 April 2009].

International Confederation of Free Trade Unions (ICFTU), 2004. *A Trade Union Guide to Globalization*. 2nd edn. Brussels: ICFTU.

International Energy Agency (IEA), 2008. *Energy Technology Perspectives 2008: Scenarios and Strategies to 2050*. Paris: OECD/IEA

    2009. *World Energy Outlook*. Paris: OECD/IEA

International Finance Corporation (IFC), United Nations Global Compact and International Business Leaders Forum, 2007. *Guide to Human Rights Impact Assessment and Management*. London: IFC.

International Labour Organization (ILO), 2006. *Tripartite Declaration of Principles Concerning Multinational Enterprises and Social Policy.* Geneva: ILO

2008. *The Labour Principles of the United Nations Global Compact: A Guide for Business.* Geneva: ILO.

Jacques, M., 2009. 'Face to face with history', *New Statesman*, 27 April 2009: 13

Jarillo, J. C., 1990. 'Comments on transaction costs and networks', *Strategic Management Journal* 11: 497–9.

Jones, C., Hesterly, W. and Borgatti, S., 1997. 'A general theory of network governance: exchange conditions and social mechanisms', *Academy of Management Review* 22: 911–45.

Kaelin, W., Mueller, L. and Wyttenbach, J. (eds.), 2004. *The Face of Human Rights.* Baden: Lars Müller.

Kale, P., Singh, H. and Perlmutter, H., 2000. 'Learning and protection of proprietary assets in strategic alliances: building relational capital', *Strategic Management Journal* 21: 217–37.

Kaplan, R. S. and Norton, D. P., 1996. *Balanced Scorecard: Translating Strategy into Action.* Cambridge, MA: Harvard Business School Press.

Katz, D., 1994. *Just Do It: The Nike Spirit in the Corporate World.* New York: Random House.

Kaufmann, D., 2004. Interview with Daniel Kaufmann on 'Corruption: can it ever be controlled?', published online at: http://discuss. worldbank.org/content/interview/detail/1196 [Retrieved 20 January 2010].

Kaul, I., Conceicao, P., Le Goulven, K. and Mendoza, R. U. (eds.), 2003. *Providing Public Goods: Managing Globalization.* New York: Oxford University Press.

Kaul, I., Grunberg, I. and Stern, M. A. (eds.), 1999. *Global Public Goods: International Cooperation in the 21st Century.* New York: Oxford University Press.

Kell, G., 2005. 'The Global Compact: selected experiences and reflections', *Journal of Business Ethics* 59 (1/2): 69–79.

Kell, G. and Levin, D., 2003. 'The Global Compact network: an historic experiment in learning and action', *Business and Society Review* 108 (2): 151–81.

Kell, G. and Ruggie, J. G., 1999. 'Global markets and social legitimacy: the case for the "Global Compact"', *Transnational Corporations* 8 (3): 101–20.

Khurana, R., 2007. *From Higher Aims to Hired Hands.* Princeton, NJ: Princeton University Press.

Kibert, N.C., 2003. 'Extended producer responsibility: a tool for achieving sustainable development', *Journal of Land Use & Environmental Law* 19: 503–23.

Kinley, D. and Tadaki, J., 2004. 'From talk to walk: the emergence of human rights responsibilities for corporations at international law', *Virginia Journal of International Law* 44: 931–1022.

Kolb, D. A, 1984. *Experiential Learning*. New York: Prentice Hall

Kolk, A. and Pinske, J., 2005. 'Business responses to climate change: identifying emergent strategies', *California Management Review* 47 (3): 6–20.

KPMG, 2008. *KPMG International Survey of Corporate Responsibility Reporting 2008*. London: KPMG.

Laufer, W. S., 2006. *Corporate Bodies and Guilty Minds: The Failure of Corporate Criminal Liability*. Chicago, IL: University of Chicago Press.

Laufer Green Issac (LGI), 2004. *Hidden Agendas: Stereotypes and Cultural Barriers to Corporate–Community Partnerships*, published online at: www.lgicommunications.com/foundations/PublicationsPortfolio/index.htm [Retrieved 20 May 2009].

Leipziger, D., 2003. *The Corporate Responsibility Code Book*. Sheffield: Greenleaf.

Leisinger K.M., 2007. 'Capitalism with a human face: the UN Global Compact', *Journal of Corporate Citizenship* 28: 113–32.

Leonard-Barton, D., 1992. 'Core capabilities and core rigidities: a paradox in managing new product development', *Strategic Management Journal* 13: 111–25.

Mahler, D., Erhard. A. and Callieri, C., 2007. *Chain Reaction: Your Firm Cannot Become 'Sustainable' unless your Supply Chains Become Sustainable First*. Chicago, IL: AT Kearney Report.

Margolis, J. D. and Walsh, J. P., 2003. 'Misery loves companies: rethinking social initiatives by business', *Administrative Science Quarterly* 48: 268–305.

Martin, F., 2009. *Moving Toward Sustainability: Household Product Research, Development, and Engineering: The Greenlist Project*, published online at: www.scjohnson.com/community/pdf/Greenlist_Case_Study.pdf [Retrieved 15 August 2009].

Martin-Luther University Halle-Wittenberg, 2008. *Principles for Responsible Management Education (PRME) Communication on Progress report 2007*, published online at: www.unprme.org/reports/PRMECOPApr2008.pdf [Retrieved 20 March 2009].

Matten, D. and Crane, A., 2005. 'Corporate citizenship: towards an extended theoretical conceptualization', *Academy of Management Review* 29: 166–79.

McCormick, J., 1995. 'Environmental policy and the European Union', *Contributions in Political Science* 355: 37–50.

McIntosh, M., 2010. *Thinking aloud: What is a Sustainable Enterprise Economy?*, published online at: www.griffith.edu.au/business/sustainable-enterprise [Retrieved 30 May 2009]

McIntosh, M. and Hunter, A. (eds.), 2010. *Perspectives on Human Security.* Sheffield: Greenleaf.

McIntosh, M., Waddock, S. and Kell, G., 2004. *Learning to Talk: Corporate Citizenship and the Development of the UN Global Compact.* Sheffield: Greenleaf.

McKinsey & Company, 2004. *Assessing the Global Compact's Impact.* New York: United Nations Global Compact Office.

Meaney, M. and Pung, C., 2008. 'Creating organizational transformations: McKinsey Global Survey Results', *The McKinsey Quarterly Online* August: 1–7.

Merieau L., 2008. 'The human factor: addressing United Nations staff perceptions of the business community when forming cross-sector partnerships', *Journal of Corporate Citizenship* 31: 23–5.

Miles, R. E. and Snow, C. C., 1986. 'Organizations: new concepts for new forms', *California Management Review* 28 (3): 62–73.

Miller, D., 1993. 'The architecture of simplicity', *Academy of Management Review* 18: 116–38.

Mirvis, P. and Googins, B., 2006. 'Stages of corporate citizenship', *California Management Review* 48 (2): 104–25.

Misangyi, V. F., Weaver, G. R. and Elms, H., 2008. 'Ending corruption: the interplay among institutional logics, resources, and institutional entrepreneurs', *Academy of Management Review* 33: 750–70.

Monash University, International Business Leaders Forum, Office of the High Commissioner for Human Rights and United Nations Global Compact, 2007. *Human Rights Translated: A Business Reference Guide.* New York: United Nations.

Morrison, E. W. and Milliken, F., 2000. 'Organizational silence: a barrier to change and development in a pluralistic world', *Academy of Management Review* 25: 706–25.

Mosley, S., 2001. *The Chimney of the World: A History of Smoke Pollution in Victorian and Edwardian Manchester.* Cambridge: White Horse Press.

Newell, P., 2000. *Climate for Change: Non-State Actors and the Global Politics of the Greenhouse.* Cambridge: Cambridge University Press.

Oppenheim, J., Bonini, S., Bielak, D., Kehm, T. and Lacy, P., 2007. *Shaping the New Rules of Competition: UN Global Compact Participant Mirror.* London: McKinsey & Company

O'Riordan, T. and Cameron, J., 1994. *Interpreting the Precautionary Principle*. London: Earthscan.

Organization for Economic Cooperation and Development (OECD) 2008a. *OECD Guidelines for Multinational Enterprises*. Paris: OECD Publishing.

  2008b. *Overview of Selected Initiatives and Instruments Relevant to Corporate Social Responsibility*. Paris: OECD Publishing.

Pacific Institute and United Nations Global Compact, 2009. *Climate Change and the Global Water Crisis: What Businesses need to Know and Do*, published online at: www.unglobalcompact.org/docs/issues_doc/ Environment/ceo_water_mandate/UNGC-PI_climate-water_whitepaper_FINAL.pdf [Retrieved 3 October 2009].

Paine, L. S., 1994. 'Managing for organizational integrity', *Harvard Business Review* 72 (12): 106–17.

Palan, R., 2003. *The Offshore World: Sovereign Markets, Virtual Places, and Nomad Millionaires*. Ithaca, NY: Cornell University Press.

Palazzo, G. and Scherer, A. G., 2006. 'Corporate legitimacy as deliberation: a communicative framework', *Journal of Business Ethics* 66: 71–88.

Petrobras, 2009. *2008 Social and Environmental Report*. Rio de Janeiro: Petrobras.

Pfeffer, J., 2007. *What were they Thinking: Unconventional Wisdom about Management*. Boston, MA: Harvard Business School Press.

Piasecki, B., 2007. *World Inc*. Naperville, IL: Sourcebooks.

Polanyi, K., 2001. *The Great Transformation: The Political and Economic Origins of our Time*. Boston, MA: Beacon.

Post, J. E. and Altman, B. W., 1992. 'Models of corporate greening: how corporate social policy and organizational learning inform leading edge environmental management', *Research in Corporate Social Performance and Policy* 13: 3–29.

Prahalad, C.K., 2005. *The Fortune at the Bottom of the Pyramid: Eradicating Poverty through Profits*. New Delhi: Pearson Education/ Wharton School Publishing.

Prahalad, C.K. and Hammond, A., 2002. 'Serving the world's poor profitably', *Harvard Business Review* 80 (9): 48–57.

PricewaterhouseCoopers, 2007. *The Right Combination: Corporate Responsibility Reports: The Role of Assurance Providers and Stakeholder Panels*. London: PricewaterhouseCoopers International Limited.

  2008a. *Confronting Corruption: The Business Case for an Effective Anti-Corruption Programme*. New York: PricewaterhouseCoopers International Limited.

2008b. *Corporate Responsibility at PricewaterhouseCoopers: Taking Responsibility in Our Communities*. London: PricewaterhouseCoopers International Limited.

Principles for Responsible Investment (PRI), 2009. *PRI Annual Report on Progress: A Review of Signatories' Progress and Guidance on Implementation*. London: PRI.

Principles for Responsible Management Education (PRME), 2009. *PRME Mission Statement*, published online at: www.unprme.org [Retrieved 12 May 2009].

Rasche, A., 2009a. '"A necessary supplement": what the United Nations Global Compact is and is not', *Business & Society* 48 (4): 511–37

2009b. 'Toward a model to compare and analyse accountability standards: the case of the UN Global Compact', *Corporate Social Responsibility and Environmental Management* 16 (4): 192–205.

Realff, M. J., Ammons, J. and Newton, D., 1999. 'Carpet recycling: determining the reverse production system design', *Polymer Plastics Technology and Engineering* 38 (3): 547–68.

Reinhardt, F., 2000. *Down to Earth: Applying Business Principles to Environmental Management*. Boston, MA: Harvard Business School Press.

Rieth, L., Zimmer, M., Hanmann, R. and Hanks, J., 2007. 'The UN Global Compact in Sub-Saharan Africa: decentralization and effectiveness', *Journal of Corporate Citizenship* 28: 99–112.

Robinson, M., 2002. *RSA World Leaders Lecture*, published online at: www.unglobalcompact.org/newsandevents/speeches_and_statements/ rsa_world_leaders_lecture.html [Retrieved 14 September 2009].

Roome, N., 1992. 'Developing environmental management strategies', *Business Strategy and the Environment* 1: 11–24.

Rosenau, J. N. and Czempiel E.-O. (eds.), 1992. *Governance without Government. Order and Change in World Politics*. Cambridge: Cambridge University Press.

Rowlands, I. H., 2000. 'Beauty and the beast? BP's and Exxon's positions on global climate change', *Environment and Planning* 18 (3): 339–54.

Rowley, T. J., 1997. 'Moving beyond dyadic ties: a network theory of stakeholder influences', *Academy of Management Review* 22: 887–910.

Rowley T. J. and Moldoveanu, M., 2003. 'When will stakeholder groups act? An interest- and identity-based model of stakeholder group mobilization', *Academy of Management Review* 28: 204–19.

Ruggie, J., 2000. *Remarks on the UN Global Compact to the NGO community (Geneva, 13 October 2000)*, published online at: www. unglobalcompact.org/newsandevents/speeches_and_statements/john_ ruggie_ngo_community_geneva.html [Retrieved 26 July 2009].

2001. 'global_governance.net: The Global Compact as learning network', *Global Governance* 7 (4): 371–8.

2003. 'The United Nations and globalization: patterns and limits of institutional adaptation', *Global Governance* 9 (3): 301–21.

2008. *Report of the Special Representative of the Secretary-General on the Issue of Human Rights and Transnational Corporations and Other Business Enterprises*. New York: UN Human Rights Council.

Runhaar, H. and Lafferty, H., 2009. 'Governing corporate social responsibility: an assessment of the contribution of the UN Global Compact to CSR strategies in the telecommunications industry', *Journal of Business Ethics* 84 (4): 479–95.

Sagafi-Nejad, T., 2008. *The UN and Transnational Corporations: From Code of Conduct to Global Compact*. Bloomington/Indianapolis, IN: Indiana University Press.

Schaefer, A. and Harvey, B., 1998. 'Rethinking research methods for the resource-based perspective: isolating sources of sustainable competitive advantage', *Strategic Management Journal* 20: 487–94.

Scherer, A. G., 2003. *Multinationale Unternehmen und Globalisierung*. Heidelberg: Physica.

Scherer, A. G. and Palazzo, G., 2007. 'Toward a political conception of corporate responsibility: business and society seen from a Habermasian perspective', *Academy of Management Review* 32: 1096–1120.

2008. 'Globalization and corporate social responsibility', in A. Crane, A. McWilliams, D. Matten, J. Moon and D. Siegel (eds.), *The Oxford Handbook of Corporate Social Responsibility*. Oxford: Oxford University Press: 413–31.

Scherer, A. G., Palazzo, G. and Baumann, D., 2006. 'Global rules and private actors: towards a new role of the TNC in the global governance', *Business Ethics Quarterly* 16 (4): 505–532.

Scherer, A. G. and Smid, M., 2000. 'The downward spiral and the US Model Business Principles: why MNEs should take responsibility for the improvement of world-wide social and environmental conditions', *Management International Review* 40: 351–71.

Scholte, J. A., 2005. *Globalization: A Critical Introduction*, 2nd edn. Houndmills: Palgrave.

Schreyögg, G. and Steinmann, H., 1987. 'Strategic control: a new perspective', *Academy of Management Review* 12: 91–103.

Schumpeter, J., 1975. *Socialism and Democracy*. New York: Harper.

Senge, P., 1990. *The Fifth Discipline*. New York: Free Press.

2006. *The Fifth Discipline: The Art and Practice of the Learning Organization*, MV. edn. New York: Currency Doubleday.

Sethi, S. P., 2003. *Global Compact is another Exercise in Futility*, published online at: www.financialexpress.com/fe full story.php?content_id=41523 [Retrieved 12 August 2009].

Shabecoff, P., 1993. *A Fierce Green Fire: The American Environmental Movement*. New York: Hill & Wang.

Shelton, D. (ed.), 2000. *Commitment and Compliance: The Role of Non-Binding Norms in the International Legal System*. Cambridge: Cambridge University Press.

Simons, R., 1995. *Levers of Control: How Managers use Innovative Control Systems to Drive Strategic Renewal*. Boston, MA: Harvard Business School Press.

Sperling, D., 1995. *Future Drive: Electric Vehicles and Sustainable Transportation*. Washington, DC: Island Press.

Stansbury, J., and Barry, B., 2007. 'Ethics programs and the paradox of control', *Business Ethics Quarterly* 17: 239–61.

Steinmann, H. and Kustermann, B., 1998. 'Management theory on the way to a new paradigm? Critical reflections on the concept of Robert Simons', in S. Urban (ed.), *Europe's Economic Future*. Wiesbaden: Gabler: 317–34.

Stern, N., 2006. *Stern Review: The Economics of Climate Change*, published online at: www.hm-treasury.gov.uk/d/Executive_Summary.pdf [Retrieved 13 March 2009].

Streeck, W., 1989. 'Skills and the limits of coliberalism: the enterprise of the future as place of learning! *Work, Employment and Society* 3 (1): 89–104

Stubbart, C. I. and Smalley, R. D., 1999. 'The deceptive allure of stage models of strategic processes', *Journal of Management Inquiry* 8: 273–86.

Suchman, M. C., 1995. 'Managing legitimacy: strategic and institutional approaches', *Academy of Management Review* 20: 571–610

Sundaram, A. K. and Inkpen, A. C., 2004. 'The corporate objective revisited', *Organization Science* 15 (3): 350–63.

Susskind, L., Moomaw, W. and Gallagher, K. (eds.) 2002. *Transboundary Environmental Negotiation: New Approaches to Global Cooperation*. San Francisco: Jossey-Bass.

Swithern, S., 2003. 'From Bhopal to Doha: business and the right to health', *New Academy Review* 2: 50–61.

Szasz, A., 1994. *EcoPopulism: Toxic Waste and the Movement for Environmental Justice, Social Movements, Protest, and Contention*. Minneapolis, MN: University of Minnesota Press.

Tarr, J. A., 1996. *The Search for the Ultimate Sink: Urban Pollution in Historical Perspective*. Akron, OH: University of Akron Press.

TeBrake, W. H., 1975. 'Air pollution and fuel crises in pre-industrial London, 1250–1650', *Technology and Culture* 16: 337–58.

Thérien, J.-P. and Pouliot, V., 2006. 'The Global Compact: shifting the politics of international development?', *Global Governance* 12: 55–75.

Torbert, W. R., 2004. *Action Inquiry: The Secret of Timely and Transforming Leadership*. San Francisco: Berrett–Koehler.

Transparency International (TI), 2002. *The Integrity Pact: The Concept, the Model and the Present Applications: A Status Report*. Berlin: Transparency International.

    2003. *Business Principles for Countering Bribery: An Essential Tool for Business*. Berlin: Transparency International.

    2008a. *Business Principles for Countering Bribery: Small and Medium Enterprise (SME) Edition*. Berlin: Transparency International.

    2008b. *Corruption Perception Index*, published online at: www.transparency.org/policy_research/surveys_indices/cpi [Retrieved 15 March 2009].

    2009a. *TRAC: Transparency in Reporting on Anti-Corruption: A Report of Corporate Practices*. Berlin: Transparency International.

    2009b. *CEOs Call for Greater Adherence to UN Anti-Corruption Convention*, published online at: www.transparency.org/news_room/latest_news/press_releases/2009/2009_05_07_ceo_uncac [Retrieved 15 July 2009].

Umlas, E., 2009. *Human Rights and SRI in North America: An Overview*, published online at: www.business-humanrights.org/Links/Repository/320729 [Retrieved 15 May 2009].

United Nations, 1999. *Secretary-General Address to the World Economic Forum in Davos*. United Nations Press Release SG/SM/6881.

    2004. *Addressing Business Leaders at Global Compact Summit, Secretary-General Says Experience Shows that Voluntary Initiatives 'Can and Do Work'*. United Nations Press Release SG/SM/9387 ECO/71.

    2007. *The Secretary-General: Closing Remarks at United Nations Global Compact Leaders Summit*, published online at: www.unglobalcompact.orgnewsandevents/event_archives/2007_Leaders_Summit/Closing_Secretary_General.pdf [Retrieved 24 April 2009].

    2008. *Global Forum for Responsible Management Education can Raise Bar for Business*. United Nations Press Release: SG/SM/11990 ECO 142.

    2009a. *Charter of the United Nations*, published online at: www.un.org/en/documents/charter [Retrieved 15 July 2009].

    2009b. *Universal Declaration of Human Rights*, published online at: www.un.org/en/documents/udhr [Retrieved 23 April 2009].

    2009c. *Agenda 21*, published online at: www.un.org/esa/dsd/agenda21 [Retrieved 14 March 2009].

2009d. *The Secretary-General: Remarks at Luncheon with Leaders of the Global Compact Korea Network,* published online at: www.un.org/apps/news/infocus/sgspeeches/search_full.asp?statID=285 [Retrieved 23 April 2009].

2009e. *The Global Compact: Creating Sustainable Markets (Address of Secretary-General Ban Ki-moon at the World Economic Forum in Davos).* United Nations Press Release: SG/SM/12073 ECO/145.

2009f. *World Summit for Sustainable Development (WSSD) Plan of Implementation,* published online at: www.un.org/jsummit/html/documents/summit_docs/2309_planfinal.htm [Retrieved 15 March 2009].

United Nations Conference on Trade and Development (UNCTAD), 2009. *Statements by Supachai Panitchpakdi, Secretary-General of UNCTAD (2008–2009),* published online at: www.unctad.org/TEMPLATES/Webflyer.asp?docID=6969&intItemID=3549&lang=1 [Retrieved 15 August 2009].

United Nations Development Programme (UNDP), 2005. *Human Development Report 2005: Argentina (Informe de Desarrollo Humano 2005).* New York: UNDP.

United Nations Development Programme (UNDP) Poland, 2007. *Equal Opportunities Company: Good Practice Guide*: Washington: UNDP Poland.

United Nations Economic and Social Council (UN–ECOSOC), 2003. *Human Rights, Trade and Investment.* United Nations Press Release E/CN.4/Sub.2/2003/9, 2.

United Nations Educational, Scientific, and Cultural Organization (UNESCO), 2009a. *The Universal Declaration on the Human Genome and Human Rights,* published online at: www.unesco.org/ibc/en/genome/index.htm [Retrieved 14 April 2009].

2009b. 'Human Cloning once again Stirs a Heated Debate at the United Nations', *UNESCO Social and Human Science Sector Magazine* 4: 3.

United Nations Environment Programme (UNEP), 2008. *Looking Back and Looking Forward: The Year of Environmental Challenge Makes Way for a Year of Opportunity,* published online at: www.unep.org/Documents.Multilingual/Default.asp?DocumentID=553&ArticleID=6032&l=en&t=long [Retrieved 13 March 2009].

2009. *Rio Declaration on Environment and Development,* published online at: www.unep.org/Documents.Multilingual/Default.asp?DocumentID=78&ArticleID=1163 [Retrieved 15 May 2009].

United Nations Environmental Programme Finance Initiative (UNEP FI), 2005. *A Legal Framework for the Integration of Environmental, Social and Governance Issues into Institutional Investment.* Châtelaine: UNEP FI.

United Nations Environmental Programme (UNEP) and KPMG, 2007. *Carrots and Sticks: Trends in Mandatory and Voluntary Reporting.* Nairobi: UNEP and KPMG.

United Nations Framework Convention on Climate Change (UNFCCC). 2008. *Report of the Conference of the Parties on its Thirteenth Session.* United Nations Press Release: FCCC/CP/2007/6.

United Nations Human Rights Council, 2008a. *Mandate of the Special Representative of the Secretary-General on the Issue of Human Rights and Transnational Corporations and other Business Enterprises* (Resolution A/HRC/8/L.8). New York: United Nations.

  2008b. *Summary of Five Multi-Stakeholder Consultations* (Report A/HRC/8/5/Add.1). New York: United Nations.

Unruh, G., 2008. 'The Biosphere Rules', *Harvard Business Review* 86 (2): 111–17.

  2010. *Earth, Inc.* Boston, MA: Harvard Business School Press.

Unruh, G. and Konolla, T., 2007. 'Really changing the course', *Business Strategy and the Environment* 16 (8): 525–37.

Victor, D., Raustiala, K. and Skolnikoff, E.B. (eds.), 1998. *The Implementation and Effectiveness of International Environmental Commitments: Theory and Practice.* Cambridge, MA: MIT Press.

Vigeo, 2008. *La norme publique internationale dans la conception et l'exercice de la responsabilité sociale des grandes entreprises européennes,* published online at: www.vigeo.com/csr-rating-agency/images/PDF/Communiquepresse/Francais/vigeo_etude_referentiels_internationaux_oct2008.pdf [Retrieved 22 April 2009].

Waddock, S. and McIntosh, M., forthcoming. *SEE Change: The Emerging Sustainable Enterprise Economy* (working title).

Waddock, S., Rasche, A., Werhane, P.H. and Unruh G., 2009. 'New Questions Raised by the Principles for Responsible Management Education: a commentary', in D.L. Swanson and D.G. Fisher (eds.), *Towards Assessing Business Ethics Education.* Greenwich, CT: Information Age Publishing, forthcoming: 2–24 (in draft).

Walsh, J. P., 2005. 'Book review essay: taking stock of stakeholder management', *Academy of Management Review* 30: 426–52.

Wargo, J., 1996. *Our Children's Toxic Legacy: How Science and Law Fail to Protect us from Pesticides.* New Haven, CT: Yale University Press.

Were, M., 2003. 'Implementing corporate responsibility: the Chiquita case', *Journal of Business Ethics* 44: 247–60.

West LB., 2007. *GRI Reporting: Aiming to Uncover True Performance.* Düsseldorf: West LB.

Williams, O. F., 2004. 'The UN Global Compact: the challenge and the promise', *Business Ethics Quarterly* 14 (4): 755–74.

2008. *Peace through Commerce: Responsible Corporate Citizenship and the Ideals of the United Nations Global Compact.* Notre Dame: University of Notre Dame Press, IN

Williamson, O. E., 1985. *The Economic Institutions of Capitalism: Firms, Markets, Relational Contracting.* New York/London: Free Press.

1995. 'The economics of governance', *American Economic Review* 95 (2): 1–18.

Witte, J.M. and Reinicke, W., 2005. *Business UNusual: Facilitating United Nations Reform through Partnerships.* New York: United Nations.

World Bank, 2009. *Governance Matters: A Blog about Governance and Development for all,* published online at: http://governanceblog.world-bank.org [Retrieved 18 September 2009].

World Trade Organization (WTO). 2009. *Relations with Non-Governmental Organizations/Civil Society,* published online at: www.wto.org/english/forums_e/ ngo_e/intro_e.htm [Retrieved 15 May 2009].

Worldwatch Institute, 2009. *State of the World 2009 Report,* published online at: www.worldwatch.org/sow09 [Retrieved 27 July 2009].

Zadek, S., 2004. 'The path to corporate responsibility', *Harvard Business Review* 82 (12): 125–32.

Zürn, M., 2004. 'Global governance and legitimacy problems', *Government and Opposition* 39: 260–87.

Index

n = footnote; *t* = table/diagram.